The Lives of Jean Toomer

Jean Toomer at mid-life, New Jersey shore, 1937

The Lives of

JEAN TOOMER

A Hunger for Wholeness

Cynthia Earl Kerman

Richard Eldridge

LOUISIANA STATE UNIVERSITY PRESS *Baton Rouge and London*

Copyright © 1987 by Louisiana State University Press
All rights reserved
Manufactured in the United States of America
Designer: Patricia Douglas Crowder
Typeface: Linotron 202 Garamond #3
Typesetter: G & S Typesetters, Inc.
Printer: Thomson-Shore, Inc.
Binder: John H. Dekker & Sons, Inc.

Louisiana Paperback Edition, 1989
98 97 96 95 94 93 92 91 90 89   5 4 3 2 1

Library of Congress Cataloging-in-Publication Data

Kerman, Cynthia Earl.
    The lives of Jean Toomer.

    Bibliography: p.
    Includes index.
    1. Toomer, Jean, 1894–1967—Biography.   2. Authors,
American—20th century—Biography.   3. Society of
Friends—United States—Biography.   4. Gurdjieff,
Georges Ivanovitch, 1872–1949—Influence.   I. Eldridge,
Richard, 1940–   . II. Title.
PS3539.O478Z7   1987   813'.52 [B]   86-27622

    ISBN 0-8071-1548-7
    ISBN 0-8071-1354-9

Published with the assistance of a grant from the National Endowment for the Humanities.

The authors are grateful to Éditions Seghers for permission to translate one of Léopold Sédar
Senghor's poems from *Chants pour Naëtt* (Paris, 1949).

Frontispiece photo by Marjorie Content Toomer, from Marjorie Toomer Collection

To Marjorie Content Toomer

How many lives must I build? From death, how many lives?

. . . .

I have formed systems of significances, bodies of meaning,
        scales of value.
I have forgotten or replaced them.

. . . .

I have had faiths and hopes destroyed and rebuilt.
A mind, and lost it.

. . . . . .

I have loved;
Yes, and forgotten those I felt I would forever love—
To love again.

. . . .

How many more lives must I build
To become One Eternal Individual?

—Jean Toomer, "How Many Lives?"

Contents

Illustrations

Preface

Jean Toomer is an American author, born in 1894, who bloomed briefly at the time of the Harlem Renaissance with the publication of his novel *Cane*, then disappeared from sight. It was only after his death in 1967, with the burgeoning of the drive for Afro-American studies, that interest in him was revived and resulted in two new editions of *Cane*, a spate of articles, inclusion of his work in anthologies, and some brief biographical attention. Ironically, it was the minimal black element in his heritage that brought the public back to the man who wrote, and deeply felt, "I am of no particular race. I am of the human race, a man at large in the human world, preparing a new race." Most of his life was spent in a search that went well beyond the issues of race or of literature.

Anyone who knows a little or even a lot about Jean Toomer is left with questions. It seems the more we know, the harder he is to explain. The first striking conclusion by an observer of Toomer's life is that it was a series of lives, a segmented sequence. Being a writer was only the first of at least three careers for him. His childhood and youth were fragmented by a checkerboard racial upbringing—he jumped back and forth several times between the white and black cultures—and a chaotic education. He then became three different men, one after another: a writer of fiction and poetry, devoted to the pursuit of elusive Art; a disciple of Georges Gurdjieff and a teacher of his spiritual-mental-physical system for making people whole; and a religious leader among Quakers who at the same time was seeking, sometimes desperately, his own physical and spiritual wholeness. During the last fifteen years of his life, he withdrew into a state of invalidism. At each stage—artist-writer, Gurdjieff teacher, and Quaker leader—he seemed to become a different person, to step out of one role and setting and into another.

How could Jean Toomer contain so many apparent contradictions? He claimed to be an archetypal American, yet all his adult life he used an assumed French name. He was equalitarian but aristocratic, could be tender and callous to the same person, wanted to lay out his whole self before the world but was a highly secretive marriage partner. He declared a mystical attachment to the soil, yet seldom got his fingers into it. He was black and white and abdicated from both groups. He was a writer who renounced writing but kept on writing all his life. Eaten by the strongest imaginable yearning for achievement far beyond most people's dreams, he consecrated his life to the attainment of a transcending greatness, but in his last years his situation evoked not admiration but pity and regret. Yet of course he displayed persistent traits also, and he made lasting contributions in each of his "incarnations." How did these continuities and contradictions arise in him, what did they contribute to his greatness, and how did he in turn affect the people and events of his time? What is this strange figure's niche in history?

To find the answers to these questions, we went primarily to the records Jean Toomer himself left—correspondence with his friends and publishers, his notes and journals and voluminous writings. We also asked questions and listened to people who had known him and sought out letters and records in other collections, always looking for patterns or clues that could give us keys to understanding.

Acknowledgments

Writing a biography is something like reading a mystery story. Little pieces fall into place as the whole begins to take shape, and if the writer is lucky, there is a kind of disclosure as the end is neared, when finally everything begins to make some sort of sense. Of course life drops its red herrings in the researcher's path also, and nowhere is reality as neat as the well-crafted mystery story.

However, it helps to find willing and honest guides, as objective as may be, and we have been blessed with a number of them. First and without parallel is Jean Toomer's wife, Marjorie Content Toomer, who gave us countless hours of interviews and whose patience under fire never failed. We are grateful to her also for permission to use letters, manuscripts, and family photographs, and for checking on the accuracy of many chapters, as well as for repeated hospitality and a cherished friendship. Second, it has been a real joy to meet and learn from her daughter, Susan Sandberg, and Jean's daughter, Margery Toomer Latimer, both of whom have searched for materials for us and generously allowed us into their lives. Others in the Doylestown area, where Toomer lived the last half of his life, are to be thanked for sharing their memories of him: Frank and Lee Bjornsgaard, Franklin Davenport, Georges and Elizabeth Duval, Sally Fell, Nancy Geiger, Charles Ingerman, Lawrence and Ruth Miller, Byron and Betty Morehouse, Dorothy Paxson, and Miryam Ralph.

In the New York area, several who knew Toomer in the Gurdjieff work were very kind in giving us time and information: Dr. and Mrs. William Welch, Elizabeth Delza Munson, and Mavis McIntosh. Dr. Welch's gifts to us included a manuscript written at his urging, Toomer's description of his first visit to Fontainebleau. Our special gratitude goes to Elizabeth Delza Munson for permission to use the text of "Postscript," which Gorham Munson wrote about Jean Toomer in 1969, and for her careful reading and detailed comments on repeated drafts of many chapters. With her invaluable help, we increased our understanding and improved our text, though she and Louise Welch, who also commented on some chapters, cannot be held responsible for any errors that may remain in our interpretation of the Gurdjieff material.

Friends of Toomer's in other places were helpful in interviews also: Marian Fuson, Priscilla Jenness Mitchell, Edith Passmore, and Douglas and Dorothy Steere. Vena Kaufman added a sidelight on Toomer's work. In addition, we made use of the interview of Katharine Green by Robert Twombly, courtesy State Historical Society of Wisconsin, Madison, and that of Gorham Munson by India Watterson, courtesy Amistad Research Center, New Orleans. We are greatly indebted to Gerald G. May, M.D., for his evaluation of Jean Toomer's life story from both psychiatric and spiritual perspectives, and to Kathleen Peoples, Ph.D., for her psychological commentary. Many others have given us information in correspondence or access to their research: Morley Ayearst, Nancy Breitsprecher, Mrs. Douglas Campbell, Walter Driscoll, Jessie Gruner, Michael Jay Krasny, Meridel LeSueur, Daniel McCarthy, Paul Taylor, Darwin Turner, and Robert Twombly. Lewis Benson has our gratitude for the extensive background material he gave us, in person, by letter, and in printed form, on the early Gurdjieff groups in New York and on his distinctions between the Gurdjieff and Quaker positions.

We would like to thank the following people and institutions for their assistance in helping us find materials: Jessie Carney Smith, Ann Shockley, and Beth Howse of Fisk University Library, where we worked with the Jean Toomer papers; Lyman Riley and Daniel Traister, University of Pennsylvania Van Pelt Library, Waldo Frank Collection; Anne Whelpley and David Schoonover, Yale University Beinecke Rare Book and Manuscript Library, Alfred Stieglitz and related collections; Elizabeth A. Swaim, Wesleyan University Olin Library Special Collections, Gorham Munson Collection; Katherine Thompson and Harold L. Miller, State Historical Society of Wisconsin, materials of Zona Gale, Margery Latimer, and Katharine Green; Clifton H. Johnson and India Watterson, Amistad Research Center; and Albert W. Fowler and Ray Turbey, Friends Historical Library of Swarthmore College. We are very grateful for permission from Yale University to use the considerable quotations from the Jean Toomer Papers and also the collections of Alfred Stieglitz and James Weldon Johnson, and from Friends Historical Library of Swarthmore College for the use of Quaker materials consulted there.

The resource in shortest supply all through the period of composition was time. For making this available at the critical point when the final strands of the story had to be drawn together, we are indebted to the National Endowment for the Humanities for an NEH Fellowship for College Teachers in 1983, which allowed Cynthia Kerman to spend a six-month leave of absence from teaching on full-time research and writing.

Appreciation is extended to Barbara Mallonee for critical reading of a large part of the manuscript, and to our two typists who both adjusted cheerfully to an erratic schedule: Gloria Henson, who added pickup and delivery to the typing job, and Loretta Reynolds, who provided not only accuracy and utter dependability but also a sure sense of aesthetics and unfailing patience.

Finally, we thank our spouses, Ralph Kerman and Lucy Reeder Eldridge, for their enduring love and optimism.

The Lives of Jean Toomer

Chronology

1894   March 29: Nina Pinchback
marries Nathan Toomer. December 26: Nathan Pinchback
Toomer born, Washington,
D.C.

1895   Father, Nathan Toomer, deserts family.

1896   Nina returns to her parents'
home with infant son, who is
given name Eugene. Live on
Bacon Street in mainly white
neighborhood.

1899   Nina divorces Nathan.

1901–
1905   Eugene or "Pinchy" attends
[black] Garnet School,
U Street.

1905   Fall: Eugene ill. Misses whole
year of school.

1906   Nina marries Archibald
Combes; moves to Brooklyn

with Eugene. Grandparents
sell house on Bacon Street.

1907 Moves to New Rochelle, N.Y.

1909 June 9: Nina dies. Eugene returns with grandparents to
live with his uncle in
Washington.

1910 Enters Dunbar High School.

1912 Moves to apartment on
U Street with grandparents.

1914 January: graduates from high
school. Summer: enters agricultural program at University
of Wisconsin.

1915 January: drops out of U. of
Wisconsin. Fall: applies to
Massachusetts College of Agriculture; arrives on campus
but does not enroll.

1916 January: Enters American
College of Physical Training
in Chicago. Explores atheism
and socialism. Fall: also attends classes at University of
Chicago.

1917 Spring: drops out of American
College. Summer and fall:
takes classes at New York University and City College of
New York.

1918 Begins intensive reading and   "Bona and Paul" written.
writing in Chicago, Mil-
waukee, and New York. Two
jobs, hectic schedule.

1919 Physical collapse; recuperates in Ellenville, N.Y. Back to Washington.

1920 In New York again until fall, devotes self to music and literature; meets Waldo Frank; changes name to Jean Toomer.

Writes "The First American," "Withered Skin of Berries."

1921 In Washington, writes full time, poetry and short stories. Fall: goes to Sparta, Ga., for two months as substitute principal. December: grandfather dies.

Writes "Meridian Hill—An Autobiographical Story." Finishes "Georgia Night," "Kabnis," and most of his southern sketches.

1922 Close friendship with Waldo Frank, both travel to Spartanburg. Falls in love with Mae Wright. Finishes *Cane* in December. Extols black elements in his background.

Writes "Natalie Mann." "Song of the Son" and "Banking Coal" published in *Crisis*; "Storm Ending," "Calling Jesus," and "Harvest Song" in *Double Dealer*; "Becky," "Carma," and "Reapers" in *Liberator*; "Face," "Portrait in Georgia," and "Conversion" in *Modern Review*; and "Seventh Street" in *Broom*.

1923 Moves to New York. Meets and falls in love with Margaret Naumburg; estranged from Waldo Frank. Introduced to Gurdjieff philosophy.

Cane published. "Fern" published in *Little Review*; "Open Letter to Gorham Munson" in *S4N*; and "Gum" in *Chapbook*. "Withered Skin of Berries" rejected by *Little Review*.

1924 Studies under Orage. Uncle Bismarck dies. Goes to Reno with Margaret Naumburg; attends Gurdjieff's institute at Fontainebleau; begins Gurdjieff dance group. Emphasizes concept of "Universal Man."

Finishes "The Negro Emergent." "The Critic of Waldo Frank" published in *S4N*, and "Oxen Cart and Warfare" in *Little Review*.

1925 Begins Gurdjieff work in Harlem. Spends summer with

"Easter" published in *Little Review*. Finishes "Values and Fictions" (re-

Paul Rosenfeld at York Beach and October at Lake George with Alfred Stieglitz. Visits Mabel Luhan in Taos at Christmas; she urges him to set up Gurdjieff institute there.

jected for publication).

1926 Breaks with Margaret Naumburg. Mystical experience, beginning at Sixty-sixth Street el station. Summer in Fontainebleau and then to Chicago to be a Gurdjieff leader.

1927 Works with groups in Chicago; summer in Fontainebleau.

"Balo" published in *Plays of Negro Life*. Writes "The Gallonwerps" and "The Sacred Factory" (both rejected for publication).

1928 Continues Gurdjieff groups in Chicago; visits York Beach in summer. September: grandmother dies.

"Winter on Earth" published in *The Second American Caravan*; "Mr. Costyve Duditch" in *Dial*. Writes "The Crock of Problems" and "Skilful Dr. Coville" (both rejected).

1929 Continues Chicago groups, summer in Fontainebleau. December: falls in love with Emily Otis.

"York Beach" published in *The New American Caravan*; "White Arrow" and "Reflections" in *Dial*; "Race Problems and Modern Society" in *Problems of Civilization*; "American Letter" ("Lettre D'Amerique") in *Bifur*. Writes "Transatlantic" and "Essentials" (both rejected). Completes short-story collection "Lost and Dominant," including "Drackman," "Mr. Costyve Duditch," "Love on a Train," "Break," "Easter," "Two Professors," "Mr. Limph Krok's Famous 'L' Ride," "Fronts," "Pure Pleasure," and "Winter on Earth" (rejected for publication).

1930   Gurdjieff visits Chicago; friction with New York group over money for Gurdjieff; Chicago group in uncertain state.

Finishes "Earth-Being—The Autobiography of Jean Toomer" (rejected).

1931   Portage experiment. October 30: marries Margery Latimer. Visits New Mexico.

Essentials privately published. Finishes "Blue Meridian" (rejected). Writes "A New Force for Cooperation" and poetry collection "Bride of Air" (both rejected). Writes "Outline of an Autobiography."

1932   The Toomers live in Carmel, return to Chicago after adverse publicity. August 16: Margery dies in childbirth; Margery Toomer born.

"Brown River Smile" published in *Pagany,* "As the Eagle Soars" in *Crisis.* Finishes "Portage Potential" and "Caromb" (both rejected).

1933   Lives in Portage with Latimers, collecting Margery's letters. To New York in October and Lake George in December.

Writes "Man's Home Companion."

1934   Gurdjieff in New York, pressing JT for money. JT marries Marjorie Content, September 1 in Taos; Toomers live in New York with young Argie.

"A New Force for Cooperation" published in *Adelphi,* and "The Hill" in *America and Alfred Stieglitz.* Writes "On Being an American"; finishes "Eight-Day World," "The Letters of Margery Latimer" (both rejected).

1935   Breaks with Gurdjieff. Summer in Taos.

Writes "A Drama of the Southwest" and "Book X."

1936   Toomers move to Doylestown, Pa.; JT has plan for a Gurdjieff center.

"Blue Meridian" published in *The New Caravan.* "Lump" written near this time.

1937   Leads group modeled on Gurdjieff work; gives lectures

Three meditations published in *New Mexico Literary Sentinel.* Privately

in New York; begins using pen name Nathan Jean Toomer. Uncle Walter dies.

publishes *Living is Developing, Work-Ideas I,* and, probably, *A Fiction and Some Facts.* Writes "Talks with Peter," "Psychologic Papers," and "Remember and Return" (all rejected). Begins "From Exile into Being" (works on this until 1946).

1938 Begins attending Friends Meeting.

1939 August to December: Toomers in India in unsuccessful search for spiritual enlightenment.

"Roads, People, and Principles" published in Doylestown *Daily Intelligencer* and also privately published as pamphlet.

1940 January: return to Doylestown. May: JT has kidney removed. August: Toomers join Society of Friends.

Begins "The Angel Begori," "The Colombo-Madras Mail."

1941 JT appointed to four Friends committees in local Meeting.

"Socratic Dialogue" published in *New Mexico Literary Sentinel.* Finishes collection "Blue Meridian and Other Poems" (rejected). Begins "Incredible Journey" (works on until 1948).

1942 Begins work with high school age group at Friends General Conference (1942–48). Starts new Gurdjieff group at Mill House.

1943 Health difficulties increasing; gets a "physical reading" from Edgar Cayce. Becomes clerk of Ministry and Counsel Committee, Bucks Quarterly Meeting (1943–48). Much speaking among Friends groups (1943–47). Ap-

"These Three" and "Santa Claus Will Not Bring Peace" published in *Friends Intelligencer.*

pointed to Ministry and Counsel Executive Committee, Philadelphia Yearly Meeting (1943–55).

1944 Becomes advisor to college-age Young Friends (1944–48). Trip to Midwest for Friends General Conference.

"The Days Ripen" (poem), "The Other Invasion," and "The Presence of Love" published in *Friends Intelligencer*. "From Exile into Being" rejected by three publishers.

1945 Added to Religious Life Committee headed by Douglas Steere (1945–47).

"Today May We Do It" and "Keep the Inward Watch" published in *Friends Intelligencer*.

1946 Continued widespread speaking; asked to write pamphlet on worship.

"The Uncommon Man" and "Worship and Love" published in *Friends Intelligencer*. "From Exile into Being" rejected twice.

1947 Becomes assistant clerk, Ministry and Counsel Executive Committee, Philadelphia Yearly Meeting (1947–51). Summer in New Mexico; Margery enters George School in fall.

An Interpretation of Friends Worship published. "Authority, Inner and Outer," "See the Heart" (poem), and "Chips" (aphorisms) published in *Friends Intelligencer*. "From Exile into Being" and poem collection "The Wayward and the Seeking" both rejected twice.

1948 More physical difficulties; summer in New York working on Alexander technique. Resigns as Young Friends advisor; resigns as clerk of Ministry and Counsel Committee, Bucks Quarterly Meeting.

Two poems, "Prayer" and "Here," published in *Friends Intelligencer*.

1949 Gives William Penn Lecture at Yearly Meeting. Begins Jungian analysis. Dwindling number of talks to Friends

The Flavor of Man published. "Spiritual Scarcity" published in *Philadelphia Enquirer*.

groups. October 29: Gurdjieff dies.

1950 Stops analysis, begins exploring dianetics.

"Something More" and "Blessing and Curse" published in *Friends Intelligencer*.

1951 Takes six-week course in dianetics. Gives six-week lecture series at Doylestown Friends Meeting.

Lecture series: "The Persistent Challenge."

1952 Experiments with nutrition and diet. Hears John G. Bennett lecture on Gurdjieff in New York.

Begins writing "Why I Entered the Gurdjieff Work" (works on until 1954).

1953 Recommits self to Gurdjieff work. Attends Gurdjieff groups in New York. Gives course in New Hope, Pa., workshop.

1954 Continuing abdominal problems. Resigns from Ministry and Counsel Committee, Buckingham Meeting. Attends Louise Welch's Gurdjieff group in Princeton (1954–57). Starts own Gurdjieff group (1954–57).

1955 "Voices for Peace" interview by Doylestown newspaper. Toomers sell Mill House, move to remodeled barn.

1956 Last literary effort.

Writes First Trip to Fontainebleau.

1957 Ill health makes it impossible for JT to continue attending or leading Gurdjieff groups.

1962 Toomer papers housed at Fisk University. JT in and out of nursing homes; final entry about 1965.

1967 March 30: dies.

1969 *Cane* reissued for first time in paperback.

Abbreviations

ASC   Alfred Stieglitz Collection, The Beinecke Rare Book and Manuscript Library, Yale University, New Haven

FHLS   Friends Historical Library, Swarthmore College, Swarthmore, Pa.

GM   Gorham Munson

GMC   Gorham Munson Collection, Olin Library, Wesleyan University, Middletown, Conn. (copies of material from Jean Toomer Papers)

JT   Jean Toomer

JTP   Jean Toomer Papers, Collection of American Literature, The Beinecke Rare Book and Manuscript Library, Yale University, New Haven

MC   Marjorie Content

MCT   Marjorie Content Toomer

ML   Margery Latimer

MLeS   Meridel LeSueur

MLT   Margery Latimer Toomer

MTC   Marjorie Toomer Collection, in possession of Margery Toomer Latimer, Pineville, Pa.

N of E   Notations of Events (JT notes)

W&S   *The Wayward and the Seeking,* edited by Darwin Turner

WF   Waldo Frank

WFC   Waldo Frank Collection, Special Collections, Van Pelt Library, University of Pennsylvania, Philadelphia

I.

REACHING FOR MANHOOD

The Grandfather

Between his thirtieth and fiftieth years, in what most people consider the prime of life, through one marriage cut short, another begun, and professional, emotional, and spiritual upheavals, Jean Toomer came back again and again to the writing of his autobiography. He was trying to explain something that he felt was very important—his own peculiar place in the world—and the work drew him back repeatedly to his childhood. He never finished the autobiography. Although he developed a table of contents that took the story into middle life, the parts he actually wrote were concentrated on the early years. These sections were written and rewritten, an incident expanded here or an interpretation there, the most fully developed manuscript filling 226 pages with only his first twelve years. His analysis is not that of a Freudian, who might look to the first five years for basic clues, and strangely enough he claims to have felt detached from his family, much as if he were a being from another planet. Yet he focused his search on these early roots, digging and digging around them.

Jean was a child of a broken home and an extended family. The family that sheltered him, and from which he detached himself, revolved around his grandfather. Toomer, giving much space to him in the account, consciously recognized his influence. It may also be, however, that part of the key he was searching for is hidden in the grandfather in ways that Toomer did not see.

Jean Toomer's grandfather has a public history as well as a private one, and this was always important to Jean. We all arise from a sea of anonymous ancestors, about some of whom we know a few facts, but rarely can we find the name of a forebear rising above the surface to appear in encyclopedias and history books. For Jean to grow up in a house with a grandfather who had been the only black governor of any state in the Union, for that man to continue to uphold his majesty among his cronies, and for him to carry unquestioned authority in his home, even with his grown children, could not help shaping the perceptions and attitudes of the fatherless boy. The fragility of that unusual status, growing out of the facts that P. B. S. Pinchback was governor of Louisiana for less than two months, that he was elected but not admitted to the U.S. Senate, and that his election to the state senate depended on a constitution just adopted, with military backing, and soon superseded, probably served to strengthen rather than weaken his lifelong air of authority.

Son of a white planter and a mulatto former slave, Pinckney B. S. Pinchback was born free. His father, Major William Pinchback, apparently maintained a legal wife and family on his Virginia plantation as well as a second family by his slave Eliza Stewart. Eliza, according to Toomer's notes, was of English, Scotch, Welsh, German, African, and Indian stock. He had studied a picture of her and noted her fair complexion, high cheekbones, firmly held lips, and set chin. Eliza bore William ten children, the first when she was fifteen, in 1829. Seven years and six children later (though only two of these had lived), he took her to Philadelphia and made out manumission papers for her and the children. Pinckney was born in 1837 in Macon, Georgia, as the family was journeying on to western Mississippi, at a time when treaties, following bloody battles, were displacing the Indian tribes there in favor of white settlers.[1]

Pinckney and his brother Napoleon, seven years older, were sent in 1846 to a school run by the Reverend Hiram S. Gilmore in Cincinnati, which Arna Bontemps in a sketch of Pinckney's life characterizes as "a private academy catering to the offspring of just such unions as the Major and his mulatto helpmate." Unfortunately, two years later their father died, and the provision he had made for his second family during his lifetime abruptly ceased. In fact, the administrator of the estate, instead of giving the family a share of the legacy, warned them that if they did not leave Mississippi immediately, the remaining relatives would reenslave them. With eighteen-year-old Napoleon to guide them, Eliza and the children made their way to Cincinnati, and for a year or so the family was kept together. But young Napoleon, apparently overwhelmed by the responsibility of being substitute father to the large family, lost his

1. Jean Toomer, autobiographical notes (MS in Jean Toomer Papers, Box 15, File 3, Collection of American Literature, The Beinecke Rare Book and Manuscript Library, Yale University, New Haven). Later references to similar sources will be abbreviated—for example, JT notes (JTP 15:3). This material is also covered, with some further detail, in James Haskins' *Pinckney Benton Stewart Pinchback* (New York, 1973), 1–4.

mind. The family disintegrated, and twelve-year-old Pinckney was forced out on his own.[2]

He found work on the canalboats then carrying cargo between Cincinnati and Toledo, gradually moving on to the larger boats on the Mississippi and Missouri rivers. In a few years he had attained the rank of steward (the highest post a black could hold on the riverboats), built a reputation as a gambler, and formed a home base in New Orleans, where in 1860 he married Nina Hethorn. Nina, then sixteen or seventeen, is described by Jean Toomer in his autobiography as a "white Creole," "reputed to be English and French," about whom he says he "never heard any implication she had Negro blood."[3] The word *Creole* is most commonly used today to mean Caucasian descendants of French immigrants to Louisiana, but in the mid nineteenth century it also included such French-speaking descendants with some black ancestry.[4] Toomer's phrase seems to indicate the former, but Arna Bontemps's description suggests the latter: "When he was about twenty-three, [Pinchback] married beautiful Nina Emily Hawthorne [*sic*] who, like himself, was practically white in appearance." Two pictures of her in the family's possession show a classic oval face with fair complexion and slightly rounded nose, smooth straight hair of medium shade, which was parted in the middle and pulled up to the top of her head or toward the back, a sharp chin, and a firm and sober expression about the mouth. The pictures of her husband from the same period (perhaps in the 1870s or 1880s) are just as sober, and his racial heritage is almost as indistinguishable, except for the tight curliness of his beard. In about 1874 a reporter described him: "Pinchback glides around the chamber like a bronze Mephistopheles, smiling sardonically. . . . He is . . . not darker than an Arab. . . . His features are regular, just perceptibly African, his eyes intensely black and brilliant, with a keen, restless glance."[5]

By 1862, the Mississippi was blockaded and New Orleans occupied by Union forces under General Butler. Up to that time, the Union forces had not encouraged or accepted enlistment from blacks, but Butler had welcomed freedmen or escaping slaves and employed them in supporting jobs around the

---

2. Arna Bontemps, *One Hundred Years of Negro Freedom* (New York, 1961), 35–36.

3. *Ibid.*, 36–38; JT notes (JTP 15:3).

4. George Washington Cable, New Orleans writer in the last quarter of the nineteenth century, was apparently responsible for restricting the meaning of the term, as noted by Sister Frances Woods in her *Marginality and Identity: A Colored Creole Family Through Ten Generations* (Baton Rouge, 1972), 7.

5. Washington correspondent of New York *Commercial Advertiser,* quoted in Reverend William J. Simmons' *Men of Mark* (1887; rpr. Chicago, 1970), 539.

army camps. In 1862 he issued a call for freedmen to enlist in the Union forces. When the boat on which Pinchback was employed had to make a run to escape the U.S. Navy, the young steward left his ship and made his way through the blockade back to New Orleans. Whether he thought of enlisting at that time is not known; Nina was expecting a baby and he may have wanted only to be near her. But very soon after he arrived, he was involved in a fracas on a street corner and arrested for stabbing his brother-in-law. The Union authorities gave him a two-year sentence and jailed him, but three months later he was released on condition he would enlist. He was then assigned to recruit a company of free blacks, a task quickly accomplished. He and other black leaders of this company chafed for a year under unequal treatment, then resigned. Almost immediately he undertook to raise a company of black cavalry on the promise of being made its captain, but when the company was formed he was denied the commission. Later he apparently planned to see Lincoln for permission to raise black troops in Ohio and Indiana, but before this happened, the war ended.[6]

Jean Toomer questioned, in some versions of his autobiography, the authenticity of his grandfather's attachment to the cause of blacks. In fact, he asked in print whether Pinchback really was black, suggesting it was to his political advantage at the time to play the part. Pinchback's motives are certainly a matter of conjecture—probably they were multiple—and there is no real way of establishing them. But two facts are clear from the records. First, he was the son of a former slave who was of mixed racial background but had some African heritage. Thus he was black according to the definition traditional in American society. Second, his skin was so light in color that he could have chosen not to be a black. His sister Adeline B. Saffold wrote him from Sidney, Ohio, on April 30, 1863, while Pinchback was in the army unit of the Second Louisiana Regiment. Enclosed in a tiny, black-bordered envelope bearing a three-cent stamp, the letter was preserved by Pinchback and later by his grandson Jean in the box where he kept his most precious, private possessions. In this letter Addie had strong advice for her brother:

If I were you Pink I would not let my ambition die. I would seek to rise and not in that class either but I would take my position in the world as a white man as you are and let the other go for be assured of this as the other you will never get your rights. Know this that mobs are constantly breaking out in different parts of the north and even in Canada against the oppressed colored race. Right in Cincinnati they can hardly walk the streets but they are attacked. . . . Reuben established his position here as a white man, voted as one and volunteered in the services of his country as one. He was insulted by the negroes here right at the public hotel and called every insulting

6. Bontemps, *One Hundred Years,* 38–41.

name. . . . I have nothing to do with the negroes am <u>not</u> one of them. Take my advise dear brother and do the same.[7]

She could see clearly, living in "free" Ohio, that legal freedom was not to be equated with full citizenship. In fact it did not even mean suffrage, though northerners were agitating for blacks' right to vote in the South. In 1867 the Reconstruction Acts required the former Confederate states to form new constitutions based on Negro suffrage and adoption of the Fourteenth Amendment. At that time, of the eighteen northern and four border states, only six permitted blacks to vote.

But in spite of Addie's urging, Pinchback's choice had evidently been made. Perhaps he had already invested too much in his image; perhaps the gambler in him saw that the stakes were high and there might be a handsome payoff; perhaps he had a basic allegiance and an honest dedication to defending the human rights of the black race. In any case he was publicly identified as a black and remained so all his life. At the end of the war he appeared on platforms in Alabama, protesting the maltreatment of the newly freed blacks. After considerable violence against blacks had occurred in the reshuffling of Louisiana's civil government in 1866, he stepped into the Republican party there by organizing the Fourth Ward Republican Club soon after Congress passed the Reconstruction Acts in 1867. In short order he was elected to the new constitutional convention, and then, with the ratification of the new state constitution the following April, he was chosen as a state senator. He was riding the crest: 1868 was the high point for black participation in government in the southern states. Fifty percent of the delegates to that Louisiana constitutional convention were Negroes; three Negro lieutenant governors and many state officers and national senators and representatives were elected that year. But already the opposing forces were gaining in strength. There were pardons and amnesty for former white leaders, and threats and brutality from such groups as the recently founded Ku Klux Klan, the Knights of the White Camelia, and other terrorist organizations. Manipulation, fraud, and violence came increasingly to dominate the elections.

But Pinchback used his opportunities. While he served in the state senate he did not neglect his financial affairs. In 1869, with a partner in Shreveport, he opened an office as a commission merchant, transporting and trading in com-

---

7. Spelling and emphasis as in original. The box where this letter was kept was available only to Jean Toomer during his lifetime, according to his wife, Marjorie Content Toomer. On showing it to us, she said she had not disturbed the contents. It is in the Marjorie Toomer Collection, in possession of Margery Toomer Latimer, Pineville, Pa. Hereinafter this source will be cited as JT tin box (MTC).

modities, principally cotton. Late in 1870 he acquired control of a semiweekly newspaper, the New Orleans *Louisianian*. He was making enough to invest in stocks and bonds (no doubt more successful in his speculation because of his influence in the legislature and knowledge of forthcoming actions), and his paper gave him an editorial forum. In 1871 he was also appointed director of New Orleans schools.[8]

Not only were the Democrats pitted against the Republicans in the political arena, but the Republicans were split into two factions. Some, led by Governor Warmoth, wished to make compromises with the Democrats, and others (among whom was Pinchback) held to the more radical civil rights positions. All sides, white and black, shared in the corruption during this unstable period, and Pinchback received his share of accusations; but the black lieutenant governor, Oscar Dunn, was by all reports incorruptible. Suddenly and mysteriously Dunn died in November of 1871, and Pinchback was narrowly elected lieutenant governor to replace him. Pinchback tested his power in several contests with Governor Warmoth in 1872. There was, for example, a great train race from New York City to get back to Louisiana in time to sign, in the governor's absence, some registration and election bills that would give the Republicans a better chance in the next election. Warmoth succeeded in having Pinchback detained at a way station until he himself arrived, so the bills were not signed. In the next trial of strength, however, Pinchback as president of the state senate swore in (in a surprise predawn ceremony) all the recently elected Republican members of the new senate, many of whose seats were contested by Democrats favored by Warmoth. The new legislature promptly impeached Governor Warmoth, charging him with attempted bribery and other misdemeanors, and Lieutenant Governor Pinchback became governor of Louisiana for the month and a half remaining in the term.

Pinchback had been elected congressman-at-large in November, but he stepped down in favor of the Democrat who also claimed election to that post. When his short term as governor was up, the legislature elected him a senator from Louisiana. Unfortunately this seat was also contested by a Democrat. Although the new Louisiana governor William P. Kellogg was a Republican elected on the same ticket as Pinchback and also opposed by a rival "elected" Democrat, Kellogg served in office and Pinchback did not. For the next three years he worked for his Senate position, spending much time on the Senate floor, stumping the state of Louisiana to protest the election frauds, and even

8. This and the following paragraphs are summarized from accounts of Pinchback's life in Bontemps, *One Hundred Years*; and Haskins, *Pinckney Pinchback*.

going afield to speak to large crowds in Cincinnati, Indianapolis, and Memphis. A reporter covering the Senate sketched his appearance:

His most repellent point is a sardonic smile which, hovering continuously over his lips, gives him an evil look, undeniably handsome as the man is. It seems as though the scorn which must rage within him at the sight of the dirty, ignorant men from the South who affect to look down upon him on account of his color, finds play imperceptibly about his lips. His manner is reserved but polite, exhibiting a modesty rarely seen in a successful politician—a model indeed of good breeding to those Texas and Louisiana Yahoos who shout "nigger, nigger, nigger," in default of common sense or logic. Mr. Pinchback is the best dressed Southern man we have had in Congress from the South since the days when gentlemen were Democrats.[9]

It was a long fight. Arna Bontemps reports, "Pinchback eventually concluded that 'traitors' of his own party had double-crossed him 'on account of his race.' Frederick Douglass, the foremost Negro in the country and the one most responsible for the early affiliation of American Negroes with the Republican party, called the denial of the Senate seat to Pinchback 'an outrage.'"[10] Despite the support of Douglass and some northern newspapers and his continued commuting between New Orleans and Washington, Pinchback was never confirmed in his Senate seat, and in the spring of 1876 the fight ended with a definite vote against him. Eventually, however, he was allowed a senator's pay plus mileage, amounting to more than sixteen thousand dollars, as compensation for his ungranted seat.

In the same year, a delegate to both the national and state Republican conventions, he wangled the chairmanship of the state Republican Executive Committee and a resolution naming him the unanimous choice for senator from Louisiana. However, the election confusion in 1876 in Louisiana was such that two governors, a Republican and a Democrat, were sworn in and both took office. When the state senate formed under the Republican governor elected two other men as U.S. senators, ignoring the directive from the state convention to appoint Pinchback, he struck back. He used his personal power and Executive Committee chairmanship to prevent a quorum in the Republican session and to give recognition and support to the Democratic governor and his legislature. Other Republicans, perceiving the swelling southern tide, then swung in with him. By that time in all the other southern states except two, Democrats were in full control. In 1877, when federal troops were withdrawn from the South, the white Democrats took over everywhere.

9. New York *Commercial Advertiser* correspondent, quoted in Simmons, *Men of Mark*, 539–40.

10. Bontemps, *One Hundred Years*, 58.

Although Pinchback did not permanently desert the Republican party and did collect a few more favors from its national wing, his time had come and gone. The official edifice in which blacks could have a high place was crumbling, but there remained a level of black society where he could continue to hold the honor and distinction he had won. In February, 1879, he was appointed an internal revenue agent. He served only a few months, resigning in favor of election to the state constitutional convention that summer, where he had a part in establishing a state-supported "university for the education of persons of color." But the convention was dominated by forces eager to return political power to the prewar leaders. The strategy involved terror and led to mass emigration on the part of blacks who had seen local black officials forced to resign at gunpoint, and feared even worse to come. Pinchback himself described the scene, in a report as internal revenue agent, March 8, 1879: "On nearing the Delta ferry landing [I found] . . . the banks of the river literally covered with colored people and their little store of worldly goods [waiting for transportation to Kansas] . . . . They . . . believe that the constitutional convention bodes them no good; that it has been called for the express purpose of abridging their rights and liberties. . . . They are absolutely panic stricken. Every road leading to the river is filled with wagons." [11]

For a while Pinchback kept on speaking to conferences and political gatherings, defending the rights of freedmen, but his editorial outlet was cut off when his newspaper, suffering financial difficulties and losing its managing editor to yellow fever, had to discontinue publication in 1879. Political feuds had ended his business partnership. An 1881 appointment as surveyor of customs for the Port of New Orleans lasted until 1885, and may have been fairly lucrative, for the family moved into a larger mansion in a more fashionable neighborhood. But when the Democrats took power nationally, it began to seem that Pinchback should gather up his winnings and leave the game.

His "winnings" must have been considerable, in addition to the sizable sum he had received from the Senate. Many people called him "Governor" from then on, and he appears to have lived mainly on earnings from investments, perhaps supplemented by gambling, for the rest of his life. When he resigned as surveyor of customs, he began the study of law at Straight University, which was the "university for the education of persons of color" he had helped found in 1880 and on whose Board of Trustees he was then serving. After a year, his studies enhanced by the knowledge he had gained from his political experience, he was admitted to the Louisiana bar. There is no mention of his actually

11. Pinchback quoted in Bontemps, *One Hundred Years*, 61.

practicing, though he was listed as a "retired lawyer" in the 1889–1900 edition of *Who's Who*. He was described about 1887 as a "prudent economical financier" with an income of "about $10,000 a year from stocks and bonds." (This sum was inflated to $50,000 in his obituary.) Later he was granted a job that resembled his old government position as an internal revenue agent, as indicated by an article from the New York *Amsterdam News*. Dated July 13, probably 1910, it notes that Pinchback "has been covered into the Civil Service, by order of President Taft. This will insure the retention of the race's 'grand old man' in the Federal employ for life." Confirmation is found in a record of his working in 1910–1911 on internal revenue affairs in Boston. But he was rather desperately attempting to recoup something of his former status. Jean Toomer recalls his grandfather's continued penchant for gambling, especially his fondness for horse races, as long as he had money at all.[12]

In any case, Pinchback was able to support his growing family in style and comfort. Children were born at about two-year intervals after his marriage. One reference indicates that the couple had six altogether, but one boy and one girl died; Pinckney (born 1862), Bismarck (*ca.* 1864), Nina (1866), and Walter (*ca.* 1868) survived. His mother, Eliza Stewart, made a comfortable home with them from 1867 until her death in 1884. Pinchback had ample means through the years to support a royal mansion in New Orleans; servants to care for it; sumptuous entertaining; heavy traveling, speaking, and campaigning schedules; and generous vacation trips with his family. On one occasion in the summer of 1871, he reserved berths on a Pullman car for his wife and children when he sent them north, but they were denied the accommodations because of their race. The family's usual summer excursion was to fashionable Saratoga Springs for the horse racing. In 1879, for example, after a leisurely weekend in Washington, they spent five weeks in Saratoga, a week at the Hoffman House in New York, then some time in Sidney, Ohio, before returning in October to their home in New Orleans.[13] In Sidney that year, Pinchback may have visited his sister or other relatives. It is interesting to speculate, in light of Addie's letter of 1863, whether she would have welcomed a visit from so well known a representative of blacks in state and national politics—even though, or perhaps particularly if, he was her brother.

Pinchback left New Orleans about 1892 and moved his establishment to Washington. He decided to build just off Fourteenth Street, northwest of the

12. Records and notes from JT tin box (MTC); obituary editorial in Baltimore *Afro-American*, December 30, 1921, n.p.

13. JT notes on genealogy (JTP 14:5); Haskins, *Pinckney Pinchback*, 55; JT notes (JTP 14:4); Bontemps, *One Hundred Years*, 64.

city, in an area that was still semirural. The house he built, where Jean Toomer grew up, was a metaphoric extension of the grandfather: "It had a sort of aggressive tower-like effect. In this it was typical of Pinchback."[14] From the front, in fact, it seemed to be mostly tower, this huge three-story brick cylinder surmounted by a sharp-pointed conical roof taking up more than half of the house's narrow width. Tall and brusquely cut off on both sides, the red brick and brownstone house invaded the area and took its stand in an open space near smaller, old frame houses, looking dominant and out of place until later years and urban growth brought other similar houses to the block.

Toomer tried to guess why his grandfather built such a constricted-looking house when the six lots he owned could have held a larger or better proportioned structure, wondering if already his grandfather was feeling cramped by reduced income. (One source of Pinchback's income, the Louisiana lottery, in which he held shares, had recently been outlawed amid charges of corruption.) The house was a narrow half duplex without its other half. But it was architecturally fashionable, reflecting the popularity of the massive castlelike Richardson style, still represented by many homes in that section of Washington. And inside, as Toomer notes, the house was not cramped but expansive and luxurious, with high ceilings, lace curtains, and heavy oak and mahogany furniture. There was an entrance hall, with a straight steep stairway on the right leading to four rooms on the second floor. On the third floor were two more bedrooms and a small area that could be used for storage or as a maid's room. The living room and two front bedrooms boasted wide bay windows opening from the tower, and the seven fireplaces meant one in almost every room. In the rear of the house was a stable for the horse and carriage.

Here Pinchback brought his family. Only his oldest son, Pinckney, was established on his own, as a pharmacist in Philadelphia; the other three children, ranging in age from twenty-two to twenty-six, were still living at home. And here Pinchback entertained friends and associates, and then "there would be a swirl of people and the house would blaze with lights." It was a practice he had enjoyed in New Orleans, where he once gave a reception for President Grant, and at the Hoffman House in New York, which was convenient for grand dinner-theater parties. He loved to be admired, and he was an impressive figure, his forehead broader now, his hair and beard white. He wore a different suit each day of the week and "always dressed well, usually in the habit of a diplomat with cut-away coat." In fact, Toomer notes, he remarkably

14. JT, "Earth-Being" (Typescript of autobiography in MTC), 35, also in Darwin Turner (ed.), *The Wayward and the Seeking: A Collection of Writings by Jean Toomer* (Washington, D.C., 1980), 29.

resembled Andrew Carnegie and was occasionally mistaken for him, which was a source of gratification to Pinchback. This image and style of life, Toomer recognized, were powerfully engraved on him, "later to function as an unconscious ideal for myself, for how I wished to look and be; and also to serve as standards by means of which I measured men and life." [15]

Beyond the conspicuous affluence, other qualities of his grandfather were impressed on Jean. He did things "with dash and flair"; he was "masculine, active, daring, full of energy, vital, never ill, hearty eating, hearty laughing, drink enjoying, able to command, clean, upstanding, forceful, intelligent, well-dressed, well-kept, well-off, noble in bearing, serious, fun-loving, stormy if need be, full of feeling, a grand speaker, a center of influence and attraction, having many friends, much exciting business, and an air of adventure." [16] All this entered into Jean's ideal picture of a man.

Jean remembered his grandmother with tenderness. She took special care of her lace curtains, and she no doubt made sure that the cook provided well for festive occasions and for the family's five o'clock dinner. She was the only one who ever—and that was seldom—talked about the days in New Orleans. Sometimes she would tell him stories of Mardi Gras or of the big house, with its lush tangerine trees and high iron fence, which her husband and his friends had once had to defend against a mob while she and the children huddled upstairs. She was gentle, sensitive, timid, but strong and enduring; she lived, in fact, seven years beyond her husband. She was something of a moralist—a letter to Jean when he was thirty includes the admonition, "I hope you will keep away from all bad company women as well as men"—and she could be stubborn, as in an argument over financial obligations with Nina's second husband. But she was the only one in the household, Jean claims, who supported him through all his struggles in the time "after I turned black sheep." [17]

She and Jean's mother Nina shared in the excitement of the entertainments and balls and banquets that were so much a part of their genteel life. Jean loved to watch his mother and grandmother get ready for balls, powdering and perfuming, dressing in velvet and silk, putting on their diamonds, "a few large sparkling stones set in brooches or ear-rings—gifts from my grandfather, souvenirs of his trip to Europe." [18] There was always money for an elegant gift to his wife or his daughter—but never money for them to spend as they chose. Pinchback kept tight control.

15. *Ibid.*, 37–38, also in *W&S*, 29–30.
16. JT notes (JTP 14:6).
17. JT tin box (MTC); JT, "Earth-Being," 25, also in *W&S*, 23.
18. JT, "Earth-Being," 116.

He also kept control of the goals and daily behavior of his family. Toomer later had the idea that his grandfather dreamed of founding a bourgeois, land-owning, political dynasty. Deciding on the appropriate career for each of his children, he had Pinckney trained as a pharmacist at the University of Pennsylvania. Bismarck was to be a doctor and was sent to Yale, but he was unable to complete the course there. He returned to Howard University and graduated, but his tastes were more for art, music, and literature than for medicine. Although his father sent him to rural Mississippi, he was miserable there and failed in his medical practice. He was then placed in the Civil Service on an Indian reservation in the West, where he was unhappy again, and finally he came home to take a minor government job, which Toomer guessed was in the auditing division of the navy.[19] But in his thirties, living at home and holding a job, he still chafed under his father's strictures. Walter was marked for a lawyer and went to Andover, but apparently returned to Washington before finishing his studies. He had a government job and studied law at night.

Nina, of course, was prepared for a brilliant marriage. She was packed off to Riverside School, a finishing school near Northampton, Massachusetts, and displayed in daily life at home her skill in writing poetry, crocheting, sewing, embroidering, singing, playing the piano, and handling servants and a horse and carriage. There is no telling how many inappropriate suitors had come and gone under her father's watchful eye before she met Nathan Toomer, a previously married man twenty-seven years older than she and reputed to be wealthy, who appeared suddenly and magnificently on the Washington social scene. Although Pinchback did not approve of Toomer, considering him unreliable, Nina evidently loved him and defied her father by marrying him on March 29, 1894. Had her father approved, Nina's wedding would no doubt have been a great society affair. As it was, at least the ceremony was performed by a well-known minister who was also a family friend. He was the Reverend Francis J. Grimké, nephew of the Grimké sisters, who had been active in the women's rights and abolition movements. When they made the unnerving discovery that their brother had children by one of his slaves, they sponsored their two black nephews and paid for their college education. Francis Grimké had become a leading minister in Washington, Archibald a leading lawyer in Boston.[20]

Toomer in his autobiographies paid special attention to the racial characteristics of various family members. According to the information Jean, as an

19. JT notes (JTP 14:7).
20. JT notes (JTP 14:9); Gerda Lerner, *The Grimké Sisters from South Carolina: Pioneers for Women's Rights and Abolition* (New York, 1971), 359–60, 365.

adult, got from his grandfather, Nathan Toomer was the son of a prosperous southern planter, of English, Dutch, and Spanish stock, and had inherited land and money when his father died. His mother was a "woman of mixed blood, including Negro and Indian." Living in Georgia between Augusta and Macon, he was "known to have some colored blood . . . [but] lived with both white and colored people. The rigid division of white and Negro did not apply in his case." Born in North Carolina in 1841, he was only four years younger than Pinchback himself, and their early situations were closely parallel, but the record does not say whether Nathan Toomer was born a slave or free. Nina's complexion was a little darker than that of her parents (Jean described it as an "olive complexion")[21] and her hair curlier; she resembled her father about the nose and eyes. Both Nathan and Nina listed themselves on their marriage license as "colored."

Nathan Toomer shared at least one quality of Pinchback's: the flair for dressing well and making an impression. Jean later recorded, "The only worldly possessions that came to me from him were some beautiful large silk handkerchiefs, a set of small diamond shirt studs, and a slender ebony cane with a gold head."[22] With a splash of gallantry at the time of his marriage to Nina, he bought a home on Twelfth Street between R and S streets, paid cash in full, and had the deed made out in Nina's name. Although repairs and alterations took about two months and the couple had to live at the Pinchbacks' for that time, they soon moved into their own house. But the splash at that point began dribbling away. The home was provided but not the servants to take care of it, so Nina had to cook and scrub, jobs she had never done before; and shortly she knew she was pregnant too.

According to Nina's account, Nathan left three months after they were married and did not return until three days before the baby was born; six weeks later, he left her again. During the next eight months, he was there intermittently but gave her little money and no help. She was ill and had to borrow on a diamond ring to buy herself and the baby a little respite from the hot Washington summer at Harpers Ferry, a vacation spot at the deep cut in the Appalachians where the Shenandoah River joins the Potomac. Nathan claimed he had to return south to repair his financial affairs; but after he finally left in October, 1895, he sent Nina only $141, then stopped answering her letters.[23]

21. JT notes (JTP 14:9, 15:1).
22. JT notes (JTP 14:9), 10.
23. Nina Pinchback Toomer to Nathan Toomer, July 8, 1897, in JTP 9:9. Mary Church Terrell, a contemporary and friend of Jean's mother and grandmother, reports that black visitors at Harpers Ferry, not welcome in the white tourist accommodations, often had quarters at Storer College, a school for blacks. The broad, shaded campus, high above the river, was on the west

Nina, stubborn and high-spirited though she was, was simply not raised to struggle against the world to support herself and her child. Pride pitted against need, she finally broke down and sought her father's support. In September, 1895, she drew up a will: her son would inherit her property, and her mother (not her husband) would be guardian of her son in case of her death. That November she moved from her house and rented it, living with a friend until the fall of 1896 when she finally returned to her father's house. In September, 1898, she petitioned for alimony, and in January, 1899, a divorce was granted. Jean by this time was four years old. He never knew his father, having only a vague memory of meeting him once in his life, later pictures, some correspondence, and what information he could get from his grandfather when he summoned enough courage to ask. His mother had never mentioned Nathan Toomer except once or twice to warn Jean against him. Much later he heard that his father had died in January, 1906.[24]

But the grandfather set conditions for readmitting his wayward daughter and her infant son. The biggest stumbling block was the boy's name. At birth he was officially given the name Nathan Pinchback Toomer. P. B. S. Pinchback, if he was to support the baby, would have none of it—he wanted the last name legally changed to Pinchback and the first name changed to anything else. Nina rejected that proposed legal action but accepted the family's informal adaptation. The first name was soon replaced by Eugene, after Eugene Laval, his godfather, and he was called "Pinchy" by his friends. His grandmother and grandfather addressed him, when they wrote, as Eugene Pinchback; his mother addressed him as Eugene Toomer. In school and college he was Eugene Pinchback Toomer. But in the family, all these names slipped away in favor of nicknames. To his mother he was "Booty" (derived from *beauty*); Uncle Bismarck called him "Kid" and Uncle Walter called him "Snoots" or "Snootze." His grandfather mostly called him "Little Whippersnapper" but on occasion used other names according to his mood. When he saw the growing boy begin to demonstrate a devious cleverness, he dubbed Jean "Foxy Grandpop," after a character in the Sunday comics.[25]

Jean liked this individualization of names and absorbed from his grandfather the penchant for creating names to suit the person, occasion, and mood. It was one of the qualities that marked his interaction with others all his life.

---

side of the town. Mary Church Terrell, *A Colored Woman in a White World* (1940; rpr. New York, 1980), 239.

    24. JT notes (JTP 15:1, 14:4, 14:9).

    25. JT, "Earth-Being," 47, 149, also part in *W&S*, 114.

He also saw the comic quality of names, including the name Toomer. In his fiction later he chose the most ridiculous names possible, each of course having some relationship to the character who bore it: the angel Begori, Mr. Costyve Duditch, Mr. Limph Krok, Prince Klondike, Wistwold and Wimepime Gallonwerp, Mr. Doofle Tack, Kalimorn Rumprires. To his wife was delegated the responsibility of picking out strange and ear-catching names from the newspaper and passing them along to him for possible use in his writing. As to his own names, he wrote (about 1929), "I don't think I would have chosen either name for myself. I mean, the sounds of them—Pinchback, Toomer—do not strike my ear well. In fact, few names strike my ear well. I think the names we human beings attach to ourselves are among the most ridiculous features of our existence."[26]

But there was a deeper level at which the shifting of names, and the lack of a name, had great significance for Toomer. In the tin box which during his lifetime he kept closed even to his wife are scraps of family records and a few selected letters, pictures, and postcards. There is also an undated poem typed on a page that has been crumpled and straightened out again:

> Above my sleep
> Tortured in deprival
> Stripped of the warmth of a name
> My life breaks madly. . . .
> Breaks against world
> Like a pale moth breaking
> Against sun.

Some twenty-five years after his birth, the overnamed and nameless young man took another name: Jean. "I gave it to myself when I began writing. The name Eugene Toomer seemed not to have the sound, the flare [*sic*], the flavor proper to a poet, a man of letters, a philosopher." It was a serious move at the time, though he makes light of it later. And in another twenty years he made another serious choice, calling himself Nathan Jean Toomer, partly to indicate clearly that he was male, since the name Jean had caused some confusion. More, it seemed to mark a hope for a new quality in his life: "I am tired of minor changes of all kinds, but with my whole heart would welcome a major transformation, a radical sharp rise upwards into a new being, a new consciousness, a new birth."[27] Although he hoped this would be his "final name till death," in fact it was signed on manuscripts for a few years and retained in his

26. *Ibid.*, 11.
27. JT notes (JTP 14:3), 34–35.

official name among Quakers as N. Jean Toomer, but faded out in daily use in favor of just Jean Toomer. The name Jean was self-chosen, adapted from a name never legally his, but it was the name by which he was known for all of his public life and by his friends throughout his adulthood.

His first chosen name, at twenty-five, eliminated his grandfather from his identity, and his second chosen name, at forty-five, brought his father's connection back as part of an effort to find inner wholeness. The struggle to shape a satisfying image of himself, of which these name changes were markers, was an extremely important element of his life.

2.

Confluence and Divergence

For Jean, his father inhabited only the realm of remote and pleasant fantasy. In spite of his mother's and grandmother's warning that his father might be in the neighborhood and might steal him (once at least they told Jean this at Saratoga), such a devil image refused to stick in Jean's mind. He was sure, as he recounted in his autobiography, that he actually did see his father once, coming up to him as he played on the sidewalk, swinging him up in his arms, talking to him briefly, and leaving him bemused with a half-dollar in his hand. This friendly image confirmed the feeling he persistently harbored that his father lived somewhere and loved him. "Way back in me he became a sort of mystery, part real, part legendary, a kindly portentous figure quite outside the ordinary run of life." [1]

His mother, of course, had the daily care of him, and it was something of a burden. She did not exercise a great deal of control. Although, as Jean later felt, she was more conscious of her husband's absence than of her son's presence and was not a "natural mother," still she was often a vivacious companion, almost like a teenager. Sometimes they would ride the streetcar out past Rock Creek Bridge to Chevy Chase, watching for a particular house on a hill that they called the "witch house." Sometimes they would go shopping, or to the zoo. Sometimes they would lie in a hammock swung between two trees on the lot next door, and his mother would sing to him. On summer vacations, on a farm he calls "Uncle Bob's" in Virginia, they would sit in rocking chairs or hammocks on the porch while she would sing. He remembered best the song about hanging her heart on a weeping willow tree.

1. JT notes (JTP 15:1).

Indeed, as she returned, now past thirty, to the round of balls and gentleman callers, her father actually treated her like a teenager. When a caller remained in the parlor after ten o'clock, Pinchback would begin pacing back and forth in his room upstairs. If that didn't dislodge the guest, the blinds would slam, and then an alarm clock would go off. Finally, all else failing, Pinchback would call down the stairs, "Nina! It is after ten o'clock!"[2] While Nina must have found her father's behavior intolerable, young Jean, jealous of the callers, became his grandfather's ally, enjoying the whole game of eviction.

In fact, there grew a warm relationship between Pinchback and his small grandson. Jean idolized his grandfather and felt overwhelmed with honor when Pinchback took the small sharp scissors he kept to trim his beard and sat Jean up on a high stool to cut his hair. Sometimes he took Jean downtown to "have lunch with 'the men' who made much to-do over me, giving me a feeling that I was the scion of a great family."[3] After his grandfather came home from downtown in the evening, there would be a light supper laid out for him. When he got old enough, Jean could wait up and listen to his grandfather tell of his adventures while he ate his supper. Once in a while Jean got a little of the cold turkey or other tidbits, and though they joked about it, both clearly understood that the great man had the prerogative and the boy never got more than a taste. In the evenings, occasionally, Pinchback would invite Jean to climb into his bed. In the dark he had a chance to talk about his friends and school and whatever he was most interested in at the moment, and his grandfather would listen sympathetically. The grandfather listened to him, too, as the boy learned to recite poetry and orations, at times asking him to declaim a special favorite for company. Jean got his share of applause and praise, developing a flair for playing up to an audience.

The grandfather's greatness was, in the boy's eyes, all-pervasive. Thinking of it later, he described a small white frame cottage the family occupied one summer at Saratoga, saying, "It fit him like a tight out-grown suit which you dare not stretch in lest it burst. Grandfather should have been in one of the grand villas." His grandfather's character he described in 1941 as "affectionate and domineering, loving and tyrannical" in the family and "indomitable" in the world of public affairs. Toomer summarized the sequence of the small boy's striving for his own independent being: he was three before he could conquer his nurse, seven when he conquered his mother and grandmother, but he was not able to conquer his grandfather until the year Pinchback died.[4]

2. JT, "Earth-Being," 123, also in W&S, 37.
3. Ibid., 121, also in W&S, 36.
4. Ibid., 134; JT notes (JTP 14:6); JT, "Earth-Being," 11, also in W&S, 17.

Jean's Uncle Bismarck, however, supplied a certain complement to his grandfather in the influences on the young boy. Named for the powerful founder of the German empire, whom his father greatly admired, Bismarck himself would rather have been named for Napoleon.[5] But Uncle Bismarck's admiration for Napoleon, which rubbed off onto Jean, must have been a compensatory fantasy, for, according to Toomer, he was gentle, sensitive, intellectual, artistic, and displayed so little drive for achievement that he could not satisfy his father's expectations for him. He spent, instead, his days in clerical drudgery and his evenings lying in bed reading, drawing, or writing short stories. But when Jean was old enough to absorb information about what was beyond his neighborhood, he found his Uncle Bis a kindred soul and a rich source of all sorts of knowledge. Thanks to a picture in a book Uncle Bis had, Jean took in the concept of the earth as a relatively small ball orbiting a much larger sun. He began to see stars, weather, and man from perspectives he had never dreamed of. Uncle Bis had books that were far more intriguing than school books, on the way the world was made and on the wider world of fantasy. Lying in bed, snacking on a dish of sliced peaches, his uncle read or sometimes told in his own words myths, fairy tales, and adventures, peopling Jean's mind with gods and heroes, abandoned sons and wicked stepmothers, and princes in disguise. Bismarck's curiosity about science and love for art and literature fed Jean's eagerness for investigating, reading, and writing.

Jean became entranced, curiously enough, not only by the pursuit of knowledge but by Bismarck's customary horizontal position for that pursuit: "This position—my uncle in bed surrounded by the materials of a literary man—was impressed upon me as one of the desirable positions in life. It is no wonder that later on I responded positively to pictures of Robert Louis Stevenson and other writers spending most of their lives in bed."[6] Later, when Jean himself became a writer, he wrote not lying down but standing up. Yet he could not have known that for years, at the end of his life, he would spend most of his days a semi-invalid, receiving guests and having his meals in just such a position, lying on a couch in his living room.

Bismarck, nearing forty, still, like Nina, had his troubles with his father. Toomer suggests in his later account that the grandfather was disappointed in his son's failure to become a doctor or to achieve anything spectacular, and his

5. Both generations of Pinchback's family tended to name their sons after military leaders. Pinchback, of course, had a brother Napoleon, and his own name, Pinckney, could well have been chosen for the Pinckney brothers of North Carolina, leaders in the American Revolution and in shaping the state and federal constitutions.

6. JT, "Earth-Being," 153, also in *W&S*, 42.

frustration came out in disguised forms. Perhaps Bismarck's habit of retiring right after dinner for his solitary intellectual and artistic pursuits, the opposite of the man of action and connections who is out socializing with his cronies, did rankle his father. In any case his "out by ten o'clock" rule was applied to the lights in Bismarck's room. But to Jean's delight, Uncle Bis did not submit. First he covered his transom, but this did not protect him from his father's opening the door and discovering the light. So he rigged a system with a matchstick and two black threads: at his father's step in the hall, Uncle Bis could pull the string from his bed and turn off the gas jet on the opposite wall.

Except for the matter of reading late at night, Bismarck caused little dissension. He did not openly defy Pinchback; in fact, Toomer recalls him as something of a reconciler. Such a function was needed, with an "active dominant man like grandfather, a passive woman like grandmother, [and] a resistant force like mother."[7] Bismarck soothed and jollied Nina and her mother in turn, helped Jean exercise his lively intellect, served as mediator when views became extreme, and smoothed over the sharp words. He was sorely missed when he finally left the family home to marry, in 1905. Toomer does not say so, but Uncle Bis also took over much of a father's teaching role and provided an image of the ideal man to supplement or, rather, compete with the one Jean held of his grandfather. In contrast to the public, group-oriented, dominating political man, often an irritant to those around him, focused on wealth and influence, Bismarck showed the solitary, inner-oriented, intellectual reconciler, vitally interested in art and literature. Jean somehow in his personality had to combine both ideals—a strange mixture. But it may be noted that each man was, in his field, clever. From an early age, Jean worked at developing this quality.

The dynamics of the extended family were fairly complete, the various members representing dominance, submission, a measure of defiance, and reconciliation. It had been a family before Jean came, and he was in a sense an extra member. They made room for him, but there was no particular part left for him to take on the family stage. Therefore he could go his own way, forming his relationships primarily with his friends on the block, concealing his real feelings from the family, pursuing his inner learnings and sensitivities, being an essentially private child. His family, he says, "seemed in a sense to follow a feeling I induced in them which made them keep their hands off me; keep, as it were, a respectful distance." His mother did not require much of him, but she represented a buffer against his grandfather, so Pinchback did not have much

7. *Ibid.*, 190, also in *W&S*, 70–71.

to do with Jean's being disciplined and trained. In the autobiography Jean records that he came in late one evening, and his mother spanked him. He deserved a punishment, he felt, but spanking was too severe, and he responded by remarking stoically to his grandmother, "She can do no more than kill me." Both his mother and grandmother were shocked at the words, but Jean would have nothing to do with them for several days. As he recalled it later, he felt that the attitude represented in this statement was frequently his throughout his life when he encountered treatment he thought unfair.[8] It is a kind of detached martyrdom: one may feel quite brave, but one is cut off from all communication with the perceived offender.

Jean appreciated his freedom, but the strained relationships among family members were upsetting. His mother's misuse by her husband, oversheltering by her father, and lack of her own domain constantly grated against her proud nature and caused friction in the family. Jean, as we have seen, sided with his grandfather against his mother, his uncle against his grandfather, and when necessary, himself against the world. In later life he felt that all the adults in his home, though well-meaning, failed him in various ways, gave him erroneous answers to questions, or were sources of disillusionment—all but Uncle Bis.[9]

Toomer in his autobiography traced a parallel between his learning process as a child and the learning process that went on for the rest of his life. He felt he had always learned best from informal, independent sources such as Uncle Bis. As he grew he developed enthusiasms for many things. Uncle Walter used to say "Snootze has a new bump" when Jean got curious or excited about collecting or learning something new. He investigated many materials, wood and metal and wire, at the shop of a neighborhood resident who was a sort of inventor. He liked stamp collecting and experimented with electricity. He wanted to be, by turns, "a bicycle cop, a street car conductor, a locomotive engineer, a baseball pitcher, a builder of houses, an electrician and inventor."[10] On the long train trips to Saratoga, he liked to shoot his toy gun at the passing billboards, pretending to be Buffalo Bill shooting Indians. At the racetrack one year he was possessed with the desire to collect the men's badges that were labeled Grandstand, Club, or Paddock, and went to some lengths to get them in pristine condition. On a visit to New York, he was fascinated with the big buildings, ocean liners, and horsecars. He suddenly wanted to learn to play a mandolin when he met a boy his own age who had one. When he met someone with a camera, again, he wanted one immediately.

8. JT notes (JTP 15:5); JT, "Earth-Being," 169–71, also in W&S, 62–63.
9. JT, "Earth-Being," 158, also in W&S, 45.
10. Ibid., 111; JT notes (JTP 15:3).

School learning, on the other hand, was hard for him. Being able to read, like telling time, came in a flash, as though the mystery suddenly cleared. Reading had seemed impossible, but when his teacher threatened severe punishment for all those in his class who could not read after a certain day, "I did indeed succeed. . . . Before judgement day arrived I had rent the veil."[11] He sounds, as he tells the story, like a child utterly alone. He does not mention asking, or getting, help from anyone, his teacher or his family.

School, in general, was a bore. Garnet School on U Street—the "colored" school to which he was sent—he describes as a prisonlike building. There he threw crayons and erasers around, rolled inkwells up the aisles, sent notes, and teased the girls—often by releasing a captured fly from his closed fist into their faces. Once he had to stand for an hour in front of the class in a girl's dress and apron for teasing girls. But he made faces and jubilantly distracted the students: "There I was, outstanding and distinguished, even if ignominiously so. . . . My prestige mounted." He altered his marks in deportment before showing his report cards to his family. He felt entitled to special privilege and immunity "owing to grandfather's position and influence."[12]

His list of reasons why he did not do well in school includes jealousy of his mother's callers, an inborn resistance to authority, a sense that his grandfather's position protected him, and the false philosophy of education that relied on forcing information into children. In this catalog of reasons he does not mention his separation from his friends or the fact that it was a black school, but both of these must have weighed heavily. Surely resentment at being arbitrarily shut out of his group, as well as the inevitable lack of resources at a black school in Washington at the height of the Jim Crow era, would have affected what was offered him and how Jean could accept it. Later, when he was in a white school in New Rochelle, New York, he seems to have gotten what school was meant to give him.

School was a place to test how much one could get away with, and home was necessary for food and shelter, but the center of young Jean's life was his friends. The children on his block did not attend Garnet School. Their families were white, some recent immigrants, of middle- and upper-class occupations. One man was in insurance, one the owner of a music store, others were contractors or in the ornamental-iron business, one the head of a government bureau, and one a senator. The senator's house was so big, it seemed like a maze when small boys had to find their way out after playing there. In terms of status and afflu-

11. JT, "Earth-Being," 159–60, also in *W&S*, 46.
12. *Ibid.*, 163, 161, also part in *W&S*, 47.

ence, his grandfather fitted into the neighborhood comfortably. Jean was not really aware of any racial difference between himself and the others until the school assignment made it sharply clear.

The neighborhood was a combination of city and country. The street, beginning at Fourteenth Street and ending at a farm east of Sixteenth Street, was dirt, with mostly red brick sidewalks, gas lights, and new trees in boxes beside the road—boxes that were to reappear years later in some of Jean Toomer's fiction. A field across the street was a summer treasure of weeds and wild flowers, an overgrown jungle at the fullness of its growth for games of hiding and pursuit. On cold fall days, he and his friends built packed-earth campfires there for roasting potatoes, apples, or frankfurters stolen from nearby stores. It was a ball diamond and a football field and, when weather cooperated, a hockey rink or a site for snow forts. In a tulip tree in Jean's yard was a tree house, a useful retreat for smoking corn-silk cigars, and the one cement sidewalk formed a roller-skating arena. A few blocks to the south, Meridian Hill provided steep banks where they dug caves. Less than a mile to the north were woods and, in Piney Branch, a swimming hole. Nearby were a stable and a lumberyard, new houses going up, and at one time a church being built. All these supplied many opportunities for exploration and adventure.

This was his kingdom, and until he was ten, Jean was—in his later perception, at least—the king. There were about eight children, boys and girls, in his "gang"; he remembered them well and could name and describe them many years later. From time to time they fought with the "Girard Street boys" or the "16th Street boys" (the black youngsters from the tenant shacks on the farm) but only occasionally among each other. Any kingdom has to be fought for, and this was a testing area in terms of power and leadership. Jean ("Pinchy" to his friends) was not large, but he was healthy and strong and could run, climb, fight, and think up Halloween pranks better than most. "We harrassed [sic] the staid adults, peppering with [sic] windows with beans and putty, slamming doors, ringing bells. If we had it in for the people of any particular house, this was the time to take it out on them. We'd steal their mats, lift their gates off the hinges, sometimes burn them—and, to one party, we made a present of a large carefully wrapped package of juicy horse-turds." It was Pinchy who set the fires in the empty lot so the gang could play firemen and practice putting them out. When the fence caught fire, the adults working on the block had to charge in with rags, brooms, and pails of water to save the neighboring houses. When the policeman came to the door, Jean was hiding upstairs, and his grandmother claimed she did not know who had started the fire. From the beginning, though almost the same age as his best friend, Jean seemed to feel that he was older and more protective, one who knew just what to do, bossed the others, and "often assumed the pose of a little Napoleon." [13]

One of the areas of learning in Jean's young life that is traced in some detail in the autobiographies is that of love and sex. His first love, long before he started to school, was Dorothy, a little fair girl with curly blond hair who lived directly across the street. At the special sound of her screen door opening, he would dash out to the street to play with her. The mothers customarily bathed their children at the open front windows in the afternoon, standing them up to wave to each other afterward. Jean's innocent enjoyment of this process was marred when an older boy began making snide remarks about the afternoon baths, and the mothers then stopped the practice. Soon after this, his interest passed from Dorothy, but fastened on other girls in succession: "I was so obviously fond of the girls that had I not been able to give a good account of myself as a fighter and runner and tree-climber I would doubtless have lost caste." [14] His sexual knowledge at this age, however, was not gained primarily from girls. The boys shared half-knowledge and bawdy songs. An older boy taught Jean to masturbate. But after one boy took a girl under a porch, the girls in the neighborhood were forbidden to play with the boys. The proscription was not enforced for long, but the early naturalness was never regained.

At this stage of life, Jean had three personal symbols. First was the arrow, which he carved on every tree and fence. Second was the eagle, proud and brave and recognized king of birds, fierce, soaring, and magnificent. He visited the eagle at the zoo, drew eagles on his school books, and found a papier-mâché model eagle to hang from the chandelier in his bedroom. Third was the heart, which he drew and doodled. In one series of sketches, a heart gradually turned into a girl's face, meant to be Dorothy's.

As he got older, yearning for such things as bicycles, mandolins, and cameras, Jean also recognized the need for money and began to find ways to get it. Pinchback, who at the height of his financial success had forced his sons to make their own way and whose resources were declining, could not be expected to provide his grandson with an ample allowance. So Jean took it on himself. In the days when candy was all he wanted to buy, he picked up pins from the floor after the dressmaker had been there or his mother or grandmother had been sewing, and sold them back, so many for a penny. Later he carefully collected unfinished cigarettes that Uncle Bis or Walter had left about, cut off the burned ends, and took the paper off, keeping the tobacco in a box to be resold

13. *Ibid.*, 86–87 (also in *W&S*, 59), 45.
14. *Ibid.*, 64–65, also in *W&S*, 52–53.

to his uncles. His crowning scheme, in his early school days, was to crack the code on cereal boxes and win prize after coveted prize. A new brand of oatmeal was promoting its sales by enclosing cards, a different animal or "kinderbeast," in each box. With a full set, a child could send in for a prize. All the kinderbeast varieties were easy to get except one, and Jean discovered that the boxes containing the hard-to-get animal had a different number stamped on the outside. He arranged with the neighborhood grocer that he would get first chance at each new carton of oatmeal boxes, bought all the boxes with the special number, and was able to get as prizes a camera, a mandolin, and a gold-plated watch. To retain his advantage, of course, he had to keep this method secret from the other children. He also kept it secret from his family and claimed he had never told it to anybody until he recounted it in his autobiography. At about this time, his grandfather adopted the "Foxy Grandpop" appellation for him. "Grandfather admired shrewdness in any form," Toomer added.[15] Keeping his own counsel was important to a boy determined to have an inner life that he did not share with anyone.

He was also developing a curious pattern of moral behavior. Doing something that was allowed, for example, he might act in such a way as to create suspicion. He did this with his collection of tobacco, sneaking into his uncles' rooms only when they were not there and keeping his supply hidden. When he was caught and accused of wrongdoing, maybe even punished, he would persist as long as possible without saying anything. Finally he would lay out his innocence, trapping his accuser or punisher in an injustice and establishing his moral ascendancy. Perhaps it was a kind of teasing, but he viewed it as a need to prove to those about him that he was above all doubt, that he was morally superior: "It was a quick turn-over, a kind of moral or emotional jiu-jitsu. . . . For this moral triumph I would undergo considerable physical or emotional discomfort."[16] It was in fact deliberate manipulation, inducing an attack by the other, designed to humble the parent and exalt the child, to overcome by cleverness his naturally lesser role.

A sense of participation in nature was basic to the growing inner life of young Jean Toomer. He describes the joy of walking in the woods and his sometimes overwhelming exhilaration in the blooming field in the summertime. On one occasion he almost seemed to fuse with the steaming grass and the flowers alive with bees: "More intense than the heat was a strange charge in the atmosphere. . . . What the heat would have drooped and wilted, this mag-

15. *Ibid.*, 246–49.
16. *Ibid.*, 145–46, also in *W&S*, 40.

netic force infused and vitalized. . . . The beauty of it seized me. It swept me with and into it. . . . I remember finding myself stretched in the grass, belly on the ground, breathing Nature into me through every pore, myself blending with it."[17]

Another interest was the observation of people. At the track at Saratoga he began to guess what people were thinking or feeling by looking at their faces, to try to "read" people—the genesis of a lifelong fascination with motivations and inner complexities, which served him both in his fiction and in his later efforts to reshape that mixture in people themselves. In addition, his mother's best friend's brother had a camera and taught Jean to use it. He learned through photography the art of selection and arrangement of detail, the building of pattern from existing materials, essential to any creative process.

Jean was practicing, then, by the time he was ten, the cleverness and dominance of his grandfather, which he used to gain material, social, and moral advantages. But he was also using the aesthetic appreciation and investigative intellect of his Uncle Bis, as well as perception, observation, and solitary analysis that would show up later in his fiction and poetry. And at the same time he saw himself as a king, even a dictator, physically and intellectually superior to his friends, morally superior to his elders. Uncle Walter had identified each new "bump" of eager curiosity as it surfaced, but, the adult Toomer recognized, "Walter seems to have overlooked one bump, namely, the bump of egotism. It was sizeable even then."[18]

The young Napoleon did not realize, however, that his tenth year would bring his Waterloo. The old order was to be overturned: his mother would no longer be ruled by her father and her son, and Pinchy would no longer rule the neighborhood. It did not happen all at once. First, beloved Uncle Bis, the reconciler, left to get married. Then in the spring of 1905, Jean noticed intense bursts of conversation between his mother and grandfather or grandmother, from which he was excluded. Late in the spring, Jean's mother told him she was going away for a while, to Atlantic City and other places, and was not taking him along. This plight might have been endurable, had Jean had his usual vacation with his grandparents, but before long, Jean found out that they were also going off for the summer without him. He was to spend his days with some people (later he could not even remember whether they were friends, relatives, or someone paid), be picked up after work by Uncle Walter, and brought back for the night to the empty house. No mother, no grandmother or grandfather, no Uncle Bis, no playmates—all the mainstays of his life were

17. *Ibid.*, 60.
18. *Ibid.*, 111.

suddenly snatched away. The summer became for him a "dark night streaked with nightmares." The postcards his mother sent him almost every day, from Atlantic City and Brooklyn, said little and could hardly relieve his anxiety, though he saved them carefully to the end of his life.[19]

Walter had served briefly in Cuba in the Spanish-American War, and his room was decorated with souvenirs, including a sword and a revolver. At this time, there had been some reports of burglaries in the area, and because there was no one home all day, Walter devised a warning system. He took his old pistol and laid it in the front hall each morning when they left, assuming that if a burglar broke in, he would surely take the pistol. Each evening when they unlocked the front door, they would look for the pistol—it was always there—but Walter insisted on going through the house in the dark, revolver in hand, searching for the burglar, before he would turn on the lights. Only then did the "gloomy ghost-ridden burglar-infested bat house" become again its familiar warm haven to Jean. This nightly ritual, coupled with the removal of almost all the figures he had leaned on, could not have failed to shake Jean's self-assurance.

Nightmares were not new to him. For three or four years of his childhood, Jean was subject to nightmares so persistent that he could recall five of the scenarios in detail when writing his autobiography thirty or forty years later. This "dark summer" of 1905 in his memory was a living rehearsal of these nightmares.

The figures in these recurring dreams are varied, but they are all chasing him, and his home in each case offers a false shelter. The first is a monster, chasing him outdoors. If he can reach a certain landing on the stairs in his house, he will be safe, but the monster does not let him get there. The second is a group of ghosts filing into the sanctum of his bedroom. Even though his mother is beside him, she cannot be waked, cannot help him. Again in his room, he bolts the door against a huge brown bear, but the animal breaks the door and bursts in. Nor can his grandfather protect him: in the dining room, Jean faces another series of ghosts, each bigger than the last. He has only to be taller than each one to win the contest, but the last is as tall as the ceiling, and Jean even on his grandfather's shoulders cannot beat that one. Outside in the fifth dream, running up an alley behind his house, he is overtaken and overcome by some immense shapeless doom, like a chicken being crushed by an automobile.[20]

These dreams must have carried a freight of anxiety about some emotion

19. JT notes (JTP 15:15, JT tin box [MTC]).
20. JT, "Earth-Being," 105, 111–13.

Jean feared would be overwhelming if it were given rein. Often children, taught not to express it, are afraid of the aggression or anger they feel. Jean's reaction to the possibility that his mother might marry again, his jealousy of the men who called on her, suggest one kind of strong conflicting feeling. She was more of a mainstay to his security than he would realize or admit. It is possible, too, that the underlying tension in his house between his frustrated, resistant mother, her dominated brothers, and her overbearing father, all covered over with a fabric of amenities, was communicated to the child as a simmering volcano about to explode or a monster that could pounce at any moment.

His summer thus was marked by emptiness and fear. Jean felt the portents of the collapse of his familiar world: his grandfather and his mother had suddenly, albeit temporarily, slipped out of his life. Although they had tried to hide their negative feelings about each other, neither could keep him from the destructive effects of the tensions they had created—but he loved and needed them both.

That his mother needed to get away from her father's coercive oppression of her social life is not surprising, and she must have been desperate enough in 1905 to defy him and insist on a summer alone. Why Jean's grandparents did not take him with them on the usual summer vacation is not so clear. It is not hard to believe, however, that the abandoned ten-year-old, when the family reassembled, would find some extraordinary means to bind them all to him so it would not happen again.

Nina's venture seems to have been successful from her point of view. When she returned in the fall, she asked Jean if he would like to have a father. He did not answer, and she dropped the subject; life seemed to resume in the Pinchback house as usual. But early in the school year, Jean had a cold and fever, unusual for him, and was out of school for some time. When he went back he found he was behind the other children, so he began faking illness to stay out rather than appear stupid (or apply himself enough to make up the work). In the afternoons, saying he felt better, he would go out to play. Since the other children ate later than the Pinchback family, he would often stay out past dinnertime and eat some candy instead, pretending at home that he was not hungry.

It was, he guesses, a combination of the physical and psychological stresses that brought on a vomiting attack in December that lasted for more than ten days, long enough, in the days before intravenous feeding, for his condition to become precarious. His mother, calling in three doctors in succession, finally got some help from the third: a prescription of some "nasty medicine" and a diet of plain boiled rice and milk. For months Jean stayed in bed, unable to tolerate any other food, and his mother was in constant attendance. He had achieved some basic desires—his mother's total care and concern, and the "desirable" reclining position of his literary uncle. His earliest, infantile memory of calling imperiously for milk and warm blankets was being played out again. The clever maneuverer was operating, this time below the conscious level, but he did not yet know what the cost would be.

When, in March, Jean was finally able to go out again to play, both he and his friends had changed. Instead of a display of his usual power the first time he ran to meet the gang, he began vomiting. He found he only looked foolish when he tried to run or climb. Nor was he strong enough to fight—when he went back to school, a bully beat up on him. His best friend Dutch, who had faithfully come to see him for a long time, finally faded away, growing closer to other children; his most recent girl friend made an unkind remark that finished the relationship for Jean; and in his months in bed, he had been supplanted as leader by a bigger, stronger boy. Rather than protesting, pleading, contesting for his lost leadership, or taking on a different role in the group until he could become stronger, Jean withdrew. He retreated within himself and kept his own counsel, providing inward solace for outward abuse. Physically he was outdoors, but not one of the group. He sat for hours on the rounded stone post flanking his front steps, watching and listening, "Pinchy on his post." Of course he did not stay on his post all the time. Sometimes he would venture to join an activity, but he was assigned a minor role, which did not suit him. He gave up on school for the year and spent some time alone on his bicycle in Rock Creek Park and areas farther from home, but he fell and ruptured himself. Reminded constantly to be careful, he came to think of himself as both a physical and psychological cripple.

There was nothing left for him in Eden. His friends had turned into "alien figures in a dissolving land—and mother floated in, and she was an alien figure in a dissolving house—and Washington reeled in and they all reeled off into the mist of a sweet April night—and I walked through the mist not knowing where I was going but knowing that I was lonely and alone, the deposed solitary keeper of kingdoms that had broken and gone forever."[21] As when his favorite trees for the hammock were cut down by mistake, as when his beloved rabbit disappeared from the backyard, a good thing was ending and, in his view, nothing could be done about it. The experience of his tenth to eleventh year proved to him the impermanence of the good, and left him (as he pictured it afterward) with a stoical acceptance of what life provides.

21. JT notes (JTP 15:5).

Having been a natural leader, he knew he could be a leader now only by working and struggling. He was bruised and sensitive. Having been a group member, he was now an isolate among his peers as he had been in his family. With a streak of self-pity he records: "Bacon Street did not want me, or at least it was indifferent to me. Well I had accustomed myself to not wanting it."[22] And as his physical activities were reduced, mental activities became more important. His mother had bought him, when he was in bed, some cardboard models of buildings, castles, and churches he could set up. These had caught his imagination, and in this fantasy town, he played out myths, fairy tales, and romances. Also he was fond of sketching, and a number of sketches are extant, in his school notebooks. One, labeled "The Evolution of Love," can be dated by the address at a time close to this period. It is a series of faces, beginning with a fresh, attractive one and moving to a few withered lines at the end. Now the internal, intangible world began to fill the space the external world was yielding, and his own thoughts, observations, and feelings flowed together to shape the beginning of a rich inner life.

When, in the early summer of 1906, Nina told Jean she was leaving for a while, it seemed to him that the inevitable was playing itself out. He and his grandmother sheltered each other through the soft warm evenings while his grandfather went downtown grouchy and returned to his table of delicacies still unshared with wife or grandson. Uncle Walter was courting a young woman and was not spending much time at home. Word soon came—a shock but not a surprise to Jean—that his mother was married and would be living in Brooklyn or New Rochelle, New York. For Jean, the thought of leaving his grandmother was harder to manage than the thought of facing a new father. Although he never knew whether his reluctance was a factor in the decision, his grandparents did manage to stay near him. A family council including Nina, Bis, and Walter produced an agreement to sell the Bacon Street house. (Pinckney, who was not close to the family, had died before this time.) Walter, like Bis, would have a place of his own in Washington, and the Pinchbacks, Nina, and Jean would move to New York, near one another but no longer in the same house.

For a time the grandparents and grandson boarded with a couple in Brooklyn, people from Boston who had the peculiar habit of serving beans for breakfast, according to Jean's memory. There Nina brought her new husband, Archibald Combes, for his first inspection by her wary family. Then Jean was taken to live with his mother and stepfather, for the first few hot months in a stuffy fur-

22. JT, "Earth-Being," 208.

nished apartment they rented in New York. Combes was working for the Metropolitan Life Insurance Company, and this required his moving about. After that summer, the three settled into a flat in Brooklyn, and the following year they moved to a house in suburban New Rochelle, on Long Island Sound.

Archibald Combes was a rough man with little sensitivity, but he tried to be nice to Jean. To Jean, however, Combes seemed "flabby and inferior" in contrast to his grandfather, and he held himself aloof. He resented his mother too, except when he pitied her for having to do all the housework. His school at first was just another aspect of his sense of dislocation. He was set back a year, starting the fourth grade again—not surprisingly, since he had been ill and out of school almost the whole preceding year. There he turned to his old mischief-making role, regarding classwork as not worth his attention. However, after a month he was transferred to his age level. In this fifth-grade class, the teacher took his measure and said she "was sure that within a very short time I would be one of the best pupils in the room." This shock brought him up short and caused a major change. He had never before worked in school, but now he "became regenerated at once, . . . studied seriously, . . . won prizes for excellence, and fulfilled her expectations." His account of this time shows considerable gratitude and respect for the teacher who believed in him, Miss Farrell.[23] Suddenly he was more interested in scholarship and less in being leader of the extracurricular exploits. Several neat notebooks and an essay from this period remain with his papers, many of the lessons marked B + or A. About this time, too, he submitted his first formal writing to public view. He entered a paper on Lincoln in a contest and won honorable mention.

He also took on a broad spectrum of other activities. A boy in Jean's first neighborhood in Brooklyn introduced him to the underworld of gangster mobs, and Jean believed that he, too, could be a detective secretly on the lookout for members of the mysterious gang of the Black Hand. Later he adopted a new strategy to give him a place among a new group of children: he toadied to the leader and became his sidekick. And pursuing the bent for fantasy and romance that had been nourished during his illness, he began to read extensively, particularly books on knighthood and chivalry. As a result, he made wooden swords and shields, properly emblazoned with coats of arms, for medieval tournaments, and developed some strongly entrenched ideas about the proper roles of men and women.

In his school notebooks from 1906 through 1907, he sketched swords and a fantasy of flying in space, perhaps landing on the moon or a planet. A similar

23. JT, "Book X" (Typescript of autobiography in JTP 16:1), 25.

though undated notebook contains pictures of trees, a whale, a submarine, a kite, a man (smoking a pipe, looking backward, and running, all at the same time), many pictures of women's and girls' heads, and a man with a robot's square boxlike body. Jean's early symbols, the arrow, the eagle, and the heart, are still implicit here, the arrow supplemented by swords and shields, the papier-mâché eagle (in actuality carefully packed and put into his mother's trunk for shipment to Brooklyn) evolving symbolically into the images of space flight and kingship. Crowns, scepters, jewels, and ermine supplanted the eagle's feathers as symbols of royalty and remained attached to his self-image: a much later invitation to a party at a café remains in the files, stating that "The Black Prince Toomer" will be there, with a sketch of a crowned figure in royal robes. Jean reports he was fond of the power of battleships and grew to a strong awareness of Dante's *Inferno* at this time. His mental world was one of extreme heights and depths.[24]

Besides the blossoming of his mind, his body was developing too. He welcomed the move to New Rochelle, which brought him back to a green lawn, open space, and especially the world of water and boats in Long Island Sound, which years before had helped nourish the soul of Walt Whitman. With swimming, fishing, and sailing, Jean became strong again. He picked up enough knowledge about boats to earn some money repairing and refurbishing them. Another girl took the place of those he had lost.

But this interlude of growth was brief. Nina's second marriage was showing signs of strain. Nina and Jean had apparently fitted into the white neighborhood of New Rochelle, but Jean later concluded that Archibald Combes was Nina's inferior in intellect and refinement and that also he had "misrepresented his income." Before these factors produced open cracks in the marriage, Nina fell ill with appendicitis in the summer of 1909. For some reason, Combes had to get consent—or felt he had to—from his wife's parents for an operation to be performed. The delay was too long, and Nina died.

Jean returned immediately to his grandparents, who had moved back to Washington and were living with Bismarck and his wife. He had no further contact with his stepfather, though his grandmother engaged in some acrimonious correspondence with Combes about whose responsibility it was to pay Nina's last doctor bills. The whole episode, with its tragic ending, turned sour. Nina's first husband, however, had dropped even further out of sight: her tombstone was inscribed Nina Pinchback Combes.[25]

24. JT notes (JTP 14:1, 14:3, 15:7, 16:1); JT school notes (JTP 13:4, 13:5).
25. JT, "Outline of an Autobiography" (JTP 14:1), 6; Metairie Cemetery Association, New Orleans, to JT, June 26, 1941, in JT tin box (MTC).

Jean had by this time developed inner shields against loss and misfortune. He had become guarded and more conscious of himself, so much so that he appeared almost callous. At this juncture, he says, "I came to meet life with my mind" rather than with his emotions. Although he had distanced himself partially from his mother when she married, he had now to accept that she was irrevocably lost and make a new beginning in a new setting. It was surely helpful that his grandparents were still there, though of course older and much reduced in income, to provide a measure of stability, even if the magic Bacon Street house of his childhood was no longer theirs. Jean had inherited his mother's house on Twelfth Street, but the family continued to rent this out until 1920, when it was sold.[26]

Living with his grandparents and Uncle Bismarck on Florida Avenue, near families who were his grandparents' friends, Jean experienced for the first time—at the age of fourteen—immersion into black culture. Washington was one of the few U.S. cities at the time where a significant population of blacks had sufficient economic resources to build their own society. Jean described it in two passages from different autobiographies:

With this world—an aristocracy—such as never existed before and perhaps never will exist again in America—mid-way between the white and negro worlds. For the first time I lived in a colored world.

In the Washington of those days . . . there was a flowering of a natural but transient aristocracy, thrown up by the, for them, creative conditions of the post-war period. These people, whose racial strains were mixed and for the most part unknown, happened to find themselves in the colored group. They had a personal refinement, a certain inward culture and beauty, a warmth of feeling such as I have seldom encountered elsewhere or again. . . . All were comfortably fixed financially, and they had a social life that satisfied them. They were not pushing to get anywhere or be anything other than what they were. . . . The children of these families became my friends.[27]

Although the date is a little earlier, a curious sidelight on this description exists in a newspaper article in the Baltimore *Afro-American* of August 10, 1895: "The colored people of Washington, who, as everyone knows, comprise the most cultured, most advanced and intelligent as well as the wealthiest of the members of the colored race in the United States are displaying marked evidence of intellectual and social progress."

It seemed to Jean as he looked back in memory that this was a place where his inner and outer worlds could come together: "It was a gay, bright, sweet life" and "I began to have my emotions fed directly from life." Boys and girls

26. JT, "Book X," 33; settlement papers (JT tin box [MTC]).
27. JT, "Outline," 8; JT, "On Being an American" (JTP 15:10), also in *W&S*, 84–85.

were more natural with each other than they had been in New Rochelle. He mentions excursions down the Potomac and the excitement of playing Bassanio in the eighth grade's production of *The Merchant of Venice*. Full of eagerness and enthusiasm, over his grandmother's objections but with Bismarck's help, he built up a route to deliver the *Saturday Evening Post*.[28]

But during the summer of 1910, while they were at Harpers Ferry, Jean's grandmother became very ill. She was brought back to Washington in a special car and placed in a hospital, where Jean and his grandfather visited daily. They had taken a room with "good people of some refinement," as it seemed better for all concerned if they did not stay on at Bismarck's house. On into the fall, Jean was dismally alone here, his grandfather giving him expense money for the day, then going off to his usual haunts with his friends. Jean would go to school, stop to see his grandmother, get supper at a restaurant, then return to do his homework by gas light. Worrying about his grandmother's dying, tortured by the "vapor of loneliness and desolation in the room," he finally walked the streets at night and did all his studying in the morning. It seemed almost that the nightmare summer he experienced as a ten-year-old was recurring. But now his mother was permanently lost to death and the possibility that he might also lose his grandmother was too close. Eventually, however, she recovered—mostly because, as he claims she told him later, "she felt she had to live for me."[29]

Jean had had dreams of going to Andover or Exeter, then Harvard and maybe Harvard Law School. But his grandfather's resources by now were considerably reduced, partly by gambling losses over the years. And at sixty-five, after a lifetime of high living, he was trying to use political influence to get a job. Pinchback had campaigned for Taft and was hoping for a political appointment as a result, which might provide the extra income to send Jean to prep school. But it soon became clear that this would not happen in time for fall enrollment. Although he feared that a black high school would limit his college chances, Jean entered Dunbar High School in the fall of 1910. It is intriguing to note that the poet Angelina Grimké, daughter of Archibald Grimké of Boston, was teaching English there at the time Toomer was enrolled, but there is no evidence that he was ever in her class. Actually Jean records that he did not like poetry in high school but liked composition and rhetoric, rules and structure and order. The business of drilling and discipline was attractive to him. Toomer describes himself at the time as less rough than

28. JT, "Outline," 8.
29. *Ibid.*; JT, "Book X," 47.

other boys, and as constantly pursuing (as he had in earlier years) some special girl. He shot up in height, but was quite thin.

In October his grandfather's long-awaited appointment came through. It was a position in New York with the Department of Internal Revenue. While Pinchback took an apartment in New York, Jean and his grandmother stayed in Washington, moving into a "fairly large house" with Walter and his wife. Although Jean had to give up "night prowlings with the boys" to keep his grandmother company on the frequent nights they were alone in the house, "I didn't mind. I had her. And I had my room with a work bench and my wireless and all sorts of electrical things."[30] He felt established and secure again. It was a good year. He used the fifty dollars he had saved from the *Saturday Evening Post* route to buy a used motorcycle; after riding grandly about for a while, he decided to earn some money with it and arranged to deliver packages for a cleaner and dyer. His grandmother was horrified at the prospect but gave in to his persistence, and Jean enjoyed both the job and the money. He and a new friend Kennedy found much in common as they shared "iconoclastic views," though they came from different social strata—Kennedy was used to struggling for survival, Jean for self-improvement. They cut school to read books and took long walks reading Shakespeare and Milton aloud. Jean had a growing sense of himself as different from the other students, except for Kennedy: he saw his own interests changing while theirs appeared rigidly permanent, and he began to withdraw and isolate himself.

In his second and third years in high school, negative experiences seemed to pile up. In the second year, an accident in the laboratory quenched his passion for electricity and experimentation with physical substances. He had other preoccupations, and the quality of his schoolwork fell off. In the middle of this year, while he was "going with" a girl, an intense sexual drive and his continuing to masturbate brought him to the "beginning of acute emotional and sex problems . . . the beginning of my stress and strain period."[31] Walter's house had come to feel like "a big gloomy barn," and staying in to keep his grandmother company at night was beginning to wear on Jean. He had recurring periods of depression and was increasingly bored with school.

His third year in high school was the worst. His grandfather returned from New York and the three of them took an apartment at 1341 U Street, bringing out the old furnishings that had been stored when the Bacon Street house was sold. They could not afford a cook or a maid, and Pinchback was tired of restau-

30. JT, "Book X," 47.
31. JT, "Outline," 11.

rants, so Jean's grandmother, frail as she was, had to cook. Jean learned to cook to relieve her burden when she was ill, and he took over all the shopping.

He was then six feet tall but weighed only about 135 pounds—in his words, "my fine boned skinny body, with the shoulders drooping and the chest curving in and not enough in the rear or in the legs to fill the pants." And the sex battle loomed so large, it seemed to have become the pennant-strewn field of the final match between the kingdoms of Good and Evil. Sex had been a powerful force in Jean's life from his earliest days: he remembers falling in love with a girl before he started school and becoming conscious of sex in the sexual organs before that. When he began secretly masturbating, a few years later, his mother was suspicious but provided no help or useful information: "She was failing the chance to intercept the forming of a practice which, as the years unfolded, gave rise to the most desperate struggles of my life." This continuing practice, loaded with fear and guilt, increased to an unbearable level and devoured him in an "avalanche of sex indulgences. I felt and looked wretched. . . . I saw myself falling to pieces."[32] Toomer made up his mind to fight back.

He tried physical training to build himself up, weight lifting, dieting, a nature cure following Bernarr McFadden. He bought McFadden's *Encyclopedia of Physical Culture.* He turned his room into a gymnasium where he worked out privately. He took so many cold baths, his grandfather complained about his using too much water. He filled scrapbooks with pictures of Greek statues and men in body-building poses. He devoted himself totally to physical combat against what he considered a destructive, evil practice, "that practice which more than any other bleeds away the body and soul of growing beings on earth." Although he never spoke to her about it, he felt that his grandmother was praying for him. No one else knew the "critical nature" of his struggle. All, it seemed, was to no avail: "And then there came another spell of sex, which reduced me so low I feared I was going into decline. In a desperate condition I began breathing exercises, living more carefully than ever, and, by sheer force of will, pulled myself out. . . . I have, as it were, gone down to the depths, and have come out."[33] He had won the battle at last.

The crowning episode of this struggle occurred during the summer after Jean's graduation from high school. Since blacks were barred from most summer resort areas, one of Frederick Douglass' sons had purchased some property

32. JT, "Book X," 60–61; JT, "Earth-Being," 93; JT notes (JTP 15:3); JT, "Outline," 12, also in W&S, 89.

33. JT, "Earth-Being," 94; JT, "Outline," 13, also in W&S, 90.

on Chesapeake Bay between Washington and Baltimore and invited a number of members of the black community to buy lots. Several of the Pinchbacks' friends, including the Terrells, had cottages there, and Jean's family visited from time to time. That summer in a tent on the shore of the bay, Toomer had his first sex experience with a girl. It gave him a feeling of fulfillment and manliness, not tinged, apparently, with any of the guilt attached to masturbation—or with any burden of commitment.[34]

Jean's high school years, then, came to a more or less peaceful close. In his final year, thinking of becoming a pharmacist, he got a job as a soda jerk and drugstore clerk. Kennedy worked in the same store, and they played practical jokes on the customers and the owner. Once, for example, they stoked up the furnace on a hot summer day to increase the sale of ice cream. Jean finished high school in three and a half years, then in the spring after a knee injury had healed, had a quiet period of reading Jack London and Joseph Conrad and taking long walks, often to Meridian Hill, where he had played as a child. With his new job as usher in a theater, he had a chance to see road shows, vaudeville, and movies. And Uncle Bismarck introduced him to the eating, drinking, and flirting customs of a more sophisticated society of older men and women.

Toomer felt a sense of maturity, of trial by fire, a certain distance from his companions. In an observation that suggests a repetitive pattern (as when, rejected by his playmates on Bacon Street, he withdrew from them and felt superior on his observation post), adolescent Jean looked down on the ordinary mortal who had not gone through the struggle he had, and questioned the shallow life of the people around him: "I see and feel more in life than they will if they live to be a thousand years old." After fourteen years in the white group, by his count, and four in the black, he was ready to be done with groups and find his place as an individual. He already saw himself as something of a deviant and longed to be "somewhere off, where no one else had been, doing something that no one else had done."[35]

34. Terrell, *Colored Woman*, 239–40; JT, "Book X," Chap. 15.
35. JT, "Outline," 14; JT, "Book X," 81.

P. B. S. Pinchback in his prime, San Francisco
From Marjorie Toomer Collection

Henry Clay Warmoth, governor of Louisiana
From Marjorie Toomer Collection

Nina Emily Hethorn Pinchback, Jean's grandmother, New Orleans
From Marjorie Toomer Collection

Pinchback in later years
From Marjorie Toomer Collection

Nina Pinchback Toomer, Jean's mother, Boston
From Marjorie Toomer Collection

The Pinchback house where Jean grew up, Washington, D.C.
From Marjorie Toomer Collection

The Pinchback house in the 1980s
Photo by Cynthia Kerman

"Pinchy on his post"
From Marjorie Toomer Collection

Jean as an older boy
From Marjorie Toomer Collection

Jean Toomer with Uncle Bismarck
From Marjorie Toomer Collection

3.

Offshore Without an Anchor

Jean Toomer had been shifted and shunted from one place to another, Washington to New York and white world to black, by the exigencies of his family's fortunes. Now it was his turn to make some decisions for himself about where he would go. In the primary choice of worlds, his grandfather had chosen the black, but the grandson thought it better (and more realistic, given the college opportunities for blacks in 1914) to appear as white. He had wanted a year in prep school to erase the record of his attendance at a "colored school" when he applied to a college. Since this was not possible, he decided simply to list himself as white where such a notation was called for; otherwise, he would be silent about the issue. His first two weeks away at school were tense because he was afraid he would be asked about his race, but he never was.

Why he chose the agriculture program at the University of Wisconsin was hard even for him to explain as he narrated it later. He ascribed the choice to some half-recognized yearning for a "landed gentry" status derived from his fantasy image of his father, coupled with a mystical attraction to the Middle West. He had no real interest in agriculture, and he came to realize that the dream farm was only a symbol, drawn from his perception of the beneficent city-country blend that nourished him as a child. This image had both the closeness to nature he had felt when he played in the vacant lot and took walks in the woods, and the civilized attractions including the excitement of new building that he observed on his block and the enjoyment of the sophisticated prerogatives of a moneyed class. The combination seemed to point to a role as manager of a "magnificent farm" or "huge country estate."[1]

1. JT, "Outline," 15.

At Jean's urging, his grandfather had mortgaged the house on Twelfth Street to provide money for college expenses. Armed with the necessary funds, he set off gaily for the summer term and did well both in his subjects and in the matters then more important to him—sailing, playing tennis, swimming, and dancing. He spent a month's vacation in Washington, and his "brief passion for a girl" coincided, we may assume, with the sexual experience he recorded for this summer. Back at Wisconsin in high confidence, he ran for class president. But in the course of the campaign, after the sophomores caught him painting a big red '18 on the grandstand roof, he was somehow convinced that the politics in the freshman and sophomore classes guaranteed the election of someone else. Rather than risk defeat, he withdrew from the contest. First, he retreated to his familiar pattern of consolation: "My star immediately begins going down. In no time at all I am left with no more than a couple of friends and the men who are living in the same house. But my room continues to be a gathering place, the place of beer parties and fun, for our small group." Then came the self-assurance of superiority: "But the lack of emotions and feelings and color in the people began to affect me. The men and girls I met were cruder and far less warm than those I had known in Washington."[2]

His English teacher, urging him to write, started him reading literary periodicals, but he, by his later analysis, was not yet ready. He "affirmed athletics and rejected literature," devoting much time to sports and social life and switching out of the agriculture curriculum. During his Christmas vacation in Washington, he fell in love with a former acquaintance, Phyllis Terrell. At the end of the semester, he quit the program at Wisconsin in order, he says, to be near her. He spent the following summer with her, "one of the most lyric and joyous periods of my life," but during the spring she was at school in Vermont and the excuse for quitting in January seems farfetched. Probably, when he left the agriculture program, Jean had no clear idea about his intention in college and was not doing well in his subjects—as he said, learning was, with him, "a passion or nothing." If he was no longer a star among his peers, we can guess that there was little incentive for him to stay. He had decided to "live from the heart," and in this noble cause the university had little function. He admits to self-deception: "True, I was building up a case for myself against the university in order to put the blame on it and save myself from a sense of failure that would have been unbearable." Indeed, he succeeded. Comparing himself to Melville's Ishmael, he mentally turned failure to triumph: "I was to some extent at war with society, but I was not, nor did I feel myself to be, an outcast, I

2. *Ibid.*, 18.

had, on the contrary, a distinct feeling of superiority, of superior position and placement and destiny."[3]

In the fall of 1915, though he had discarded agriculture at Wisconsin, Jean for some unexplained reason applied to the Massachusetts College of Agriculture at Amherst. He went there to enroll, but there was some red tape in the transfer of his credentials from Wisconsin. Getting impatient, he quit before he started, though the transcript eventually arrived. In his words, he "fooled around New York till my money gave out," then went home again. Not surprisingly, his grandfather disapproved. Already the feeling was growing that he was a "black sheep," disappointing the normal expectations—that he was, to put it bluntly, a failure. His scenario was beginning to bear an almost uncanny resemblance to Uncle Bismarck's series of trials and failures in his early life. It is no wonder his grandfather was not eager to repeat that history. Against the accusations of failure, Jean, as he had in childhood, started to shape his defense. "Here began the notion that I was a strange queer fellow, different from everybody else. . . . For myself, here was the beginning of my individualization. . . . I felt the need to justify my position. I became articulate. On the one hand, I began building up a world of my own based on fancies and rationalizations. On the other, I began a deeper and sincere and penetrating questioning of myself and of life."[4]

By New Year's, he was ready to try college again, this time at the American College of Physical Training in Chicago. This was a two-year course, and he began in January, 1916, his grandfather loaning him some more money against Jean's Washington property. His interest had grown partly out of his fondness for athletics, partly out of his obsession in high school with body building, for the school had originally been directed by Bernarr McFadden. Toomer had knocked about enough to feel less special and more in need of a way of making a living, such as being a physical education teacher and coach. He also liked the thought of himself "rapping out commands," drilling a class as though he were "a general with his army." After a year of living "from the heart," he was ready to let his physical self be primary again.

The school was congenial, with a democratic atmosphere and friendly companions, more women than men enrolled. With little smoking, no drinking, and a diet he worked out for himself, Jean soon was in excellent physical condition, able to date a different woman every night, study fifteen minutes between classes, "and give brilliant recitations," according to his account. In contrast to

3. JT, "Book X," 127, 129, 146; JT, Outline," 21, also in *W&S*, 97.
4. JT, "Book X," back of 166; JT, "Outline," 22, 10, also in *W&S*, 99, 97.

this image of remembered gaiety is the memory of another student there at the time. She remembered Jean Toomer as reserved, isolated, perceived as an Indian by the rest of the students. Jean, in turn, could not remember Meridel LeSueur as a classmate at all when, as a close friend of the woman who was to become his wife, she reappeared in his life fifteen years later.[5]

Involved in the school, however, Toomer grew fascinated with his work in anatomy, and becoming a doctor began to seem attractive. With the help of his anatomy teacher, he was almost committed to enter a small local medical school in the fall, but was diverted by the dream of being a basketball star at a big famous college. He decided therefore to enroll in premed at the University of Chicago, without telling his grandparents.

Meanwhile, Jean's intellectual horizons were expanding to the point of explosion. His boxing instructor introduced him to the theory of socialism. At first he fought this new notion, defending his family aristocracy and the Republican party, but the ideas sank in. Social gaiety began to be replaced by serious talks about the organization of society with his special friend Eleanor Davis. A bit later in the spring, he attended a public lecture on naturalism and atheism given in downtown Chicago. Deeply shaken by the speaker's combination of impressive, broad-ranging intelligence and thoroughgoing materialism, he vowed never to go back. The following week, however, he went to hear Clarence Darrow, and he found himself returning again and again as the series of radical lectures and debates continued. He had been brought to the point of swallowing "the bait of reality" and was "unable to let go, ever." It proved a heavy shock to his system.[6]

What he had previously learned about evolution was either very little or made no impression on him. But Darrow was sketching a picture of the universe according to Darwin and Haeckel that was so vivid and systematic, it was overwhelming to Jean. Although Darwin had refused to pontificate on religious questions from the viewpoint of his scientific theory of evolution, his follower Ernst Haeckel, a German zoologist of high reputation, was not so careful in distinguishing scientific from religious truth. A popular writer, he was still living, and his major publications had appeared within the preceding two decades, contemporary with Jean's young lifetime. Jean devoured Haeckel's works. With a unified analysis derived from the connections he discovered between the simplest and the most complicated life-forms and between simple organisms and nonliving carbon compounds, Haeckel asserted the total in-

5. Meridel LeSueur (hereinafter MLeS) to the authors, August, 1982. JT quotations in this and the previous paragraph are from "Book X," 180, 188, 198.
6. JT, "Book X," 218.

clusiveness of the material world and the absence of the spiritual. He considered psychology only a branch of physiology, and there was in his scheme no place for free will, immortality, or any kind of personal God.

Jean had never had a strong or specific religious faith, but a general sense of a benevolent protective power to whom one could pray was an important part of his world view. The more he read and thought about the doctrines of the naturalists, the more he became convinced that they were right, despite the extreme atheistic implications. Returning to his studies and continuing with the summer term at the American College, he submerged these new ideas for a time, but toward the end of the summer, when he was staying with his good friend Harry Karstens, the whole undigested mass came back up with explosive force:

My old world suddenly and completely collapsed. I found myself in a world without a God. I felt that the foundations of the earth had been pulled out from under me. I felt like a condemned man swinging with a rope about his neck. For several days I was so stunned and broken that I could hardly do more than lay [sic] on my bed in a darkened room and feel I was dying. Also, I felt as if I had been somehow betrayed. I didn't want to see anyone. I didn't want to see the light. In truth, I did not want to live.[7]

However, after this intense withdrawal, Jean managed to tap some new resources. This time his tactic was not a retreat into a fantasy world but a bold descent into the destructive element. Although he dropped his fall classes at the University of Chicago and cut most of those at the College of Physical Training, he found his remedy in venturing deeper into the threatening ideas. He went back to the books that had traumatized him—writings on evolution, naturalism, socialism—and also to novels, especially Victor Hugo's tales of Jean Valjean. He read voraciously. And he talked with Eleanor. Suddenly things started coming together for him, and he wanted to tell people about it. His fondness for applause was probably a factor, but the inner dynamic of accumulating and consolidating a mass of new knowledge that was restructuring his view of the world must also have pushed him to share this excitement. The systematizing quality of socialism particularly had an appeal:

I had been, I suppose, unconsciously seeking—as man must ever seek—an intelligible scheme of things, a sort of whole into which everything fit, or seemed to fit, a body of ideas which held a consistent view of life and which enabled one to see and understand as one does when he sees a map. Socialism was the first thing of this kind I had encountered. I responded accordingly. It was not so much the facts or ideas, taken singly, that aroused me—though certainly I was challenged and stimulated by them. More, it was the *body*, the *scheme*, the order and inclusion. These evoked and promised

7. JT, "Outline," 26, also in *W&S,* 101–102.

to satisfy all in me that had been groping for form amid the disorder and chaos of my personal experiences.[8]

Getting permission from the College of Physical Training to use one of their rooms, he gave a lecture there one evening a week, with a fair attendance, on anything he chose: philosophy, economics, Victor Hugo, evolution, society, the nebular hypothesis of the origin of the universe. Finally he met his nemesis in a talk entitled "The Intelligence of Women," having drawn his ideas from Herbert Spencer, to which both the female audience and the dean of women objected. His audience lost its enthusiasm and his series was ended. But it had been a heady experience, and the breakup of his universe of ideas, with the following recovery and regained sense of order and power, was a marvelously integrating step for him.

In fact, he felt so self-sufficient that he quit both colleges in which he was enrolled. The biology course at the University of Chicago had been too taxing, and his fall crisis may have kept him from passing his American College courses. If he had completed the fall and spring terms, he would have graduated. In the 1917 yearbook of the American College of Physical Training, he is shown among the graduates, only the words "Special Student" indicating a difference. His activities listed there include basketball '16, baseball '16, vice president Athletic Association '16, and membership in what appears to be the only fraternity, Alpha Delta Gamma. Returning to Washington before the end of the spring term, he did indeed somehow pretend to have graduated. To himself he excused this deviousness with the idea he had learned everything Chicago could teach him: "I had derived from my stay in Chicago a thousand times more value than any graduation from college could possibly have given me. I was in living and vital contact with the ideas and thoughts of my century. Chicago had indeed witnessed and brought about the birth of my mind. And, of equal importance, I was again full of strength, physical and moral and mental, again with zest for life, with greater self-confidence."[9]

He dreamed of getting an M.A. or a Ph.D., to "get a job in a school or university, and devote my leisure hours to the life of a scholar." Having read Lester Ward's *Dynamic Sociology* and wanting to pursue this new "bump" of curiosity, he took one course of sociology at New York University summer school, getting a grade of B. Next he took up history, doing so well in it at City College of New York that he was recommended for a job as assistant to the librarian there. He was staying with Uncle Walter, whose wife had died and who was

8. *Ibid.*, back of 25, also in *W&S*, 101.
9. *Ibid.*, 17, 28, also in *W&S*, 102, 103.

working in New York. Jean was still running in high gear, working at his job and his studies, as well as drinking, playing tennis, and dancing. "My strength and zest seemed to be inexhaustible," he reports.[10] His interests were moving on to psychology, he was pledged to a fraternity, and at the library he was starting to explore George Bernard Shaw, when the structure of this circle of emotional and intellectual fulfillment began to crumble.

In his narrative he states he was upset by the conscription act. On April 6, 1917, the U.S. had declared war, and the Selective Service Act was passed in May. Jean's period of high satisfaction with his self-directed intellectual search seems to have lasted from the winter of 1916–1917 through the fall of 1917, considerably beyond the imposition of conscription. Certainly he made no immediate response to the war situation, but perhaps it is true that his uneasiness grew as he waited to be drafted, and he suggests that a speech by Harry Overstreet gave him a nudge. Perhaps, on the other hand, his interest in college courses lagged again. Opposed to war but attracted to soldiering, as he described himself, he finally went to volunteer, before the end of the term. He was classified as physically unfit "because of bad eyes and a hernia gotten in a basketball game." But instead of going back to college, secure in his freedom from the draft, he began another period of drifting, which he euphemistically characterized to himself as doing "something more active" because a war was on.[11]

He found his way first to Chicago, where he stayed with Harry Karstens again and sold cars for a Ford dealer. But something important happened: it was there that he did his first writing, including "Bona and Paul." Unsettled and casting about for something else, in February he got a short-term job at a school in Milwaukee as a substitute physical education director, and went on reading. His library card shows nine books checked out during the two months he was there. He concentrated on G. B. Shaw and discovered Shaw's "real message" for him. Jean had been concealing his failures by "bluffing" (his word); Shaw convinced him it was better to be candid: "I experienced a sudden turn over—a spiritual bath, a complete cleansing. I became candid. And the minute I did so, I felt myself for the first time in years, standing squarely and frankly on my own feet. I was what I was. The world could take me or leave me."[12]

Although Jean was happy with himself, his family was not happy with him. When he returned to Washington without a job and without plans, his grand-

10. *Ibid.*, 29, 30, also in *W&S*, 103, 104.
11. *Ibid.*, 34, also in *W&S*, 106.
12. *Ibid.*, 35, also in *W&S*, 107.

father let him know he was thoroughly upset with him. In order to get out from under this stream of criticism, Jean found a job in New York as a clerk with a prominent grocery firm, Acker, Merrill and Condit Company, where he had worked part time before. Then he added a round of activities to feed his soul. He became acquainted with the Rand School and began meeting radicals and literati. Still a socialist, blending Lester Ward's and Bernard Shaw's positions, he kept a notebook of his thoughts and discoveries, reading a lot and writing a little. Music suddenly reappeared as an interest. He thought of becoming a composer and got a second job as physical education director in a settlement house to pay for piano lessons and renting a piano. He heard Scott Nearing and Alfred Kreymborg, read Ibsen, Santayana, and Goethe, went to concerts at Carnegie Hall—and became ill from exhaustion.

Quitting all his activities in the late spring of 1919, he headed for Ellenville, New York, a resort town full of white clapboard houses on a canal at the foot of the Catskills. Jean knew a farm family near there, and asked them to take him in as a paying guest for a month. Later he claimed to have cured himself by fasting and dieting. He was also spending more time writing, and he sent mimeographed copies of his work to his friends and his grandfather. With a friend, he "bummed around" upstate New York for the summer, then returned to Washington—in Pinchback's eyes, a failure again.[13]

Jean had come, though perhaps he did not yet know it, almost to the end of his self-styled "four years of chaos." It was a period when he himself could surely have been called "The Wayward and the Seeking," a title he later gave to an unpublished collection of poems.[14] Only his grandmother and his high school friend Kennedy had not lost faith in him. Against his grandfather's intensified criticisms he built intensified defenses. First, the world was not fair. He felt that his experience had "exploded the myth that an ablebodied young man could start at the bottom of American business or industry and work his way up"—it took pull or a lucky break to make money. Second, he was special in his use of experience, so the ordinary standards of completing what one started could not be applied: "Whatever I believed, I did; and whatever I did, I did with my whole heart and mind as far as was possible to do so—and thus I gained in intensity of experience what may have taken a less intense person a much longer time. So that, though I finished a thing not long after having begun it, and certainly prematurely from an ordinary point of view, I have reason to believe that at least in several cases, I got and gave all that was to be

13. *Ibid.*, 35–38, also in *W&S*, 107–10; JT notes, n.d. (JTP 18:10).
14. This was the source of the title chosen by Darwin Turner for his Jean Toomer anthology.

had." Third, he was misused. He recounts being "pushed out" from his group of playmates at ten or eleven, from his mother at thirteen, and from his college career at nineteen. In actual fact, the first age is accurate, but he was fourteen when his mother died, and not yet through high school when he turned nineteen. It is difficult to connect his college record with the concept of being "pushed out." Significantly, he remembered himself as younger and therefore more vulnerable at each of these crucial points than he really was. Fourth, there was a destiny that ruled his affairs, superior to any mortal's understanding. His rejection of many alternatives rested on "a sustaining sureness, an unshakeable faith that the way of life was a superior destiny leading to the inevitable goal that I, just this person myself, must reach, at whatever price." [15]

But shore himself up as he might, Jean could not withstand his grandfather's unloading his frustrations on a wayward grandson. In December, in desperation, he left the Washington apartment with ten dollars in his pocket, walked to Baltimore, where he took a cheap room for the night, and then on to Wilmington, Delaware. From there he hitchhiked on an army truck to Rahway, New Jersey. Finally he got a job as a fitter in the New Jersey shipyards. Ten days of this cramped, cold, tough work were enough to cure him of ideas about life as a laborer and of his dream of socialism. For the first time he had met the "proletariat" and he was convinced that they "had two main interests: playing craps and sleeping with women." Socialism was too good for them; it was meant for intellectuals only. [16]

At this point in his life, it must have seemed to Toomer that the disturbing vision he had had on leaving the University of Wisconsin—the first of a long series of cut-off commitments—was prescient: "I saw myself as if on a boat which the nations would allow to put up at no port. I could come in for food and supplies. This done, I'd have to put out to sea again, and again to sea, and again, never having a harbor which I could call my own, never knowing a port in which I could come to rest—always at sea, . . . stopping at many places, staying at none, by order of the government of the universe." [17] But in fact he was drawing near to his first home port.

Jean drifted again to Acker, Merrill to support himself, and filled his mind with Whitman. In February of 1920 his grandfather sold the house on Twelfth Street that had been willed to Jean. It brought $3,800, but after the mortgage was paid off, there was only $600 left. Jean decided to stay in New York, quit

15. JT, "Outline," 41, also in W&S, 111; JT, "On Being an American" (JTP 15:11).
16. JT, "Outline," 42, also in W&S, 111–12.
17. JT, "Book X," 141–42.

his job, and use the money to devote himself to music and literature. It was again a period of voracious reading—Dostoevski, Tolstoi, Flaubert, Baudelaire, Sinclair Lewis, Dreiser, Waldo Frank, Freud, Coleridge, Blake, Pater, and a group of American poets. But the outstanding flavor came from Goethe's *Wilhelm Meister,* which gave Jean a vision for the first time of what he felt was his own real world.

It was the world of the aristocrat—but not the social aristocrat; the aristocrat of culture, of spirit and character, of ideas, of true nobility. And for the first time in years and years I breathed the air of own my land [*sic*]. My God! how far I had wandered from it! Through the cities of America, through colleges, through socialism and naturalism and atheism, through the breakup of family and my home, through arid philosophies, Herbert Spencer and all the rest,—and now at last I saw it again. . . . In fact, of course, I was seeing it for the first time. . . . I resolved to devote myself to the making of myself such a person as I caught glimpses of in the pages of *Wilhelm Meister.* For my specialized work, I would write. I would put music aside forever, as a possible career. And indeed I did just this.

Wilhelm Meister, taking him to the peak of an identity choice, led him back to extensive reading of and about Whitman, because in contrast to the German hero, "he was of America, and I felt he had something to give me in terms of the American world." [18] It seems likely that this was the time when he fully adopted the name Jean Toomer, since this moment is the first indication that he saw himself and his goals with some clarity. It was an appropriate time to break away from his grandfather and his grandfather's name, which he had been using as late as 1919. He had tried out the name Jean as his listing in the American College yearbook in 1917, soon after his first encounter with Jean Valjean, his first real step into literature, and the first powerful integration of his maturing thinking. Included in his recent reading also was another alienated hero named Jean, misused by society, with whom he could identify: Romain Rolland's Jean-Christophe. Now he was ready to abandon Eugene Pinchback Toomer and declare his allegiance to Uncle Bis's ideals—as represented by the choice of cultural rather than social aristocracy—as his own true world.

Writing accompanied the reading, and whenever he could, he shared what he wrote with those who he thought might be helpful. Toomer so far had had little contact with the literary coterie in New York. However, in August of 1920, he attended a literary lecture and was invited to a party given by Lola Ridge, an editor for the fledgling "little magazine" *Broom.* It was a typical gathering of the day, where the cultural legislators and budding artists shared ideas, conducted readings, viewed paintings, presented recitals—in short,

18. JT, "Outline," 43–44, also in *W&S,* 112.

tried to impress one another. There Toomer met Waldo Frank, one of his literary idols, who held a somewhat mystical vision of the connections among nature, humanity, and the American Dream. The following day, meeting by chance in Central Park, they engaged in talk about music, literature, art, and American values. Toomer held that conversation before him as inspiration during the subsequent months of writing poems and sketches principally about Washington and more rarely about his Chicago and Wisconsin days.

Armed with Frank's encouragement and with his newfound determination about his calling, his six hundred dollars having given out, Jean returned to Washington and persuaded (his word is "forced") his grandfather to let him live there in the old apartment and give him an allowance of five dollars a week so he could write. "Grandfather put up a fight but I beat him. His age and enfeebled condition were no match for the strength and singleness of my determination. At last I was wholly convinced that I had found my true direction in life, and no one was going to stop me. . . . In truth, I was so ready and so eager to help myself, whatever the pain and sacrifice, that, in comparison, I felt I was demanding hardly anything of him. So it was done." [19]

It did involve pain and sacrifice. His grandfather, "a game fighting cock to the end," was feebler in body but sharper in mind and tongue. Jean endured the criticism rather than ducking out. The only able-bodied resident, Jean had to manage the household affairs, cooking, sweeping, and cleaning, though Walter and Bismarck dropped in occasionally. Aside from his household duties, Jean spent most of his day as a recluse. The small apartment crammed with furniture from finer, more prosperous days was, for him, physically cramped and psychologically stifling. Yet, because of the narrow dimensions of his regimen, Toomer could spend much of the day free to read and write without the necessity of a full-time job. The decline of his grandfather's fortunes and the general malaise of the household were burdensome; but, as he stated in an autobiographical story written at this time, he was sustained because he "had a purpose": "To have a purpose in life offsets any and all surrounding declines. Just what this purpose was he could not say in his mind. He felt it as a power, as a hive, as a destiny, a force that made him sure he had something in him that was bound to fulfill itself, whatever his own mistakes and weaknesses, whatever the external obstacles. It upheld him. He believed in it." [20]

When he was writing, his life was bound to the large oak table in what had been a second-floor living room of the row house but was at that point used

19. *Ibid.*, 48, also in *W&S*, 114–15.
20. JT, "Meridian Hill—An Autobiographical Story" (Typescript, n.d. [*ca.* 1921], in MTC), paragraph handwritten between pp. 1 and 2.

entirely as his study. The only break in his routine might be a walk with his friend Kennedy, who discussed with Toomer in particular the black experience in America, or an occasional late-night visit by a girl friend, an arrangement that offended his grandmother's sense of discretion. (His earlier love Phyllis had married someone else.) Sometimes during the evening hours he would take a meditative walk through Meridian Hill, the park that was the site of his childhood digging forays as well as the setting for his story "Avey." With his high sense of commitment, no longer the playboy, Jean carved out the time from housekeeping and nursing to continue reading—French, Russian, American novelists, English and American poets, literary magazines—and writing "essays, articles, poems, short stories, reviews, and a long piece somewhere between a novel and a play, . . . a trunk full of manuscripts." But he considered all of this to be his literary apprenticeship and did not attempt publication.

There came finally the moment of reward, when he was suddenly certain his apprenticeship was over. Although not an outward recognition, it seemed a quantum leap, like his learning to tell time or to read: "And then, after several years of work, suddenly, it was as if a door opened and I knew without doubt that I was *inside. I knew literature!* And what was my joy!" At the same time, he had acquired the faculty for seeing inside people: "As if a veil had been taken from my eyes I began seeing into the lives of grandmother, . . . everyone, as never before."[21] The failures, the false starts, were now behind him. At last he knew what and where he was, and he had the tools to begin his work.

Still, his struggle with his grandfather was not over. Out of necessity, Jean chose to live with his grandparents—it was the cheapest place for him to stay. But in a way, that choice resembled the method he used to cure his deep depression upon encountering atheism: to go back to what gave him the trouble, and consume more of it. Going back to his grandfather was placing himself in the environment where he experienced the greatest conflict between the values he had absorbed from his grandfather, still pounded into him daily, and those he had gained from Uncle Bis, broadened and deepened by his voluminous reading and his exposure to lectures and conversations with intellectuals and literary people. Class and status, wealth, loyalty, fine appearance, and power were held up against sensitivity, fantasy, intricate blood-confused human relationships, pain, beauty, and truth. Yet even in rejecting his grandfather and stubbornly choosing his own way to fame, Jean was reflecting his grandfather's independence and grasp of power. Later he tended to credit his grandfather, not

21. JT, "Outline," 51, 53, also in *W&S*, 117, 119.

Bismarck, for qualities he saw in himself. Here, deliberately immersing his body and soul in the conflict, he was finding his own voice.

The difficult winter of 1920–1921 passed. Jean had produced a long poem, "The First American," and felt drained. The continuing conflict, though perhaps generating creativity, was taking its toll. He saw his grandfather as the locus of his energy loss, likening the process to being bled: "Just so . . . had my grandfather taken energy from me. He was still taking it; and I began to see the situation as a struggle for life between him and myself. It was a question of who would die first. . . . [I felt] caught and trapped. It was as if life were a huge snake that had coiled about me—and now it had me at almost my last breath."[22] In the late spring and summer of 1921, he was exhausted, though not organically ill. He did some drinking and, like his mother in her tortured first year after his birth, got away for a week in Harpers Ferry. Then he was suddenly offered a post as temporary head of a black agricultural and industrial school in Sparta, Georgia. He seized on the job as a way out of his cul-de-sac. Putting his grandfather in a hospital and hiring a woman to look after his grandmother, he left for the South.

This job was to prove an end and a beginning. Although capped by his grandfather's death, it would bring him "one of those revelations, a 'particular appropriate disclosure to which the gods at some moment treat the artist unless they happen too perversely to conspire against him,' which Henry James writes about."[23] At its completion, he would have the materials and the means to become the writer he dreamed of—the stuff of experience and the forms to shape it—and would stand on the threshold of his major literary accomplishment.

22. *Ibid.*, 56–57, also in *W&S*, 122–23.
23. JT to Samuel Pessin, March 25, 1923, in JTP 8:5.

II.

THE LITERARY PERIOD

4.

The Convolution of Cane

Good writers inherit before they create, and Jean Toomer was no exception. In his writing he was selecting what fit his own emerging voice, from the storehouse he had been precipitately filling for the past five years. Whitman's universality, sensualism, and portrayal of the American experience remained central. Readings in Buddhism and other Eastern philosophies (though he thought that much of this had been written by "fourth rate minds") had somewhat softened his hard, cold, atheist-naturalist position, so there was again some room for a mystical, organic connection between earth and spirit. Life experiences left him concerned with the alienation of soul from soil and of soul from soul, and especially with the peculiar alienation he had observed arising from racial differences in society.

While Toomer later claimed that *Cane* was a unified book that should not be reprinted in segments, the writing of the pieces occurred in fragments and unfolded over three years. Stories, sketches, and poems were published separately in various magazines and journals. When he thought of putting some of his works into book form, he reviewed his writings, discarding some, revising others, and creating new pieces to fit into his scheme. As the formation of the book evolved, Toomer could join the parts together into a whole because the motive for his writing stemmed from a single source: fitting his own racial parts into a unified whole. His experience in upper-class black Washington society was but limited exposure to Afro-American life. In order to unify the segments of his own life, he had to seek out what he probably knew least, his African inheritance. The crucial piece in this puzzle, as is clear from his later accounts, was his experience in Georgia.

From the beginning, his writings centered on the relationship of black and white. Here he was able to focus his reading, his experience, and his acute perceptions. Racial conflict sometimes occurred between people, sometimes within the individual. In his early piece "Bona and Paul," written when he was in Chicago, Jean Toomer explored the expectations and fears, how one is "natural" yet defensive about one's behavior, in those who are racially self-conscious. While mulatto Paul rhapsodizes to a skeptical doorman about his hopes for a future with the white Bona, she disappears into the night.

Toomer allowed a more successful relationship between two mulattoes in another early story, written in Washington and based on his Wisconsin and Washington experiences. Called "Withered Skin of Berries," it is a clear statement of Jean's own version of American racial amalgamation. A mulatto woman, Vera, unable to find satisfaction with men, dates a white man Carl, who, ignorant that she has Negro blood, makes insulting comments about blacks. However, he tells her about a mulatto visionary at the University of Wisconsin (Jean Toomer in disguise) who believes in preserving dying races in art and has proposed a new race consisting of a mixture of red, black, and white. Vera's second date is with a man of pure African ancestry whom Vera, repelled by his advances, calls "nigger beast," failing to recognize how shameful the words are. Her third date is with the young mulatto from the University of Wisconsin, who happens to be in Washington. With him she finds for the first time satisfying love and is determined to be part of his vision of a new American race. The coupling of the two mulattoes in this story is one of the few portrayals of mutually fulfilling love that Toomer wrote during the *Cane* period.

One of the key images is the Potomac River, upon whose banks David and Vera consummate their destiny. The river, as David describes it, embodies all the races and cultures that constitute America. Similarly, the Mississippi was the touchstone for Toomer's long poem "The First American," written in the winter of 1920–1921, which finally evolved as "Blue Meridian," completed by 1931 and published in 1936. In the poem he explores the definition of the new race, a blend of all European, African, Asian, and American Indian cultures. Jean realized that racial conditioning would force most Americans to wear "queer bifocals" that would prevent their accepting the concept of the American blend. Toomer recalled reading his poem to "a man of intellect" who insisted afterward that he was black and Toomer was white, and any thought of a new blend was nonsense. Jean's response to the man whose skin color was just a shade darker than his own discloses his early commitment to a supraracial identity:

So far as I knew, they never realized that racial strains do not exist separately in a man but blend to form a new product. . . . They never understood that the real factors operating in the United States . . . are creating a new people in this world, a people to whom all Americans, without exception, belong. . . . At one time they would live in the colored world, at another, in the white world. They were under the compulsion to be this or that. They could have been self-determined to be this *and* that.[1]

In feeling his way to this definition, Toomer needed an emotional identification with his African heritage similar to his sense of ecstatic connection with Whitman and Goethe. Developments leading to this had begun in March of 1921. When one of his grandfather's cronies stopped by the house one day, he mentioned that a friend needed a substitute principal at his school. The friend, principal of the all-black Sparta Agricultural and Industrial Institute in Georgia, was going north to try to raise funds for the school. Feeling imprisoned by a dying grandfather and a grandmother in failing health, and pulled taut by the tensions in his own life between white world and black, between materialism and art, and between the aborted desire for music and the struggle to create literature, Jean saw the job possibility as an escape and offered his services.

When the Sparta administrator came to Washington on his way north, the two agreed that Jean would start as substitute principal at the beginning of the September semester. Arranging for the care of his grandfather and grandmother, he took the train to Georgia. In Sparta he took up residence at the small school, a short way from the center of town.

Like most of the southern black schools founded after the Civil War, the Sparta institution was modeled on Tuskegee Institute, which intended to provide the student both a practical occupation and an attitude of self-respect. Booker T. Washington's educational model had been the object of much scorn from activists like W. E. B. Du Bois as being too placating and demeaning. But southern black schools with northern support could follow Washington's example as a pragmatic step away from occupational and psychological servitude. The school, therefore, served the black community in Sparta and its outlying areas. A commercial course was offered, but the emphasis was clearly on training boys and girls for professions related to agriculture and light industry. The school was a rectangular, boxlike two-story stucco building on a hill a mile from town. The teachers, like Toomer, lived in adjacent residences. As the principal, Jean was required to visit homes, businesses, and churches. Sparta was then, as it is now, principally a rural community, a small center for the farmers, with its courthouse and such industries as the mill for the tall Georgia pines. Roads leading to the town cut through the red clay over low hills. Atlanta is some eighty miles to the northwest.

1. JT, "On Being an American" (JTP 15:2).

Small as the Sparta center was, Toomer was struck by the differences between the rural community surrounding the school and the town just a mile away. A family of backcountry blacks had moved into a shack not far from his own, and their songs expressed with rustic simplicity the pains and joys of their hard life. Even in the town of Sparta, the black families, trying to escape their past, pointedly ignored such "out-landish" people as these rustics and worked at stifling this heritage. Jean saw this inclination exaggerated as blacks migrated from the smaller towns to the larger towns, and thence to Washington and beyond.

As in most parts of the South, the rural areas were beautiful but also scarred by poverty and discrimination, bound by tradition as permanent as the unpainted shacks—in short, an ideal place for an urban, somewhat sophisticated poet to be. It is incongruous that pastoral works have been almost wholly written by urban poets, but not surprising: the shepherd and farmer seldom have time or inclination to detach themselves from their drudgery and see beauty in their routine. Toomer, however, saw that beauty and added to it the recognition of waste and despair in the experience of southern blacks and whites. He reacts to the South as he did to his southern roots, with ambivalence that could be expressed but not resolved, as he speaks through the persona of Kabnis: "God Almighty, dear God, dear Jesus, do not torture me with beauty. Take it away. Give me an ugly world. Ha, ugly. Stinking like unwashed niggers. Dear Jesus, do not chain me to myself and set these hills and valleys, heaving with folk-songs, so close to me that I cannot reach them. There is a radiant beauty in the night that touches and . . . tortures me." Later, again through Kabnis, Toomer expresses the torment of the writer who is trying to shape words to fit his soul: "Th form thats burned int my soul is some twisted awful thing that crept in from a dream, a godam nightmare, an wont stay still unless I feed it. An it lives on words. Not beautiful words. God Almighty no. Misshapen, split-gut, tortured, twisted words."[2]

Jean remained in Sparta for only two months, until the principal returned from Boston. Nevertheless, he had had time to begin sorting out the mysterious pulls of his inner life toward the culture in which he was participating. He was living and working in a black community with an intensity he had never known before. "There was a valley," he writes in his autobiography, "the valley of 'Cane,' with smoke-wreaths during the day and mist at night." He had lived with urban blacks and whites and had seen how they mixed in the city, but now he was experiencing for the first time the rural, mostly black folk-

2. JT, *Cane* (New York, 1923), 161–62, 224.

culture that in his vision had formed the roots of the transplanted urbanites: "There, for the first time I really saw the Negro, not as a ps[eu]do-urbanized and vulgarized, a semi-Americanized product, but the Negro peasant, strong with the tang of fields and soil. It was there that I first heard the folk-songs rolling up the valley at twilight, heard them as spontaneous and native utterances. They filled me with gold, and tints of an eternal purple. Love? Man they gave birth to a whole new life."[3] Seldom a joiner, Toomer discovered a group sense that was bound as much by geography as by race, for he identified with the black experience principally as it was manifested in the rural South. And, as he describes in "Kabnis," that identity was more a spiritual than an ethnic union.

James Weldon Johnson describes a similar reaction to his own experience as a teacher in rural Georgia. Johnson and Toomer were both brought up in fairly prosperous families with little emphasis on being black. Although no two lives are duplicated, Johnson's memory of his summer teaching is probably a close parallel of Toomer's:

In all of my experience there has been no period so brief that has meant so much in my education as the three months I spent in the backwoods of Georgia. . . . It was this period that marked the beginning of my psychological change from boyhood to manhood. It was this period which marked also the beginning of my own people as a "race." . . .

As I worked with my children in school and met with their parents in the homes, on the farms, and in church, I found myself studying them all with a sympathetic objectivity, as I could realize they were something apart; but in an instant's reflection I could realize that they were me, and I was they; that a force stronger than blood made us one.[4]

Toomer had spent his teenage years in a society that seemed to him a culturally rich aristocracy—but that by its nature was an isolated pocket. Waldo Frank called it the most "conscious community of American Negroes. . . . They were aware of their ghetto and their awareness corroded their instinctual relation with the Negro peasant and with the earth of the South." Langston Hughes was even unkinder about the society in which Jean had grown up: "They were on the whole as unbearable and snobbish a group of people as I have ever come in contact with anywhere," he wrote, adding that they "seemed to me lacking in real culture, kindness, or good common sense."[5]

3. JT to Waldo Frank (hereinafter WF), April 26, 1922, in Waldo Frank Collection, Special Collections, Van Pelt Library, University of Pennsylvania, Philadelphia (hereinafter WFC).

4. James Weldon Johnson, *Along This Way* (New York, 1933), 118–19.

5. Alan Trachtenberg (ed.), *The Memoirs of Waldo Frank* (Amherst, Mass., 1973), 106; Langston Hughes, *The Big Sea* (New York, 1940), 106–107.

In contrast to Washington's black middle-class society was Seventh Street, the major stopping place for those who had recently arrived from the South and who were embedded in Washington's labor force as unskilled or partially skilled workers. It was along Seventh Street that Toomer and others like Hughes saw the raw-boned "crude new life" that would appeal to the poet interested in recording the song of "a new people."[6]

Toomer was turning away from the genteel residences to the shanties, in order to find a genuine black spirit, and that search carried him back to the South. This spirit is described by Nathan Merilh, the code name for Jean Toomer, in "Natalie Mann," a play Toomer wrote in 1922 soon after his return from Georgia to Washington. In the play, Nathan shocks Natalie Mann and her friends because he publicly insults the bourgeois parlor culture and seeks alternative outlets for his creative energy. Therman Law, a detached observer of the Mann-Merilh conflict, analyzes what it is that Nathan is revolting against:

[F]or three hundred years at least, an unsympathetic and unscientific white posture has gestured with scorn and condemnation at what it calls the benighted moral looseness of the Negro. It has used its own moral pretensions as a foot-rule of universal measurement. . . . The Negro, cursed by his ignorance of moral evolution, of moral relativity, and lack of any sense of autonomous development, has . . . knuckled to. He has cupped his whole nature in an imitation of bigotry just to prove to the white man that what he says is not true. The result is obvious: what should be the most colorful and robust of our racial segments is approaching a sterile and denuded hypocrisy as its goal. What has become of the almost obligatory heritage of folk-songs? Jazz on the one hand, and on the other, a respectability which is never so vigorous as when it denounces and rejects the true art of the race's past. They are ashamed of the past made permanent by the spirituals.[7]

Jean Toomer found "the true art of the race's past" in Georgia. As he explained later in a letter to Sherwood Anderson, "My seed was planted in the cane- and cotton-fields, and in the souls of the black and white people in the small southern town. My seed was planted in *myself* down there." The enchantment of pine trees, smoke from the sawmills, cane and cotton fields overwhelmed his sensibilities. "Here were cabins. Here negroes and their singing. I had never heard the spirituals and work songs. They were like a part of me. At times, I identified with my whole sense so intensely that I lost my own identity."[8]

6. JT to WF, n.d., in WFC.
7. JT, *Natalie Mann*, Act II, Scene 2, in *W&S*, 289–90, also in JTP 49:9.
8. JT to Sherwood Anderson, December 18, 1922, in JTP 1:1; JT, "On Being an American" (JTP 15:11).

If Toomer found sustenance in the folk spirit of the people and their union with the land, the awareness of his heritage deepened when he discovered that his father had returned to Georgia perhaps twenty-five years earlier. While Toomer resided in Sparta he met a barber who claimed he remembered Jean's father. Jean asked whether his father had been regarded by the community as white or "colored." The barber replied that Nathan stayed at the white hotel, did business with white men, and courted a black woman. At that moment both the barber and Jean became embarrassed, and the conversation shifted to other topics. But Toomer received the answer that for him could not have been a surprise: his father had lived in both the black world and the white.

Toomer's sojourn in Georgia produced an emotional intensity not unlike that of a summer romance. He despaired at the tenuousness of his visit, yet it had given him unparalleled exhilaration. Toomer grieved over the demise of an era marked by the folk spirit, but his grief may well have been for his having lost touch with that same spirit: "The folk-spirit was walking in to die on the modern desert. That spirit was so beautiful. Its death was so tragic. Just this seemed to sum life for me. And this was the feeling I put into 'Cane.' 'Cane' was a swan-song. It was a song of an end."[9]

His experience of Georgia gave Jean Toomer not only material for writing but also the impetus to try to get his work published. Full of enthusiasm, he returned to his grandparents' home in Washington. He had tucked his manuscripts in a trunk long enough. Before he had gone south he had shown his writings to a few of his friends only, but the day before he left Sparta he had already written to *Liberator* about publishing "Georgia Night." A periodical with leftist leanings, whose associate editor was Claude McKay, *Liberator* was one of the few magazines that printed material by black writers alongside that by whites. For Jean, it was the ideal place to initiate his career in print. But *Liberator* was not yet ready for Jean. McKay returned the poem and subsequent pieces to "Miss Toomer" and stated that Jean's work lacked focus.

Nevertheless, Toomer wrote with renewed purpose, stimulated by the vision of seeing his work in print. In December of 1921, one month after he had returned and one day before his grandfather died, he finished the first draft of "Kabnis," which "sprang up almost in a day" and reflected most closely his relationship to the South. Pinchback was buried in the family plot in New Orleans. With only his grandmother left to take care of, Jean found that his writing virtually flowed. After finishing "Kabnis," for example, he wrote

9. JT, "Outline," 59, also in *W&S,* 123.

"Fern" immediately and almost without revision. By April of 1922 he completed most of the pieces that were eventually to go into *Cane*.

By April, too, Waldo Frank had become Jean's correspondent and confidant. In Jean's reaching toward acceptance as a writer, he had become reacquainted with Waldo Frank by letter in January. Frank, by then one of the prime forces in American literary and cultural life, wrote back encouraging correspondence and friendship. In early April, Jean responded to the offer. "I have never had such a deep and wonderful experience from a letter," Jean wrote. Waldo's impression on Jean from two years before had not diminished: "Almost the first, and surely the last real talk was the one I had with you in Central Park." With a self-effacement that betrayed his tentativeness with someone of Frank's stature, Jean sent him "The First American," which Jean described as "uneven" with "easy" themes, and other material whose "artistic value is at a minimum—I send them as human records."[10]

Quickly their correspondence became warm and intimate, by May their greetings being "Brother" and "Brother Mine" and their closings, "Love." Waldo Frank found in Jean a protégé, someone who believed, as he did, in a new American ethic and in art as a personal and mystical expression. In turn he served Jean by criticizing his pieces, responding to phrases and ideas. He acknowledged the strength of many of Jean's southern sketches and poems such as "Becky" and "Evening Song" and concluded that Jean should concentrate on the South and not on his Washington pieces. "Keep yourself warm underneath, in the soil, where the throb is," he warned Jean, "and use every decent means in your reach to protect yourself from a too early pushing to the surface." In May, Jean wrote Waldo that his creative well tapped in Georgia was still there: "The skeleton is knot by my cartilage of the two races. But what are bones! The flesh and blood and spirit are my own." He was now trying to "grasp Washington" with the "stamp of a personal vision," to write with the same fervor that had inspired him in Georgia: "And at evening, when the theater signs are lighted, Washington opens to a dusk-bloom. . . . Their [blacks'] rhythm approaches the soft slow music of the black belt South. But above the stems of streets and pavements, their faces are deep clusters of macadam flowers."[11]

Jean and Waldo's friendship was truly a product of their correspondence. While much of what they wrote to each other had to do with their writings and art in general, the letters were, for Jean especially, a way to release emotion that

10. JT to WF, April 4, 1922, in WFC.
11. WF to JT, April 25, 1922, in JTP 3:6; JT to WF, May 5, 1922, and n.d. [probably April or May, 1922], both in WFC.

helped him articulate his apparent purpose in life. Not merely literary, the letters quickly became discourses between friends of a kindred spirit—for Jean, the first kindred spirit who could really understand him. He felt bold enough, indeed, to criticize Frank's recent book:

In your Our America I missed your not including the Negro. I have often wondered about it. . . . Of the Negro, what facts are known have too often been perverted for the purpose of propaganda, one way or the other. It has been necessary, therefore, that I spend a disproportionate time in Negro study. Recently, facts and possibilities discovered have lead [*sic*] to an interest mainly artistic and interpretive. . . . No picture of a southern person is complete without its bit of Negro-determined psychology.

That Waldo was also one of the artistic leaders of the country created in Jean a kind of euphoria. "You have definitely linked me to the purpose and vision of what is best in creative America," Jean wrote Waldo soon after their renewed correspondence began. "You have touched me, you have held me; you have released me to myself." [12]

Writing about Washington proved more difficult than Toomer had expected. By July he reported to Waldo that he was mentally exhausted and needed physical stimulation. "The impulse which sprang from Sparta, Georgia last fall has just about fulfilled and spent itself." He decided to spend a few days in mid July at his favorite retreat, the Mountain View Home at Harpers Ferry. There he met Mae Wright, eleven years younger than he, a "wonderfully emotional, rich dark-skinned, large-eyed girl." The daughter of a Baltimore physician, she succumbed to Jean's good looks and sense of purpose, and in many ways she was the counterpart to Vera in "Withered Skin of Berries," Jean's partner in his new-race theory. To Mrs. Wright, Jean wrote that he loved her daughter and sought the parents' support. Since Mae was only sixteen and was intending to enter Tufts University in the fall, Jean admitted that she needed a few more years of maturity. But he implied that he would wait until Mae was ready for marriage. Meanwhile, he wrote her letters of gratuitous advice and philosophical commentary. Mae emerged as the first of a number of women Jean fell in love with and then promptly tried to mold to his design of the fulfilled woman. He was to write Waldo Frank several months later about his relationship with Mae: "I kid her, and share with her my deepest thoughts, that is, I talk to myself in her presence! But she has a mind. Yea! Only it is not quite nimble or profound enough to follow me, hence the kidding and joshing and general tomfoolery." Nevertheless, she was important enough for him to write her in

12. JT to WF, March 24, April 26, 1922, both in WFC.

August, one month after they had met, that they both had a special destiny, Jean's momentarily being that of a writer. He felt that his life was beginning to fulfill "a quickening of higher impulses." He sent her a list of books to read, including McKay's poems and Rolland's *Jean-Christophe,* in which the central character was "true to me. Many of his trials and problems are or have been or will be mine. To know him is to know the most difficult side of Jean Toomer." Mae, through no fault of her own, also presented a difficulty. Jean called her an example of "the complete tragedy of color": Jean's near-white friends in Washington considered her blackness objectionable. "Mae's lov[e]liness didn't get a chance to show. Only her skin. She really seemed insignificant—and black. And my friends didn't fail to take her (or rather, not take her) in terms of her color and in terms of what she seemed." Jean was determined to free her—and himself—from this demeaning state. He revealed his mission to her to break "the Tyranny of the Anglo-Saxon Ideal." "We of the darker skins, we who have Negro blood in our veins," he wrote her, were still prisoners of the notion that white skins, minds, and souls were superior to any others. It was up to them to show the equal and distinctive beauties in blacks and to be true to their own individual natures.[13] He stayed with the mission longer than he stayed with Mae. Before a year was out, she was to be supplanted in his affections, probably without knowing how or why, as he was swept up in a new passion.

But a partial statement of this attack on "the Tyranny of the Anglo-Saxon Ideal" could be made more powerfully by compiling some of his pieces into a book. Accordingly, in July of 1922, Toomer announced to Waldo Frank and John McClure his decision to put together his sketches into a book called *Cane.* It was to be divided into three parts: "Cane Stalks and Choruses" for his Georgia sketches and stories (including "Kabnis"), "Leaves and Syrup Songs" for his poems, and "Leaf Traceries in Washington" for what eventually became the second section of *Cane.* The decision to combine the pieces into one volume came because "a precipitant is urgently needed just at this time. The concentrated volume will do a good deal more than isolated pieces possibly could."[14]

Having come to something of a stopping place in his writing and revising, Jean proposed that he and Waldo travel together in the fall to recapture the spirit that so fired Jean's inspiration in Georgia. Rejecting Harpers Ferry as too tame, Jean suggested that they travel farther south to catch the true southern flavor. "Have you ever been in a Negro church?" Jean wrote Waldo enthusi-

13. JT to Mae Wright, August 15, 1922, in WFC; JT to Mae Wright, August 22, 4, 1922, both in JTP 10:10; JT to WF, n.d. [probably March, 1923, and December, 1922], both in WFC.

14. JT to WF, July 19, 1922, in WFC; JT to John McClure, July 22, 1922, in JTP 7:22.

astically in August. "Not the white-washed article of respectable colored folks; but the shanty of the peasant Negro. God, but they *feel* the thing. Sometimes too violently for sensitive nerves; always sincerely, powerfully, deeply. And when they overflow in song, there is no singing that has so touched me. Their theology is a farce (Christ is so immediate); their religious emotion, elemental, and for that reason, very near sublime." Jean felt, too, that the trip would help both of them confirm their collective impressions of the South. Waldo had also visited the South in 1920—he had spent some time in Tuskegee and in New Orleans—and had found southerners "superlatively shallow, cultureless, cruel and ugly minded folk." Nevertheless he, like Jean, was engaged in writing a story of the South, akin to Jean's "Blood-Burning Moon." Frank's book, an account of a lynching, was called *Holiday,* and he had by February of 1922 finished the first section. Jean wanted Waldo to return with him, for by summer he felt that his and Waldo's literary missions were inseparable. "I cannot think of myself," he wrote to Waldo in August, "as being separated from you in the dual task of creating an American literature, and of developing a public, however large or small, capable of responding to our creations. Those who read and know me, should read and know you." [15]

Toomer worked out the plans. He had contacts in Washington who could help him find a place to visit. These, Waldo's agreement, and expected assistance from his grandmother's pension were all he needed to confirm the trip for September. Jesse Moorland, a YMCA official, made the arrangements. "What I want is the bite and crudity of pure Negro: White southern life," Jean wrote him. "A fresh contact with this nature would give my work an immediacy and vigor which could come to it in no other way." Trying to ensure Moorland's patronage, he continued in another letter: "The shallow observation, and loose thinking which have hitherto formed the bulk matter written about the Negro are now in a position to do double injury." Wanting to do a scientific study but not having the tools to do so, he felt he could "tone down my desires to a modest work, which, while claiming nothing in the way of scholarship, realizes those fundamentals of vision and observation that you have heard me express." [16]

Toomer and Frank found their place of racial antithesis in Spartanburg, South Carolina. There, as a means to sharpen their perceptions of the South, they traveled as blood brothers. Jean had cautioned Waldo about their roles:

15. JT to WF, August 21, 1922, in WFC; WF to Alfred Stieglitz, December 4, 1920, in Alfred Stieglitz Collection, The Beinecke Rare Book and Manuscript Library, Yale University, New Haven (hereinafter ASC); JT to WF, August 2, 1922, in WFC.
16. JT quoted in Jesse Moorland to R. S. Wilkerson, July 31, 1922 (copy sent to JT), JT to Jesse Moorland, July 28, 1922, both in JTP 7:10.

"At whatever town we stay, I'll have to be known as a Negro. First, because only by experiencing white pressure can the venture bear its fullest fruit for me. Second, because the color of my skin (it is nearly black from sun) at the present time makes such a course a physical necessity. This, however, will not hinder our intercourse. Should make the exchange complete, in fact." Frank, dark-skinned himself, stayed with Jean at homes, attended churches, and mingled with laborers in southern black society. Since Toomer and Frank were northern celebrities, they were asked to give talks to various assemblies. Waldo Frank in his memoirs tells of the time Jean arranged to have Waldo speak at a gathering in a small rural church. Waldo spoke about the value of science and its place in religion, and the audience applauded enthusiastically. Waldo felt pleased with what he had said and asked Jean whether it had been appropriate. Jean, no doubt with some superiority at being knowledgeable about such things, said that the audience had appreciated his talk very much, but the people did not know the meaning of "science." [17]

For a week, Jean was Waldo's host in a black world that Jean had himself lived in for only two months. In a letter to a friend soon after his return from Spartanburg, Toomer revealed how the experience, like his time in Georgia, had sensitized him and had clarified the direction of his writing and life:

The city, with all its beauty and hideousness had come inside of me; I wasn't Jean, but a sort of sensitized embodiment of the place.

My life here has been painful. And this body of mine has had all that it could do to survive the pressure it has been subjected to. But from it all I've won to a certain extent spiritual clarity which is still many spaces ahead of my ability to express it. One illusion after another has fallen off. God after God has died. But, unlike the generation which preceeded [sic] me, in loosing [sic] these I have built up an edifice in which reverence and mystery may still find their altar. I kneel and pray before new gods come into a godless age. [18]

The new gods—investing separate historical strands of various ethnic groups with religious significance as they were woven into a mystic national fabric, a collective group consciousness—had already been outlined in Waldo Frank's works. Toomer had been learning his catechism well on their trip.

Jean and Waldo's trip to Spartanburg increased the bond between them. Having returned from their trip, one to Washington and the other to New York, the two writers commented on each other's drafts of *Cane* and *Holiday* by mail during the ensuing months, exchanged and sharpened their shared vision of art in America, and anticipated as a final gesture of unity that their books

17. JT to WF, August 15, 1922, in WFC; Trachtenberg (ed.), *Memoirs of Waldo Frank,* 106.
18. JT to [?], October 9, 1922, in JTP 7:11.

would be issued by Boni and Liveright on the same day. It was as close to a collaboration as two separate books could ever come. "Spartanburg (how curiously, painfully creative is the South!) gave us each other perhaps as no other place could," Jean wrote Waldo. [19]

Toomer criticized and sharpened Frank's ear for dialect; Frank made more fundamental suggestions, such as what to leave out. At Frank's suggestion, for instance, the poem "Sonnet," where bitingly sharp imagery fades into a lackluster conclusion, was removed from *Cane* and never published:

> There is no transcience [*sic*] of twilight in
> The beauty of your soft dusk-dimpled face,
> No flicker of slender flame in space,
> In crucibles, fragilely crystalline.
> There is no fragrance of the jessamine
> About you, no pathos of some old place
> At dusk, that crumbles like moth-eaten lace
> Beneath the tomb. Nor has there ever been.
>
> Your love is like the folk-song's flaming rise
> In cane-lipped southern people, like their soul
> Which burst its bondage in a bold travail;
> Your voice is like them singing, soft and wise,
> Your face, sweetly effulgent of the whole,
> Inviolate of ways that would defile. [20]

When Jean returned from Spartanburg, he worked for two weeks at the Howard Theater in Washington. The theater, famous for burlesque, was a night spot popular among black Washington society. As an assistant to the manager, Jean could watch the actors and theater crowd without having to participate, and he used his observations in his writing. Two of these pieces, "Theater" and "Box Seat," he sent to Waldo for comments. Toomer credited Frank with overseeing his writing "at a time when my own artistic efforts were at the phase where they most needed the criticism of a deeply intuitive and sympathetic mind, of a mind as honest in its judgments as it was sympathetic." [21] Jean did the creating, but Waldo's critical eye was extremely important to the final quality of *Cane*.

Waldo Frank, however, was not the only literary figure in Jean Toomer's world. From the beginning of 1922 he had been strenuously sending out manuscripts and writing to anyone he thought might help him publish. He became an occasional visitor to the home of Alain Locke, a Howard University professor who

19. JT to WF, n.d. [*ca*. November, 1922], in WFC.
20. "Sonnet" was included in correspondence from JT to WF, July, 1922, in WFC.
21. JT to WF, July 31, 1922, in WFC.

was soon to be one of the catalysts in changing Afro-American culture. It was at Locke's home that Jean met some of the bright young authors, among them Countee Cullen. Through Alain Locke's arrangement, Jean had his first piece of writing published in a major journal, *Crisis,* the organ of the NAACP. "Song of the Son," a poem expressing Toomer's purpose in writing his southern pieces, was printed in April of 1922; "Banking Coal," a poem in imitation of Robert Frost, was printed in June. Toomer also submitted "Balo" to Locke for an anthology entitled *Plays of Negro Life,* published five years later. Further, Locke wanted to review a preliminary draft of *Cane* in late 1922 to incorporate it into an article on artistic shifts by contemporary black writers, a piece that was published in 1924 in *Crisis* and expanded as the introduction to his famous anthology *The New Negro* in 1925.

Jean's persistence with Claude McKay finally gained him publication in *Liberator* in August and September of 1922, with "Carma," "Reapers," and "Becky," all from his southern sketches. McKay was by then the most famous of the young black writers, and his help was invaluable for Toomer's gaining entry to the literary world. Jean invited McKay to take a trip with him to Harpers Ferry. McKay, declining the invitation but impressed not only with Toomer the writer but also with Toomer the person, instead asked Jean to New York before McKay set out for the Soviet Union.

Jean sought other outlets for his works, mostly via the "little magazines" that were in vogue. In the spring of 1922 he submitted material to *Double Dealer,* principally because, as a New Orleans publication, it might be interested in his southern pieces. John McClure, editor of the journal, discerned in Toomer's writing a powerful force—too powerful for his southern white reading audience. McClure rejected "Fern" and "Karintha" on that basis and suggested that they be sent to *Dial*—which also rejected them and several other pieces, calling them "unfulfilled." McClure, nevertheless, wanted to champion this new writer and encouraged him to submit other pieces and tell about himself.

Waldo Frank, too, broadened Jean's contacts. On one of Jean's visits to New York, Waldo arranged a dinner for him with another guest, a friend and admirer of Waldo's, Gorham Munson. Jean made an instant impression on Munson as a "tall, vital, handsome young man." [22] At that time Munson was editor of the little magazine *Secession,* so he represented for Toomer a literary outlet. On his return to Washington, Jean sent Gorham some of his material as well as

22. Interview of Gorham Munson (hereinafter GM) by India Watterson, New York, June 27, 1969 (Amistad Research Center, New Orleans).

his own long commentaries on art. Toomer never had any of his works published in *Secession,* since Matthew Josephson and Kenneth Burke, co-editors with Munson, did not find Jean's style acceptable. But between Jean and Gorham a friendship emerged that was to last for the remainder of their lives.

Munson was part of the Greenwich Village group that sustained itself by intellectual and creative interchanges, living freely with one another as funds fluctuated whimsically. Hart Crane and Munson were close friends in the early 1920s, Crane living in Munson's apartment just before Toomer came to New York. Munson, later a major proponent of Social Credit, was writing verse, short stories, and plays and, through his magazine, was also functioning as a critic of young authors' works. He took the time to write back to Toomer about his contributions: "The spirit I write you in is not that of an editor on a pedestal, but that of a young writer to another." He complimented Toomer for having a "demon" inside of him that created moments of spectacular art. However, Munson functioned, appropriately, as a skeptic and gave some pertinent and sharp criticism. He accused Toomer, for instance, of "violating the principle of the crescendo" in the short story "Theater." And after he read Toomer's vignette entitled "Fern," he expressed his concern that it sounded too "Andersonian." [23]

It was not, however, too Andersonian for Sherwood Anderson, who took interest in Toomer in December of 1922, mainly through his friend John Mc-Clure. McClure had written to Jean in December that he was featuring "Harvest Song" in the December issue of *Double Dealer* and had added that Sherwood Anderson had dropped by the office and was impressed with Jean's writing. Soon after, Anderson sent Toomer a letter stating his prediction that the writer of *Cane* would be of major importance to the emerging Negro literature. Toomer responded with appropriate reverence:

Just before I went down to Georgia I read Winesburg, Ohio. And while there, living in a cabin whose floorboards permitted the soil to come up between them, listening to the old folk melodies that Negro women sang at sun-down, The Triumph of the Egg [one of Anderson's stories] came to me. The beauty, and the full sense of life that these books contain are natural elements, like the rain and sunshine, of my own sprouting. . . . Your Yea! to life is one of the clear fine tones in our medley of harsh discordant sounds. Life is measured by your own glowing, and you find life, you find its possibilities deeply hopeful and beautiful. It seems to me that art in our day, other than its purely aesthetic phase, has a sort of religious function. It is a religion, a spiritualization of the immediate. [24]

23. GM to JT, October 29, 1922, February 22, 1923, both in Gorham Munson Collection, Olin Library, Wesleyan University, Middletown, Conn. (hereinafter GMC).
24. JT to Anderson, December 18, 1922, in JTP 1:1.

Anderson wrote at once and offered to write the introduction to *Cane,* but Jean was unable to accept the offer, since Waldo Frank was already doing that.

Toomer was encouraged, too, by Georgia Douglas Johnson, then a teacher at the De Witt Clinton High School in Washington. Just at the point of establishing a national reputation for her poetry, she initiated a Saturday evening literary club that was Washington's equivalent to the New York salons. Jean read her some of his work, but he himself thought little of her poetry. He commented to John McClure, "Too much poetic jargon, too many inhibitions check the flow of what I think to be real (if slender) lyric gift." [25]

All this activity was great stimulus for writing, but Jean was primarily writing to others about his work and life, or reworking his previously written pieces, rather than concentrating on new work. Jean wrote to Waldo in October that the trip to Spartanburg had not stimulated him to write anything new. What he was doing was sending letters to anyone who might assist him in his literary cause. Each time he sent a manuscript he included an explanation of himself or his purpose for writing. To Lola Ridge of *Broom* he explained, "The South needs consciousness." To Jane Heap of *Little Review* he praised the literary magazine with self-conscious hype: "Little Review is an existence. This issue. It is itself germinal." Jean was, in fact, marketing himself, and he was doing it well. *Liberator* published "Becky" in the fall of 1922; *Modern Review* elected to use "Conversion," "Face," and "Portrait in Georgia"; Lola Ridge was becoming interested in him; *Dial* was reviewing his material. Even later, while *Cane* was being edited for publication at Boni and Liveright, Jean was hard at work, getting sections of the larger work published elsewhere. Although the final section of the book, "Kabnis," had been revised from a play to a narrative, Toomer was still interested in having it produced as a play. He sent it to Kenneth Macgowan of *Theatre Arts Magazine,* describing it as an attempt to achieve a "close-knit, deep rolling, dynamic structure whose language tends more towards poetry than towards what is flat and commonplace." [26] Macgowan returned the manuscript, saying it was too long, but suggested that Jean send other material. Responding to the polite note with his now characteristic fervor, Jean wrote Macgowan a lengthy description of his experiences, preferences, and motivations. It was typical of the letters he was sending to people who might help him gain literary prominence.

Jean's efforts at publicizing himself were far-reaching, and sometimes the

25. JT to McClure, October 6, 1922, in JTP 7:22.

26. JT to WF, October 4, 1922, in WFC; JT to Lola Ridge, September 20, 1922, in JTP 8:8; JT to Jane Heap, January 12, 1923 [dated 1922], in JTP 4:5; JT to Kenneth Macgowan, March 21, 1923, in JTP 7:7.

results were unexpected. Once he applied to be a member of a southern poetry society. On his trip to the South with Waldo Frank, Toomer learned that South Carolina had a poetry society, led at that time by DuBose Heyward, author of *Porgy.* In May of 1923, Jean wrote to "Mr. Heywood" seeking membership in the society and describing his credentials as the author of a still unpublished book: "Both black and white folk come into *Cane*'s pages. For me, this is artistically inevitable. But in no instance am I concerned primarily with race; always, I drive straight for my own spiritual reality, and for the spiritual truth of the South." Heyward accepted his application, but when the advertisement of *Cane* was read by a member of the society, irate letters began to be written. South Carolinians—Charlestonians, at that—did not take kindly to the news that someone alleged to be of African ancestry was actually a member of the all-white group.[27]

There was another issue that occupied him in his correspondence. In order to write *Cane,* Jean Toomer had had to embrace a part of his background that had not been familiar to him. With pieces of the book now appearing in many places, it was inevitable that he would have to define his relationship with that background. Further, it is not surprising that the psychological movement which swung him so fully toward his heritage might complete its cycle in the opposite direction.

Jean's early awareness of his own race was something like the mottled pattern of sunlight shining through leaves, shifting as a breeze rises or the sun slowly moves. His first playmates were white; he assumed he was just like them and was surprised when he looked darker in a group picture. The difference was sharply brought home to him when he was put in the black elementary school, but he never felt he belonged there. He continued to function in the white group, though he was aware that his family had black friends and that among the Pinchbacks, there were variations in complexions. Not until the eighth grade, back in Washington with his grandparents, was he plunged into a fully black environment; even there, encountering a racial gang fight with his black friends, he found he could not take either side. He was nineteen before he dared ask his grandfather about his ancestry. Then he made his first conscious racial choice: to be white when he enrolled in college. He carried the image of a fair girl, his first love, next to that of his dark mother, "and so the two, dark and fair, existed side by side, to govern my taste throughout life."[28]

27. JT to DuBose Heyward, May 16, 1923, in JT tin box (MTC); Frank Durham, "The Only Negro Member of the Poetry Society," in Frank Durham (ed.), *The Merrill Studies in "Cane"* (Columbus, Ohio, 1971), 12–13.

28. JT, "Earth-Being," 66.

Now for the first time, though still trying to hold all parts of his background in harmony, he passionately affirmed one of those parts in writing *Cane*. In the summer of 1922, he was emphasizing this affirmation. A letter to Claude McKay explained that *Cane* was a

spiritual form analogous to the fact of racial intermingling. Without denying a single element in me, with no desire to subdue one to the other, I have sought to let them function as complements. I have tried to let them live in harmony. Within the last two or three years, however, my growing need for artistic expression has pulled me deeper and deeper into the Negro group. And as my powers of receptivity increased, I found myself loving it in a way that I could never love the other. It has stimulated and fertilized whatever creative talent I may contain within me.

A slightly more passive acceptance of a similar position was included in Toomer's letter to John McClure that accompanied "Storm Ending" and "Calling Jesus" (printed in *Double Dealer* as "Nora"):

I alone, as far as I know, have striven for a spiritual fusion, analogous to the fact of racial intermingling. It has been rough riding. Nor am I through. Have just begun, in fact. This, however, has neither social nor political implications. My concern is solely with art. What am I? From my own point of view, naturally and inevitably an American. Viewed from the world of race distinctions, I take the color of whatever group I at the time am sojourning in. As I become known, I shall doubtless be classed as a Negro. I shall neither fight nor resent it. There will be more truth than they know in what they say, for my writing takes much of its worth from that source.[29]

Readers of such descriptions tended to ignore the complex part about "spiritual fusion" and concentrate on the black identification. John McClure, in a letter to Sherwood Anderson, said of Toomer, "If he follows that African urge and rhapsodizes, he will be a commanding solitary figure."[30] Anderson, too, wrote Jean several times that he feared that the white would overtake the black in Jean's writing.

Jean, in turn, tried to share with Anderson his view of the black consciousness, since Anderson, too, was attempting in some of his writing to record the black experience. "The Negro's curious position in this western civilization," Toomer wrote,

invariably forces him into one or the other of two extremes: either he denies Negro entirely (as much as he can) and seeks approximation to an Anglo-Saxon (white) ideal, or, . . . he over-emphasizes what is Negro. Both of these attitudes have their source in

29. JT to Claude McKay, August 9, 1922, in JTP 6:10; JT to McClure, July 22, 1922, in JTP 7:22.
30. McClure quoted in Anderson to JT, July 22, 1922, in JTP 1:1.

a feeling of (a desire not to feel) inferiority. I refer here, of course, to those whose consciousness and condition make them keenly aware of white dominance. The mass of negroes, the peasants, like the mass of Russians or Jews or Irish or what not, are too instinctive to be anything but themselves. Here and there one finds a high type Negro who shares this virtue with his more primitive brothers.

Whether the last comment was intended as a self-compliment, it is clear that Toomer was connecting his art and, by extension, himself to the black experience. "I feel that in time, in its social phase, my art will aid in giving the negro to himself." Later in the same letter, Toomer attempted to interest Anderson in a new magazine, "American, but concentrating on the significant contributions, or possible contributions of the Negro to the western world. A magazine that would consciously hoist, and perhaps a trifle over emphasize a negroid ideal." While he felt that such a magazine would initially meet resistance, the need, he claimed, was "great. . . . With the youth of the race, unguided or misguided as they now are, there is a tragic need."[31] Anderson concluded that Jean should abandon plans for the magazine. He should concentrate on writing and let others do the publishing.

These discussions by letter with Anderson would surely reinforce in Anderson's mind a view that Toomer was primarily interested in drawing out his Negro background, and his letters to Toomer do so attest. The emotional impact of the trips to Sparta and Spartanburg had evidently brought Jean at this point in his life to an integration around his African heritage. Yet he did not wholly want to be called "black." Jean was to write Waldo a short time after his initial contact with Anderson, "Sherwood limits me to Negro. As an approach, as a constant element (part of a larger whole) of interest, Negro is good. But try to tie me to one of my parts is surely to loose [*sic*] me. My own letters have taken Negro as a point, and from there have circled out. Sherwood, for the most part, ignores the circles."[32]

Like Kabnis, who was ambivalent about his racial identification, Jean was working out his racial identity as he was shaping his book. "The only time I think 'Negro,'" he wrote Waldo, "is when I want a particular emotion which is associated with his name. As a usual thing, I actually do not see differences of color and contour. I see differences of life and experience, and often enough these lead me to physical coverings." A long passage from another of his letters to Waldo reveals the connectedness between his views on blackness and the shape he was giving *Cane*:

31. JT to Anderson, December 29, 1922, in JTP 1:1.
32. JT to WF, n.d. [*ca*. March, 1923], in JTP 7:7.

There is one thing about the Negro in America which most thoughtful persons seem to ignore: The Negro is in solution, in the process of solution. As an entity, the race is loosing [*sic*] its body, and its soul is approaching a common soul. If one holds his eyes to individuals and sections, race is starkly evident, and racial continuity seems assured. One is even led to believe that the thing we call Negro beauty will always be attributable to a clearly defined physical source. But the fact is, that if anything comes up now, pure Negro, it will be a swan-song. The Negro of the folk-song has all but passed away: the Negro of the emotional church is fading. A hundred years from now these Negroes, if they exist at all will live in art. . . . The supreme fact of mechanical civilization is that you become part of it, or get sloughed off (under). Negroes have no culture to resist it with (and if they had, their position would be identical to that of the Indians), hence industrialism the more readily transforms them. A few generations from now, the Negro will still be dark, and a portion of his psychology will spring from this fact, but in all else he will be a conformist to the general outlines of American civilization, or of American chaos. In my own stuff, in those pieces that come nearest to the old Negro, to the spirit saturate with folk-song: Karintha and Fern, the dominant emotion is a sadness derived from a sense of fading, from a knowledge of my futility to check solution. There is nothing about these pieces of the bouyant [*sic*] expression of a new race. The folk-songs themselves are of the same order. The deepest of them, "I ain't got long to stay here." Religiously: "I [am going] to cross over into camp ground." Socially: "my position here is transient. I'm going to die, or be absorbed."

When I come up to Seventh Street and Theatre, a wholly new life confronts me. A life, I am afraid, that Sherwood Anderson would not get his beauty from. For it is jagged, strident, modern. Seventh Street is the song of a crude new life. Of a new people. Negro? Only in the *boldness* of its expression. In its healthy freedom. American. For the shows that please Seventh Street make their fortunes on Broadway. And both Theatre and Box-Seat, of course, spring from a complex civilization, and are directed to it. And Kabnis is *me*.[33]

However, even his spiritual brother could not seem to interpret Jean's view to his satisfaction. He had declared that Waldo "not only understood *Cane*; you are *in* it, specifically here and there, mystically because of the spiritual bond there is between us." When Waldo sought advice on the content of the introduction he was to write for *Cane,* Jean answered, "Sure, feature Negro." Nevertheless, when Waldo sent a draft of the introduction to Jean, Jean was disappointed that "he did not get my racial position. . . . What was I to do? How could I take issue with a man who had responded to the art of 'Cane' so firmly and fully? Besides, what did it matter, the question of race? I was what I was—to be called a Negro would not change me in the least. All right, go ahead. And so it was." Jean did not ask that the introduction be changed. In fact, he complimented Frank on his sensitive description. "The one thing I was uneasy about in a foreword was this: that in doing the necessary cataloging and

33. JT to WF, n.d., and n.d. [*ca.* October, 1922], both in WFC.

naming etc. the very elements which the book does *not* possess would get plastered across its first pages. I was sure of *you*. I knew you could do the thing. You *have*." [34]

This apparent unconcern was again present in a letter in the spring of 1923 to Samuel Pessin of the magazine *Prairie,* which was to publish "Blood-Burning Moon." "It is stupid and absurd to call me anything other than an American. . . . When I live with the blacks I'm a Negro. When I live with the whites, I'm white, or, better, a foreigner. I used to puzzle my own brain with the question. But now I'm done with it. My concern is with the art of literature. Call me what you like." [35] Jean was sending out mixed signals, and increasingly he was to find himself misinterpreted. Hence, increasingly, he was to harden his position against classification.

Although Toomer's racial philosophy was embedded in *Cane,* discussing it in letters did not get the book written. Through the fall of 1922, Jean was working over the pieces to be included, having more trouble with the Washington sketches than with the Georgia pieces. Waldo's comments on "Box Seat" and "Theater" had not been favorable. He suggested that Jean had "introduced things that are forced, formless, alien" and asked him to make extensive revisions. Jean responded positively, leaving out four poems that Waldo felt were inferior, but retaining "Prayer" because it completed a "spiritual curve, the only companion piece to Harvest Song." He was not a slave to Waldo's every suggestion, but Jean appreciated his extensive help. "Your marginal notes through out [*sic*] the mss are splendid," he wrote. "Your sensitivity to muddy, ragged lines and passages is unerring." He added that "all of my stuff gains in the second trial." Particularly rewarding was his year-long wait before completing "Kabnis." "It took a year to grow within me. For it to have been wrong—foundations and everything else would shake." [36]

Finally, Jean's struggle to get the book finished was over. In early December of 1922 he completed the final copy and sent it to Waldo Frank with an explanatory letter:

For two weeks I have worked steadily at it. The book is done. From three angles, CANE's design is a circle. Aesthetically, from simple forms to complex ones, and back to simple forms. Regionally, from the South up into the North, and back into the South again. . . . From the point of view of the spiritual entity behind the work, the curve really starts with Bona and Paul (awakening), plunges into Kabnis, emerges

34. JT to WF, n.d., in JTP 7:7; JT, "Outline," 61; JT to WF, n.d. [*ca*. November or December, 1922], in WFC.

35. JT to Samuel Pessin, March 25, 1923, in JTP 8:5.

36. JT to WF, n.d., in JTP 3:7; JT to WF, n.d. [*ca*. November, 1922], in WFC.

with Karintha etc. swings upward into Theatre and Box Seat, and ends (pauses) in Harvest Song. . . . You will understand the inscription, brother mine: the book to grandma; Kabnis, the spirit and the soil, to you. . . . Between each of the three sections, a curve. These, to vaguely indicate the design.[37]

The celebration of the book's completion was undercut somewhat by Jean's announcement that at least for a while he was through doing any "real writing." Perhaps this was because of the tremendous effort it had taken to produce *Cane.* As he described it later,

Life had me in a knot, hard and fast. Even in Georgia, I was horribly conflicted, strained and tense—more so here. The deep releases caused by my experiences there could not liberate and harmonize the sum of me. Cane was a lyric essence forced out with great effort despite my knotted state. People have remarked its simple easy-flowing lyricism, its rich natural poetry, and they may assume that it came to bloom as easily as a flower. In truth, it was born in an agony of internal tightness, conflict, and chaos. . . . During its writing, and after it, I felt that I had by sheer force emptied myself and given to that book my last blood.[38]

However, it was done. Frank took the manuscript to Horace Liveright and telegraphed Jean on January 2, 1923, that it had been accepted.

While he was arranging and polishing the parts of *Cane,* Toomer had announced plans for another book of short pieces emphasizing a creative tension between the two races, the black spirit pressing against the white consciousness to make it change. "The upward heaving," he concluded in a moment of enthusiasm, "to be symbolic of the subconscious penetration of the conscious mind. . . . Great gains, brother! Whenever I get a real glimpse of the thing, a terrific emotion sweeps me."[39] "Balo," "Natalie Mann," and "Withered Skin of Berries" were to be the central pieces in the book, which he expected to have finished by the following fall. Liveright, in agreeing to publish *Cane,* also took an option on this or whatever two books he might write next.

Toomer's future seemed set. He had patrons and protectors, a publisher, a growing audience of admirers, and material for further writing as soon as he should gain energy to tackle it. The carefully crafted arrow of *Cane* had left the bow. Where else could it take Jean Toomer but straight to the target of literary success?

37. JT to WF, December 12, 1922, in JTP 3:6.
38. JT notes, n.d. (JTP 32:6).
39. JT to WF, n.d., in WFC.

5.

The Charmed Circle

When *Cane* shot onto the literary scene in 1923, it was distinctive but not unique. It fitted, rather, into a literary and social milieu that existed before Jean Toomer stepped into the New York world of artists, social movers, and climbers. His immediate literary forebears were a group of avant-garde artists who, like Jean, were eager to see a transformation of American letters. This desire was not unique to New York, and New York certainly contained more than one group seeking similar ends. The post–Great War era was ripe for social and artistic change in America, and artists were banding together in loose or, in some cases, tightly knit groups whose common purpose was to change the status quo. Those congregating in Harlem, Nashville, Chicago, Taos, Carmel, Paris, and elsewhere were all seeking to give new direction to American culture.

Among the various New York groups vying for cultural leadership was a loose assemblage of artists and intellectuals including Waldo Frank, Randolph Bourne, and Van Wyck Brooks, who collaborated in 1916 on a short-lived but influential magazine called *Seven Arts*. The magazine supported a cultural revolution based on the ideas of several American and European writers, the most prominent of whom were Walt Whitman and Romain Rolland. Rolland's epic novel *Jean-Christophe* portrays a musician whose persistent search for new forms of art always places him outside the expectations of a society that does homage to stability. The heroic outcast can find solace and even pride in being misunderstood by the ignorant masses he is trying to change. This Byronic role, very much a part of Waldo Frank and other aspiring social movers of the day, also suited Jean Toomer's self-image. Independently of Frank but carried by the same cultural currents, Toomer by 1920 had added the tales of Jean-

Christophe to his Whitman discipleship and enthusiastic absorption of Jean Valjean.

Rolland was a proponent of what was called *unanisme,* a mystical union of symbols and sensibilities that joined people into a collective group consciousness. This theory of how individuals are united had already been explored by Yeats and Jung as well. It was but part of several causes and effects in international thought that gradually linked such disparate persons as Sherwood Anderson, Waldo Frank, Carl Van Vechten, Mabel Dodge, Alain Locke, Gertrude Stein, Alfred Stieglitz, Kenneth Burke, and a host of others who wanted to create a new American idiom.

It was, as has been indicated, Waldo Frank who wielded the most influence over Toomer during the *Cane* period. Toomer wrote in October of 1922, "With the exception of Sherwood Anderson some years ago (and to a less extent Frost and Sandburg) Waldo is the only modern writer who has immediately influenced me. . . . I must *grow* out of him."[1] In his attitude toward art and society, Frank helped shape Toomer's and other young writers' purpose for writing. Rejecting the wasteland image held by many postwar American writers, Frank chose to take a more positive stance. This he outlined in 1919 in a social criticism entitled *Our America.* His composite of American culture centered on the "organic, mystic Whole," a transnationalism that blended geographical and cultural differences while preserving the validity of the source of those differences. Frank felt that the postwar era was the time to reshape American culture by infusing shattered symbols with new, essentially religious, meanings. Puritanism, he believed, was a dead husk, but a deep sense of brotherhood rooted in a divine Oneness could replace its morality. Man's sense of dignity could no longer rest on belief in a special creation—even man's faith in linear time, space, and reason had to crumble under Einstein and Freud. The writer or artist, however, could see through appearances to spiritual meanings and bring to life the organic connections between walled-off segments of society. This cultural "revolution" required an "uprising generation" of writers, whose task was to find the "buried cultures" of America and use them to break Main Street sterility.[2]

Several writers and critics responded to Waldo Frank's challenge, among them Hart Crane, Alfred Kreymborg, Paul Rosenfeld, Gorham Munson, and, with Munson's and Frank's encouragement, Jean Toomer in 1922. They attempted to create an American art that had as its basis an affirmation of a

---

1. JT to GM, October 21, 1922, in GMC.
2. Waldo Frank, *Our America* (New York, 1919).

unique American ethic and aesthetic. *Our America* used as a central metaphor
the native Indian traditions, which Frank described as dying cultures. He felt
that these traditions should be preserved, in art if nowhere else, as an emblem
of the diversity of life that could and does add texture to the larger social
model. Toomer, already feeling that he was a physical and spiritual embodiment of this diversity, quickly became for Frank the symbol of synthesis that
Our America purported to characterize.

Toomer's aesthetic was in large part also Waldo Frank's. He thought of art as a
spiritual emanation having its own reality. And yet he perceived art as a mover
of people, a catalyst for reshaping symbols that give our lives meaning. The
artist's burden is to record a people's spirit with a detached, often lonely and
misunderstood, compassion. In Toomer's case, he felt compelled to record a
spirit that was dying in the rural South and contrast it with a spirit that was
already dead in the urban North. Most contemporary writing, Jean was convinced, was composed of "clever gestures [substituted] for true songs and life."
His view was different: "When I use words I wish to create those things which
can only come to life in them. I am violated to think of literature as nothing
more than a vicarious experience of what one should be strong enough to wring
from the social life." Form was to evolve from the charged moment, fragments
were to blend of their own accord into a whole. Frank's followers emphasized
emotion as a spiritual experience and an exalted lyricism, which linked earth
images to the human condition and unified abstract meanings and concrete
references. This spiritual and emotional function of literature Jean described
again as his goal in the spring of 1923: "I do not want art to be a mere transcription of life, technically OK; I want it to be the most vital and thrilling
experience that life has to give."[3] Toomer had applied these ideas to the shaping of *Cane* and constantly tested them on his mentor, Waldo Frank.

Thus Toomer, though relatively isolated in Washington much of the time he
was writing, felt that he was part of a larger literary context. While he was
arranging his fragments of American life into *Cane,* other writers, shaped by
similar influences, were doing their share of experimentation. Hart Crane was
linking myth to present reality in poetic forms that became the first passages of
The Bridge; and Frank, just finished with *Rahab,* was joining white with black
in *Holiday.* The construction of *Cane* resembled many other literary experiments
of that era, the most noteworthy being, for Jean, *Winesburg, Ohio.* Winesburg
continued the trend of Robinson's Tilbury Town and Masters' Spoon River, and

3. JT to WF, May 5, 1922, in WFC; JT to John McClure, July 22, 1922, JT to Kenneth
Macgowan, March 21, 1923, both in JTP 7:22, 7:7.

this technique of storytelling continued in Hemingway's *In Our Time,* Dos Passos' *Manhattan Transfer,* Faulkner's *The Sound and the Fury,* and Steinbeck's *The Pastures of Heaven.* All of these were fragments creating a sum greater than the parts, with an experimental style that attempted to go beyond dialect to find deeper measures of the American voice. In content, they sought a definition of the American experience as universal.

It is understandable, then, that Jean was anxious to move to New York and live in this milieu. The death of his grandfather had in a way removed the yoke that he had felt bound him to Washington. Uncle Walter had remarried and had bought a house. Jean's grandmother urged him to go to New York, since she could move in with Walter and be taken care of. Although he thought that his close ties with Washington and his grandmother would not let him stay elsewhere permanently, Jean made efforts to get to New York. Once his book was accepted, he attempted to get a loan from a potential patron through the assistance of Alain Locke. At the same time, he applied for jobs in the city, one of which involved his being a social worker at St. Cyprian's Chapel. Nothing was offered, but it was only a matter of time until the means to go to New York would be provided.

In the meantime, Jean settled for friendship by correspondence, particularly with Waldo, who received a battery of enthusiastic plans from Jean. Having received no positive reply from Sherwood Anderson about collaborating on a magazine, Jean tried the idea on Waldo. Most of the literary magazines, Jean argued, were inferior: *Broom* was formless, *Dial* was too Continental, *Little Review* was personal and uncertain, *Secession* was too narrow. He wanted to start a magazine with Waldo and Gorham that would do away with these limitations. Jean stated that he wanted to see Waldo in the spring and was writing an article on him. And in his first reference to Waldo's wife Margaret Naumburg, Jean was pleased that she had "loved" *Cane,* the manuscript of which Waldo had undoubtedly shown her.[4]

Gorham Munson offered to have Jean stay at his apartment on Grove Street once Hart Crane had moved out. Reacting to the invitation and to Munson's suggestion that Jean write a review of Munson's *Waldo Frank: A Study,* Jean was prompted to say, "I'm beginning to feel *in* things. And its [*sic*] a damn good feeling."[5]

When the proofs of *Cane* arrived in late April of 1923, Jean wrote Waldo a letter filled with good cheer and humor, praising him for at last finishing *Holi-*

4. JT to WF, n.d., in WFC.
5. *Ibid.*

day. Jean felt good, he said; he was exercising, he was thinking seriously of going to New York, and he had been in love steadily with "ONE girl for the past eight months." With an expansive view of himself and his intellectual power, he finished the proofreading and sent Boni and Liveright his comments, consisting of a few strictly technical suggestions.[6] Then he prepared to go to New York himself.

Jean had been asked by Will Marion Cook, a jazz musician, to stay at his home in New York. The offer was tempting, for Jean felt that Cook was "the only person within the negroid segment of this country who has touched me to artistic love, even to reverence." But in May, Hart Crane finally moved out of Munson's apartment and into his own quarters, leaving a spot for Jean. Jean left Washington and never again really considered it his home. He moved in with Gorham Munson on Grove Street and became automatically part of the life his host was experiencing. Their days were filled with making as many contacts with artists as possible, with sharing ideas about current trends, with trying to discover new talent or trying to be discovered by others. "It was very exciting life and work," Toomer writes in his autobiography, "giving me a taste and an experience of the literary life such as I had never known before and have never experienced since. There was an excitement in the air. Writing was a living thing. We had programs and aims, and we were all caught up in a ferment. These were the last days of *Secession* and *Broom.* But the *Dial* and the *Little Review* were still going, and what was not yet an actuality we had as a glowing potentiality in our minds."[7]

Soon Jean moved out of the cramped quarters into a small row-house apartment on Gay Street, a side street one block long, distinctive then as being a predominantly black settlement in an otherwise white part of town. Toomer spent his days in the backyard reading or in the apartment writing. During that summer he was trying to establish himself as a free-lance writer for various New York journals and little magazines.

It was important to work for and to be published in the little magazines, for they were acknowledged as among the cultural arbiters of the day. *Poetry, Dial,* and *Little Review* were relatively long-lived. Others, like *S4N, Fire, Secession, Double Dealer,* and *Broom,* while short-lived by choice or because of financial problems and haphazard management, were also vehicles for recognition. Harold Loeb's *Broom* was among the more important for Toomer, because the American editor, Lola Ridge, was impressed with Jean's writing and was

6. JT to WF, May 1, 1923, in JTP 64:15.
7. JT to WF, n.d., in WFC; JT, "On Being an American" (JTP 15:10), also in *W&S,* 127.

eager to champion him. Loeb, who printed the magazine in Rome and later in Dresden because printing was so much cheaper there, relied on his assistant editor in America to make contacts with new authors and to screen their works.

Lola Ridge was an indomitable spirit in the frailest of bodies. She made the *Broom* office a center of intellectual activity. The office, located in the basement of Marjorie Content Loeb's house on East Ninth Street, was only two rooms, but on Thursday afternoons and occasional evenings, Lola and her husband would play host to a multitude of artists. With the help of an awed Kay Boyle, who served Lola as a secretary and occasional cook, Lola offered tea and had guests read their works. Jean was among them.

In one of the *Broom* issues, Lola featured Jean's sketch "Seventh Street" as the opening piece, and she accepted several of his reviews. She also urged Marjorie Content, whose marriage to Loeb was dissolving, to meet this dashing man Toomer. But Marjorie, described by Kay Boyle as having a "warm, shy, generous heart" and a "madonna face," stayed upstairs and never met him.[8] It was not until eleven years later that the urging of two other good friends finally brought her to meet Jean, who eventually became her fourth husband.

Toomer entered the world of literary contacts with great excitement but considerable aplomb. Munson, Frank, Kenneth Burke, Matthew Josephson, Malcolm Cowley, Paul Rosenfeld, Van Wyck Brooks, and Robert Littel—all were figures Toomer says he met that summer. There was much literary cross-fertilizing, as each of the young group of writers publicized the others in his enthusiasm. By that summer, for instance, Munson's book on the early Frank novels had been published. Jean's review of Munson's book had been printed in *S4N*. Frank's introduction to *Cane* completed the circuit. And so it went.

Hart Crane was also important in Jean's life that summer. He was part of Waldo Frank's inner circle, as well as a good friend of Munson's. Crane's own discovery of America was tangential to Frank's and as such was a valuable stimulus to Toomer. In 1921, Crane had written "Black Tambourine," a poem eventually included in the collection *White Buildings,* dedicated to Waldo Frank. The poem presaged a description of Jean's Father John in "Kabnis." Crane describes an old black man sitting in a darkened cellar with his tambourine tacked to the wall, and waiting for a day when society will recognize in him the dignity he has earned:

> The black man, forlorn in the cellar,
> Wanders in some mid-kingdom, dark, that lies,

8. Kay Boyle and Robert McAlmon, *Being Geniuses Together* (1938; rpr. Garden City, N.Y., 1968), 18.

> Between his tambourine, stuck on the wall,
> And, in Africa, a carcass quick with flies.[9]

Crane also had a fascination with the mystical, which appealed to Toomer. Crane had reported in a letter to Munson the preceding year an experience under ether in the dentist's chair when his mind "spiraled to a kind of seventh heaven of consciousness and egoistic dance among the seven spheres" and he heard a voice declaring his genius. Crane tried his hand at making a sketch of Jean, and he wrote to his mother, "Toomer and I are great friends."[10] He did his part for Jean's potential fame, writing to friends such as Allen Tate about Jean's artistry and helping Jean start corresponding with literary leaders who, like Tate, were not in the immediate vicinity of New York.

It was an extraordinary time for the neophyte writer, to be thrust into an elite circle of artists who had achieved the kind of fame attained only by the few.

To "arrive" meant a great deal in those days of the early 20's. If you were doing anything worthwhile in any of the arts, and in the modern idiom, to arrive meant that you were welcomed, officially as it were, into the most remarkable up-swing yet to occur in our national culture. It meant that you found yourself not only with name and place in a local movement or "school" but with function in a regenerative life which transcended national boundaries and quickened people in every country of the post-war world. You were part of a living world of great promise. And in this world, if you so felt it, there was not only art but something of religion.[11]

Crane, Toomer, Munson, and Frank not only derived great intellectual stimulation from one another; they also enjoyed one another's company. Munson's quiet, professorial demeanor complemented Crane's mercurial behavior, and Frank's fatherly patience fed upon Toomer's adulation. Together they made frequent forays to a restaurant in Chinatown, a ritual that Jean later kept up with Munson.

It was a fraternity, however, that was as exhausting as it was stimulating. Jean wrote to Countee Cullen, "I have not only been rushed, but, what is worse, greatly fatigued. These few months are the tail-end of a labored period.

---

9. Brom Weber (ed.), *The Complete Poems and Selected Letters and Prose of Hart Crane* (New York, 1966), 4. See Victor Kramer's "The Mid-Kingdom of Crane's 'Black Tambourine' and Toomer's *Cane*," *CLA Journal*, XVII (1974), 486–97, for a closer analysis of the poem's relationship to Toomer's book.

10. Hart Crane to GM, n.d. [*ca.* June 18, 1922], Hart Crane to his mother, September 23, October 12, 1923, all in Brom Weber (ed.), *The Letters of Hart Crane, 1916–1932* (New York, 1952), 91–92, 149, 150.

11. JT, "The Second River" (JTP 66:8), 3.

I bear them with certainly no great relish or surplus."[12] As had happened at other times in his life, the very intensity of experience was the root of exhaustion and disillusionment. The charmed circle was soon to be utterly broken, and by Jean himself.

The most puzzling question for students of Jean Toomer's life is why he turned away from literature at a time when he seemed to be well launched on a spectacular career. There were many interwoven reasons for this; at least four can be identified. The first, Toomer's reaction to the literary world itself, had to do with the limited sales of *Cane,* with Jean's closer view of that world, and mostly with his own psychological pattern.

The publication of *Cane* was not immediately recorded as a major literary event. It was advertised by Liveright in August of 1923, and by September the book was out and Jean had copies he could give away. No more than one thousand copies were sold, in spite of generally favorable reviews, though some bookstores had calls for more copies than they could secure. The little magazines, and the writers and critics who read them, praised the book. But the readership of the magazines was small. The book did receive wider publicity in reviews such as that by Robert Littel in the *New Republic.* He praised *Cane* for its unstereotyped view of the South, a view that regrettably was "unfamiliar and bafflingly subterranean." Allen Tate responded with an immediate and continuing admiration for it, indicating in both a personal letter to Toomer and a review in the book section of the Nashville *Tennessean* that Toomer's innovative technique in places rivaled some of the best work of his literary contemporaries. Reviews were published in NAACP's *Crisis* and in *Opportunity,* the organ of the newly established Urban League. Roger Didier, for the Associated Negro Press, praised his courage, truthfulness, and originality, saying, "Jean Toomer is a lover who paints pictures and then sings to them." W. E. B. Du Bois and Alain Locke, writing an article in early 1924 entitled "The Younger Literary Movement," chose to feature Jean Toomer as one of the bright young black authors. In Alain Locke's *The New Negro* in 1925, William Stanley Braithwaite called Toomer the "very first artist of the race, who . . . can write about the Negro without the surrender or compromise of the artist's vision." Countee Cullen wrote Jean a note expressing his happiness that *Cane* was a "classical portrayal of things as they are," a comment that Jean particularly appreciated. In October, Edward O'Brien wrote from England requesting that "Blood-Burning Moon," the story that ends Part I of *Cane,* be used in the an-

12. JT to Countee Cullen, August 17, 1923, in The Countee Cullen Papers, Amistad Research Center, New Orleans, Box 6, Folder 3.

thology *The Best Short Stories of 1923*. The book indeed had its recognition, and while sales were not high, those who bought the book (or borrowed a friend's copy) had influential opinions.[13]

All in all, this was not a bad reception for a first book. Jean, in fact, was pleased with the response, though three years later he was convinced that the book was "not successful." However, by its date of publication, "[w]hat was happening to 'Cane' seemed a long way off, . . . not a vital concern of mine."[14] Jean was occupied, rather, in observing what seemed to him chaos and trying to bring about some sort of order. The group of literati he had been so eager to join, the cultural aristocracy, was discovered, once he was inside, to be something less than a harmonious circle. Although all may have held high principles, they fought for their different views of what art should be, and the economic pressure to survive forced them into competitive positions. While the constant interchange of ideas and creativity encouraged a climate of artistic fervor, Toomer began to have questions about their characters.

One rivalry in 1923 that may have fed this reaction helped dissolve the group of artists and thinkers of which Toomer was a part. An article Munson sent to *Broom* was rejected with cutting criticism, leading to an exchange of increasingly abusive letters between him and Matthew Josephson, new American editor of *Broom*. They had had literary and managerial differences when Josephson was working on Munson's magazine *Secession*. Eventually Kenneth Burke called a meeting to make peace between the two. Munson, out of town, sent a letter stating that he declined to "participate in any group which contained so vulnerable a member as Josephson—a literary opportunist and intellectual faker." This caused "a great rumpus," with people taking sides. Josephson, who was then trying to promote dadaism, which attacks accepted values and seeks out the deliberately outrageous, made a journey to where Munson was staying and demanded that he come out and fight—it was a dadaist's "significant gesture." Hart Crane stood up for Munson, and when Toomer understood some of the ways they differed in principle from other literary people, he also took Munson's side. After that event, Frank's group was

13. Robert Littel, Review of Toomer's *Cane*, in *New Republic*, December 26, 1923, p. 137; Allen Tate to JT, November 7, 1923, in JTP 8:15; Roger Didier note (JTP 64:16); W. E. B. Du Bois and Alain Locke, "The Younger Literary Movement," *Crisis*, XXVII (February, 1924), 161–63; William Stanley Braithwaite, "The Negro in American Literature," in Alain Locke (ed.), *The New Negro: An Interpretation* (New York, 1925), 44; Countee Cullen to JT, September 29, 1923, in JTP 1:12; JT to Cullen, October, 1923, in Cullen Papers; Edward O'Brien to JT, October 9, 1923, in JTP 8:1.

14. JT to Horace Liveright, January 27, 1926, in JTP 1:5; JT, "Outline," 63.

reduced to Crane, Munson, and Toomer, with a few others, like Paul Rosenfeld, delicately bridging the rift. Burke began taking literary potshots at Crane and Munson, who returned in kind. Jean himself in the last published review during his literary period, printed in *Little Review* in the fall of 1924, commented unfavorably on Burke's writing.[15]

Such excursions into the politics of art left Toomer wondering about an artist's quality of life. Just as in each of his college experiences, the enthusiasm had faded; being "inside" was not so good as it had seemed from the outside. With his jaundiced view of life and people, he peppered his friends with questions about meaning and values, getting a reputation "for being a sort of genius of chaos." He formulated two sayings, "In a sick world, it is the first duty of an artist to get well" and "The forming of a man is more important than the forming of a book." It was not until he was considerably older that he realized that his chaos arose largely from within himself: "I passed into a condition which gathered up the results of all my past difficulties, struggles, fatigues, discontents, and searchings. I became a severe critic of values and ways. . . . I turned on myself and on my friends. I whipped and lashed everything I came in contact with. . . . What I said was true for myself [but] . . . untrue or untimely for most of [my friends]."[16] At this time, he says, he found himself becoming a pretentious poseur, one of a community of exhibitionists whose sole intention was self-advertisement as a ploy for getting ahead.

A second cause of Toomer's unhappiness with the literary world had been building since before he left Washington for New York. This was the increased battle he was fighting in regard to the intent of his book and to his own racial affiliation. His ambivalence on these issues caused the first rift between Frank and Toomer, over the introduction to *Cane*. His definition of his multipartite self continued to be little understood as his publication date approached. Liveright, aware of the craze for Afro-American literature that was blossoming in the 1920s and was eventually called a renaissance, ignored all but that one element. In May, when the publisher was promoting Jean's review of Munson's *Waldo Frank: A Study,* Horace Liveright described Toomer as "a colored genius whose remarkable book we're bringing out in the fall." Boni and Liveright returned Jean's self-description, written to be used in advertising, and urged him to stress his "colored blood" more emphatically. In a September, 1923, letter, Toomer replied, "My racial composition and my position in the world are reali-

15. Elizabeth Delza Munson to the authors, July 27, 1982; JT, "Oxen Cart and Warfare," *Little Review,* X (Autumn-Winter, 1924-25), 44-48.
16. JT, "Outline," 63, back of 62.

ties which I alone may determine. . . . As a unit in the social milieu, I expect and demand acceptance of myself on [that] basis. . . . I have told you . . . to make use of whatever racial factors you wish. Feature Negro if you wish, but do not expect me to feature it in advertisement for you. For myself, I have sufficiently featured Negro in *Cane*. Whatever statement I give will inevitably come from a sympathetic human and art point of view; not from a racial one." [17]

Toomer was not the only one to be pressured in this way, but he may have been more inwardly detached than most from the black identification. The pressure on those partly black to fit into "being black" was particularly acute in the 1920s. Harlem nightclubs excluded black patrons in favor of the moneyed, daring whites who wanted to experience the "primitivism" of jazz and the blues; the publishers, all white, had no less an inclination to profit from a fad. Jean was aware of these molds, but found them more and more irritating as they were applied to him—without reason, he felt. Not long after this, he wrote an essay called "The Negro Emergent," which portrayed something he had observed. The inner selves of many black individuals were slipping the bonds of societal expectations, "transforming rejections to acceptances, denials to affirmations," and these blacks were exploring the new persons they might become. When he wrote this, he said, he had become aware of the ferment in the Negro world, but he was merely offering an observation. [18]

Toomer's continued fight against being called a "Negro" increased after the publication of *Cane*. While Du Bois, Locke, and others were urging him to make an even more fruitful "race contribution," as Countee Cullen called *Cane* in a complimentary letter to Toomer, the harassed young author elected instead to risk friendships and associations. Tensions arose between himself and people like Alain Locke, who had printed excerpts from *Cane* in *The New Negro* without Toomer's later permission. (Before the publication of *Cane*, Toomer had been delighted at the prospect of having Locke as a patron.) The aim of this popular anthology was to present new, mostly young, black writers and artists who were breaking away from old stereotypes of the Negro in American art. In the essay "Negro Youth Speaks," which introduces the book, Locke was careful to praise Toomer as being racial "purely for the sake of art." Toomer's universality as an artist was reinforced in that essay by a quotation from Toomer himself: "There [in Georgia] one finds the soil, soil in the sense the Russians know it—the soil every art and literature that is to live must be embedded in."

17. Horace Liveright to John Macy of the *Nation*, March 17, 1923, copy in JTP 7:8; Liveright to JT, August 29, 1923, JT to Liveright, September 7, 1923, both in JTP 1:5.

18. JT, "The Negro Emergent" (MTC); JT "On Being an American" (JTP 15:11).

Nevertheless, Toomer by this time was minimizing his past close identity with black people. He thought the new "negro movement" a "splendid thing, but . . . something that had no special meaning for me." Thus, at a time when Toomer was considered one of the originators of the Harlem Renaissance, he was quite methodically detaching himself from association with it. He felt that Locke had "tricked" him into posing for a portrait for the book and then had used the sketch without Toomer's permission. Jean was also distressed that Locke had put into *The New Negro* sections from *Cane,* which Toomer did not want "dismembered." If that were not enough, Locke's comments in the preface and introduction praising Toomer "in their way, have caused as much or more misunderstanding than Waldo Frank's!" This new American did not want to be a New Negro, and the writing and publishing world kept pushing him in that direction.[19]

A third important change for Jean Toomer in 1923 was a love that was unique in his experience thus far. Through all his close relationship with Waldo Frank, their contacts had been by letter or at hotels, restaurants, and friends' parties in New York City, except for their trip south together. Until Jean moved to New York at the end of May, he had never had occasion to visit Frank's home in Darien, Connecticut, or to meet his wife Margaret Naumburg. That occasion came in the early summer. It brought fireworks: Jean and Margaret were entranced with each other from the first time they met.

Margaret was a professional educator. She was dark-haired, powerful, and self-assured, and seems never to have used her husband's last name. Eight years earlier she had founded the Walden School in New York; the first students were very young children, and she added a class every year. The school was conceived as an organic society, where the children put out their own newspaper, planned and bought food for their lunches, and derived all their study from actual life processes. Its aim was "independent children who can think, act, express themselves on their own basis."[20] Naumburg also had published some poetry and was very interested, as were Jean and Waldo, in a mystical view of the world. Although she and Waldo had a son about a year old, their marriage was not going well; and it did not take her long to make a final break.

From Jean's point of view, his meeting with Margaret started him on a series of remarkable experiences that could be likened to the terror and elation of a roller coaster, without the assurance that it was all in fun. These experiences,

19. Countee Cullen to JT, September 24, 1923, in JTP 1:12; Alain Locke, "Negro Youth Speaks," in Locke (ed.), *New Negro,* 51; JT, "On Being an American" (JTP 15:11), also in *W&S,* 132.

20. Brochure of Walden School, 1923–24 (JTP 24:51).

more fully described later, led him to the conviction that the making of a man was more important than the making of a book. Margaret helped him plunge into the unknown, demolish and reassemble his personality. What writing he was contemplating then had Margaret as its focus. He described in a letter to her "the outline of my first real work," which sounds transparently derived from Jean's own experiences in New York, Georgia, and Washington, and culminates with "Birth in New York. And the final expansion, inclusion, digestion, adjustment, integration." He went on, "I could write its individual scenes without you . . perhaps. But no matter how violent an episode may be, beneath it, as the soil from which it springs, there *must exist* that calm, tender spiritual strength and beauty of which we that evening spoke. . . . And I may attain and sustain that beauty only through you. The notion I once entertained of an isolated, self-sufficient art existence is exploded. In its place I have the vision—I have something more than vision—I have the vision and the *experience,* Marge, of a linked, interacting, completed Life." [21] The bonds between them formed very quickly and were, for a time, very tight.

Of course this caused strains in Jean's friendship with Waldo. At first he seemed to take Margaret and Jean's relationship in stride, but that became more and more difficult. The literary collaboration, the "brother mine," the joint effort to save American culture, dissolved. In August, Jean, needing time to put himself together after his first trip to the top of the roller coaster, went to his old retreat at Ellenville, New York. In the same month Mae Wright, the "ONE girl" he had been in love with for more than eight months, warmly invited him to her family's place on the Chesapeake Bay and asked again for the picture of himself that he had promised her. But there was no longer any room in Jean's life for her. In September, Jean wrote Waldo from Ellenville that he was worried about his friend's "crucial torment": "Ever since I came to you that day at Darien there has been a most cruel silence on the sheer life-plane, on the plane where we have had such deep and sustaining contacts. . . . I know that I am a factor of it. How could I not know?" But though it begins in a conciliatory tone, the letter goes on to accuse Frank of a life and writing full of evasions, and to challenge him from Toomer's new state of illumination to a "sheer facing and a pure resolution of fundamentals." [22] This did nothing to heal the breach. By October, the split between Margaret and Waldo became official; Waldo took an extended trip to Europe, and Margaret moved from Darien to an apartment in New York. By this time, Gorham Munson and other

21. JT to Margaret Naumburg, n.d. [1923?], in JTP 7:17.
22. JT to WF, September 9, 1923, in WFC.

close friends were thinking of Jean and Margaret as a couple. The small, tight circle of Toomer, Frank, Munson, and Crane was broken.

The fourth and major factor that arose in the complexity of 1923 to turn his attention away from literature was Jean's introduction to the thought of George Gurdjieff. Actually it was a work of one of Gurdjieff's disciples, P. D. Ouspensky, that was most accessible. Gurdjieff was teaching in France and had not yet written anything for publication. Ouspensky's *Tertium Organum* was published in English translation in 1920 and was becoming popular reading among Toomer's circle of literary friends. Hart Crane was discussing it from the time Jean met him, and Munson was also fascinated. Frank, too, sampled these new ideas, and Margaret pursued them with the same hunger that Jean developed. Jean, however, did not actually read Ouspensky until December of 1923.

Ouspensky's thesis, worked out empirically with constant illustrations from daily experience, is that human beings live in three dimensions and use three levels of perception: sensation, representation, and concept. But there is a fourth dimension, one totally different from the three we know, and a fourth level of perception, of which mystics have had glimpses. The world of the fourth dimension, the "noumenal world," is the world of causes, beyond time and space and dualistic logic. Such forms—time, space, logic—are the products of our limited perception, not the condition of the universe. One of our first steps in appreciating this view of reality is to "recognize the unity of all opposites." The goal presented by Ouspensky is the development, on the part of those who can do so, of a "cosmic consciousness," one more extended than that of the mystics: "For the appearance of cosmic consciousness it is necessary that the centre of gravity of *the whole* of man should be in self-consciousness and not in the sense of the external." And he cautions this can only be "the result of great labour, great work, demanding daring both in thought and feeling." [23]

The noumenal world pictured by Ouspensky, with its unity of opposites, rejection of logic, interpenetration of living and nonliving, and causality lodged in the unseen, could not have seemed too foreign to Jean Toomer. A universe that joins space and time into a continuous flow of "now," in which fragments of past and future are revealed in a present moment, could accommodate his and Frank's mystical philosophy of the development of the new American race. In *Cane* the living spirits of the trees, moon, songs, and dusk conspire to change the lives of the people. Jean did not read *Tertium Organum*

---

23. P. D. Ouspensky, *Tertium Organum,* trans. Ouspensky and E. Kadloubovsky (Rev. ed.; New York, 1981), esp. 163, 225, 286–87.

until after he had finished *Cane,* but Ouspensky's ideas were compatible with Toomer's view of art and the world. A closer embrace of these views in late 1923 helped shift his commitment from art to philosophy.

This change was not, in fact, a significant departure from Toomer's interests while working on *Cane.* The book reflects one stage in his developing a picture of self that attempted to universalize the individual's experience. While others may have read *Cane* to see how a man could fit his human view into his blackness, Jean was trying to fit the blackness that was a part of him into a more comprehensive human view. Nor was he trying to "pass" in a racial sense; rather, he was passing from preoccupation with external, visible reality to concentration on internal, invisible reality.

The method of doing this, however, remained to be explored. The philosophy of the "Fourth Way," which Gurdjieff had developed, represented a system into which Ouspensky's ideas fitted. This system stressed vigorous discipline of the mind, emotions, and body in an effort to free and empower the basic essence at the center of the self. The activities of these three parts of the self—the mental, emotional, and physical—should be balanced and fused into a higher activity called Being, according to Gurdjieff. To achieve Being, one must transform outer-world energies by connecting with the inner-world energy that is the spirit of the universe. This new power is to be tapped through a series of exercises in intense awareness and control, to bring the competitive segments of the organism into balance and harmony.

Jean, recently taken to emotional heights and depths that seemed beyond his control, was looking for just such a balance and just such a method. Being knowledgeable about oneself rather than successful in the external world therefore appealed to him particularly at this moment and served to separate him as to motivation from many in New York literary society. Art became, instead of a high goal, a minor means, and the form of his art changed as a result.

Toomer's disenchantment with the writer's role grew gradually, but when the change was completed, it was a radical one. For many reasons, he could no longer feel that he was part of the charmed circle. Trying for a time to communicate his inwardly broken state, which had distanced him from his friends, he wrote to Waldo: "'During the past months I have been through many deaths and many births.' These have given me fractions of knowledge, and a great fatigue. No inclusive vision, no synthesis has come. . . . I have heard that this has been a time of deep search and discovery for you. Search and discovery bind us in the spirit, though no words break through the flesh." But the strain of hurt egos and changing relationships found expression in letters they all wrote to one another. Some of Jean's notes to Waldo were curt, stating how blind

Waldo was to new world forces that had passed him by. Waldo replied with equal frigidity that Toomer was the one who was misguided. Munson, urged by both Frank and Toomer to take sides, remained scrupulously neutral at the risk of, in particular, losing Frank's friendship. Naumburg, herself admitting that "deep spiritual shifts" were occurring among them, took the Gurdjieffian view that "work can be no purer and completer than the individual who creates" and urged that Waldo "give up creation wholly in the external world, and return into oneself."[24] This was what she also was urging Toomer to do. While he continued to take part in events in New York, attending a dinner party with Burke at Margaret's apartment, Jean was turning inward. At this time, as he states in his autobiography, he began to annoy his fellow writers with his persistent questions about the value of the person as opposed to the brilliance of the work created. His world centered on Margaret, and when she wrote to Waldo in December that she was planning a spring trip to Reno for a divorce, Jean planned to go with her.

With all this activity, Toomer's literary output dwindled to nothing. A new philosophy and a new lover were quite enough to occupy him. He suffered from indigestion as well as from a spiritual crisis. When he had finally come to a decision, Toomer wrote to Munson about his transition: "I have given up art," he stated, "as we have practiced it. And I am about . . . to undertake the Gurdjieff discipline." He continued, "I too had to pass through Waldo—I am not entirely through and without Waldo God knows where I would be. . . . To me, Waldo stands for what *not* to do, whereas Gurdjieff stands for what *to do*."[25]

In his autobiography, Toomer implied that the swan song that was *Cane* was in many ways his own: "Yes, the modern world was uprooted, the modern world was breaking down, *but we could not go back.* There was nothing to go back to. . . . The soil, the earth was still there, . . . [b]ut such peasantry as America had had . . . was swiftly disappearing. . . . 'Back to Nature,' even if desirable, was no longer possible, because industry had taken Nature unto itself. . . . So then, whether we wished it or not, *we had to go on*."[26]

24. JT to WF, n.d. [November, 1923?], Naumburg to WF, December 14, 1923, both in WFC.

25. JT to GM, July 17, 1924, in GMC.

26. JT, "On Being an American" (JTP 15:11), also in *W&S*, 129.

III.

THE GURDJIEFF PERIOD

6.

Spiritual Search

Jean Toomer's dissatisfaction with writing as an art form and his experimentation with writing as a means of self-exploration and teaching may have grown up like exotic, suddenly blooming flowers, but they did not spring from sterile ground. His life had long been ready for a religious, mystical principle.

His early religious training served to make Jean favorably inclined toward the idea of God, but bound him with no particular denominational cords. The crisp but nurturant imagery he uses to describe his christening in St. Paul's Church in Washington suggests that this connection with his grandmother's Catholicism was important to him, though it was the only formal religious act of his childhood and youth: "I always see it as a cross of white and green, for the stone is crystal white and the lawn around is vivid green. . . . I recall the marble bowl and the stained-glass window with sunlight coming through." His grandmother also taught him "Now I lay me," and he repeated that each night, replacing it later with the Lord's Prayer. He was so intent on the practice, except in some periods of stress when it was temporarily forgotten, that he resorted to subterfuges in order to pray without being noticed when he spent the night with a friend or roommate. Although he was taught about Heaven, the concept was not presented as a reward for good behavior on earth, nor was Hell a punishment for bad. He knew Doré's illustrations of Dante's *Inferno*, but he thought they were in the same realm as the *Arabian Nights* (his mother confirmed his view that these ideas were purely imaginary). The Devil, often present in his grandfather's vocabulary, "was a roguish energetic fellow whom you could evoke to help you express your anger or high spirits." The concept and even the word for sin were foreign to him until his college days, though guilt was a familiar companion at his time of uncontrollable masturbation. In contrast to his scorn for the "organized religious machine" leading to persecutions and wars, and the "vices and vanities . . . that hide under religious cloaks . . . the oily piety, the sweet sugar frosting, the hypocrisy, the infidelity," was his continuing sense of the presence of God.[1]

"I grew up," he reports, "without benefit of organized religion . . . [but] I did have religious experiences and I did somehow form feelings and notions of God." What these religious experiences were is spelled out in a pamphlet he wrote in 1947. He is talking of attitudes or feelings that would suddenly arise in the midst of some childhood experience: "Such religion as I had was life-centered, not book-centered. . . . It consisted in my response to flowers, trees, birds, snow, the smell of the earth after a spring rain, sunsets and the starry sky. It consisted of my devotion to pet rabbits and dogs, and to some interest or project that caught my imagination. . . . Worship . . . spontaneously arose as I beheld the wonders of the world which God created." The prayers he said regularly were directed to a "celestial Santa Claus" who became, as Jean matured, "an invisible but felt Presence whose existence was interwoven with and quite necessary to the earth and all life." In other words, all his intense moments of perception, love, appreciation, or enthusiasm were *ordered* in terms of a concept of an understanding, creative, benevolent God who was the basic web connecting all parts of the universe. "Indeed there formed in me, despite or because of the lack of formal training, a deep, powerful, interior religious sense. Until my twenty-second year my main attitudes to life arose from religious views. So firmly and completely did my universe have God, so related was I to this religious world, that when the then to me irrefutable logic of atheism compelled me to accept it, not only did my ideational world collapse, but my very form of life, my life itself, was broken."[2]

That event, however, ended neither his physical life nor his religious life. As he went on with his multifaceted reading, he found books on Eastern philosophies. He tried some exercises (presumably yoga or zen), wrote haiku, and experienced something of the nonmaterial beyond the tangible realm. He went back to the Bible, reading it as "grand literature," and then "my religious nature, given a cruel blow by Clarence Darrow and naturalism and atheism, but

1. JT, "Earth-Being," 174–78 (quotations on 175, 176), also in *W&S*, 64–66.
2. JT, "Incredible Journey" (JTP 15:3), 3; JT, *An Interpretation of Friends Worship* (1947; rpr. Philadelphia, 1979), 4; JT, "Earth-Being," 178, also in *W&S*, 66.

not, as I found, destroyed by them—my religious nature which had been sleeping was vigorously aroused."[3]

Interestingly enough, he uses religious imagery to describe the bout with atheism: when his "descent into purgatory" ended, he says, he "found new energy, lucidity, sense of power, keenness of sensation." This of course was an integration, a reshaping of his world view around new knowledge. After another low period, his next experience of wholeness, so far the most complete in his life, was his choice of vocation, drawn from the literary ideal of *Wilhelm Meister,* in 1920. The burst of reading and writing persisted until 1923, when the direction, the wholeness, no longer seemed so clear. "During the winter of 1923, owing to a complex of causes, my writing stopped; and my disharmony became distressingly prominent. So it became clear that my literary occupations had not worked deep to make of me an integrated man. Had it done so for others? Now I looked questioningly, not at the book, but at the writer of it."[4]

The need for wholeness, within himself and between him and the universe, was especially strong in Jean Toomer. Things had to fit together in some sort of a system. It was the *system* that gave socialism most of its appeal; it was the regimen of body building that seemed to promise a way out of a difficult habit. And the system of the naturalists was so powerful, it overcame temporarily the strongly ingrained, but not yet systematized, attachment that Jean had to the supernatural. Each integration had released a flow of energies, only to break eventually on the rocks of incompleteness. The *Wilhelm Meister* ideal now seemed incomplete; the integration it had promised was false. Focusing on the interior of the self, Toomer now recognized conflicts among mind, soul, and body. He began to see himself as an inner being versus an outer personality— the inner was real but the outer was false. Earlier he had thought it sufficient to take Shaw's simple advice, "Be candid," but now he was looking for some more effectual process to bring his soul and his personality into closer harmony. It was at this point that Jean Toomer was introduced, principally through his New York literary friends, to the ideas of Georges Ivanovitch Gurdjieff.

Gurdjieff and his system became widely known among the New York intelligentsia through his most important pupils in the West, P. D. Ouspensky and A. R. Orage. The Russian Ouspensky, author of the book *Tertium Organum* that had so impressed Hart Crane and others, followed his mentor west after endur-

3. JT, "Outline," 54. An example of one of his haikus is "The old man, at ninety, / Eating peaches. / Is he not afraid of worms?" (JTP 50:16).
4. JT, "On Being an American" (JTP 15:11, 15:10), also in *W&S,* 128.

ing with him the dangers of the Russian Revolution and eventually began his principal work in England with his wife. Orage, who was English and had attained literary fame as the editor of *New Age,* was attracted by Ouspensky's lectures and became the one far more involved in setting up the institute at Fontainebleau, the center of Gurdjieff learning and the model for Jean Toomer's later social experiments. Several commentators have presumed that Gurdjieff was trying to wean Ouspensky from him by cutting off emotional ties, hence the lack of association between them during the critical time when Gurdjieff was working to establish his Institute for the Harmonious Development of Man. Whatever the reason, Ouspensky had broken with Gurdjieff and was continuing his work independently in England by the time Orage decided to carry the Gurdjieff work to America.

Ouspensky and Orage did become leaders in their own right and continued an uneasy relationship with Gurdjieff and with each other. As disciples frequently do, they developed different styles and methods, and each had devoted followers. Each in his own way was teaching Gurdjieff's complex cosmological system through an experiential process by which people could work on themselves to attain more awareness of that system, true individuality, the development of a higher consciousness—the goals Gurdjieff espoused. Both approaches were derived from principles Gurdjieff had tried to incorporate into his institute.

Gurdjieff by this time was nearly fifty years old. He wore a copious, flowing moustache but kept his head as clean-shaven as an egg. Solid in body but mercurial in spirit, he might appear to the visitor as forbidding, arbitrarily cruel, or serene and utterly wise. Wearing a fez and holding audience with one leg tucked underneath him, he would sometimes comment on man's foibles and possibilities with seeming indifference to the individuals around him, but with surprisingly pointed application. In private, he might move the visitor to an unexpected confession, or evaporate a premeditated question with a long look from his penetrating eyes, or simply exude an easy, very quiet calm. To the people who stayed by his side for some time, his most apparent qualities were his dramatic unpredictability and his tremendous power.

In 1922, Gurdjieff had bought in Avon, just outside of Fontainebleau, near Paris, a château for his institute. The building had not been inhabited for more than ten years, but it was an ideal setting for his eclectic strategies. The ground floor had a slightly run-down elegance that would appeal to Gurdjieff's flair for the dramatic: a grand salon where he would lead the singing (he played the harmonium) or hold his lectures; a library (without books); an attached kitchen where meals were prepared for all the pupils and guests—often more than sixty or seventy. On the second floor, called the "Ritz," were the more elaborate private rooms where Gurdjieff, his immediate family, and honored guests stayed (such as Jean Toomer when he first arrived). The third floor, known as the "Monks' Corridor," held the bedrooms for the more permanent pupils and ordinary visitors, sometimes four to a room with mattresses on the floor. The back rooms overlooked the stable yard, called "Cow Alley." The meals, frequently the centerpiece for conversation and lectures, were served either in the dining room, called the "Russian Room," or in the parlor, called the "English Room," the place for more elaborate meals and celebrations. Sometimes both were used at the same time, and then the Russians and the English—the two major groups there—were often separated by their choice of the room in which each felt more comfortable.

The grounds, also well suited for Gurdjieff's purposes, included a huge lawn in front, a fountain, some houses in back for Gurdjieff's extended family who had followed him from Russia, and a large patch of woods. This diversity allowed Gurdjieff to require of his pupils the many physical tasks conducive to The Work, such as building walks, sawing firewood, creating a vegetable garden, digging ditches—and filling them up again. In 1923, Gurdjieff had had his pupils build the Study House, its basic structure a purchased airplane hangar, and its interior designed as a dervish *tekke*. This staging area for dances and other physical exercises was furnished with Orientalia: carpets on the dirt floor, drapes with painted aphorisms in an Eastern script, and a partially curtained review stand where Gurdjieff could watch the proceedings in private.

This was the setting for the institute, which Orage began advertising in New York in the late winter of 1923–1924. America was a good place to locate pupils, Gurdjieff had decided. There, he might find people idealistic enough and—perhaps as important—wealthy enough to enhance the impact of the institute. To raise money and to spread the Gurdjieff movement, Orage planned the U.S. engagement under Gurdjieff's instruction, the highlight being a visit to New York City by Gurdjieff himself. Orage had come to New York in December to publicize and interpret the demonstrations in preparation for Gurdjieff's visit. Orage, widely respected in America because of his association with *New Age,* had ready contacts with progressive magazines such as Margaret Anderson's *Little Review* and Herbert Croly's *New Republic.* It was relatively easy for Orage to marshal interest in the Gurdjieff principles through the network of intellectuals and artists associated with these and similar publications and with other establishments such as the avant-garde bookstores.

Jean Toomer was ready for the Gurdjieffian message. For much of the summer of 1923 he had been struggling with feelings of dislocation and dissatisfaction.

Because of my personal experience, my ups and downs, my I-am-I states, and my I-am-nothing states, I was fairly well convinced that in man there was a curious duality—an "I," a something that was not I; an inner being, an outer personality. I was further convinced that the inner being was the real thing, that the outer personality was the false thing; that the "I" was the source of life, that the personality was the sack of poison. . . .

Also because of my personal experiences, my disorganization of parts, I was convinced that the parts of man—his mind, emotions, and body—were radically out of harmony with each other. But how to bring them into harmony? I did not have a means of doing this.[5]

It was in July, not long after they first met, that he had with Margaret Naumburg an experience so intense that it "culminated in my birth into another life."

Through a love-experience I discovered the reality of the soul. . . .

My flood-gates were thrown open by inward surging and out poured the accumulated suffering of my entire life . . . as though my innermost pockets were being opened and the contents washed out; and all became sweet before it left me, so that what I gave back to the world was not hurt but tenderness, not hate but love. . . .

And after the dross was swept away, . . . I was moved to an utter surrender of myself. And as I did surrender I was made [to] realize that never before in this life had I altogether relinquished my final hold upon my falsely precious self. . . . There was holy union. . . . And I was made [to] realize that separateness is unholy.

I found myself on the frontiers of, if not within, the great and radiant world reported by Walt Whitman, Dante, Plato. . . . Here was beauty. Here was wonder. Here was meaning. Here was realness. Here was the resurrection of my deepest life out [of] its long death.

Clearly, a sexual experience became for him a spiritual experience. Calling this "an actual but partial experience of a higher world," he distinguishes it carefully, in a description written late in his life, from a different order of consciousness. But it was as close as one could get, he says, without passing from one to the other, from what he called the First River to the Second River. The normal consciousness was "transformed and enlarged." He was given what he called "an astonishing fertility," and he began putting down notes. They seemed to write themselves, and their style ranged from the lush and florid to the stripped and bare:

5. *Ibid.* (JTP 15:10), 47–48, also in W&S, 130–31.

Figure of a world within, what flesh, what fire! And all around, sun-dew, dancing points, luminous and sparkling fill the air. They blind my eyes, and suddenly the whole world is haloed. The hard, tough bolts of past experience, infused, melt and disappear into a stream of life whose upward surging sings a hymnal [*sic*] to complete surrender.

                                        Equation
            The cruel cycles:
                Death . . . life . . . death . . . life . . .
                Birth . . . dying . . . birth . . . dying . . .
                                          and
            The dual existence:
                Living in death
                Dying in life.
                    Survival,
                    equals:
                TRANSFIGURATION[6]

Unfortunately but inevitably, the roller coaster went down as well as up. Rather shortly, his "conscious and subconscious parted company." He felt, in fact, as if his soul had departed and what was left was simply dissolving. At this juncture he spent August and September in the rural hills of Ellenville, New York, to gather himself together again. Thus, when *Cane* was finally issued in New York City, Jean was in hiding in the Catskills, visited occasionally by friends like Gorham but otherwise staying by himself. Not apparently affected by the book's poor sales, Jean wrote to Waldo in late September, "Well, old soldier, it looks as if *Holiday* and *Cane* are *going over*. Not best sellers—hell no—but the sort of selling and notice that really counts." Jean's growing disassociation from his former life is revealed in the same letter: he was planning to use an assumed name when he submitted his article "The South in Literature" to the *Call*.[7]

In Ellenville he experienced a new synthesis and another low, an onset as if of demons. He determined now that inward progress was far more important than outward success: "One ought to *be* something before one essayed to *say* something." Back in New York City, he began testing his ideas on friends and acquaintances, often attacking their values, trying to build "a frame of reference . . . compounded of moral, aesthetic, psychological and mystical ele-

6. JT, "The Second River" (JTP 66:8), 30–32; JT, "How I Found the Gurdjieff Work" ("The Second River," part VII; JTP 67:5), 15, 2; JT, "The Second River," 35. "Equation," dated July 19, 1923, is also found in JT notes (JTP 50:12).
    7. JT to WF, September 29, 1923, in WFC.

ments." If people did not agree with him, he concluded that they were still asleep and tried to shake them awake, until he had alienated almost everyone.[8]

Margaret, however, stayed by his side, though they had to deal with the tensions of their feelings for Waldo and of the give-and-take between themselves amid the wild swings of Jean's psyche. She was interested in deep ideas, hungry for information if she thought it could help her development, and she was stimulating to his growth, as he was to hers. In mid November, Jean had another peak experience with her, embodying reconciliation—whether with Margaret, with himself, with the universe, or with all three, is not clear. He wrote in his notebook, "Let the evening of November 17, 1923 mark the time of my greatest illumination, of my purest vision, of the most comprehensive experience that has yet come to me." Recalling it later, he described this as the moment he was pushed out of the literary world, as he had earlier been pushed out of other worlds. "So we enter a world, develop in it, develop through it, and, in time, develop out of it. . . . The essential concern seems to be the unending moving of human beings through life after life, through world after world, towards a long-range objective which remains undefined."[9]

The following month he began in earnest his exploration of Ouspensky and Gurdjieff. His notebook records his first reading of Ouspensky on December 12, 1923. A poem accompanies this note:

> I am of a consciousness whose earth-eye is my body;
> I am of a consciousness which is beyond me.
> My intellect is its brilliance in the third dimension:
> My emotions are its glow.
> The world is as radiant as a sun-flood on eyes whose lids are folded.
> When will these lids rise?
> My eyes expand?
> When will my body open?

Close to this same time, Jean first saw the brochure describing Gurdjieff's Institute for the Harmonious Development of Man, which made an overwhelming impression on him. The design on the cover of some copies is a symbolic summary of Gurdjieff's ideas. "TO KNOW—TO UNDERSTAND—TO BE" is inscribed at the top. An angel and a devil flank an enneagram, the emblem used by the Seekers After Truth, the religious community that supposedly had inspired Gurdjieff's own system. Inside the nine-sided geometrical shape, a figure embraces a Manichaean duality: the lion and the lamb, and the condor and the dove. At the bottom of the cover is a clutter of tools representing various

---

8. JT, "The Second River," 26.
9. *Ibid.*, 33.

aspects of the Gurdjieffian method—a lute, sewing machine, anvil, globe, telescope, rake, scale, quill pen, ax, microscope—and a portrait of G. I. Gurdjieff. It was a program that tempered the esoteric with the practical.[10]

The brochure outlined the essence of the Gurdjieffian way. For a person to become whole, the three centers of the self—intellect, emotions, and instinct—must work together harmoniously. Only then would the self rise to a higher level of development. Having read the material, Toomer responded as though he had already found his mentor: "The first words made me feel that I was close to what I sought. . . . I gave cries of joy as I came upon statement after statement that said what I wanted to hear said. . . . At last I had come upon something that 'spoke to my condition.'"[11] The language here reflects that used by George Fox, founder of Quakerism, in speaking of the time of his greatest illumination.

Jean was so inspired that he went with Margaret Naumburg to one of the early demonstrations in New York in January, 1924. Typically, these consisted of a series of dances and a lecture by Orage. The dances combined preparatory gymnastic exercises and sacred gymnastics requiring tremendous concentration to unify the intricate and asymmetrical body movements, dervish and other religious dances commemorating events and rituals, and graceful priestess ceremonies. And directing the presentation, moving in and around the audience, pacing the aisles, assessing the viewers' reactions, was Gurdjieff himself.

Jean's first impression of Gurdjieff at the demonstration was a lasting one:

His head was shaved. You could not miss the shape of it. His forehead was high and wide. His dark eyes looked. His nose was finely moulded and almost delicate in comparison to the strong jaw. And then his mustache, most unusual and large, curving down and sweeping up to the tips. His complexion was dark. He wore a tuxedo. . . .

All of him came together. He was a unit, a unit of senseable but unknown power. As he moved around, . . . there was something panther-like about him.

For someone who had previously studied and taught gymnastics, these demonstrations were "amazing events that satisfied and exceeded anything I could have asked for. . . . By twelve o'clock most of the on-lookers had left. . . . I stayed to the very last, for I was endlessly fascinated and would have been happy had the program gone on through the night, every night." Something had touched him, like a preconscious "memory of a music I had once known, a life I had once lived, a world that had been mine and that I had left and forgot-

10. JT notebook, December 12, 1923 (JTP 57:8); C. S. Nott, *Teachings of Gurdjieff: A Pupil's Journal* (London, 1961), 7.
11. JT, "The Second River," 7.

ten. It made me feel as a wayfarer who was being recalled to his rightful way and destiny." [12]

As if anticipating the inevitable connection that was to occur, Gurdjieff sat down beside Jean in a seat recently vacated, toward the very end of the performance. "At first I dared not turn my head to look. Then I did. What I saw, as my impressions registered it, was not a strong man, not a great man, not a man. I saw a little shrunken old person who bore almost no resemblance to the Gurdjieff I had seen moving around." This double identity Jean was to carry with him to Fontainebleau and later as well, when Gurdjieff's credibility teetered and Jean wavered between total belief and disillusionment. But at that moment, Gurdjieff spoke to Toomer's deeper needs, needs that had not taken root in New York's artistic life. At the demonstration Jean caught a glimpse of a more esoteric approach to "place." Toomer felt that the Gurdjieff teaching answered the types of questions he believed should be addressed: What is the world? Are there cosmic laws? What is man's relationship to the world? How can a man become whole? The system seeker was on the scent of a new system: "Here was work whose scope was greater and more complete than anything I had dreamed of. Here, in fine, was truth." [13]

Soon after, Jean returned with a group of friends to the next demonstration, held at the Neighborhood Playhouse. Elizabeth Delza, a dancer by profession, discovered that night "the greatest aspect of Dance and Movement she had ever imagined." Her husband Gorham Munson, too, was so elated by the experience that both stayed up all night, exhilarated. Hart Crane was very impressed with the "astonishing dances and psychic feats . . . that would stump the Russian Ballet." However, he lost interest more quickly than did others, for he thought the Gurdjieff way required too much discipline and not enough intuition. [14]

Jean promptly sought out Orage for further instruction and enlightenment. He requested an appointment for both himself and Margaret: "Miss Naumburg and I have both worked through experience to an awareness of dissociated selves and we are painfully conscious of the fact that no instrument (till now) available to us could effect the necessary cleansing and correlation." Jean and Margaret attended the early meetings with Orage among a group of about fifteen, uptown in a small and unpretentious apartment. From their talks with

12. JT, account of first trip to Fontainebleau, untitled, written in 1955–56 at the request of Dr. William Welch (given to authors by Dr. Welch), 17–18; JT, "The Second River," 12, 13.

13. JT, First Trip, 28; JT, "On Being an American" (JTP 15:10), 49, also in W&S, 131.

14. Elizabeth Delza Munson to the authors, November 22, 1982; Hart Crane to his mother, February 3, 1924, in Weber (ed.), *Letters of Hart Crane*, 174.

Orage, Jean drew comfort—here was someone who had answers to his questions. Orage had ended a discussion about how most humans are in hopeless bondage, asserting, "Yes, but there is a way out." [15] Jean was convinced that Orage could show him the way.

They were not, however, quick friends. Perhaps sensing Orage's complete self-possession and strong grace, Jean felt that he was at a loss in such company. Perhaps he was overaggressive in expecting to move right into the inner circle of the initiated. In any case, his stubborn individuality stood between him and immediate allegiance to either Orage or Gurdjieff. He was unwilling to follow so soon the work of the Eastern mystic who, impressive as he was, seemed overpowering. Gurdjieff would occasionally attend the early meetings with Orage, smiling, fielding questions, allowing his commentary to be translated by a companion, or himself commenting in broken English, "I say like before, we all sleep. Our aim, wake" or "No ordinary life, just life." The group would pull closer, Jean no less than the others asking him questions. Jean thought Gurdjieff truly had the status of a master, and that stature alone was enough to caution him. "Knowledge, integration, many-sidedness, power—in fact he had a bit too much power for my comfort." [16] Like someone resisting hypnosis, Jean was as yet unwilling to submit his life to someone else's control. His reluctance was a way to postpone a commitment to go to the institute at Fontainebleau.

It seems clear that Jean was trying to come to grips with various pressures he was feeling from different sources. While he was breaking new ground in self-exploration, his friends in New York were battling over the philosophy of literature. They were indignant that Ernest Boyd in a winter issue of *American Mercury* had condemned the "young Aesthetes" (Munson, Frank, Crane, Kreymborg, Tate, Brooks, Josephson, and Burke) as upstarts who carried formalism to the point of empty rhetoric. On the other hand, they themselves diminished one another in small ways, in critical articles printed in the network of little magazines. The group led by Malcolm Cowley began to isolate Munson and Frank for being too mystical in their approach to literature. Crane, himself espousing a personal brand of mysticism rather than being tempted to participate seriously in the Gurdjieff work, wavered between the Munson-Frank group and the Cowley-Burke group. They all still gathered at large parties and carried on their literary movements with a certain amount of

15. JT to A. R. Orage, January 30, 1924, in JTP 8:2; JT, "The Second River," 14.
16. Interview of Mavis McIntosh (who attended the early Gurdjieff demonstrations and Orage groups), Sag Harbor, N.Y., August 1, 1982; JT, "The Second River," 15.

cooperative rivalry. But attitudes toward each other approached mockery. Cowley, lacking any acquaintance with Gurdjieff's ideas, wrote to Harold Loeb of Munson: "Munson is a gurgeyite, galooshiously gurgling Gurdjieff growling Gurdjieff gargling Gurdjieff." [17]

While Jean was very much with the Munson group, his relationship with Gorham was filled with strain. Munson refused to take sides in the Naumburg-Toomer-Frank triangle, even though Jean insisted that he do so. It was, then, a circle of friends that was not altogether comfortable for Jean in January of 1924. But his erstwhile literary companions were themselves so beleaguered that his own turmoil went relatively unnoticed. Hart Crane, in fact, commented on Jean's equanimity. "Jean's new hygiene for himself," he wrote to Gorham, "is very interesting to me. He seems to be able to keep himself solid and undismayed. Certain organic changes are occurring in us all, I think, but I believe that his is more steady and direct than I have been permitted." [18]

Jean's steadiness was superficial at best. He received new stimulation from seeing Alfred Stieglitz and Georgia O'Keeffe, and his letters to them after his evenings at their home show that he was infatuated by their offering of friendship. Stieglitz's age and temperament made him a father figure for many of the artists in New York. Waldo Frank expressed a genuine filial attitude in his letters to Stieglitz; Paul Rosenfeld literally treated Stieglitz as a father and received from him much-needed paternal advice and encouragement. Jean quickly adopted this kind of relationship, and he was able to tell Stieglitz what he might have been uncomfortable revealing to friends like Crane. In February he wrote to Stieglitz from Washington a letter suggesting his continued state of confusion: "Words, pure words, do not come from the motion that accompanies internal break-ups, inward re-buildings. I am broken glass, shifting, now here, now there, to a new design. And because I am in this city, physically soft and quiet, I am glass fragments blown by a low wind over asphalt pavements." [19]

In temporarily shelving a commitment to Gurdjieff, Jean decided to concentrate on Margaret Naumburg; but to do so meant leaving New York. The appeal of Gurdjieff was "as strong and authentic as ever, though I continued having my reservations and questions," Jean writes. "I still had faith in the transforming power of personal love, I still believed in my own resources as a

17. Malcolm Cowley to Harold Loeb, September 15, 1923, in Harold Loeb, *The Way It Was* (New York, 1959), 221.

18. Hart Crane to GM, December 20, 1923, in Weber (ed.), *Letters of Hart Crane,* 162.

19. JT to Alfred Stieglitz, February 20, 1924, in ASC.

source of force and guidance, and Margy and I had still to test what actually living together would do for us."[20]

Margaret had determined to go to Reno for a divorce, and the two of them decided that if they lived together there, they would undergo an appropriate experiment as husband and wife before actually getting married. Although Jean's friends in New York that winter learned to find him as a matter of course at Margaret's apartment, he and she had maintained separate living quarters. Knowing that Waldo might hold up the divorce proceedings or withhold support for his and Margaret's young son if he knew of their conjugal experiment, they decided that their stay in Reno would be an absolute secret. They hoped they would not meet Sherwood Anderson, who would also be there going through a divorce from his wife Tennessee Mitchell. Jean let it be known that he would be in Washington and asked friends to write him there in care of his grandmother.

But before it was time to leave for Reno, Jean actually did have to go to Washington: A letter from his family told him Bismarck was dying. His favorite uncle had, as much as anyone, been a companion and a father to Jean, so he felt he should be there. Although aware that he could not heal, Jean lifted the burden from Bismarck's exhausted wife. He sat with his uncle in the same room Jean and his grandparents had shared when they returned to Washington after his mother's death sixteen years before. Surrounded by furniture from the old house on Bacon Street, he saw his uncle dying too early, a victim of "an overworked and all too actual sensuality. Not drink . . . but sex, women, running around, poker, staying up all night and trying to hold a responsible job by day." He summed up the episode in Gurdjieff's terms: "Man has deflected from his true course."[21]

His duty to his family completed, Jean told Munson that he would be in the country outside Washington visiting a Rosicrucian center. Then he headed in early March for Reno, where Margaret had arrived shortly before. It was a trip very few ever knew about. Jean's grandmother—still calling him Eugene and somewhat bewildered about what Jean was doing—nonetheless for the next three months faithfully forwarded packets of letters to him.

During his time in Reno, Jean began an intense regimen of writing, the first since early the previous summer. He concentrated almost entirely on autobiographical material of a psychological nature, though he took time to write criticism. One such article, never published, was a critique of Paul Rosenfeld's

20. JT, "The Death of Bismarck Pinchback" (JTP 16:2).
21. *Ibid.*

latest book *Port of New York,* a collection of short sketches that included one of Margaret Naumburg. Paul had become a friend and supporter of Jean's new work, and Jean was furthering the friendship by an article of praise. Jean had by now lost touch with his New York associates—*Dial* rejected his article, Munson wrote that he was dismayed that Jean's "great reconstruction period is a paper on Rosenfeld," and Jean's other compatriots were planning a satire on Rosenfeld called "Rhapsodic Criticism with 39 Metaphors and no ideas, by Paulina Roseyfield."[22] Trying to elicit more esoteric views from his literary and artistic friends in New York, Jean planned to compile their definitions of *experience*. He sent his own definition to many people and asked them to write theirs in reply. Some treated the task seriously and sympathetically—Stieglitz, Waldo Frank, and others wrote several pages each. Others, like Burke, dismissed the project with curt, humorous replies. It was a project Jean did not pursue further.

Suddenly, late in the spring, everything he had done until then seemed worthless. He had a "feeling of total, utter ignorance. . . . A realization that must have been coming on for a long time, crashed full into my consciousness. . . . I realized I knew nothing. . . . I but manipulated ideas without knowledge of the underlying reality." At last he agreed he could not achieve his own salvation and needed help "to exist as a man." He was drawn full circle back to Gurdjieff.[23]

Gurdjieff all this time had never been forgotten. Margaret and Jean had been practicing the few exercises they knew and reading whatever they could that related to their search. Superconfident Jean had even been selecting and suggesting exercises for Margaret. Now both grew in their eagerness to join the master at Fontainebleau. By the beginning of July, Jean could no longer contain his determination to go, but Margaret had to hold back because of her divorce proceedings. Jean's peremptory note to Munson announcing his intentions drew a warning: see Orage in New York first, since Orage was the "American agent and Americans are supposed to apply for admission through him." Jean heeded his friend's advice. After returning to New York on July 9, he immediately wrote Orage, regretting that he had missed Orage's preparatory sessions for potential institute pupils. He added that "though more or less in isolation, I have now ended a phase of many years duration and am open, with no backward reservations whatever, to the next discipline. In fact, I am actively

22. GM to JT, July, 1924, in GMC; Brom Weber, *Hart Crane: A Biographical and Critical Study* (New York, 1948), 240.
23. GM to JT, July, 1924, in GMC; JT to Orage, July 9, 1924, in JTP 8:2.

searching for it." [24] He urgently asked to see Orage, determined that nothing now would stop him from attending the institute.

Jean stayed at the Hotel Albert and received private instruction from Orage while he waited for the ship to depart. His talks with Orage were extremely informative. "I had not been drawn to Orage primarily, amazing person though he was," Jean noted in a reminiscence. "I can still see him seated there in the hot New York room, he in shirt sleeves and wearing suspenders. His eyes were keen and sparkling, his face aglow, all of him alive and with zest for the ideas and work." Orage was not enough, however. "I had wanted Gurdjieff." [25] Jean saw this trip as a tangible break from his past. In a letter to Gorham, he claimed a final break from Waldo Frank and urged Gorham to do the same.

Margaret in spirit accompanied Jean. Tucked into a basket of fruit she sent him July 19, the day his ship sailed, was a note of encouragement: "All crevices not filled with other nourishment brimming with love and such deep wishes for this trip and all it may come to be." She had to content herself with applying to Orage to join Jean at the institute and with cherishing "a sense of oneness I feel entirely with you in this great adventure. Take all my love and devotion." [26] Through summer and early fall, she worked toward being able to be with him in France. Jean, however, had a way of ignoring people close to him when he was afire with some great new cause. It appears he was never again as close to her as they had been that spring. At last he was on his way to Fontainebleau, filled with the expectation of a glorious new life that one year previously he had been hoping to find among the literary circles in New York.

His new life, by now one in a series of new lives, was based wholly on being the pupil of "the only real man I had ever seen." His entire purpose was

to work with and under Gurdjieff, to follow his instructions, to attempt whatever he indicated I should do. If he accepted me as one of his pupils. I was so thoroughly convinced that he would that I had no serious doubt about it. Perhaps I regarded myself as something special. Maybe I believed I was among the chosen ones. And also maybe, the current ran deeper—deeper, and of a nature and duration that we ordinary men know little or nothing about. All we know is that we are moved, in a certain direction, if and when we are. And there seems to be, at certain times, in relation to a person and a work, a mysterious but authentic recognition, as if what we are finding is really a re-finding, after a long exile. [27]

24. JT, "How I Found the Gurdjieff Work," 23.
25. JT, First Trip, 20.
26. Margaret Naumburg to JT, July 19, 18, 1924, both in JTP 7:17.
27. JT, First Trip, 3, 20.

7.

Fontainebleau and New York

When Jean Toomer arrived at Fontainebleau that summer of 1924, he found a place different from what had been advertised in the pamphlets and lectures. Gurdjieff had been in an automobile accident on July 5, two weeks before Jean left for Fontainebleau. Either Orage had not known, or he had not told Jean. Gurdjieff's recovery was slow, and there was some doubt whether he would live at all. There was a distinct pall hanging over the institute. The veteran pupils attempted to go on as best they could, according to Gurdjieff's principles. Under these circumstances, there was little interest in newcomers.

Jean's first impressions of the institute were not encouraging. The cab driver had no idea which estate in Fontainebleau was Gurdjieff's. Only after several attempts did they find it, since there was no sign by the gate bell except *Sonnez Fort*. Jean was shown in first by two young men and greeted by a woman who spoke English but demonstrated no inclination to be more than barely civil—a letdown for someone who thought while on his way that he might want to stay there for the rest of his life. As a guest he was shown to the Ritz, an altogether too fancy spot for a pupil, Jean thought. But other than his own room, there was little to be construed as a welcome. He was not called to dinner, and when he did manage to find the dining area, he sat in a hard chair at the long table. No one gave a sign of greeting. "If anyone spoke at all," he recollects, "it was only briefly. They ate, much as animals would eat. In a way they were occupied, completely so. In a way they were pre-occupied with matters I knew nothing of." [1]

1. JT, First Trip, 5.

Jean was not aware of Gurdjieff's serious accident, but he was certainly aware of the gloom that it—something—had cast on the institute. Le Prieuré seemed almost deserted except when meals were served. The only person he noticed, Dr. Stjoernval, one of Gurdjieff's oldest pupils, was standing motionless in the hallway shadows, head bent, oblivious of anyone else. It was not until several days later when he met Bernard Metz that he began to feel part of the institute's work. Metz, a member of Ouspensky's London group, engaged Toomer in working at the chicken houses. Toomer had his first taste of physical work as "inner work." Very quickly he had all he wanted of it, but learned to continue on, remembering the words of Orage, "Will begins when desire stops."[2] Still a neophyte, Jean had to quit early in the day, impressed that his friend could continue laboring long after.

Later, Metz took Toomer to the Study House, and it was there, with the soft light, the grand piano, the tiered seats, and the dancing area, that he recalled the dances in New York. Painted on the curtains in Eastern script was a saying that Toomer learned later, one which impressed him more than any other did: "You are here having realized that you have only yourself chiefly to contend with. Therefore thank those who give you the opportunity." Jean quickly grew to understand the meaning that this directive had for him:

I am to struggle with myself, first and last. Not with you. Not with something in you I do not like. And I am to thank you for giving me the opportunity—really thank you, inwardly, and on occasion perhaps outwardly too.

This is not the way we usually behave. We merely react, according to which button is pushed.

I had had no such realization before coming to the Institute. I wondered how many of the other people had.[3]

Jean learned soon enough about Gurdjieff's accident, hence the explanation for no music, no feasting, little organized work, and little comradeship beyond that of Metz. Subduing his disappointment, he tried to become part of whatever routine was being maintained. Meals broke the day into four parts: breakfast usually of "soggy bread," lunch of soup, afternoon tea, then late in the evening a dinner again of soup and bread. It was at the informal meals and at work sessions that Metz introduced Jean to various members of the institute, and people slowly acknowledged Jean's presence.

Nevertheless, it was clear that those present were considerably more interested in their "inner work" than in having a social time. Mostly in silence, Jean shared in hard work with the others. Gradually he built himself up by working

2. *Ibid.*, 11.
3. *Ibid.*, 14, 15.

on projects around the grounds. He helped clear a space for a larger kitchen garden, and cut felled trees into three-foot lengths, using a two-man saw with a pace-setting Englishwoman. Here was a method he could respond to, thinking out word or number problems, for example, while doing physical labor, and harmonizing both efforts. The result was a self-awareness and a self-assurance he claims he had never known before:

One was simply to be aware, aware of bodily movements. . . . Not to think about them, not examine and try to understand them, not be critical, not want to improve or change them in any way. Just be aware, and for as long as possible any times of any given day. . . . So one might increase and develop awareness as such, a faculty, mostly dormant in most people most of the time, that is capable of functioning provided it receives the right stimulus and proper guidance. . . .

After searching as long as I had before hearing of Gurdjieff and his teaching, and then finding it in the Gurdjieff work—well, I felt I had received something priceless, something that would enable me to give my life a real significance from then on.[4]

The real significance expanded with Gurdjieff's recovery. Jean recalls the first time he saw Mr. G. after the accident, walking "deliberately, as though his legs were not moving of themselves, as though each forward step was made possible only by his will. One woman was on his right, the other on his left, both either supporting him by the arms or close by in case he needed support." As Gurdjieff's health improved, the pace of life at the institute steadily increased, and Jean found his niche in the day-to-day operations. He wrote to the skeptical Alfred Stieglitz that the institute was "by all odds the best *general* instrument that I have found." To Waldo Frank he was more cryptic: "Neither past experience nor speculative knowledge adequately measure the difficulties, the acute psychic states that each day confront me. I am inarticulate. Never before have I been so intense and conscious; and I cannot recall the time when I have been so dead." Withal, Jean's devotion to Gurdjieff allowed little criticism from others, whether they were back home or in France. A friend recalls a gathering in Paris where Gurdjieff was accused of being a charlatan and a scoundrel. Jean defended his master with such fury that he had to leave the party after his outburst.[5]

Toomer had intended that Margaret and her son Tom come to Fontainebleau that summer, as soon as the divorce proceedings were completed. Margaret and Jean exchanged long letters sustaining their love. She wrote that his several letters "brought much joy and peace. How concentrate they are with the inten-

4. *Ibid.*, 26–27.
5. *Ibid.*, 32; JT to Alfred Stieglitz, October 7, 1924, in ASC; JT to WF, October 1, 1924, in WFC; Morley Ayearst to the authors, July 21, 1982.

sity of the deep and significant forces you have touched for us both."[6] In late July, Margaret received from Orage permission to attend the institute, but because of further delays in obtaining the divorce, she had to put off her trip until mid October.

Meanwhile, Gurdjieff challenged the dedication of his pupils once more. He peremptorily announced that he was dismantling the institute, that thereafter the mansion and grounds would be his home and would be called "The Priory" (le Prieuré). Many left, particularly the students from England; but Gurdjieff's immediate family, several of his old-time Russian followers, and some Americans, including Jean, remained. Margaret was still determined to go to Fontainebleau, but she was also trying to hide her relationship with Jean. She had Jean type her address when he sent letters to her through her brother-in-law Melville Cane. Something, however, prevented her coming—perhaps Jean's decision to return in October, or perhaps Orage's discouraging her traveling so far to the institute, which would likely be closed. Gurdjieff had decided to spend his time writing rather than actively teaching. For this reason, or possibly as inexplicably as he had been drawn to Gurdjieff at the beginning of the summer, Jean felt "something click" in him that pushed him toward New York. He felt he would learn more about Gurdjieff's ideas from Orage than from Gurdjieff. He returned to New York in late October with Orage and Jessmin Howarth, who had assisted in Gurdjieff's dance and movement classes.

For the next year and a half, from November, 1924, through the middle of April, 1926, Toomer was fully occupied in learning and teaching the Gurdjieffian Fourth Way in New York. Almost immediately after his return from Fontainebleau, he began an ill-starred venture as an instructor of Gurdjieff dances, gathering a group of about thirty to meet once a week, working with Jessmin Howarth. First he acted as an assistant dance master, but then he began to teach elementary exercises and hoped to be business manager for the group. He used Russian commands as Gurdjieff had, and he affected certain of Gurdjieff's mannerisms. His fervor for this teaching startled some of his friends, such as the Munsons, for it was clear to them that Jean was neither a good enough dancer nor knowledgeable enough about the complex Gurdjieff movements to be an adequate instructor. He had been entranced with the dances, and the adult was following the patterns of the child who had pursued one "bump" of curiosity after another, caught up totally in each new enthusiasm, so that it seemed the most essential thing in the world—until something else came along. The common thread was the longing to find himself, his "real essence." No matter how excessive some of his behavior might have appeared, he was genuinely trying to make the outer self conform to the perceived inner truth. Enthusiasm, however, was not enough. After five or six frustrating sessions, the dance group dissolved.[7]

Jean, too, evidently realized that he needed to learn more before he could teach. He had been working more or less by himself, but in early January of 1925 he wrote Orage, asking to work with him more closely. Orage had started a number of groups to study and practice Gurdjieff methods, each formed of six to ten men and women, who chose their own time and place, afternoon or evening, to meet once a week. One of these groups met at Jane Heap's *Little Review* gallery; among the members were architect Hugh Ferriss and radical socialite Mabel Dodge Luhan with her husband Tony. The fee was two dollars to five dollars a session, but those who could not pay would empty ashtrays or set up chairs. Jean regularly attended the group that met at the home of Wim Nyland, who lived in Brewster, New York, and who eventually became a prominent teacher of the Gurdjieff method. Jean and other members would take the train from New York or would drive together and stay for the evening and night. After the meeting they would pull out blankets and pillows and sleep on the benches lining the walls of the living room. Mavis McIntosh, who attended these meetings, recalls that Jean brought a "depth" to the discussions that few others had. He was known to those in his group as a writer—they read *Cane* with interest—but it appears that he himself seldom mentioned his past writing.[8]

Orage conducted his groups with a subtle combination of lectures or short introductory remarks, prodding questions, and discussions led in such a way that participants discovered more about themselves than they had ever expected. What kept bringing people back "was not alone Orage's brilliant exposition," Louise Welch declares. "It was much more the way he was toward the people who came. . . . Each person existed for him as an individual; he never swept up their problems in metaphysical generalizations. At the same time, he could put them into a large, more inclusive perspective that made it possible to take a fresh look and not drown in one's subjectivity." Other members of Orage's groups report this same combination of astounding mental stature and human warmth. One was "bowled over" by his "capacity to anticipate every question"; another writes, "Orage felt as well as thought, and though

7. Interview of GM by India Watterson, New York, June 27, 1969 (Amistad Research Center, New Orleans).

8. JT to A. R. Orage, January 9, 1925, in JTP 8:2; interview of Lewis Benson, Wallingford, Pa., March 12, 1983; McIntosh interview.

none of us, and no intellectual, . . . was ever a match for him, Orage could, like Gurdjieff, put a simple person at his ease."[9]

Orage in meetings with new people would state the purpose of the groups, "to be introduced to ourselves as objects of scientific observation and study." He began by illustrating individual and cultural frustrations, aware that first "one must become convinced that he is not conscious, that he does not know, that he cannot do," that people must realize they are in prison before they can agree they want to get out. Then he would develop the basic Gurdjieff theory that man is mechanical, determined, a product of heredity and environment that have warped his proper being. A person is formed of many "I"'s, ruled in chaotic sequence by the three centers, instinctive, emotional, intellectual. But the real "I" is potential, to be gained only by conscious effort and a special method, "the aim being to conceive it, develop it, in order that it may control the organism." Man's duty and high calling is to develop himself as an essential unit in the hierarchical organization of the universe, fitting into his place in the grand pattern of successive "octaves." Each of these, akin to the octave in the musical scale, in turn becomes a segment of the more inclusive octave at the next higher level. The various centers and functioning parts of a person, for instance, fit together as notes of one octave; man in turn becomes one note in the next larger octave. Man's development within this broader context involves four levels of consciousness: the Sleeping State, Waking State, Self-Consciousness, and Cosmic Consciousness. Most people are and remain all their lives in the first, or sleeping, state. To move from one to another requires conscious effort leading to waking from or being "born out of" the former state.[10]

Toomer went weekly to Orage's meetings through the spring and fall of 1925 and the spring of 1926. He took meticulous notes at each session. His pages on lecture-discussions, for instance, carefully elucidate the Gurdjieffian practices of self-observation and non-identification, the two fundamental exercises Orage stressed as introductory steps. All the Gurdjieff work involved trying the theories and practices in one's own life and behavior.

The effort to act upon oneself rather than being acted upon unconsciously by outside forces was one of the principal purposes of Orage's method, and one to which Jean devoted much of his own time and energy. The goal was to achieve a "higher state of consciousness" by a certain amount of objective insight, to

9. Louise Welch, *Orage with Gurdjieff in America* (Boston, 1982), 33; Benson interview; Nott, *Teachings of Gurdjieff*, 93–94.

10. JT notes, 1925–26 (JTP 66:2, 66:5); JT, "How I Found the Gurdjieff Work," (JTP 67:5), 31.

have, in a sense, two beings, one that operates at a normal level and another that can detach itself and observe what the organism is doing at the present moment, without judging or changing or reacting emotionally to the activity observed. At the beginning, only a small segment of behavior could be observed, and sometimes a study session would concentrate on one of the three centers of being—physical, emotional, or mental—or on ways in which energy is wasted in our unaware, sleeping state of normal life. To become awakened, Orage's pupils recorded a multitude of items, so that details of behavior would not go unnoticed. Toomer did so both at the sessions and at home. At one meeting, Orage required his pupils to self-observe on the basis of several exercises—forty-eight in all. Still another time, questions were given to the pupils to answer: "What do you really like? What do you really dislike? . . . Superficial likes and dislikes, superficial wishes come from personality. They are acquired. They act as obstructions to real likes." [11]

In preparation for class, Jean would answer these questions in great detail; his list of likes and dislikes extended for pages, from clothes to food. He preferred loose and flowing clothes, like the costumes of monks or ancient priests, or a military uniform with boots and cape, the colors "subdued and dignified," the materials pure silk, pure linen, or pure wool. His main dislike was "any costume that would throw into relief . . . the weak points of his anatomy: his spindle lower limbs in particular." Under "What He Looks Forward To," the first item was "having groups or an institute of his own." To attain this, "he particularly wants a large sum of money . . . to buy material placement, the power of position, and superior free locomotion." Next were set down the dreams of "travelling about the world in the position of a wealthy and learned prince" and "meeting and having the one who would combine all physical attractions with the capacity and serious wish to learn and develop from his instruction." His most inclusive wish was for "a free and reckless living of what he is in essence, unconcerned with consequences, liberated from the fears and concerns that now restrict him. . . . He would like to live, without reserve, the Devil and God in essence." [12] No petty dreams for Jean Toomer.

The listing of likes and dislikes was part of a process called "peeling the onion," that is, making "notations of the various attitudes toward life, stripping off the superficial ones in our effort to reach the fundamental attitude." One could then discover the organism's "essential wish" or "chief feature" and perhaps experiment with ways to achieve it. This exercise was supposed to fol-

11. JT notes (JTP 66:2).
12. *Ibid.*

low one's mastery of a great many simpler observations and one's understanding and applying the Gurdjieff theory and the law of the octave. Toomer, however, was eager to rush into what seemed more productive and more interesting, and he pushed through to a guess that Orage verified in a private question-and-answer session: "I decided that my chief feature was the desire for power. Orage thought that this came pretty close to the nest. And added, say that the chief feature must die." Sharply perceptive, Orage advised also that Jean was "too much given to forcing things. Too much cerebral domination." Toomer apparently was content to observe these qualities in himself "without self-criticism or aim or improvement," a dictum Orage had given earlier.[13] But it is hard to believe that Orage could have made these direct statements to Jean without hoping to see some change.

Toomer was finding great satisfaction in using his love of writing to explore his newfound self-awareness, and his notes soon turned into an autobiographical account called "Values and Fictions." This was written throughout 1925, and he spent some concentrated time on it in August and October. In August, Jean visited his friend Paul Rosenfeld at a vacation spot near York Beach, Maine. They used the morning hours for writing privately and then filled the rest of the day with long walks and discussions. In the fall, Stieglitz invited them both to use his summer home on Lake George as a kind of writers' retreat, and there, in October, Jean finished "Values and Fictions." His first manuscript since *Cane,* it was sent in January to Liveright, as was stipulated in his contract. However, recognizing how different it was from *Cane,* he did not really expect them to publish it, and they did not.

This manuscript is an extended, very personal, psychological statement. It is all the more difficult to understand because it is written in the second person, ostensibly describing the reader rather than the author, in an effort to make it universal or descriptive of Everyman. Its details, however, are so idiosyncratic as to be applicable to no one but Jean Toomer. It may be understood better as an experiment in objectivity, his attempt to gain insights in order to unmechanize himself. Although all Toomer's insights seem related to the practice of self-observation, they are really distortions of it in the direction Orage had cautioned against—intellectualization, introspection, and analysis. The pure method, as Orage emphasized and Jean noted, contains "no words, thoughts, comments, just awareness."[14] But Jean was off on his own track.

By this process, he revealed personal strengths and weaknesses he had not

13. JT notes (JTP 66:2, 66:5).
14. JT, "Values and Fictions: A Psychological Record" (MTC), v; JT, "Certain Gurdjieff Methods, Self-Observation and Non-Identification" (JTP 67:3).

noticed in what he called his preconscious life. He noted problems he intended to rectify, but many of these same characteristics were still attributed to him at a much later time. At his worst, he was a "petty moralist," an impractical idealist who preached his truth, often to an unwilling audience of lesser beings. At his best, he could relate to others by stripping off masks and penetrating to an inner significance. Intensity of experience would sometimes so overwhelm him that it would dissipate his energies and talents. Aloneness could give rise to aloofness. He imagined himself a prince traveling incognito, yet he feared that the whole world might despise him. Speaking of pride, he found "all of your actions tend to either protect, sustain, or increase it," and when these actions failed, the ego would collapse "like a wind bag." He recognized that he wished to be a master, but he did not want to seem a beginner, so he tended to step into a new subject at a level too high for his skills. He wanted to find and marry "a woman who would satisfy all of his needs for love and companionship and at the same time make no unreasonable demands upon his time, energies, and other interests." This wish, he believed, "was expressive of the highest ideal of the man-woman relationship." [15]

The characteristics he mentioned, however, were but manifestations of his interest in seeing the self all at once, a process somewhat similar to looking at a cubist painting. Fragmented observations were to be brought together into an identity that was not dependent on any one part, such as race, sex, or location. Toomer declared in "Values and Fictions," as he did in later works also, that an individual's specific attributes such as race are "prejudices" rather than realities. This reflected Orage's point, stressed in a group meeting, "that one should not be dependent upon externality for what happens to one, that this is shameful. And in this way [he] rubs against the Negro, his positions and attitudes, in a white world." [16]

This observation and description of himself, Toomer implied, was a kind of deliberate self-creation, which in his mind now became the highest form of art. "You were a man before you were an artist," he commented. "You had experienced essence before experiencing a medium of expression." Art, he felt, was meaningless unless moral. Thus his own act of self-awareness and discovery was the ultimate artistic endeavor—a creation of unity, meaning, and power. Making a grandiose leap, he envisioned himself as the first man to "utilize art as an instrument of consciousness," to use his art and genius "to increase being and demonstrate its existence." [17]

15. JT, "Values and Fictions," 43, 59, 62, 111.
16. JT notes (JTP 66:2).
17. JT, "Values and Fictions," 128, 133.

That Jean saw his earlier literary efforts and his current psychological explorations as different kinds of art and as parallel attempts to find wholeness, one replacing the other, is shown by some notes he made in September, 1925, after about two years' exposure to the Gurdjieff techniques. Recording experiments with diet and a successful effort consciously to work out of a depression through his new awareness, he writes (the third-person narrative voice is an attempt at non-identification), "His good psychological digestion is cheating America of a great(?) literature. For, owing to it, a line suffices for that process which otherwise would need a novel." [18]

This self-creation led to a pinnacle toward the end of "Values and Fictions." Almost from his first acquaintance with the Gurdjieff movement, Toomer saw himself as one of its leaders. Both in fantasy, as in the clothes he preferred (the monk's, priest's, or general's), and psychologically, in his need to be dominant, to be seen as a master, he showed this quite candidly as he described himself. The list stated it in so many words: "having groups [like Orage's] or an institute [like Gurdjieff's] of his own." [19] Near the end of the text, he is presented—despite certain specified flaws—as a developed soul, a genius, one of a kind, ready to be a leader of men and women. Perhaps, in accord with the title he gave this work, he was allowing himself some elements of fantasy or fiction in his self-creation.

In the spring of 1925, a move was made in the real world in the direction of Jean's desires. Deciding that Toomer was ready for more responsibility, Orage asked him to set up a group in Harlem for black intellectuals associated with the Harlem movement. Toomer's plan was to try to convince those with whom he had associated in his former literary life that a nonracial philosophy was preferable. Orage expressed the hope that Toomer would be an exponent not of black or of white culture, but of human culture. Jean's appearance in Harlem, and his new attitude toward life and art, were treated with some curiosity and wonder. "He had an evolved soul," Langston Hughes writes, "and that soul made him feel that nothing mattered, not even writing." [20]

Others may have agreed with Hughes's sardonic observation, for Toomer's indifference to race could easily have been interpreted as indifference to everything that was on the surface associated with *Cane*. This is not to say that Toomer felt he was a stranger in Harlem—he mixed easily with the black intel-

18. JT note in "Tennants Harbor" notebook, September 4, 1925 (JTP 17:1) (question mark in original).
19. JT notes (JTP 66:2).
20. Orage's comment, from GM interview; Langston Hughes, "Gurdjieff in Harlem," in his *Big Sea*, 242.

ligentsia as he did with the white. His work in Harlem would prove his point that he could be identified with any group in America but could not be contained within any such identification. As he stated in his essay "The Negro Emergent," which he read one evening to a gathering at Margaret Naumburg's apartment, black intellectuals have more in common with white intellectuals than with non-intellectual blacks. In other words, one establishes one's cultural preferences more by personal interests and abilities than by race. It is not surprising, then, that Jean could initially assemble those from Harlem's intellectual elite for his Gurdjieff group. He continued to be friends with acknowledged black leaders such as Alain Locke and Charles S. Johnson, editor of *Opportunity,* who themselves moved easily between black and white society. Gorham Munson recalls the time Jean invited him to have lunch with Johnson. Jean selected a small restaurant on lower Sixth Avenue, which, Jean declared in advance, "we know . . . is all right for us to eat at." At the luncheon, Munson arranged with Johnson to write a piece for *Opportunity* called "The Significance of Jean Toomer," later incorporated into his book *Destinations.*[21]

Toomer began his lectures and demonstrations in Harlem in the late spring of 1925. Like Gurdjieff, Toomer felt that those who were most likely to become absorbed in the Gurdjieffian philosophy would be educated, relatively successful people who were seeking a remedy for their "incompleteness." He attracted many to his sessions: Wallace Thurman, the self-styled bohemian of the Harlem movement; Dorothy Peterson, a writer who became fond of Toomer and corresponded with him for about ten years; Aaron Douglas, the most successful of the Harlem painters; Nella Larsen, author of two novels about the color line; and Harold Jackman, a teacher and Harlem activist. Arna Bontemps, a writer and an intense admirer of *Cane,* attended the first session but did not go back.

Consulting Orage regularly about content and method and continuing to learn by attending Orage's group, Jean met with the Harlem group for about a year. He followed very closely in his own teaching the substance, order, and methods of presentation contained in his notes from Orage's meetings. While he had wanted to be a leader partly to feed his expansive ego, he also believed in using his gifts in service to a larger method. As Orage had stated at one of his group meetings: "I am a sign post. I indicate a way. But you do not follow a sign post; you follow the road. You are not to follow me; you are to practice the method I define."[22]

21. Gorham Munson, *Destinations: A Canvass of American Literature Since 1900* (1928; rpr. New York, 1970). Incident recounted in GM interview.
22. JT, "Seventh Johnson Group" (JTP 66:2), 2.

The group in Harlem eventually faltered because few could afford the time or money necessary for full dedication to Gurdjieff's Fourth Way. Probably also, still being introduced to the materials, Jean was less effective than he would have liked to be. Langston Hughes observed somewhat bitterly that Toomer returned "downtown to drop the seeds of Gurdjieff in less dark and poverty-stricken fields," adding, "They liked him downtown because he was better-looking than Krishnamurti, some said." But it was a useful group for a time, and far from a wasted effort. Some members, like Dorothy Peterson, transferred to Orage's group and continued for years. She much appreciated Jean's leadership: "I wonder what I have done to deserve all this help which you have brought me and which seems to me divine." Aaron Douglas, too, even three years later, was reported to be very appreciative: "You would really be surprised at Aaron's enthusiasm. I have never seen him actually care about anything so much before, but he is actually transformed when he starts talking about what your groups meant to him." [23]

When Orage needed to be away from time to time, he would ask Jean to lead some of his other groups. According to one member, though, Toomer "didn't have the oomph that Orage had." [24] At the same time, Jean was exploring possibilities for extending the Gurdjieff movement in America. One potential spot was Taos, New Mexico. Taos, a picturesque collection of old and new worlds, was becoming a well-established artists' colony by the 1920s. Of the many artists who settled there either permanently or temporarily, perhaps the most flamboyant was Mabel Dodge Luhan. Moneyed, articulate, domineering, Mabel Dodge had married a Taos Indian, Tony Luhan, and tried to bridge the culture gap by immersing herself in Indian lore and by holding cocktail parties for the well-heeled. She specialized in being a patron to the intelligent and the creative and, like Gertrude Stein in Paris, helped the crosscurrent of ideas spread among her friends, among them D. H. Lawrence and Robinson Jeffers.

To accomplish her ends, she maintained two homes, one in New York and the other in Taos. In New York, she, like so many others in progressive circles, was searching for a solution to the postwar spiritual ennui. In Taos, she was attempting to complete that search by joining with the spiritual base of native American culture. Like Frank and Toomer, she looked toward a more "primitive" life as a source for regeneration and tried to convince others that her model was valid. In her book *Lorenzo in Taos*, Mabel Dodge Luhan describes her

23. Hughes, *Big Sea*, 242; Dorothy Peterson to JT, May 10, 1926, November 10, 1928, both in JTP 8:4.

24. Benson interview.

success in persuading D. H. Lawrence and his wife Frieda to visit and later to settle for a while in Taos. Lawrence's reply in November of 1921 to one of her letters illustrates his own interest in combining cultures as a form of spiritual renascence: "I believe what you say—one must somehow bring together two ends of humanity, our own thin end, and the last dark strand from the previous, pre-white era. I verily believe that. Is Taos the place?"[25]

Mabel passionately believed so. Relying on Tony's imperturbable stability (calmly silent, he wore his Indian robes with equal aplomb in a New York flat and a Taos adobe), she continued her stormy relationships with Lawrence and others like Toomer in her desire for significance. Orage's Gurdjieff movement drew her into the New York groups in 1924. In spite of Lawrence's warning her that the Institute for the Harmonious Development of Man was a "rotten, false, self-conscious place of people playing a sickly stunt,"[26] she became increasingly intrigued by the Oragean method and attached herself to one of the central proponents, Jean Toomer.

Jean represented the combination she found appealing: he embodied the fusion of races and cultures, which made him physically attractive. Beyond his personal appearance, she was drawn to his sense of mystery if not his mysticism, so that soon she was trying to control his destiny as well as hers. Within a short time after her involvement in Orage's group meetings, which were often held at her New York home, she was discussing the impact their joint lives might have on each other: "I am highly charged—I am as you know—full of explosives! It isn't so much that you can contact this force in me. . . . But you can do another thing. You can take this fire I lend to your touch and in a flash transmute it in my organism to another centre . . . and in this more lofty region—every cell is filled with light and no more weight remains in matter. . . . This is marvelous." Less than delighted when Toomer suggested that he bring Orage and Naumburg with him to Taos, Mabel Dodge Luhan nevertheless continued to explore the possibility of having Jean start a Gurdjieff institute there. She paid for his trip to Taos—without Margaret—for the Christmas holidays in 1925 and entrusted $15,000 to him for the Gurdjieffian cause. Jean sent Gurdjieff $1,000 directly in early 1926 and suggested that the rest of her money be used to establish an institute in Taos. He began his letter with the humility (exhibited by him only toward Gurdjieff) of pupil to master:

25. D. H. Lawrence to Mabel Dodge Luhan, November 5, 1921, in Luhan, *Lorenzo in Taos* (New York, 1932), 6.
26. Lawrence to Luhan, January 9, 1924, *ibid.*, 134.

After so many months of silence—months devoted with as much concentration and attention to the Work as I have well been able to concede to it—which, you may assume, signifies practically all I have in me to give—I again find myself placed in a relation to you that calls for speech.

And as no relation may exist between you and myself, or you and any other, save that of workman and master—it is of work that I am writing.

Jean describes Taos as "distant" but beautiful; Luhan's property was as extensive as the institute's grounds, and there was a spacious main house. Toward Luhan, he was less kind, describing her as a person with enormous energy that often lapsed into egotism: "I can hope for her, just in so far as she will persist in her present idea of following your method—but I cannot persuade myself to certainty in regard to her constancy since her previous record is all too evidently chiefly remarkable for changeability." [27]

Mme. Olga de Hartmann, who frequently served as Gurdjieff's corresponding secretary, replied, requesting that a sizable portion of that money be sent to Fontainebleau instead, since the existing institute and its two branches in London and New York were in need of money. Further, Gurdjieff needed the money to sustain him during the completion of *Beelzebub's Tales to His Grandson*. She urged Toomer to discuss the matter with Orage. [28] Orage was in accord with Gurdjieff, so Toomer forwarded the money in small portions to Fontainebleau and to New York. He intended to keep $2,000 in trust to help defray the cost of an American edition of *Beelzebub's Tales to His Grandson,* of which he or Orage, or perhaps both, expected to be in charge. Through a series of misunderstandings and poor bookkeeping, "Toomer's money," that is, the remaining $2,000, was thought by several, particularly Gurdjieff, to have been kept by Toomer. When he was asked to supply money for the book's publication, and still later in 1934 when Mabel Dodge Luhan asked for some money that she claimed she had loaned him, Toomer could not deliver. Instead he gathered receipts showing he had sent the full sum, and more, to Gurdjieff in response to insistent demands over the intervening years. The incident was to be a major element in his break with Gurdjieff in the 1930s.

Nevertheless, in 1926 no one could foresee that this "magnificent gift to consciousness," as Toomer called it, [29] would lead to so much confusion and ill feeling. At the time, Mabel Dodge Luhan intended to place under her care a major portion of the Gurdjieff movement in America, as well as a major Gurd-

27. Luhan to JT, n.d., in JTP 7:2; JT to Gurdjieff, n.d., draft in JTP 4:3.
28. Mme. de Hartmann to JT, February 11, 1926, in JTP 4:3.
29. JT to Luhan, November 26, 1934, in JTP 7:3.

jieff leader. She had gone so far with Jean, in fact, that she was agonizing over Tony's jealousy; but she kept pleading with Jean to let her continue to bask in his glow. For Toomer, discovering a benefactor who could aid the master's work with such munificence encouraged his aspirations to be a leader.

However, Jean was not inclined to succumb to Mabel Dodge Luhan on other than a spiritual plane. He saw the danger of being kept. Indeed, Mabel had written him: "You see Jean, I am trying to subjugate your will to mine—it is my talent—my whole mechanism works together to this end—to seduce your spirit—as I have always been doing. Why, I wonder? They are all around me— the ones I did suceed [*sic*] in and I don't like it at all, really! Why should I want to keep it up and up? And yet how defeated I will feel if I don't." [30] But also he was far too immersed in the work of Gurdjieff, and too engrossed in his relationship with Margaret Naumburg and other women closely associated with the Gurdjieff movement, to submit to Mabel's suggestions. He clearly was interested in having a group of his own, but the establishment of a Fontainebleau on American soil was going to have to wait.

30. Luhan to JT, n.d., in JTP 4:3.

8.

Epiphany

The relationship with Margaret had undergone some shifts since the summer of 1924, when she was struggling under a heavy burden of secrecy to join her lover at Fontainebleau. After Jean's return to New York in November, they resumed their lives in separate quarters, seeing a good deal of each other, but Jean was getting more and more involved with Orage's groups and his own dance groups and efforts in Harlem. Margaret, too, continued to work on the Gurdjieff exercises and to plan for the time she could learn from Gurdjieff directly. Although the institute was closed, it was "not quite closed." Gurdjieff was allowing selected Americans to come to le Prieuré, but he was not fully recovered and was spending most of his time writing rather than teaching in any organized way. In June of 1925, while Jean was in a crisis of indecision and Margaret herself felt "numb and dull and buried," she set sail for France. The report of her one private session with Gurdjieff in a summer full of frustrations perhaps best reveals the condition of her ties to Jean: "I referred to the fact that you had spoken of my coming to him. . . . He had difficulty in recalling who was who, and only associated with you, your telling him about your wife coming over. Well, it was a little difficult to make the fine distinctions in simple English. He then asked me whether we were going to be married. I smiled and said that was very much a question. And then I added something about the way ones [*sic*] outlook on life shifted with this work." She wrote him eight- to eleven-page letters detailing all sorts of information she was ferreting out of people there. But at the end of the summer, just before she came back to New York, they were both at a low point: "Your last letter a week ago, written when you got back to N.Y., continues to give me a sense of your curious state—far away and depleted of your former content. Well I sit here wondering more than ever, what the hell it all means. What has been the use of this whole trip to me anyway. I cant [*sic*] see two inches ahead of me anymore." In October, while Jean was at Lake George working on "Values and Fictions," she had again a rush of the old feeling, writing, "There is a peace for us both here I know, when you return. Peace—and perhaps a sword!" Her conclusion was warm: "Somehow to come to rest and feel truly at peace will wait for your return. For I miss you and love you deeply." [1] While Jean was in Taos with Mabel at Christmastime, Margaret took care of checking his apartment and forwarding his mail. But clearly he was spending more and more time with other people and less and less with her.

The end came abruptly in the spring of 1926. Gorham Munson speculates that Margaret was too sexually demanding; his wife Elizabeth Delza believes that Jean did not want to be tied down to a permanent relationship. It may simply be that this great enthusiasm had been crowded out by another—Toomer's leadership in the Gurdjieff movement began to hover as an imminent possibility. The Munsons, at least, felt that Jean was responsible for the break; but he was not untouched by it.

A small notebook of Jean's, with "Break with M; Being-Consciousness" on the cover, records his reactions at that moment. Dates in this diary-notebook run from the fall of 1925 to April 10, 1926. At the end of March, Toomer visited Tenant's Harbor, Maine. The following entries are from that period.

29, 30, 31 March. It is as if she were dead and a shadow was grieving for her. . . . He [Toomer] experiences extreme alternations between feeling a broken heart and the greastest [*sic*] lightness and freedom that he has known. . . . I have taken his name away from him, and he is now John Jones. The social personality named Jean Toomer is, for this moment at least, dead, and now I am attached to a nondescript organism. . . . It is without possessions, without associations: it is quite nude, new, and alone in the world. It blinks, its [*sic*] somewhat startled and fearsome, and at times feels that it would like to slip into the rather comfortable looking clothes of Jean Toomer.

4 April. I break with M. . . The face of the Earth has changed, and the essence of the World is changing.

8 April. This is my first real psychological struggle and attempt to non-identify. In comparison with this, with what this now means and implies, all that has gone before seems unbelievably superficial; psychic and in a comfortable imagination.

9 April. The final break with M. This nightmare is horrible, and it is horrible precisely because it is a nightmare—I cannot see its cause, its mainspring, what is behind it. I cannot understand it, because I am dreaming; I can only experience it.

1. Margaret Naumburg to JT, June 30, September 4, October 10, 1925, all in JTP 7:18.

Margaret had meant so much to him that many years later in his autobiography he wrote that all his past had prepared him for meeting her in 1923. At that point he "felt the whole world revolve. . . . My birth, and it was truly a birth, came from my experiences with Margaret Naumburg. . . . The very deepest centre of my being awoke to consciousness, giving me a sense of myself, an awareness of the world of values, which transcended even my dreams of high experience."[2]

When such a self-organizing principle drops away, a major upheaval in the personality can be expected, and this is exactly what happened. Jean Toomer was about to undergo an event of such proportions that it formed the keystone of his convictions for the rest of his life. There is just one more entry in the diary after April 9, specifying his hopes:

10 April. I have an intimation that this earth, instead of being my home planet—as Toomer assumes and feels that it is . . . —will become strange, foreign, and remote, while at the same time I will increasingly feel Karatas or the Sun-Absolute to be my home. [Karatas, in Gurdjieff's *Beelzebub's Tales,* is Beelzebub's home planet, from which he had been exiled.]

Let me observe where *this* remote being, Toomer, dwells. . . . Let me likewise observe the life of these other remote beings, bipeds, quadrupeds, insects, etc., seeing them all as *remote,* distant from my native planet, friends, associates, and surroundings. If I can hold this state, wherein this Earth—all of it, New York and Toomer's room and friends in New York included—is *really* the remote place, whereas Karatas is *really* home, the chief feature [segment of self with the most driving force] will then at once wish to leave this place and will become nostalgic, will wish to reach Karatas. And in this way, it can be used to aid my return.

A later copy of this entry adds the comment: "The same will hold true in regard to states of consciousness, to states of being. If the waking state can be made to feel 'not home,' whereas the self-conscious state can be made to feel and mean 'home,' the chief feature will similarly aid me in my purpose. I alone can help the organism."[3]

Jean had been experimenting with many new practices, some of which had strange effects. His notes from the spring and fall of 1925 record efforts at simultaneous functioning, such as repeating a series of numbers or a verse while remembering all the events of one's day. These exercises were supposed to bring greater power to the organizing "I," but sometimes in Jean's case they brought on the sensation of several powerful inner motions, "an internal whirl-

2. "Tennants Harbor" notebook (JTP 17:1); JT, "Outline," 62.
3. "Tennants Harbor" notebook; JT notes (JTP 66:2).

wind" that "threatens to carry my ordinary consciousness into some unknown plane beyond." Concentrating on the mental center, he discovered a "new mode of thinking"—words, apparently strung together as physical entities, emerged in something like automatic writing. With similar concentration, sometimes he felt that his forehead was being parted and wind was blowing through. At other times he experienced what he believed to be the beginning of the formation of the astral body. In Gurdjieff theory, he noted, man has the possibility of possessing up to four bodies, the physical one being the first. The other three are formed on the physical base in sequence, but only by active, conscious work. The feelings contribute to the astral body, the mind to the mental body, and the emerging "I" to the divine body. Each body is formed as its respective center (the emotional or the mental, for example) matures. Another kind of experience that came to Jean more than once in 1925 arose from his attempts at non-identification, the companion exercise to self-observation. It was a dissociation of mind from body: he would suddenly see the organism as if he were outside it, feeling completely separate from it at the time. He had experienced this before but it had not come about through his own effort. He had spelled out his expectations in his notes: "It is necessary to non-identify with the three centers, with the total organism. To be aware that the behavior we are observing is not-I. . . . It has often proved helpful to conceive of the 'I' as existing outside the organism, say a foot behind it. This 'I' then, non-identified, observes the behavior of the organism."[4] So it seemed, when it happened.

Clearly Toomer was in the midst of considering other modes of consciousness, and perhaps experimenting with altered states, though Gurdjieff did not encourage such experimentation. Orage in his teaching emphasized objective observation of self, a long hard work of sharpening consciousness that would eventually build an "I" with enough detachment from the fragmented body-mind to have the potential of attaining a higher consciousness—but even then for brief moments only. Despite this conservative image of what to expect, Jean later characterized the first two years of his study of Gurdjieff as working for just such an experience as was now to be his, an effort "to transcend the limitations of the body-personality," believing that it could be brought about deliberately if a person were properly prepared. He was always overeager, wanting to grasp immediately what there was to be had. At the same time he was familiar with accounts of people having transforming experiences of the kind usually called mystical. Ouspensky's *Tertium Organum,* for example, includes extensive quotations from Plotinus, Jakob Boehme, William James, and many others

4. JT notes, January, February, May, November, 1925 (JTP 67:11); JT, "Sayings of G. G." (JTP 69:4); JT notes on Orage groups (JTP 66:2).

describing such experiences. Ouspensky used these as samples of participation in the essential, "real" world existing beyond and within the visible, illusory one. Toomer had been particularly drawn to Plotinus, even before the *Cane* period, as representing the kind of genuine experience he himself was seeking. With these many influences, he was "preparing myself as best I could for the death of the old and the birth of the new man."[5]

Apparent shifts in the locus of the mind, whether psychic, spiritual, or pathological, were not entirely new to Jean Toomer, nor were they derived solely from the Gurdjieff teaching. One took him by surprise in the summer of 1914, between his high school and college days—the first time he had made a major decision to strike out on his own. In Madison, Wisconsin, before the summer school session began, he and a companion were walking along. Suddenly Jean felt he was rising above his body and watching it from the outside as it continued to walk and converse. "It was as if, from a position slightly above and behind my head, I were observing my body and its movements in a way that turned a spotlight on my body and made the most familiar things seem new and incredibly strange." After a few minutes, he returned to his body as before, and his companion apparently noticed nothing unusual. This occurrence, though it did not frighten him, did not fit into his understanding of religion or psychology. He put it aside and did not recall it again, he says, for ten years—the time when he began seriously studying with Gurdjieff and Orage. His memory of the event served as a datum then for further analysis in relation to the teachings about detachment and self-observation.[6]

At two other times, under less favorable circumstances, Toomer had had experiences when his mind seemed to be detached from his body. In Chicago in 1916, the defeat of his religious beliefs by what he understood as atheistic naturalism had a drastic effect on both his mind and his body. He had often before lost one theory or another, but "I had never lost myself. Now myself was lost." For three days, he lay inert in bed in his room. His roommate, concerned, tried to nudge him to awareness or response; Jean could observe this happening, but he felt as if he were not in his body but outside it. He slept a great deal and felt old, as if ready for death.[7] He cured himself only by accepting the trap, absorbing the challenge of the new ideas, and developing a new personal belief system.

Again at a time under great stress, early in the year 1919, his body rebelled.

---

5. JT, "Experience Above Being" (JTP 26:7); JT, Foreword to "From Exile into Being" (MTC), 2.

6. JT, "Book X," 104.

7. *Ibid.*, 244.

For six months, Toomer had been keeping to a schedule of taking piano lessons and studying musical theory, reading literature and doing his own writing, working as a clerk for a grocery firm half time and as physical education director at a settlement house in the evenings until eleven, together with going to concerts and other social events. Suddenly he had a serious breakdown, signaled by a sharp pain at the base of his brain. "For a day or two I was in a semicoma. . . . One or two [friends] thought I was losing my mind. But I wasn't. I was there all the time, looking out at them. Only, I couldn't do much with my body. Seemed disconnected with it." [8] This time, when he came to himself, he cured himself with fasting and dieting, rejecting the advice of a nerve specialist his friends urged him to see. Perhaps even more important to his cure was his quitting his two jobs and multiple activities and going to the place he used again and again as a retreat, Ellenville, New York.

Jean Toomer, in 1926, was ripe for another crisis of vision. For the past two years, he had consistently tried to attain a state of more universal consciousness in which his personality would wither away and only the essential "I" would remain, in which he would be separated from the conditioned body and united with the essence of all-pervasive Being. Further, he had a history of earlier experiences that seemed to indicate several kinds of separation of body and spirit. And then there was the present shock of his tortured break with his mentor and lover, who for almost three years had sustained and inspired him in a way no one else had. At the end of his "rebirth" attributed to Margaret, he now needed another. Forced on him by a "nightmare" he wanted to wake from, this rebirth, within the same month, not surprisingly took the form of waking to a sense of more inclusive Being through an experience of radically altered consciousness.

Returned from Tenant's Harbor and waiting idly one evening on the platform of the Sixty-sixth Street el station in New York, not in any hurry to get his train home, Toomer suddenly had a feeling of inner movement, as if some other power had taken over within him. Gradually, something like a soft light seemed to unfold from just behind and inside his body and to shape itself into a new body, a new form enveloping his physical body. "This was no extension of my personal self, no expansion of my ordinary awareness. I awoke to a dimensionally higher consciousness. Another being, a radically different being, became present and manifesting." He still felt identified with his everyday self, but he could clearly see both as if from outside. But the next step was a shift of

8. JT, "Outline," 39, also in W&S, 109.

identification—a change in location but without movement. Without choice, his "I" was surrendered to the larger freedom of the new being. His body stood motionless; his being was waiting to receive him: "Precisely *I* was being transported from exile into Being. Transport is the exact term. So is transcendence. . . . Liberation is the exact term. I was being freed from my ego-prison. I was going to a strange incredible place where I belonged."[9] He could not go back if he wanted to. His ordinary self, with its feelings, desires, and confusions, had disappeared for the duration of the experience. Yet within his new larger consciousness, his awareness of sensations and use of faculties remained. He was not in the kind of trance in which the body is inert.

His body then seemed small and removed from him, no longer identified with the "I": "I had been born above the body." His being towered above the platform and the streets: "I saw the dark earth, and it seemed remote, far down and removed from the center of the universe, a small globe on the outskirts. . . . Not only was I not of that world, I could not feel myself even to be within its boundaries." Somehow, feeling that he was an intrinsic part of the extended universe, he also could closely observe the people walking mechanically over the earth's surface, as little in touch with it as if it were a large metal shell, as little in touch with their bodies as if they were robots. He then felt cut off even from his own body, as if he had died: "It seems I was in the illimitable reservoir of life before it is poured into moulds"—a place that was awesome, empty, "watched over neither by man nor God."[10]

After a time—perhaps two hours, he guessed—a thought came that he might try to move his body. It seemed inconsequential whether or not he did, except that the body might be missed or noticed if it was not in its usual place. Could he move it? He found he could manipulate it, as though it were a toy, and he got it on the next train, struck by the tongue-in-cheek idea that "[i]nasmuch as I was newly come to this planet, it was lucky that I was in league with a body that had been born and reared here. It spoke the language and knew how to get about. . . . It had money in its pockets. . . . We'd get along quite well."[11] Looking at earth-beings closely for the first time, sitting on the train, he began to realize that they could see only his body, not his real being; therefore if he could see only their bodies also, they might be in the

9. JT, "From Exile," sec. 1, p. 8, sec. 2, p. 3. This manuscript is in two versions. In one, cited here, each section is paginated separately; in the other, cited in most of the following notes, the pagination is sequential throughout the whole work.

10. *Ibid.*, 19, 23, 31.

11. *Ibid.*, 34.

same state as he. Their haggard faces, however, convinced him that they had somehow lost the "wonderful Power" within them. He experienced a sharp pang for their loss.

Returned to his apartment, operating his body from somewhere above and behind it, he saw the walls as "penetrable curtains" to the universe. "A segment of my life was represented by this place, several years of unconsciousness"—there, body and he moved about, discovering things. Apprehensive that this new state might be lost when he awoke, and feeling a seemingly inexhaustible energy, yet he decided to take a chance and went to sleep full of gratitude for that evening's experience.

In the morning, however, he found himself still in the larger consciousness. His body managed its usual morning routine while familiar objects presented new wonders—water, cloth, metal, wood, and the orange, rolls, and coffee he had for breakfast were seen and felt intensely, almost as living things. His body felt free and flowing as if a weight had been lifted from it; it enjoyed food more than ever, but needed less. Riding on the top deck of a Fifth Avenue bus, he seemed to be up in the sky and down on the pavement at the same time. There emerged a radiant impression of oneness with all the people around him, "a swift contact of essences." "There was no filter between myself and things, no buffer between myself and men. . . . Each contact had an electric quality. Life crackled, and I enjoyed the sting of it." As he was walking, in the midst of pedestrians, "the impression of walking-bodies-sleeping-beings was so sharp that I had a sense of moving in a crowd of somnambulists." Lunching with a friend who was unusually sensitive and aware, he had hoped that some communication of his state would come about. But the friend noticed nothing unusual, and midway through lunch, Toomer's "being" recognized the being of the other, saw its separation from the personality, and vividly saw the friend's personal self strangling his essential being. The strong sense of kinship with all others refused to leave him. It was reinforced in his room by a vision in which he had no boundaries, was an open channel for love, and saw the people of the Earth "enter here, enter me, and go down into the sacred root, and ascend from it, as I did." This secret fraternity, the awareness of the "Brilliant Brotherhood," extended to all his meetings with people: "Walking around the Battery I came upon beings called bums, and some called cops. There were those called street walkers, and business men, Americans, foreigners, Jews, Christians, blacks, whites. And with them all, without exception, it was the same, the same radiant weaving of being into being, of beings into God." [12]

12. *Ibid.*, 89, 96, 145, 147.

At length his joy and peace were penetrated by a sharp sense of personal responsibility, a profoundly discomfiting duty, a self-dependence with no end, no external guidance, no expectation of happy accidents. The center of this feeling of responsibility began burning within him like a bright sun, the overpowering force of what he called "Being-Conscience"—as different, he says, from ordinary conscience as his new level of consciousness was from the "normal" somnambulist state. In his experience of this sense, a man feels responsible, not only for himself and his life on earth, but also "for his character, conduct and development in this life and all life, in this world and all worlds, to everyone and to everything." Being-Conscience is not formed by outward training like ordinary conscience, but purely inward and so powerful that no force in man can withstand it. Its strictures apply directly to oneself, not, like the moralist's conscience, primarily to others. The pressure of this conscience grew enormously: "It seemed that I was in an incredible furnace whose fire consumed yet renewed me. . . . The very existence of this seemingly excessive Conscience must mean that there was an inconceivable goal. . . . But I felt that I would burst long before I reached that goal." Enduring what to him was unbelievable torture, trying to affirm the suffering as positive but unable to bear more, he finally tried to dim this new conscience by sleeping (unsuccessful because the energies it generated were inexhaustible) or by temporary respites such as going to a movie. The movie escape was no use. Conscience and consciousness burned as always, showing him his small self amid circles of responsibilities, the other moviegoers in a secondary dream level beyond their daily dreaming. "There was no hiding in this house, no dreaming with this film. . . . I [was] alone, exposed." [13] However, on the way back from the movie, he found a new equilibrium, and the burning sun of conscience was beginning to subside. For the first time in days, he slept well.

Next day he was startled and appalled to notice that with the withdrawal of conscience, Being-Consciousness was leaving him too. He felt he was losing volume, losing altitude, literally falling, but he had the sense that, as in his entrance into Being, the process was directed by a Mind or a Hand. Toomer felt then he knew what Adam's fall was, "the mysterious way in which a being, through radical change of consciousness resulting in loss of Consciousness, seems to pass out of the Universe and exist apart from God." The leave-taking took about twenty-four hours. "The intolerable freedom to suffer as a being was giving way to a tolerable confinement": he was returning to exile. "The body of my being diminished until it was hardly larger than the physical body,

13. *Ibid.*, sec. 24, pp. 2, 200, sec. 30, p. 5.

and then vanished. The instant it vanished I made the reverse transit back into body-mind. . . . Fallen from the state of awakened beings, I was again one of the exiles—but, *remembering*." [14]

The whole experience lasted about two weeks. It burned into him many convictions about man and the universe, including the first conclusion that such an experience is possible. "If two weeks then two months is possible. If two months then two years, twenty years, a life-time. What can happen to one can happen to all. . . . My work as a being in this life [was] made explicit." [15] He knew then, with an unshakable conviction, that he was to demonstrate to others the truths he had discovered. The experience itself, however, was so awesome that it was twelve years before he tried to describe it on paper.

Jean Toomer fully believed he had participated in the state of Being-Consciousness, which was his name for the state of Self-Consciousness in the Gurdjieff scheme—that is, the state of being fully awake, the larger goal of all the early exercises, not to be attained until a person had developed a functioning "I." He says this "sheer consciousness," uninterrupted awareness, can never become habitual as long as we are body-bound. "When, however, I was body-free and in Being, it was natural for me in that condition." It is difficult for some other Gurdjieff followers to accept this assessment. Elizabeth Delza Munson comments,

Part of it may have been [a higher-consciousness experience]—but knowing from Orage and Gurdjieff how wary they were of such claims as real—and remembering that Orage talked of only a moment of consciousness as a rare experience, and Gurdjieff used to say "I am only a man" even when certain manifestations were remarkable—I am surprised that Jean could think he was in this higher state for that *extended time*.
. . . I feel Jean's experiences and states could rather be considered intense emotional states and to some extent imagination and rationalization rather than what he calls a true Being experience. . . . There is no doubt Jean had moments of realization. But to Gurdjieffians it would seem an experience mixed up with expectations as a result of theories rather than pure. [16]

His experience may have contained elements of imagination, exaggerated emotion, and wish fulfillment. Dr. Gerald May, a psychiatrist familiar with many kinds of mystical experience, describes what happened to Jean as closer to the psychological dissociation that occurs with psychedelic drugs than to a

14. *Ibid.*, 214, 215, 217.
15. *Ibid.*, 18, 217.
16. JT, "Certain Gurdjieff Methods, Self-Observation and Non-Identification" (JTP 67:3), 5; Elizabeth Delza Munson to the authors, March 14, 1983.

true mystical experience. Nevertheless, Toomer's coincided at several points with the classic concept of mystical experience: the powerfully direct touch, which can never be fully communicated; the authoritative knowledge of the eternal oneness of the human spirit with other beings and the cosmos; the sense of passivity, of being moved and grasped by a larger power; and the distinct impression of the onset and the end of this state within a restricted period of time. Jean's differed from other accounts in its duration—most illuminations seem to last from a moment to a few minutes or an hour—and in the lack of a sense of unity with a loving God, which resulted in an extreme dependence on himself.[17]

A vision offers the perceiver psychological "truths" that are no more susceptible to proof than are religious ones. For Toomer, the experience was undeniably a key event that crystallized his life-goals and past experiences. It seemed to conclude a search for self-identity with which he had been laboring long before he wrote *Cane*. Toomer was at a psychological threshold: he had abandoned occupational as well as emotional moorings, and he needed a quick success through the Gurdjieff method. His rebirth as a spiritual personage was self-induced, for even though he claimed to have been passive at the time of his vision, he had long been seeking a revelation. Although the specific moment was a surprise, the event could not have been altogether unexpected. What Toomer wanted was a workable definition of his identity, and he seemed to find it: instead of thinking of his temporary sojourn in time and space, even as an American, he discovered a meaning in considering himself the universal man. "One must rise above the Earth to become universal," he wrote. "One must experience the Universe, not in thought alone but with his whole being, in order to become aware of himself as a being of the Universe; and to do this, one has to rise above himself, to be born above the body, above the personal self." Freed of the body and its confinements, he felt liberated also from the definitions people impose on others—the familiar "prejudices" of race, nationality, sex. Those who feel uprooted or disinherited, he said, look for connections between the outside world and the incidental facts of geography, history, physical appearance, or occupation. They are "strangers to the way of their own be-

17. There are many collections and studies of mystical experiences, but one of the best analyses is still that of William James, *The Varieties of Religious Experience* (1902; rpr. New York, 1936), Lectures XVI and XVII, "Mysticism." Dr. May, a psychiatrist who works with clergy in the field of spiritual counseling, has analyzed the interaction between the spiritual and the psychological in *Care of Mind, Care of Spirit: Psychiatric Dimensions of Spiritual Direction* (San Francisco, 1982) and *Will and Spirit: A Contemplative Psychology* (San Francisco, 1982).

ings." They need to find their larger connections with the universe. We are earth-beings, that is all, but that is the key to our self-understanding.[18]

In contemporary parlance, Toomer was born again, not as a Christian, but certainly as one touched by a "Power." This force—"the nameless God, who once had seemed terrible"—caused an experience that, he felt, cleansed him of ignorance. Literally feeling born into a second body, he was also born into a truth that was, he believed, absolutely right for all. The need to express this vision was the controlling factor in his career as teacher and writer: art as emotional expression or as pleasure gave way to art as instruction and moralization.

Toomer's description of himself as comprising two entities, the self and the beyond-self, accounts for much of the detachment he could achieve, both from himself and from others. Heightening this philosophical schizophrenia was a belief that he was indeed different, destined by virtue of his special properties to be a cut above the rest of humanity. "And this," he wrote, "is interesting— that I, who am fashioned on no antecedent, but who will be a prototype for those to come, should have sprung to life in a standard house."[19]

With this inflated view of himself, he set out again for Fontainebleau. On May 29, 1926, he arrived in France for the summer with Gurdjieff and stayed until October 16. He studied with renewed belief that he would become a leader in his own right of a Gurdjieff center. New York and Fontainebleau could no longer contain him.

18. JT, "From Exile," section revised under title "The Second River," *ca.* 1941 (MTC), 2, 16.
19. JT, "Earth-Being," 10, also in *W&S*, 16.

Toomer (*left*) at college, Wisconsin
From Marjorie Toomer Collection

With a friend [Mae Wright?] by the Potomac
From Marjorie Toomer Collection

In the early 1920s
From Marjorie Toomer Collection

Margery Latimer
Courtesy Margery Toomer Latimer

With daughter Margery at Shirley Grove's parents' farm, Illinois, 1934
Photo by Marjorie Content Toomer, from Marjorie Toomer Collection

With Chaunce Dupee, Portage, 1934
Photo by Marjorie Content Toomer, from Marjorie Toomer Collection

Marjorie Content Toomer, Taos, 1934
From Marjorie Toomer Collection

At work in Taos, 1935
Photo by Marjorie Content Toomer, from Marjorie Toomer Collection

At leisure in Taos, 1935
Photo by Marjorie Content Toomer, from Marjorie Toomer Collection

9

"Toomer the Chicagoan"

Jean Toomer spent that summer of 1926 at Fontainebleau with Margaret Naumburg and others from New York. He and Margaret shared in the Gurdjieff work, but by this time, that was their only connection. He was in love with another woman in the movement, Edith Taylor. She was a young interior decorator, "rather good-looking, of considerable means," according to Gorham Munson. She met Jean at the dock when he returned from France in October, and he evidently tried hard to get her to marry him, but with no success.[1] They maintained a fond relationship, however, for many years, through their subsequent marriages to other people.

Toomer's vocational star was clearly rising. His felt destiny as a major teacher of Gurdjieff's ideas had been strengthened by his intense experience of Being, as he called it, and the summer's work no doubt extended his skills as a potential teacher of Gurdjieff's method. He left Fontainebleau with a commission he took as a sacred charge: to go beyond the confines of New York and attempt to found another center in the Midwest, a place where he had already made some contacts. As a result, the second major Gurdjieff center in the United States was established not in Taos, as Mabel Dodge Luhan had hoped, but in Chicago. The city, well known to Toomer from his college days, appealed to him. He thought Chicago resembled him in its contrasts, to be accepted and rejected, to suffer and enjoy. In Chicago, he said, "I am an ascetic and a Don Juan. . . . History will say, Jean Toomer of Chicago. Toomer the Chicagoan."[2]

1. Interview of GM by India Watterson, New York, June 27, 1969 (Amistad Research Center, New Orleans).
2. JT notebook, *ca.* August, 1930 (JTP 17:1).

So, in November of 1926, his home in a suitcase, he took the Twentieth Century Limited to Chicago. He had one hundred dollars, several letters of introduction, and a belief in Gurdjieff as the "central sun" of a cosmos, with "Orage, the de Hartmanns and the others as the planets of an amazing system." He was both apprehensive and expectant, for Gurdjieff's power awed and thrilled Jean and infused him with a feeling that he could do almost anything, that whatever he did would have value. Jean sent invitations to several contacts in Chicago, their names having been supplied by the New York group. He set December 10 as the date for his first lecture, to be held in a rented meeting room. He would offer an introductory explanation of the works and ideas of the Institute for the Harmonious Development of Man. "Mr. Jean Toomer, who has come to Chicago for this purpose," the invitation says, had planned subsequent meetings for "study and practice according to Mr. Gurdjieff's ideas."[3]

Rather quickly, Jean set up several groups at the homes of people who lived on the Gold Coast, which fringes the shore of Lake Michigan. Interested Chicagoans were, Jean felt, better able to prepare themselves for Gurdjieff's method—they were less fragmented and more vital than were New Yorkers. As a center for Gurdjieff thought, Chicago was "less promising and more possible" than New York. Toomer stated that he had as many as four different groups,[4] but they became fluid interchanges of the same people, engaged in Toomer's experimentation with the Oragean method. The group members were an eclectic assortment: Elise Bunnell, a widow with a practical mind; Douglas Campbell, a psychologist; Mark Turbyfill, a poet; Diana Huebert, an aspiring movie-script writer.

The backbone of an early group that lasted for more than five years grew from a sprinkling of Chicagoans who came to depend on one another outside as well as during the meetings. Fred Leighton managed The Trading Post, which sold Indian and Mexican artifacts in Chicago and New York. While he was in New Mexico on business, probably in December of 1925, he met Jean. Steady, unassuming, and enjoying a good laugh—the bull in the china shop, he called himself—he remained loyal to Gurdjieff's ideals long after the Chicago group dispersed, and he was still Jean's friend after Jean broke with Gurdjieff. Max and Shirley Grove were also devoted to Gurdjieff, who stayed at their apartment during his visit to Chicago in 1934, and they watched with delighted dismay as he virtually dismantled the kitchen in order to make an elaborate

3. JT, "Chicago Form" (Margery Toomer Latimer Collection, Pineville, Pa.); invitation (JTP 64:15).
4. JT, "Chicago—1926" (JTP 16:4); Larry Morris to JT, n.d. (in which Morris compliments Toomer for having four groups), in JTP 7:11.

meal. They relied on Jean to be their counselor, and in fact looked to Jean for help early in their marriage, Shirley's second one. By contrast, Yvonne Dupee enjoyed being single, but she felt she had a certain claim on Jean that kept other women wary. A columnist for one of the Chicago newspapers, she had a wit and detached breeziness that were at once entertaining and unsettling. Jeremy Lane, called both a "great god Pan" and a "timid soul,"[5] was indeed a curious mixture of contraries. He represented loyalty to the master teacher Toomer, willingness to challenge complacency and to grow from new humility, and dedication to the Gurdjieff teaching that in many ways characterized the ideal pupil. He was perceived by some, however, as a lost soul who was seeking a spiritual base that could never be found, a "born loser" whose restlessness was merely aimless. Old members dropped out of the group because its impact waned or because they joined other Gurdjieff groups, and new people were drawn into the group, but Jeremy Lane remained an apprentice leader throughout Jean's five years of major activity in Chicago.

Lane in some ways resembled a younger Toomer, looking for a center within himself and relying on a spiritual leader to help him find it. People were drawn into Toomer's groups for reasons related to that search. Carol Bliss, who became part of the Chicago group fairly late, stated her reason for joining:

I entered your classes in Chicago deliberately purposeful: my persistence in my purpose kept me attending; it was the method and what you had to give to me that actuated me; I came to admire and respect you but over and above this I saw you always in the role of teacher.

In the period of seven months I was in the group I came to a realization that any very noticeable change in ones [sic] functioning and growth in consciousness was a laborious inner process that might be assisted or speeded up by intensive work such as that at the Institute at Fontainbleau [sic].[6]

There were, of course, other motives besides growth of one's consciousness—the security of a group identity, mere curiosity, fascination with a handsome bachelor. Toomer was subject to the criticism that his primary objective was to attract pretty young women and rich matrons who could, in different ways, support his needs. In fact, in his early efforts to build groups he noted that a "bevy of women disciples" was not the most healthy situation. "My question—'Where are the men?'" Certainly there were women followers who did indeed gratify his sexual and financial requirements. Jean lived on the funds raised by the groups: donations given at each meeting, additional money

5. Margery Latimer to Jane Comfort, May 31, 1931, in JTP 5:17; Yvonne Dupee to JT, November 27, 1934, in JTP 2:16.
6. Caroline Bliss to JT, December 29, 1931, in JTP 1:4.

contributed to allow him fare to Fontainebleau in the summers, and subscriptions to his formal lectures on literature and psychology. He had also constantly to raise money to send to Gurdjieff in France. He had willing partners in his persistent efforts to find money for himself and for Gurdjieff. Carol Bliss, for example, was responsible for finding sponsors for Toomer's lectures, at one hundred dollars each, with the view that Jean was "too powerful and dynamic to be submerged." Diana Huebert, who became a member somewhat later in 1931, was of the other sort, attracted not only to the ideas but also to the man. And yet she was aware that Jean himself was principally devoted not to self-gratification but to the larger Gurdjieffian principles: "I must tell you what a deep impression your last lecture particularly made upon me. You were not only eloquent—but rhythmic in your delivery and there was much to be digested—all of which demonstrated so emphatically to me—your concentrated effort and your internal discipline." Yvonne Dupee was also devoted to the man, for she framed a picture of Jean for her room. And she was not the only one. Elise Bunnell kept for many years some poems that Jean wrote for her at this time:

> Lord take her to a distant place
> Inaccessible to my fate
> That my pride may not break
> Against her anviled loveliness
>
> . . . .
>
> Stop, Lord, I see her lovely there
> Within me though in far off place
> Lovelier than were she here
> And all I am is forced to yield.[7]

There is no doubt that Toomer's power as a leader was in many ways connected to his considerable sexual appeal. The intense devotion he generated in individuals as disparate as Margaret Naumburg, Dorothy Peterson, and Mabel Dodge Luhan was the result of his intellectual and emotional fervor combined with his physical attractiveness. In that respect he resembled the archetypal preacher whose exhortative flair creates in his flock an admixture of physical and spiritual drives impossible to separate. As Gorham Munson has stated, Jean was a sexual being who enjoyed healthy relationships, "a genuine lover and a genuine person in his sex contacts."[8]

7. JT note (JTP 57:10); Bliss to JT, February 4, 1933, in JTP 1:4; Diana Huebert to JT, January 24, 1931, in JTP 4:9; Elise Bunnell to JT, September 28, 1928, in JTP 1:7; JT, "I See Her Lovely There," *ca.* 1930, MTC (sent to MCT by Elise Bunnell in the 1960s).
8. GM interview.

One young divorcée, a member of Toomer's group, intended to become a writer and used the group, specifically Jean, as a source of inspiration. She recorded in copious letters how Jean overpowered her in person: "I've had evidence of your extraordinary kindness—and yet if I were talking to you, face to face, I would shrivel under the faintest twinkle in your eye—and if you started to erase a smile under the pretense of deliberately stroking your mustache I think I'd curl up and disappear." Some compliments were excessive, to the point of ignorance. One devotee wrote to her brother: "This man has been maligned by different cults and churches among them some Christian Scientists. . . . In the first place he is not a Catholic of any kind nor has he ever been. . . . I am sure he is the most wholesome, cleanest man I ever saw in my life. . . . He has always seemed like a 'big brother' to everybody who knows him."[9]

Toomer as a group leader was indeed an impressive figure. His emotionally detached but intellectually engaging style was bewildering to some, but they came back for more because of the possibilities he offered. He would lay out man's basic problem, of living mechanically, being lopsided in his development, feeling something essential is missing. Then he would give the promise, through the means at his command, of getting out of the maze, of tapping more energy, of experiencing potentialities people never knew existed. His tone was playful but serious, full of examples and analogies, intense and compelling. In one presentation he called for full attention to his rapid-fire delivery: "If you miss, you miss—I don't repeat, even for God." His studied emotional detachment, however, was the source of discomfort for some of his followers. One of his Chicago group wrote to him, stating she could never really talk to him, and another called him "removed. You didn't get close to Jean Toomer." Even as good a friend as Gorham Munson noted that Jean's new elevated stature made him less warm: "Jean's ambition was such that he began to outstrip his old friends or to set up as a leader. . . . It wasn't an arrogant process, but it was a kind of setting up of some distance between him and his development and you as a fellow striver who perhaps was not as far along as he." Still, he was capable of gathering devoted followers, many of whom were almost worshipful in their admiration. Jeremy Lane, after many years of dedication to Jean Toomer, believed Jean to be a deliverer of humankind.[10]

9. Nadja Mortimer to JT, April 8, 1934, in JTP 7:11; Blanche Leverette to her brother Deane, September 21, 1927, in JTP 8:19.

10. Taped interview of Katharine Green by Robert Twombly, Briggsville, Wis., March 21, 22, 1975 (State Historical Society of Wisconsin, Madison); GM interview; Jeremy Lane to JT, September 27, 1932, in JTP 5:12.

To inspire that kind of following was Jean's major desire. He was largely successful because of the methods he used and his detached compassion. Foremost were his projection of confidence in himself as a leader and his eloquence in presenting his ideas to others. Second, he had learned his lessons well from Orage and Gurdjieff—on the surface, at least. To be a disciple of Gurdjieff was, for Jean, almost to play Gurdjieff himself. According to Munson, Jean struck an occasional Gurdjieffian pose, even to the extent of breaking his bread in the master's coarse manner or talking with echoes of Gurdjieff's brusqueness. Gurdjieff's appeal in part was his Oriental aura. Jean, too, converted himself into a man with an exotic heritage, someone who enjoyed being thought of as an Indian, or partly native American, or perhaps Spanish. A fellow passenger on an ocean liner traveling to France in June of 1929 recalls a captain's masquerade party at which Jean appeared as a rajah, complete with dinner jacket and bath-towel turban. In Jean's autobiographical account of the trip, "Transatlantic," the passengers wonder whether the character representing him is Russian or Egyptian—and his rajah disguise serves to deepen their curiosity. Whatever the guise, he presents to his fellow passengers an image of the mysterious stranger—one who, like Gurdjieff, codes his past and hides his motives. Attraction often is the power to veil oneself effectively. Marsh, a fictionalized traveler who is attracted to the Toomer character, has submitted to that power:

"You are never like anyone else, are you?"
"Quite right," I laughed.
"And you're never what anyone thinks you are?" she pressed.
"Seldom." I shook my head. [11]

From the position of the willing isolate, one who lives "midway between the earth and sun," he is able to steer people into discovering how they can grow in self-awareness. "I am an artist," he declares. "But not someone who spends all his days fiddling with paints or words. I am, if you will, an artist in life. It is my aim to understand how life, from the point of view of balance, of contrasts, of oppositions, tensions, or harmony, of right beginnings and perfect endings, can be lived." His strategy of detailed analysis and suggestions for self-observation is made specific:

"A strong part of yourself is saying, 'I want to experience, even to experience madly the great wide world.' And just because this affirmation is so strong, it has aroused the part which has to do with the wife and mother and which says, 'I need to experience nothing beyond the limits of my home. . . .' What I have said is so, or not?"
"It is so," she said.

11. Morley Ayearst to the authors, July 21, 1982; JT, "Transatlantic" (MTC), 60.

"Well, dear Miriam, both are too strong for either to, as it were, knock the other on the head and eliminate it. And so, just these wishes, these two directions, constitute for you a cross-pull, a tension. I am suggesting that you take a positive attitude towards them; that you view them and try to make them contribute to your own further growth and individualization. Yes?" I smiled, and my serious mood relaxed.

This Toomer surrogate was not just the philosopher engaging others in serious discussions. He was also the life of the party, or at least wanted to be—the center of gossip, dancing, singing, drinking, "throwing off sparks of song and banter as I went." But rather haughtily, again not unlike Gurdjieff, he lumped the cross section of passengers into "types." [12]

At Fontainebleau, Gurdjieff frequently placed people into categories of "idiots." As a kind of test for pupils and guests to measure their own limited achievement, Gurdjieff reminded people of what he called in *Beelzebub's Tales to His Grandson* "moral shame." Each person was in some way an "idiot," that is, an imperfect human whose eccentricities of personality or habit kept him or her from attaining higher states of consciousness. Gurdjieff had names for everyone—names that alluded to a "chief feature" or "particularity" that unconsciously identified the individual. Toomer was called "Half-an-Hour Toomer" by Gurdjieff. A fellow participant explains why: "You know Jean used to talk slowly and sometimes he would think for a long time between his sentences, particularly when it was something of importance to him. . . . [Gurdjieff] would say something, and then he would say, 'Half an Hour Toomer.' And Jean would smile, and would go on thinking." The theory that people function mechanically was a source of Toomer's own tendency to typecast the ship's passengers and partly explains his endless fascination with giving bizarre names to his characters in fiction and to his friends in real life. So on the ship to France he was expecting to find the "ship's buffoon," the "candidate for ship's main elderly love affair," the "ship's drunk." Each is a type, rather than an "individualized person . . . who, by effort, has risen superior to the influences which conditioned him." Toomer similarly classified his group members in Chicago—for instance, "dissatisfied, charming Shirley," "lovely, romantic, suppressed Yvonne," "deep understanding, tolerance, love of beauty Max." [13]

Toomer's style as leader was an evolution of method. Having studied at le Prieuré in 1924, 1926, 1927, and 1929, he retained Gurdjieff's emphasis on work as a means to self-discovery, along with the master-pupil relationship

12. JT, "Transatlantic," 207, 126, 178–79.
13. Interview of Louise Welch, New York, June 25, 1982; JT, "Transatlantic," 48, 49, 38; JT notes (JTP 53:14).

that allowed for lectures, readings, and short dissertations in reply to questions. He continued to use much of what he had learned from Orage. Most of the group's activities, and also Toomer's readings and lectures, centered on self-observation and non-identification, features of the Gurdjieff philosophy Jean thought he had come to understand.

He developed, however, certain methods of his own, rejecting too much direction from above. Orage wrote him, for instance, in early 1927 to say, "I am very sorry you've not been doing my weekly reading of the [Gurdjieff] book." Many of Jean's techniques were calculated to give participants "shocks," that is, profound revelations of self-awareness intended to be a starting point for heightened consciousness and growth. In a sense, he helped pioneer experimental group techniques that came into more widespread use some forty years later in the human potential movement. The psychologist Douglas Campbell, a member of the Chicago group who was also one of Jean's best friends, describes his style: "Jean played the role of mystic as he presented the vast cosmology of the Gurdjieffian system. He was a hypnotic speaker. In his conduct of the meetings he jumped from astronomical mysticism to personal psychodynamics, obviously related to persons in the group without identifying them. It was a sort of early day group therapy." [14] An evening's session would stress in one way or another Gurdjieff's teachings, through a combination of lectures, discussions, readings, awareness exercises, group projects—and making supper. Sometimes there were readings of Gurdjieff's works, then recently translated into English by Orage. Some of Jean's own works, too, were read and discussed, like "The Gallonwerps." Often the focus would be on the individual: what "weak spots" each had, what feature made each one "idiotic," which of the three centers of being each person relied on most strongly.

Toomer set up different exercises and encounters that would be the central activity of the evening or a series of evenings. He would write aphorisms—many of which became part of his book *Essentials*—on index cards, hand them out, and have members of the group discuss the significance of the statements. One evening, for instance, they discussed the following, derived from *Beelzebub's Tales* with slight changes in wording:

> Faith with reason is freedom.
> Faith with feeling is weakness.
> Faith with body is stupidity.

14. A. R. Orage to JT, March 28, 1927, in JTP 8:2; Douglas Campbell to the authors, September 1, 1982.

> Hope with reason is strength.
> Hope with feeling is slavery.
> Hope with body is disease.

Similarly, he would write out encounters between pupils and include stipulations about their behavior:

Fred and Betty willing. To persuade Betty that Indian life is more desirable than Chicago life.

Max and Pauline agreeing. To convince Pauline that the desire for perfection is a hindrance when it prevents necessary imperfect first attempts.

Mrs. Bliss and Jerry resistant. Try to persuade Jerry that we are living at the dawn of a new and better age.

A group exercise sometimes used for self-observation was the "stop" exercise. The leader might shout "STOP!" or "OBSERVE!" in the midst of any action. Pupils would freeze and reflect instantly on the activity of body and mind, in an effort to catch the fluid moment of transition from one mechanically determined position to another. Toomer describes this as simultaneously exercising "the will, attention, thinking, feeling, and motion." Or a discussion might center on the attainment of the octave, the construct that applied to many levels of development in Gurdjieff's cosmology. Each note represented a stage of behavior and understanding. Each step up the scale brought one closer to perfect harmony, but the steps mi and ti were considered hardest to pass, because to make the next movement, to fa and the ultimate do, a more subtle half step was required. From either of these points, without extra effort, one normally would descend the scale again rather than rising. This was the place a "shock" was needed. If one could pass do, the highest note, one entered the octave above and began a new stage of growth. Participants analyzed their own relative places on the scale and the work they would have to do to move to the next higher state of integration. Mi represented a frequent plateau, for individual members and for the group as a whole.[15]

In addition to the psychological groups, which were his mainstay, Toomer set up at various times groups for reading Gurdjieff's manuscript and attempted, at least once, a weekly "evening for physical and mental exercises and gymnastics." While variety kept the meetings relatively fresh and new, Jean's Chicago groups did not remain static in membership and interest. Some key participants left—Fred Leighton decided to stay more often at his New York

---

15. Bunnell to JT, September 29, 1928, in JTP 1:7; JT notes (JTP 12:5); JT, "Certain Gurdjieff Methods, Self-Observation and Non-Identification" (JTP 67:3), 15.

residence and became a prominent member of Orage's group. Some members remained skeptics, such as William Fackert; when their lives did not perceptibly grow, they dropped out. Sometimes members did not get along, or factionalism between North Side and South Side residents would cause the group to think of itself as blocked in its spiritual growth. Jean Toomer would take several trips a year, principally to New York but also to Santa Fe, the University of Michigan, Montreal, and other places where people might respond well to a Gurdjieff group. When Toomer was gone, the group would be led by someone else, often Jeremy Lane or Fred Leighton. But in most cases, especially during the summer when Jean was at Fontainebleau or Tenant's Harbor, the group would flag. "Somebody says you are coming back the first of October," Jeremy Lane wrote Jean in 1927. "That will be a blessing. I need you and the objective stimulation of your guidance, more than anything else on this planet. We all do." Elise Bunnell, the following autumn, wrote Jean that she had been growing too slowly and needed his presence to stimulate her. "It seems to me the ability to observe has left me," she commented.[16]

Jean Toomer needed the group as much as the group needed him, to the extent that he, too, grew from the association. While Jean never attained the stature of Orage, nor did the Chicago group achieve the importance of the New York group, Chicago became under Jean's leadership an important center in America for the Gurdjieff work. Jean was the Chicago group's personal envoy from Fontainebleau, though, in subtle ways, those in Chicago took certain directives from the New York group. Orage throughout this period wrote Jean as an equal, telling of his plans for his groups in New York, advising him to do more reading of Gurdjieff's manuscripts with his groups in Chicago, and wryly sharing his frustration at Gurdjieff's continuing excessive demands for more money. Early in 1927, Orage had arranged that he and Munson would each send Gurdjieff $500 per month and that Toomer would send $200. Neither Orage nor Munson had private funds to draw on, and Toomer had only what he collected from his groups. Orage from time to time taught personal writing classes, in addition to his heavy schedule of Gurdjieff groups, in order to raise the money. He thought that $1,200 a month should be enough but doubted that it would: "Gurdjieff is really quite extraordinary about money— but not, unfortunately, unique; we've known many people at college and in life equally extraordinary. However, I'm giving him still the benefit of the doubt; and I'm only sorry I cannot give him a million if only to see if he could be impecunious within a month or so of receiving it."[17]

16. Lane to JT, August 22, 1927, in JTP 5:1; Bunnell to JT, September 28, 1928, in JTP 1:7.
17. Orage to JT, February 11, 1927, in JTP 8:2.

Some American group members went to Fontainebleau each summer, though Gurdjieff, concentrating on his writing, did little for them except make seemingly arbitrary rules about their behavior. These visitors were primarily a source of income to keep the establishment afloat. Toomer arranged for some chosen few, like the poet Mark Turbyfill and Jeremy Lane, to become temporary residents there. As the matchmaker, Jean wrote pompous letters of introduction to Gurdjieff, lacking the humility that characterized his personal writing to the master: "[H]e [Lane] is so predominantly emotional in his present state that he could not handle any work of importance. . . . He claims to be eager to reach objective life, whatever his notion of the phrase may be. Give him a task." Jean, further, received considerably more encouragement and praise from the Chicago groups about his writing than he did from any other source. They were a captive audience upon which to test his plays, essays, aphorisms, poems, and novels such as "Transatlantic," "The Gallonwerps," and "The Sacred Factory." Sometimes the symbols were rather clear and thought-provoking, as in this excerpt from "The Earth and Us":

Who says that the Earth is blind?
Who have not seen its tiger-eye
In an almond face,
Who have not met the thousand eyes
Within the Void,
And the one great eye of the belly.

What Life-force, what Sculptor within the body,
What organ is unseeing save that which we are pleased to call our consciousness?[18]

But even when his writings were not so stimulating, his group members had little inclination to be critical. If the message was too abstruse, the pupil was too dense to fathom it; if the symbols were incomprehensible, there was a hidden meaning; if the characters were two-dimensional, they were meant to represent the "chief faults" of the readers. It was, in short, a time when Jean Toomer truly had a tangible following, small and devoted, that he could call his own.

And yet his position had its strains. He wanted to be useful and spiritually advanced, but he also wanted to be famous. These desires pushed him in two directions: to veer once again toward literature, and to enact the boldest experiment of his teaching career. "A Certain Man," a poem of this period, suggests his plight:

18. JT to Gurdjieff, September 6, 1927, in JTP 4:3; JT poem, 1931 (JTP 50:11).

A certain man wishes to be a prince
Of this earth; he also wants to be
A saint and master of the being-world.
Conscience cannot exist in the first:
The second cannot exist without conscience.
Therefore he, who has enough conscience
To be disturbed but not enough to be
Compelled, can neither reject the one
Nor follow the other . . .[19]

19. JT poem, 1930–31 (JTP 50:4) (ellipses in original).

10

Portage

In many ways Jean Toomer's Chicago life was for him an enjoyably stable time. He became a confident and competent leader who knew he had a base for his teachings. Still, behind his success as a Gurdjieff leader lay a desire to build the movement into a greater cause, either through his increasingly psychological writings or through the creation somewhere in America of an institute modeled after Fontainebleau. Throughout his years in Chicago, an undercurrent of restlessness kept him traveling and writing.

Almost as soon as Jean took up permanent residence in Chicago, he continued writing. Far from lapsing, his output of manuscripts increased with his championing the Gurdjieff cause. By the time he was forty, he had written at least four plays, four novels, ten short stories, several variations of an autobiography, and countless poems and essays. What had changed was not his chosen vehicle but his style and his intention. "All of my writings are composed with the view to their effect on contemporary life and future life. . . . My main motive is to produce a to me desirable effect on living people—not to give them an experience of art. The artistic effect—though desired, is secondary." He was trying to use art to convey Gurdjieff's ideas while at the same time attempting to make his style conform to the master's description of "objective art." Ouspensky records a conversation in which Gurdjieff described significant art as "objective." Most art, Gurdjieff claimed, is subjective and therefore accidental, based on random associations and unplanned impressions both in the artist and in the perceiver of the work. Because the true artist knows and understands everything about himself and the object of his art, what he conveys to another through his art will produce one impression only. It will be as flawless as the beauty of an equation.[1] What Jean produced, however, though based on Gurdjieffian themes, did not exactly meet this test.

During his years in Chicago, Toomer wrote "The Gallonwerps," "The Sacred Factory," and "Lost and Dominant." "The Gallonwerps" was a long novel, later turned into a play, about various "types" of people in need of awakening to the Gurdjieffian understanding of life. Each character was said to be modeled on a member of his Chicago group. Jean Toomer appears in this novel as Prince Klondike, the mysterious, autocratic, and omniscient visitor to a party, who brings out the flaws of each guest (thus "waking" them to reality) and then deserts the party with the hostess, the most enlightened one in the gathering. "The Sacred Factory" was a play designed to show the mechanical character of human life, full of meaningless repetition, and as such it is composed more of gesture and symbol than of encounter and involvement. "Lost and Dominant," a collection of stories and poems with settings in New York and Chicago, contains a few powerful pieces. In the fable of Drackman, for example, the business magnate turns into a skyscraper. In "Love on a Train," the protagonist is so bent on efficiency and planning for the future that he lets the precious present slip through his fingers. But there are also turgid, stiff, and characterless explorations of Gurdjieff's ideas as Toomer interpreted them. Many pieces focus on small people who parody the foibles of forgetfulness, selfishness, timidity, ignorance, and greed. Toomer could still write vivid lines, but more often he substituted abstract, analytical statements, which came through simply as dull writing.

As Jean was sending these manuscripts fron one publisher to another, his past was still pursuing him. In the early summer of 1927, "Balo" was finally published in *Plays of Negro Life,* and Jean allowed Countee Cullen to reprint portions of *Cane* in Cullen's anthology *Caroling Dusk.* Just as Toomer was on his way to Fontainebleau that summer, Zora Neale Hurston and Langston Hughes were visiting Sparta, Georgia—a pilgrimage to the source of what was increasingly regarded in black circles as a seminal novel of the Afro-American experience. Nor had Toomer fully abandoned his concern with racial issues. Through the winter of 1927 and early 1928 he was working on a book called "The Crock of Problems," in which the major thesis is that "problems of race . . . exist in the human psyche and nowhere else." In putting this extensive manuscript together—it was a sane, fairly scholarly work—he drew on anthropologists such as Franz Boas, psychologists such as John B. Watson, philosophers such as

1. JT notes, n.d. [*ca.* 1929] (JTP 69:13); P. D. Ouspensky, *In Search of the Miraculous: Fragments of an Unknown Teaching* (New York, 1949), 26–27.

Bertrand Russell, and he gave much credit to A. R. Orage. He also developed his personal position, that he was neither black nor white. The book, rejected by several publishers, was never finished, but out of it came a long article, written in 1928 and published in 1929, called "Race Problems and Modern Society."

In the summer of 1927, however, Jean concentrated on Gurdjieff and Fontainebleau. Leaving his Chicago group under the direction of Jeremy Lane, Jean joined his New York friends and others in France. There the trio that had once been so close, Jean Toomer, Waldo Frank, and Gorham Munson, met again for the last time. For Gorham and Jean, both thoroughly imbued with Gurdjieffian principles and at home in Fontainebleau, the meeting was relatively easy. For Waldo, the brief episode was a terrible ordeal. He was by this time an international celebrity, and his fame, he felt, should count for something; but when he visited le Prieuré, Gurdjieff seemed deliberately to treat him like anyone else.

According to several accounts, Gurdjieff at first simply ignored Frank when he and his new wife Alma visited for the weekend. He was relegated to walking around the grounds with Jean, an event that must have caused Frank considerable discomfort. Finally, Gurdjieff deigned to meet him, but instead of discussing philosophy and mysticism, Gurdjieff indulged in unceremonious banter. At dinner, having seated the Franks on either side of him, Gurdjieff seemed to make them the targets of the dark side of his humor. He toasted Frank and included him in his lexicon of idiots; Elizabeth Munson, sitting next to Frank, tried to make the event humorous, but Frank was offended. By the end of the evening, Gurdjieff had implied that Margaret Naumburg was the better of Frank's wives. Frank left the next day, humiliated and determined to be his own mystic rather than a follower of Gurdjieff.[2]

Jean spent the summer at le Prieuré not only with the Munsons but also with Clare McLure, a member of one of Jean's Chicago groups who had decided to take a year's training at the institute. Her intention was to become a co-leader of the Chicago groups—apparently as Jean's wife. They had become lovers in the spring of 1927. After Jean left for Chicago at the end of the summer, she continued to write him long letters about her development as a Gurdjieff disciple, but she became increasingly suspicious that Gurdjieff was treating her only as a subject for his amusement. It seems that she was accused of theft in a Paris department store. Whether Gurdjieff encouraged her to try it as a test is

2. Interview of Elizabeth Delza Munson, New York, July 7, 1978. See also Gorham Munson, *The Awakening Twenties: A Memoir-History of a Literary Period* (Baton Rouge, 1985).

a mystery—he sometimes created unusual situations for self-observation. Toomer himself set up another ruse, pretending that he was already married, then testing her reaction. Clare first assumed that Edith Taylor had won out. All this "testing" seemed to shake her belief that living with Jean would be easy, but she tried to keep her perspective. She was sent to New York in March to continue her apprenticeship, still expecting that she would join Jean in Chicago and still hoping to marry him. "I understood the affair in France to have been a final test of my year at Prieuré," she wrote Jean in July of 1928. "At that time, from things I have been told, and from my own observations, I thought it was to see if I had the understanding and strength to meet the difficulties of your life and work with you as your wife. When you told me you would never marry except compelled to I was sure that this was the real situation, though for the moment I reacted emotionally." [3]

However misused by Gurdjieff or Toomer, Clare McLure still adhered to Gurdjieff's philosophy. Finally understanding that Jean had no plans to include her in his work, she realized she would remain enshrined only as the humorous character Mrs. Wimepime Gallonwerp in "The Gallonwerps."

Munson found "The Gallonwerps" deplorable but felt that other stories, such as "Winter on Earth," contained glimmers of Jean's old craft. Jean's correspondence with his other friends reveals his high hope about being published—he was writing a new novel, he was on the verge of a literary breakthrough. While his manuscripts were being rejected by such firms as Harcourt, Brace, Coward-McCann, and Harper and by literary agents Brandt and Brandt, Jean visited Paul Rosenfeld in August of 1928 at York Beach. There he began a novel that he first called "Istil" and later "York Beach." It was to be his "novel of American life." Nathan Antrum, the protagonist, is a writer who has realized that his life consists of phases of apparent fulfillment and nonfulfillment, but both are necessary to push him toward something superior to life on earth. Antrum was clearly based on Toomer himself, and the other major character was based on Rosenfeld. Although Jean hoped to expand the book to four hundred pages, he completed only a seventy-page version. This was published the following year with the help of Rosenfeld, who was one of the editors of *The American Caravan,* a yearbook of American literature. In fact already in 1928, Rosenfeld had helped publish "Winter on Earth," a story from the collection "Lost and Dominant." It is a heavily symbolic tale of a winter of excessive cold and a young man who jauntily walks off the edge of the world. The coldness of

3. Claire McLure to JT, July 26, 1928, in JTP 7:3.

human relationships is contrasted with the joy and wisdom and warm interchange among the angel-descended inhabitants of mythical White Island.[4]

In mid September, Jean's grandmother died. He left York Beach for her funeral in Washington, then returned to Chicago. Not satisfied with staying put, he prepared an application for a Guggenheim Fellowship in November, hoping to complete his novel with some generously supported time in Europe; but nothing came of it. Some of his friends were particularly interested in his writing and helped fund him during this period in the perennial hope that the next mail would bring an acceptance from a publisher. One of these was Eugenia Walcott, not a member of Jean's Gurdjieff groups but peripherally interested in the teaching, who lived with her husband Russell in a small community northwest of Chicago. Although Eugenia had an extremely warm regard for Jean, of which her husband might have been jealous, both she and Russell were and remained his good friends all his life. Eugenia, in addition to giving Jean a monthly stipend of $50 during 1929, with an extra $500 occasionally thrown in, would send him off to Brooks Brothers whenever they opened a temporary outlet in Chicago, for an ostensible birthday or Christmas present. With this kind of help, Jean could write in those years, "My grandmother told me, 'Dress well, even if you haven't a penny in your pocket.' It was easy for me to follow her admonition. All my life I have dressed well, in fact, have looked like a million dollars. All my life I've had hardly more than a penny to my name."[5]

The year 1929 saw him no less restless. Gurdjieff arrived in New York in January for his first visit since the early demonstrations of 1923–1924 and insisted he had to have $10,000 within three weeks. Jean was, of course, caught up in the pressure. Orage wrote him in February, when Jean was planning a visit to New York. "We strongly urge that Chicago should make that contribution of $1000 through you; and, so to say, as security for *your* return to Chicago with G's fresh material etc. . . . A subscription that should ensure your obtaining the book, etc. would surely be money well spent by Chicago. I'm very glad you are coming, but, in my opinion, 'Chicago' would be twice welcome bearing gifts."[6] In New York, Munson congratulated Jean on his presence of mind at a very difficult public meeting with Gurdjieff. In May, Jean

4. JT, "York Beach," in Alfred Kreymborg, Lewis Mumford, and Paul Rosenfeld (eds.), *The New American Caravan* (New York, 1929), 12–83; JT, "Winter on Earth," in Kreymborg, Mumford, and Rosenfeld (eds.), *The Second American Caravan: A Yearbook of American Literature* (New York, 1928), 694–715, also in *W&S*, 166–81.

5. JT notebook, 1929–30 (JTP 17:1).

6. A. R. Orage to JT, February 14, 1929, in JTP 8:2.

sent $1,050 to Fontainebleau, probably drawing at least partly on Mabel Luhan's earlier gift.

Soon after, he left to spend the summer in Fontainebleau, going by way of Toronto for a holiday with his friend and follower Douglas Campbell. Eugenia Walcott was concerned that he be properly outfitted for the trip. Had he thought of white flannels and an extra sport coat? "You know even in Toronto you can't dance, fly, play tennis, sail and lounge clad in a fountain pen." In Toronto, Jean fell in love with a young girl called Bay, eighteen or nineteen, of an elevated social set, "a sweet body, immediate and bright as the sunshine." Through the summer, staying at le Prieuré and writing "Transatlantic," he corresponded with her and his heart grew fonder. It seemed to him that marriage was what he needed to cure his restlessness—he was having trouble with drinking, with sex, with finances. For the first time he recorded feeling not the *wish* to drink but the *need* to drink "to put my body in a functioning condition." But alcohol had the opposite effect: it prevented him from functioning clearly and gave him unnaturally wakeful nights as well. He was also smoking heavily, was disgusted at his sexual dalliances, and was disturbed that his personality swung without his intending it from being dominated by his emotions to being dominated by his intellect. Somehow, when he was away from Chicago, his form and control seemed to dissolve. "I will be interested to see what effect on my form results from having a wife and sufficient money. . . . Marriage . . . I desire it in a special form moving in a special way. . . . Marriage is a sane form securing one from insane sex impulses and their consequences." Just before he left France, he wrote Bay seriously about marriage. But a visit with her on his way back to Chicago in early November must have changed his perspective, or hers. He was, of course, almost twice her age; but only after that visit did the salutation in her letters shift from "Jean dear" to "Grandfather dear." [7]

It did not take him long to recover. On December 4, at one of Fred Leighton's lectures on Indian culture, Jean met Emily Otis and was swept away on a far stronger current. Emily, like Bay, was from a moneyed family. She left a Junior League dinner to attend Jean's Gurdjieff group the week after they met, and she promptly invited Jean to the Otis ball, a grand function hosted by her parents in "the crystal ballroom of the Blackstone." She was blond and lovely; he covered her with endearing nicknames: "Angel child! Princess of earth! Bride of the air! Priestess of fire! Pride of the eagle! Beloved of the thunderbird! Dearest

7. Eugenia Walcott to JT, May 23, 1929, in JTP 10:1; JT notebooks, 1929 (JTP 17:1, 69:13); correspondence between JT and Bay, June 22 to December 29, 1929, in JTP 11:2.

of dears!" and, for everyday use, "sweetest of the gooses." He in turn was fondly called "moose" in her notes to him. He found her to be a vivid force that stimulated him to "marvelous functioning." Within a month of their meeting, he had come to the conclusion he should marry her, telling himself, "If this does not happen, the greatest gun yet fashioned in America will never fire." He thought through the consequences: her family would surely object, probably on racial and certainly on financial grounds, and "nasty publicity" about his race might force him to give up the Gurdjieff work. But if this took place, he planned to "utilize this stir as the occasion for launching my plan for the Spiritualization of America, including my ideas as to the American race. . . . My act and Emily's would cease to [be] ours alone, and would become the nation's, yea, the world's." The decision, enfolding these grand purposes, hinged in the end on his own need:

I must marry. My necessary next phase depends on this crucial factor. As long as I am unmarried, . . . my . . . forces will continue being wasted in search, in wishes, in unsatisfying expenditures. I will remain comparatively unstable, uncosmic, unconcentrated, non-building. . . . And, too, I will remain arrested this side of the world which says that because I have dark blood, no matter what else or who I may be, I shall not marry such a one as Emily. . . . I will marry. And when I marry it will be just such a one as Emily.[8]

Toomer sent to Emily, as he had recommended to Mae Wright some years before, the books that meant the most to him, *Wilhelm Meister,* Emily Dickinson, and Blake. He wrote her, during the year, a sheaf of poems—these would form the bulk of the next collection to be sent around to publishers. She, in turn, made her first attempts at creative writing and sent him pieces to criticize. He spent three idyllic days with her and her family at their summer place in Michigan on his way to Montreal and New York in July. But gradually, in early 1931, she began postponing dates with him or giving him second place. She would, for instance, agree to come to tea only if she could appear in the riding habit she wore for an outing earlier the same afternoon. In June of 1931 she wrote to tell him that she was engaged to marry someone else.[9]

Later, as Toomer was writing his autobiography, he considered his romances with Margaret Naumburg and Emily Otis. He believed that each woman had come into his life when he needed her. At a time of withdrawal, when he was questioning the values of the ordinary world, Margaret, being antisocial,

8. JT notes, Chicago, January 4, 1930 (JTP 69:13).
9. Correspondence between Emily Otis and JT, January 5, 1930, to June 29, 1931, in JTP 8:3.

helped him. And then, after he had been in Gurdjieff's extraordinary world, "having already reached a new plane of existence, having already formed my new self," he was ready to emerge again into the ordinary world. Emily, being gaily social and positive toward people, helped him with this phase.[10]

Although Jean was still fully involved with the Gurdjieff work and was still to make another major contribution to it, he was subtly pulling away. Much later he indicated that in the early years of his association with Gurdjieff, he had felt a kind of force flowing through him, which he believed came from the master himself. About a year before he stopped the Gurdjieff work, this force seemed to have left him, and after that it became increasingly difficult for him to continue. In Paris in the summer of 1929 he had noted his shift back to literature:

In the midst of my great work I am becoming literary. . . .
This begins the period of my great writing.
Years hence I will again emerge into the world of pure being.
This is an eclipse of Jean the saint, an emergence of Jean the man in the world and artist.
Salzmann [has said]: "Once you were an eagle. Now you are a sheep."[11]

For funds, he was relying more and more on his writing rather than his groups, and he fell back on his friends when publishers failed to greet his manuscripts with enthusiasm. Although a poem and a small group of aphorisms were published in 1929 in *Dial*, which had published his short story "Mr. Costyve Duditch" the year before, none of his longer manuscripts was accepted. As it turned out, emergency funds for his passage to and from Europe in 1929 came from Eugenia Walcott and Yvonne Dupee. Both times, Jean waited in vain for a publisher's advance, delaying his sailing date until he could be bailed out.

In that year of 1929 he had completed "Transatlantic" and "Essentials." He wrote "Transatlantic," his novel about a steamship passage, in seventeen days while he was at Fontainebleau. The main character, unnamed but clearly Toomer playing himself, provides psychological leadership for his fellow passengers, particularly the women, as he guides them to heightened self-awareness and fulfillment. As "a member of a new race, produced from a blending of bloods which existed in recognized races," this character's attraction for others, the secret of his power, is that he cannot be typed. Toomer plays upon that quality in the novel as he must have in real life. Allusions to his Chicago nicknames,

10. JT Autobiography (JTP 15:13).
11. JT to John Bennett, August 23, 1953, in JTP 11:9; JT notes (JTP 69:13).

such as the Black Swan and the Chicago Prince, as well as to his work as a Gurdjieff leader, make the identification very clear.

"Essentials" was an attempt to sum up all wisdom and experience—the universe according to Jean Toomer—in a collection of aphorisms. Gurdjieff used this technique at Fontainebleau, where his favorite homilies decorated the Study House. Toomer's collection, part of a larger book of essays, poems, and truisms, summarized his commitment to the universal man purveying universal truth:

I am of no particular race. I am of the human race, a man at large in the human
world, preparing a new race.
I am of no specific region. I am of earth.
I am of no particular class. I am of the human class, preparing a new class.
I am neither male nor female nor in-between. I am of sex, with male differentiation.
I am of no special field. I am of the field of being.[12]

When he returned to the United States, Jean asked Melville Cane, a poet and a lawyer who was Margaret Naumburg's brother-in-law, to help him contact publishers. Cane agreed, though he continued to express the hope that Toomer would abandon his experimental stage and return to his old publishable self. In the meantime, Melville Cane as agent could not work magic. "Transatlantic" was rejected by Cape and Smith, Harcourt, Brace, and Macmillan; "Essentials" was rejected by Doubleday, Macmillan, Farrar and Rinehart, Coward-McCann, and Knopf. Through all this and into 1930, Jean finished yet another manuscript, "Earth-Being—The Autobiography of Jean Toomer," and conducted an eight-part lecture series entitled "The Psychology and Craft of Writing." The brochure advertising his lecture series did not mention any of his past writings but projected great optimism for the future, listing his "forthcoming books" as "Transatlantic," "Essentials," "Navarin" (poems and prose), "Winter on Earth" (short stories), and, in preparation, "Individualism in America—A Psychological Study."[13]

His Gurdjieff work continued too, with the master himself visiting Chicago in March. Gurdjieff had returned from Paris to New York to assess the status of his pupils there, both spiritually and financially, and he stayed in New York for what turned out to be several years. In early March, 1930, Toomer (perhaps on the wave of his love for Emily Otis) gave a talk on Gurdjieff's ideas the transcription of which runs to the incredible length of fifty-six double-spaced

12. JT, *Essentials: Definitions and Aphorisms* (Chicago, 1931), 24.
13. Brochure, May, 1930 (JTP 7:12).

pages. Jean's words sparked an ecstatic description from Eugenia Walcott: "What a jag you were on! and the jag was contagious to say the least. I felt as if I were on the tail of a comet. I had the same impulse to shout that one has when swinging far out over a deep ravine. The near future bids fair to hold all kinds of surprises (nice ones I mean) don't you think?"[14] Yet by the end of December, Jean was beginning to withdraw, loosening his attachments and making his groups more independent of his leadership.

The year 1931 was crucial both for Toomer's writing and his Gurdjieff discipleship. Jean had been drawing more attention in Chicago, and Orage somehow displeased Gurdjieff in New York. The master may have visited Chicago in 1930 and early 1931 partly to see whether the Toomer groups adhered to his tenets more than the Orage groups did. Apparently they were no better, for Gurdjieff made no great investment of time there. Fritz Peters, who had lived as a boy at le Prieuré, described the Chicago group he had recently joined:

While Gurdjieff seemed to me to offer a means of acquiring a new point of view towards life, through work and personal struggles, the prevailing attitude of this particular group of followers was that of substituting new values for old by rote, without any consideration of the means. . . .

By and large, the Chicago "group" fitted in with other Gurdjieff "disciples" I had known—people who were content to take on certain ritualistic, physical attitudes which lacked any inner content.[15]

Meanwhile, Gurdjieff seemed to be forcing Orage to break with him and at the same time putting increasing pressure on the groups in both cities for financial support. In February he refused some money sent from Chicago, stating that the sum would have to be the entire amount owed him from Mabel Dodge Luhan's original donation and that Toomer was to deliver it personally. Jean sent a letter of explanation, which Gurdjieff would not read. In addition, Toomer heard at almost the same time that his grandmother's house in Washington, of which he was part owner, was falling into ruin, with mortgage and taxes in default.

Jean was no more successful with the publishing houses. Rejections of "Essentials," "Transatlantic," "The Gallonwerps," a collection of short stories under the title "Winter on Earth," and a collection of poems called "Blue Meridian" continued through July of 1931. Toomer, feeling that his talents were being ignored by the larger audience who still wanted from him another *Cane,* decided to spurn the established publishers and start a publishing firm on his

14. Walcott to JT, May 8, 1930, in JTP 10:1.
15. Arthur [Fritz] Peters, *Gurdjieff Remembered* (New York, 1971), 17, 21.

own. Yvonne Dupee, her brother Charles (Chaunce), and Jean joined together in the hope that such a company would help more writers than just Jean and would become more than just a vanity press. The proposal, probably written by Jean, outlines the general aim: "(1) to establish itself as a profitable publisher and seller of literary books; (2) (a) to become an instrument contributing to the cultural growth of America, (b) to become an instrument contributing to the cultural growth of Chicago in particular." The first of the stated policies explains, really, Jean's own frustrations at not being published and the reasons why he wanted to venture into self-publication:

To encourage, secure, publish, and distribute quality literature dealing with all phases of spiritual experience, but particularly with such experiences as they occur in America. By spiritual experience is meant essential experience, experience concerned with and leading to the full balanced growth and development of human beings.

The field is open for a publisher with such an interest. Most of the first-rate publishers have no particular interest in such material, and, if it is submitted to them, they are likely to reject it. This is because their tastes and their values have been conditioned by 19th century naturalism and rationalism, or by materialism, or by "back to nature and the primitive," exotic, or erotic leanings. They will publish any competent work dealing realistically with things they already know and have experienced.[16]

Jean received advice from Gorham Munson in preparation for this first attempt at private printing. Munson, though admitting later that he thought little of the book, also wrote an introduction to *Essentials,* but it was not used. He encouraged Yvonne Dupee, the primary financier of the proposed firm, to "make it appear as much like a trade edition as you can" in order to extend sales. Mock-ups of the front covers show that Jean was interested in publishing several of his works that had been rejected elsewhere, but what went to press first was *Essentials,* with the subtitle *A Philosophy of Life in Three Hundred Definitions and Aphorisms.* A flyer promoting the book reveals what Toomer was hoping to become known for: "An increasing number of thoughtful people are recognizing the power, intelligence, and literary artistry of Jean Toomer. He is already known as a lyric poet, as a writer of distinguished prose, as a brilliant lecturer. This volume will introduce him as a philosopher of crystalline understanding."[17]

This, then, was a supreme effort to move Toomer beyond the confines of his Chicago group and into national prominence as a philosopher-writer. At this time the Chicago group, too, needed a "jolt" out of its customary behavior.

16. JT proposal (JTP 64:15).
17. GM to JT, March 1, 1931, in GMC; JT flyer (JTP 65:18).

Jean's frequent and prolonged absences from Chicago caused difficulties for the group. Jeremy Lane was doubting his own ability to lead; others were convinced that the core group was static and, in some ways, even counterproductive. Max Grove, the "strong, silent one" of the central group, pinpointed the trouble and offered a solution. "The past year the group seemed to take on more and more the aspect of a funeral," he wrote, "settling into their over-stuffed coffins with sweet contentment, listening to the eloquent exposition that five years ago would have been eloquent explosions." Grove was restless and began wishing for something other than lectures or the revelation of what seemed now to be stale ideas. As an alternative, he "would wish for some kind of laboratory in fact, rather than theory, such as has now been projected." [18]

That possibility must have captured Toomer's imagination, since he too felt that the Chicago group was "though deeply satisfied, fatigued." [19] Not that there was an absence of new blood. Those in the group were constantly bringing new friends to hear Jean and to participate in the meetings. At one such gathering, a young writer from Portage by the name of Margery Latimer first met Jean, and the course of both of their lives changed from that point. More than any other event at that time, their romance and marriage were testimony to the impact that Jean Toomer could have on the lives of those around him.

When Margery Latimer first met Jean Toomer, she was thirty-one and an accomplished author, having already published three books, including her most recent novel *This Is My Body*. She was on the brink of a phenomenal career as a writer who dealt with the issues of womanhood with, for the time, uncharacteristic frankness. The writer Meridel LeSueur, who was her closest friend, recalls that Margery's books, which contained "the unmasking of the female dilemma . . . the sexual frankness and the depiction of the unromantic woman," were "revolutionary." Despite her literary accomplishments, however, her personal life was unsettled after a series of unfulfilling relationships, and she was looking for a permanence with a man that could stave off her seemingly endless turmoil. Before meeting Toomer, Margery Latimer was under the tutelage of the Wisconsin writer Zona Gale, who, while directing Margery's writing career, also managed Margery's life. Margery's parents and Zona were friends; Zona personally provided a scholarship so Margery could attend the University of Wisconsin. Zona then tried to run Margery's career, both in New York City after Margery had left the university and later back in Portage when Margery returned home to seek a less hectic environment in which to write.

18. Max Grove to JT, January 25, 1931, in JTP 4:1.
19. JT, "Portage Potential: An Adventure in Human Development" (Typescript in MTC), 3.

Margery's letters to friends indicate that she apparently felt chained to her relationship with Zona, and in many ways she feared it; yet Zona Gale's patient constancy overpowered her resistance. Her friends in turn noticed Zona's dominance in her life. Lewis Mumford wrote Margery in 1929: "I think particularly that I must have wanted to say something to you about Zona Gale: how she appears to me a King Charles's head, which keeps bobbing up in your writing, and making you take pot shots at it. Perhaps I ought to tell you: Slay that woman. Release yourself: all grudge and gratitude must vanish, perhaps, together." [20]

It was Zona Gale who first interested Margery Latimer in Gurdjieff. Soon after Margery arrived in New York City, Zona sent her and her roommate Mavis McIntosh (a University of Wisconsin graduate who had also received one of Zona's scholarships) tickets to attend a Gurdjieff demonstration in January of 1926. Both women attended and then began going to the Orage groups along with, ironically, Jean Toomer and Margaret Naumburg, though Margery and Jean were strangers in the group. Margery, before becoming fully involved, stopped attending altogether, insisting that adherence to the Gurdjieffian method would ruin her ability to write. She returned to Portage, ostensibly free of Gurdjieff's influence. [21] Yet through mutual friends she heard of Jean Toomer in late 1930, and then she obtained a copy of *Essentials*. Impressed by the book of aphorisms, she asked Shirley Grove whether she could become part of Jean's lecture series and group work in Chicago, and in May she accomplished just that.

Margery Latimer was ready for someone like Jean Toomer. The tone of most of her letters before meeting Toomer was fluttery and wildly dependent. To her friend Katharine Green she wrote: "I could hardly bear it, reading your letter, I could hardly *breathe*." She admitted to several friends, including a rejected lover, that she wanted a father figure who could give her direction without destroying her, a man who "is superior to me. I want to be in love." Her first visit to one of Jean's sessions caused an instantaneous euphoria: "Then Toomer came and sat beside me on the couch and when I didn't look at him I could feel myself changing inside, growing quieter, all merging inside, all turning to cool moving water, all my elements. . . . And Jeremy Lane and his wife and myself—I felt we were three shoots of corn, so young and tender and naive, growing from the ground and being warmed by the sun of this man who stood

20. MLeS to the authors, October, 1982; Lewis Mumford to Margery Latimer (hereinafter ML), June 21, 1929, in collection of State Historical Society of Wisconsin, Madison.
21. McIntosh interview.

looking at us." This image of regeneration was a continuing part of her description of herself with Jean Toomer. She had been so convinced of the destructive nature of relationships that when she found a group naturally supportive of each other, she could describe the experience primarily in religious terms: "I have been washed of all evil. I am clean. Now I can choose." [22]

Margery wanted so badly to continue the group experience that she invited Jean Toomer, the Lanes, the Groves, and Yvonne Dupee to stay in Portage. A small and isolated cottage near Bonnie Oaks, the estate where Katharine Green lived, was available for rent, and Margery was willing to pay the fee. This ideal retreat was in the woods near a stream called the Big Slough, yet close enough to Portage for supplies and brief respites in more comfortable homes. So Margery and Katharine prepared the cottage for guests, and Jean and some of his group came out to Portage to try living there for a week. Portage seemed an appropriate place for Jean to set up a group experiment, for it was "plain straight good American. . . . It had an atmosphere of its own, a quiet sincere quality." [23]

Although they had not yet agreed on a summer experiment, it was clear that Toomer was to be the focus of the group. By sheer activity he helped energize those around him, particularly Margery Latimer. "He was beautiful," she observed in a decidedly partial way, "in the water, dancing, playing golf, driving the car, speaking, embracing all of us, laughing, eating. . . . I got what I have longed for in men—rebirth." Later in her letter she described her initial reaction to the group experience at the Big Slough: "We worked together wonderfully and at first I resented the physical friendliness, the constant embracing and tenderness of the men for all the women, and then that thing in me that causes so much suffering seemed to change. I had a complete realization, a complete experience of life, and the following day when I realized that Jean was trying to give this to every one I thought I couldn't live." [24]

The week's trial in June solidified plans to establish an experimental workshop for group living and self-observation for the rest of the summer. While Toomer was back in Chicago gathering people and equipment, including a magnificent used Pierce-Arrow, Margery Latimer arranged to rent the cottage for the rest of the summer. During the next two months, people from Chicago, Portage, and other nearby places would come to the improbable little Gurdjieff center, but a core of devotees led by Toomer stayed the entire summer. They were undergoing what to them was a vital psychological experiment, "a labo-

22. ML to Katharine Green, March 5, 1930, in JTP 5:15; ML to MLeS, May 31, 1931, ML to Jane Comfort, May, 1931, ML to Shirley Grove, May 1, 1931, all in JTP 5:18.
23. JT, "Portage Potential," 6.
24. ML to MLeS, n.d., in JTP 5:18.

ratory of consciously controlled events." Those who were aware of the ground rules realized that they were there to be observed and, to a certain extent, controlled by Jean Toomer. It was he who organized the day's proceedings, who established household and shopping duties and the seating pattern at table—the two men, the "Captain" and "Chief Officer," at head and foot—and who gave lectures or readings after supper. Toomer would select a topic or a text, usually his own, for the evening's presentation and would explore its various theoretical and practical applications. The individual listener was expected to relate the significance of the observations to his or her own circumstances. Toomer seldom made specific references to people in the room; it was up to them to reach to the truth that was available to them. As Katharine Green pointed out, many casual visitors to the Big Slough or to Toomer's lectures, which were occasionally held in Portage homes, were intrigued more by Jean's magnificent delivery and low-key authority than by the obscure philosophy he was trying to present. But the purpose of the lectures and the readings, as of the entire summer experiment, was to explore the individual's ability to break away from behavioral patterns that by cultural expectations or by personal habit had constrained human potential.[25]

While all those who became involved in the Portage experiment were subject to the same controls, Margery Latimer was the one probably affected most, for the two fell in love. It was nevertheless love of a Pygmalion sort, with Jean's obligation being to transform her into the woman he felt she should be. This desire to "improve" her began with the first impression he had of her at the Big Slough: "She had a fine woman's body, a sensitive fine-featured face, large grey-blue eyes full of light, and a wealth of wavy golden-russet hair. . . . I noticed something, however, which I did not like. She was wearing an 'anti-feminine-male-protest garb.' . . . This habit failed to enhance her fine features; on the contrary it tended to neutralize them and bring out features which were false for [Margery]."[26] It appears from Jean's and others' accounts that he made Margery Latimer his special project for the summer. Many certainly felt changed by the experiment, but Margery's transformation was spectacular and embodied what the experience was intended to do.

It was well known to others, and later to Margery Latimer herself, that she relied on her creative talent almost entirely for her self-esteem. So when she was ignored or otherwise slighted, she felt insecure to the point of outrage.

25. JT, "Portage Potential," 10. A summary of the day-to-day proceedings and a description of the lectures are given by Katharine Green, in taped interview by Robert Twombly, March 21, 22, 1975 (State Historical Society of Wisconsin, Madison).

26. JT, "Portage Potential," 7.

Throughout the summer, Jean placed her in situations, frequently without her knowledge, where she was forced to relate to others without depending on her reputation as a writer. Sports was one example. Not especially confident or even competent, she was engaged by the group in such a way that she discovered an awkwardness that left her jealous of others and angry at herself. Jean worked with her on self-perception, usually by playing on her side at deck tennis or croquet and by swimming with her. Gradually, she attained a grace and a competence that pleased her and surprised others.

One of the best examples of Margery Latimer's creative growth that summer was her decision to read an essay by her friend Meridel LeSueur to the group after supper. In the evenings Jean, if he did not lecture, would read some of his writings; but that evening Margery Latimer made an effort, so others thought, to upstage him. Jean pointed out that Margery "had a strong and almost unshakable conviction that though she did not know much about people her judgments of literature were right and absolute." Having read the article aloud, she was dismayed that no one in the room seemed to treat the reading with more than mild interest. She could not believe that the article should fall so dead on a group of people whom she had already assumed to be among the most enlightened in America. What she failed to realize was that they were responding to her aggressiveness, not to the article. Margery exploded. "How I hate every one of you. How dare you be casual about this. You can't be casual about essential things. . . . Oh, I'd like to have a hatchet and kill every one of you." [27] Even though Jean quietly agreed that the group's reaction was extreme, it was not enough for her emotional state. She left the Big Slough.

After two days, when Toomer went to her home to ask her to come back, she returned, still worried about her "possessiveness and my vanity and my longing for special treatment." From her standpoint, she was aware that Toomer was working on her, trying particularly to move her from an "emotional type" to one whose emotional, intellectual, and physical centers were integrated. She determined to place herself "in Jean Toomer's hands, having fully experienced the peril and suffering in self surrender to others." [28]

From Jean Toomer's standpoint, he was doing what he was trying to do with others: "to break the deadlock by increasing her desire *to be free of herself* until this desire is the intense expression of all her being. She had only herself mainly to contend with. And the second thing she must do is act on herself." In trying to be psychologically free of Zona Gale, Margery was inclined to withdraw

27. *Ibid.*, 95; ML to MLeS, summer, 1931, in JTP 5:18.
28. ML to MLeS, July, 1931, in JTP 5:18; JT, "Portage Potential," 357.

into her emotions and to feel trapped. Toomer had a design to move her out of this self-pity: "Under no circumstances should she allow herself to brood, commisserate [sic] herself and work up a tragedy. If she does, she will imprison herself and her emotions, and neither her own mind or body nor any other person's mind and body will be able to reach and aid her. Her mind is not greatly involved in this thing. Her body is practically untouched. All the trouble is seated in her feelings." [29]

Margery tried to speak with Jean about her difficult relationship with Zona Gale, but she could broach the subject only indirectly. Jean, knowing the problem, did not interpret for her but patiently waited while she made several embarrassed attempts to speak to him privately. One evening she addressed a question to the group at the dinner table. Expecting a direct response, she was startled when Toomer and others shifted the conversation quite casually to other topics. Margery reacted with her usual temperament: she was so angry she wanted to strike them. "But after an instant it was gone and I realized that my question had been completely answered the night before. I glanced at Jean Toomer in humiliation and I said, 'Forgive me for asking that. You covered it all last night in your talk.' Then I felt overcome at the thought of my goose-like stupor the night before and my harping incessantly on the same kind of question. I thought of him in the world speaking to the deaf and mute like myself." This ability to look outside herself to find comfort culminated in an experience the following day when Katharine Green began to cry with happiness at the sight of a newborn calf, and Margery empathically shared in her friend's emotions. According to Jean, this moment was a turning point in her life because from then on she was able to "spiritualize experience." And indeed, this is what seemed to happen. She began feeling more comfortable as a woman and therefore more secure with men and other women. She quotes Toomer as having said one night at dinner, "You know this kind here, this Margery, thought it was enough to be the author of a book called 'This Is My Body' and all the time she was neglecting her body. My God, all the time she knew nothing about her body and wasn't even using it or expressing anything with it." [30]

The experiment was, by most accounts, a success. Jean Toomer asked each of the major participants to write him about their reactions to the summer. These letters he incorporated verbatim, having changed only the names, at the end of "Portage Potential," a book he wrote during the following winter summarizing

29. JT, "Portage Potential," 23.
30. Ibid., 28–30; ML to Carl Rakosi, August, 1931, in JTP 5:18.

the significance of the experiment. Most of the statements acknowledged a freeing of the mind from restricting habits, a greater self-perception that allowed realistic knowledge of personal limitations as well as possibilities. Some, the casual visitors, were less moved. Elise Bunnell, for instance, who came late in the summer, was impressed not with "Jean Toomer the extraordinary man of action" but with "Jean Toomer, the ordinary man in love."[31] Others, particularly the two women who battled him and each other most with their egos, Yvonne Dupee and Margery Latimer, felt indebted to him for controlling what they eventually perceived as their self-destructive impulses.

Yvonne Dupee, in a long self-analysis, described how Toomer forced individuals into situations in which they could test themselves:

I have had unconsciously always a fear of being unable to function if I became ruffled in any way. I have in consequence always avoided situations of people who might affect me in this way. Last summer it was impossible to so arrange things. Jean Toomer, knowing this trait and how it handicapped me in every way, saw to it that at the moments I wished most to appear calm and to be poised, I was most ruffled—before conducting a large group meeting, for instance; and also that I had to go on to the thing I was to do in spite of it. When I realized that this had actually happened and nothing serious in any sense occurred—that I could do even difficult things in a ruffled state—the spell was broken. This too was extremely releasing.

Margery Latimer in particular noted the sense of breaking the spell of inhibitions, especially in relation to her writing. Instead of displacing her anger into unfulfilled characters in her novels, she determined to affirm her own life through her writing: "In intensifying the positive side of me he gave me the desire to write of positive fulfilling experiences instead of the dark negative fruitless ones I had been writing about." In a letter to Meridel LeSueur, Margery Latimer revealed how Jean Toomer felt about his own transition from the destructive to the fruitful: "Jean said I belonged with the group now who affirm life and then write about all the negative things, like a crucified person recording his wounds. He said, 'I wrote the story of a negro lynching and they want me to keep on writing that over and over, feeling crucified myself. They want me to keep on with that forever.'" As a conclusion to the summer and a direction for her life, she stated in her article for Jean's book, "I want to know value, how to respect, how to love utterly with none of the sly defenses, I want to know how, after much disbelief and disillusionment, to believe with my whole being so that I would die for one valuable true thing so sure would I be of its rightness and value."[32]

31. JT, "Portage Potential," 341.

32. Ibid., 311, 359; ML to MLeS, October, 1931, in JTP 5:19 (ellipses in original); JT, "Portage Potential," 359.

It would be simplistic to attribute too much prophecy to these words, but Margery Latimer believed with her whole being that marrying Jean Toomer and having a child by him were sure and right and valuable; and she was dead within a year. There is tragedy in her death because she died before her life as a writer, wife, and mother was fulfilled. Nevertheless, from her letters to her family, her friends, and her literary colleagues, she saw that married year as the happiest time of her life, the only year she felt truly creative rather than destructive, and free of constraining relationships with those who had surrounded her since childhood. She was, as she put it, "a new person, created by him"; and to bind this "rightness," they were married in a conventional service at the Portage Episcopal Church on October 30, 1931, with many of the Big Slough participants and several Portage citizens in attendance. The local papers recorded the event with society-page neutrality, even though Jean had announced to the press two days before the wedding that their marriage heralded a symbolic union for the creation of an American race. He proclaimed "the birth of a new order, a new vision, a new ideal of man" to replace the "outworn" classification of "white, black, brown, red." Margery's response to the racial question was more personal. After describing Jean's actual background to a friend, she wrote:

People in Portage think J. is an East Indian. He looks very much like one, that color—beautiful rich skin, gold shade, very fine features, and bones, very tall and slender, beautiful mouth, very sleek hair and fine hands. My mother knew about the racial thing and for a time felt quite agitated. Then when she saw that he really is the right person for me she jumped the hurdle and now we are enormously happy. . . . You don't know how marvelously happy I am and my stomach seems leaping with golden children, millions of them, and my head is all purged of darkness and struggle and misery.[33]

As a tangible manifestation of his universal vision, Jean sought to establish a permanent institute, modeled after Fontainebleau, for continuing his experiments in group living and self-awareness. Shirley Grove, upon her return to Chicago after her summer at Portage, initiated a plan to have a group of Jean's most devoted followers purchase a house and live there under his supervision. There was a major effort to raise money. While Jean and Margery remained in Portage, some—but only a few—donated the amount that Jean required to make the offer worthwhile. Yvonne's sister Helen Dupee helped sponsor a series of eight literary evenings beginning on Wednesday, October 22, just before Jean and Margery were to be married. In a series of publicity items related to

33. ML to MLeS, October, 1931, in JTP 5:19; JT announcement superscribed "(written for publication a few days before my marriage)," October, 1931 (JTP 17:9); ML to Rakosi, October, 1931, in JTP 5:19.

the lectures, Jean reflected on the book he had published eight years ago: "There can be no cumulative and consistent movement, and of course no central plot to such a book. It is sheer vaudeville. But if it be accepted as a unit of spiritual experience, then one can find in *Cane* a beginning, a progression, a complication, and an end. It is too complex a volume to find its parallel in the Negro musical comedies so popular on Broadway. *Cane* is black vaudeville. It is black super-vaudeville out of the South."[34] Jean's efforts to move himself from "vaudeville" to aphoristic philosophy, and his friends' efforts to raise money for a house and for Jean's $5,000 fee, fell through by November. The lecture series was not successful. One thousand copies of *Essentials* were printed. Some sold for three dollars each, but sales were poor. And the Great Depression was too much for several of Jean's followers who, instead of donating money for an institute in Chicago, were discovering that their salaries were being cut back. Several agreed that the summer experience was valuable and that they wanted to continue group sessions and lectures with Jean, but a return to their own homes and to their "normal" lives seemed more important than establishing a communal society.

There was still the possibility that Mabel Dodge Luhan and her connections in New Mexico could support a Gurdjieff institute. In mid November, Jean and Margery drove to Santa Fe, where they were guests of one of Mabel's friends. There he set up groups for lectures, wrote the first draft of "The Cottage Experiment," and talked to several people about settling in Santa Fe. A permanent home for Jean's work was not forthcoming, however; the enterprise was too expensive for the economic conditions. In December the Toomers decided to continue their honeymoon in California. Evelyn Hood, a former member of one of Jean's Chicago groups, had moved to San Diego and wanted him to begin a Gurdjieff group in the West. They stayed briefly with her, Toomer giving a few lectures, and then traveled to Pasadena, where Jean gave a series of lectures sponsored by Ruth Ware, another former member of the Chicago group. Finally in March the Toomers rented a house in Carmel overlooking the ocean. Because Carmel was known for its intellectual and creative spirit, Jean thought he could successfully combine writing and lecturing. Margery and Jean quickly became part of Carmel's social milieu, which included Mabel's friends Robinson Jeffers and Lincoln Steffens.

Far from settling down into a routine, their married life became filled with unexpected pressures. By now Margery knew she was pregnant, which excited her; but her pregnancy was not easy. Jean's Chicago group was struggling along

34. JT publicity note (JTP 17:3).

without his presence, reviewing his "Cottage Experiment" manuscript, which was now called "Portage Potential." Other than that, they had no direction and were in danger of disbanding altogether. Worse, he received little encouragement from Chicago or from New York to publish his account of the Portage experiment. Toomer felt that "Portage Potential" was a just tribute to the Gurdjieffian philosophy and cause. He believed that his account was "genuine" and thus in the spirit of objective art. "One should take it as if Gurdjieff had written it," he wrote to Gorham Munson, who was still active in the New York group. "True, it has not G.'s craftiness, but neither have I nor any of us."[35]

"Portage Potential" was rejected on all sides. Munson was distressed that Toomer was trying to get it published. At first, Munson felt that Toomer was "completely out of touch with the shifts of opinion produced by Mr. G.'s stay in New York. . . . I can easily foresee how it will play precisely into the hands of Mr. G.'s enemies." Munson later attempted to tell his friend what he thought of Jean's new writing style:

One thing I will mention are the occasional traces in it of the influence of Mr. G.'s style on you. These I think unfortunate, and I have been hoping in the past that you would see for yourself that G.'s "sublime egoism" at moments is unapproachable by us when we write, and that you would see the difference between his vernacular raciness and what I must call your lapses into wooden colloquialism. . . . Many people are waiting to pounce on the first avowed Gurdjieff exposition that comes along, so we must beware, lest we ourselves work harm to the system of ideas we love.

Clifton Fadiman, then working for Simon and Schuster, rejected the manuscript (as did two other publishing houses in quick succession) with a similar warning: "I believe very deeply that since CANE (which had genius in it) you have traversed the wrong road." Toomer responded to Fadiman with an impassioned defense of the Gurdjieff work and "Portage Potential," insisting that its value was evident outside the tight New York circles: "You will pardon me for being a bit tart of this matter of audience. . . . But I have found an audience of several thousand for my lectures. And even for a book of aphorisms I found over five hundred direct readers." To Munson he wrote that there was a "wall" in the publishing world barring him from his rightful access to legitimate publication. "Well," he said, "we'll smash it."[36]

The "smash" came from the opposite direction, however, in an unexpected way, curiously playing out the script Jean had privately written in January, 1930, when he was thinking of marrying Emily. A reporter for the *Wisconsin*

35. JT to GM, March 10, 1932, in GMC.

36. GM to JT, February 29, March 4, 1932, JT to GM, February 9, 1932, all in GMC; JT to Clifton Fadiman, February 9, 1932, in JTP 3:3.

News in Milwaukee had written a story about the gossip that filled Portage after the summer experiment. A reporter from a San Francisco paper, having access to the Wisconsin story and hearing of Jean's fame and attempts to start Gurdjieff groups in California, interviewed Jean in Carmel. Jean carefully delineated his philosophical views, but the article generally ignored them and instead emphasized the sensational aspects of the communal life at the Portage experiment and the courtship and marriage of a racially mixed couple. The story was copyrighted by the syndicates and versions appeared in papers across the country. "NEGRO WHO WED WHITE WRITER SEES NEW RACE" stated one headline, hardly calculated to convince readers that traditional race definitions were outmoded. The black papers picked up the story as a form of race pride. "AMERICA, THE RACIAL MELTING POT" boasted the headline from the *Gazette* in Cleveland. The story became distorted to the point that the *Amsterdam News* in New York stated that Margery's parents—not her ancestors—were "Anne Bradstreet, poet, and John Cotton, noted clergyman and magazine writer." The culmination of this unwanted publicity was in an article in *Time* under "Races." Entitled "Just Americans," the article focused by innuendo on miscegenation and belittled what appeared to be Toomer's elaborate rationalization for marrying a white woman.[37]

This all put undue pressure on a marriage that was already suffering from too much idealization. Jean championed their union as symbolic of the new American race; Margery championed Jean as her savior. Neither view could have been sustained for long without the normal human idiosyncrasies interfering, and to have their marriage perverted so publicly was hard for two expansive yet fragile egos to bear. Part of Jean's reaction was to put his frustration on paper, this time in a narrative called "Caromb," which attempted to state yet again the significance of a marriage devoted to self-revelation and love. Caromb is the town of Carmel; the two characters, John and Marian, are Jean and Margery. If one believes that Toomer followed his own precepts of objective art, the description he gives probably reflects fairly accurately their brief, traumatic time in Carmel.

Marian is portrayed as a psychologically frail and dependent woman, so nervous about their rented cottage by the sea that she cannot go up on the balcony or the second floor at night. She sleeps in a small room off the living room in a bed just big enough for her; John sleeps in the living room, where she feels he

37. Washington *Telegram,* March 18, 1932 (Schomburg Collection, New York Public Library); Cleveland *Gazette,* March 26, 1932 (JTP 64:18); *Amsterdam News,* August 24, 1932 (Schomburg Collection); *Time,* March 28, 1932, p. 19.

can protect her without adding to her excessive fear of shadows. John has recently come out of a situation (the Portage experiment is not named but is clearly suggested here) where he took willing people down in the depths and helped them come up again and swim. This, he states, grew out of an experience of his own, when "several years ago, life took me down—and then, by grace, I came up."[38] Marian is pregnant and is subject to emotional extremes; John is presented as the one capable of keeping her in control.

John, evidently well known, is not surprised when national news media pick up publicity about him. A reporter asks if he can interview John about his theories and take pictures of both of them. They accede to the interview but are reluctant about the pictures; they finally agree on the condition that they see the photographs before publication. The reporter is fresh-faced and innocent, the kind of man that Marian intuitively fears. She holds back, but John convinces her that if they refuse the interview, they will be hounded even more. But the reporter has deceived them: his story is not just for the local paper but for a syndicate, and he uses the photos without their review. Suddenly other reporters are telephoning them, sensational headlines begin to appear, and the positive publicity they had hoped for is twisted into gossip. Unlike the real stories, Toomer's fictional description of the incident contains no hint of racial slurs. Toomer tries to illustrate the bewilderment of a couple who publicly espouse love and life when the norms of the nation conspire against this attitude. Love and life are taboo in Carmel and America: "[T]hey were violating a league of hate to love each other, . . . she was violating a league of death to have a child."[39]

The view that they were combating an entire nation may seem extreme, but at times they must have felt so persecuted. They were receiving hate mail and calls, reading about themselves as lascivious lovers (Toomer's collection of articles about their marriage was extensive), and responding to desperate letters from Portage claiming that those who had participated in the Portage experiment were about to lose their jobs. Margery herself felt ruined. One Portage friend actually sent a letter—a parallel to one in the novel—suggesting that in light of the media coverage, some people thought the book "Portage Potential," and perhaps even the experiment itself, had been set up by Jean as a publicity stunt. The friend asked him to show his good faith by stopping his efforts to publish the book.[40]

38. JT, "Caromb" (Typescript in JTP 32:4), 43.

39. *Ibid.*, 74.

40. Margery Latimer Toomer (hereinafter MLT) to Harrison Smith, April, 1932, in JTP 6:3; Sara Roberts to MLT and JT, March 17, 21, 1932, both in JTP 8:9.

Yet the support from his personal circle was significant. Fred Leighton and others from the Chicago group wrote letters to the editors denouncing the articles and sent the Toomers encouraging notes of sympathy. Zona Gale, Meridel LeSueur, and other friends of Margery's also sent letters of support; Dorothy North, though she was not a participant in the Chicago groups, sent them money to tide them over their "heavy worry." The artists' colony in Carmel also tried to make the Toomers as welcome as possible and decried the articles as scandal-mongering. A list of prominent citizens, from the mayor (who was a poet) to writers and artists and businessmen, attested to the Toomers' importance in American culture and the importance of their presence in Carmel—but even these accounts were headlined "Colored Sage, White Bride Join Art Set" and "Carmelites Greet Negro Poet, Bride." They attended social functions, often with some discomfort, not because they felt unwanted, but because their mission in life seemed utterly different from what people in Carmel were doing. Margery records how Jean endured the "stony" cynicism of Robinson Jeffers and of Lincoln Steffens, whose attitudes Toomer was determined to counter in his writing. In the face of observations such as Steffens' "Truth is an old whore pursuing people" and Jeffers' "No one ever said anything important when he was sane," Toomer remained in their company with a calm that impressed her: "And Jean was so silent, so beautiful looking, his skin so dark and smooth and gleaming, his eyes so strange and risen looking, as if he had risen from all that he was." Toomer explained to Margery his resistance to the Jeffers-Steffens frame of mind, by parable: "One way to clean a room is certainly by trying to remove the dirt. Another way is to open windows and let the sun burn it away and the clean air blow it away. In any case, it helps to have the window open when one is cleaning."[41]

Even in the midst of this turmoil Jean and Margery both tried to write with a positive point of view. Jean was working on "Caromb"; Margery began an account of the Portage experiment and then started to write a social novel. The characters' names in the book she abandoned—Mrs. Longmere, Clara Bull, Porter Meek—illustrate the influence Jean Toomer (and indirectly George Gurdjieff) had on her writing, an influence that was not necessarily good.

Nevertheless, she had publishers interested in her work in a way that her husband was still trying to obtain. During the late winter and early spring of 1932, Margery was preparing her next book for publication, a collection of short stories entitled *Guardian Angel*, the name of the first and most ambitious

41. Dorothy North to JT, June 20, 1932, in JTP 7:21; *Monterey Peninsula Herald*, March 17, 1932 (JTP 64:18), 7; MLT to MLeS, March, April, 1932, both in JTP 6:2, 6:3.

story.[42] The stories chronicle Margery's own growth from what she perceived as a childlike dependence on others. In "Guardian Angel," written in Portage before Margery's marriage, a strong older woman, Fleta, sets standards for young Vanessa. Vanessa asks Fleta whether she should marry a particular man. Fleta diminishes the man's attractiveness, calling him a "nice little fellow"; Vanessa knows she can never marry him, thus acknowledging the power Fleta still has over her. The young woman finally breaks away from the older woman's control, just as Margery Latimer forced herself to become liberated from Zona Gale.

Marriage was a difficult decision for Margery. It is clear from her letters that she was seeking a father figure, one who, in her own words, could take care of her and quiet her mercurial emotions. In two other short stories, Margery's persona asks some people whether she should marry, implying that their opinion will be her decision. In the penultimate story "Marriage Eve," the woman returns to her father's house to seek his permission to marry. With embarrassed affection, he releases her, saying "[S]ure—go ahead." Margery concludes her book with a sketch of marital happiness, though against the backdrop of her dark past. "Monday Morning" expresses Margery's joy with Jean and her hope for a family. Margot, the protagonist, moves through a morning of domestic peace. She and her husband share small moments with each other, cooking eggs and planning names for their expected child. Hardly able to contain her joy, Margot concludes with a prayer. "I have a child inside me. . . . I love my husband. I love the world. Thank you, God."[43]

In spite of Margery's expressions of marital joy, the Toomers were unable to settle into an outer stability that would allow them to feel at home. Having failed to set up a permanent Gurdjieff center in the West, they went to Portage in August and then to Chicago, where Margery was to have their child. From early on in their marriage, Margery longed to have a baby, but the discovery that she had a heart leak filled her with trepidation. The day before she gave birth, soon after reading the galley proofs of *Guardian Angel,* she wrote Meridel LeSueur, "[T]oday I feel ripe and round and ready. . . . My stomach feels *done*. Quite finished. Quite complete." The next day, with a midwife in attendance, Margery held her baby daughter Margery and smiled, then lapsed into a coma from hemorrhaging.[44]

42. Margery Latimer, *Guardian Angel and Other Stories* (1932; rpr. Freeport, N.Y., 1971; rev. ed., Old Westbury, N.Y., 1984).

43. ML, *Guardian Angel* (1971), 294, 308.

44. MLT to MLeS, September 15, 1932, in JTP 6:4; JT to Mr. Holmes, n.d., in JTP 4:9.

Margery's death was in some ways as controversial as her marriage, at least to Portage's small-town sensibilities. Zona Gale reported that Margery lived for twelve hours after the child's birth but was not taken to the hospital. Whether this was the case or not, Margery's decision to give birth at home was risky, especially in view of the known physical complications. The end of her life, a product of her ten-month marriage, by necessity encompassed Jean, whom some from Portage held responsible for Margery's fate. At the laying out, in the Latimer home in Portage, friends of the family thought that Jean and members of his Gurdjieff groups were impassive and detached to the point of indifference. When asked why Margery had died, Jean replied with a philosophical composure understandable to those in the Gurdjieff movement but probably shocking to grieving friends, "It was her time." But the Latimers never presumed any fault in Jean and retained a warm relationship with him thereafter. Jean announced at the funeral that he would soon gather close friends together and give a talk about the significance of Margery's life and death, but nothing came of this announcement.[45]

When Margery died, so in many respects did Jean Toomer's potential as a Gurdjieff leader. The hope for a permanent Gurdjieff institute led by Toomer became less of a possibility, and Toomer retreated from conspicuous leadership in group psychological experiments. Whether Margery's death or the public controversy over the marriage had much to do with this change is hard to say. In an appropriately Gurdjieffian way he considered her death as another facet of his spiritual growth. "I . . . felt Margery's amazing purity," Toomer wrote, "the sense she gave of being a special creation. I felt this while she lived, and her death gave me one of the deepest religious experiences I've ever had." While idealization is easier in memory than in the present, if Jean's description of their marriage is at all accurate in "Caromb," Margery retained her belief in the special quality of the marriage as long as she lived. Her statement of the spiritual harmony and growth that Toomer had publicly declaimed before the wedding is contained in a short piece she wrote toward the end of her life. It was published in the local paper at her death: "And inside you, Town, I had suffered, and from you, People, I had hidden and covered my face and walked alone. And now, through him and through you I have partaken of full life, you

45. Zona Gale to Ridgely Breese, September, 1923, in Nancy Breitsprecher, biography of Zona Gale (Typescript in Breitsprecher's possession, Fort Atkinson, Wis.), 440; MLeS to the authors, October, 1982; Nancy Breitsprecher to the authors, July, 1982 (Breitsprecher's information is based on an interview with Jessie Gruner of Watertown, Wis., who was asked by the Latimers to assist with Margery's laying out and funeral); Jessie Gruner to the authors, August 17, 1982; MLeS to the authors, October, 1982.

have partaken of full life. Deep in us, living its strange life, we are ripe together and complete and round with this perfect taste of living fruit. . . . O do not perish then, my perfect marriage! Live in my dark bones and burn behind my sightless eyes if I, too, am swept away forever." Meridel LeSueur, Margery's lifelong confidante, summarized Margery's life and death by using the image that most aptly characterized the Latimer-Toomer marriage: "When the ripe fruit falls it is just."[46]

46. JT to Holmes, n.d., in JTP 4:9; Latimer passage (JTP 6:4) also included in MLeS, "Afterword: A Memoir," in ML, *Guardian Angel* (1984), 235; MLeS to Caroline Bliss, September, 1932, in JTP 1:2.

IV.

EXPERIMENTS

11

Fontainebleau at Doylestown

During the ten months of Jean's marriage to Margery Latimer, both were hard at work writing, and Jean's enthusiasm for teaching was unflagging. But after Margery's death, not surprisingly, it was as if Jean withdrew from life to find a new direction. Perhaps he wanted to enhance his wife's memory—but not by concentrating on their daughter. Apparently he did not even consider making a home for little Margery himself. Rather, he accepted the foster-parenting offer of Max and Shirley Grove in Chicago. They wanted a baby; her care was their gift of love to their friends and mentor. They had been close to Margery Latimer as well as to Jean, and they had a vague hope that some unspecified spiritual benefits would come to them through service to this very special child and through the frequent exposure they assumed they would have to the child's father. In this they were disappointed; Jean's visits were rare and rushed.

Jean retreated instead to Margery's family home in Portage, where her mother still lived, and spent most of his time collecting Margery's correspondence from her friends and arranging the letters in the hope of publishing them. He was also trying to work on his own writing, having sent "Caromb" for consideration. But he realized that one editor's response was correct: The manuscript was an undigested mixture of autobiography, poetry, and philosophy. Jean felt "baffled and blocked" about what to do. "Life has brought to an end so many things. Evidently it is demanding of me, 'Start again. Begin new things. Again set to work to build your world.'"[1] He was in contact with various friends and Gurdjieff enthusiasts near Chicago, and he continued to receive

1. JT to Dorothy North, n.d. [*ca.* September 24, 1932], draft in JTP 8:11.

financial support from Dorothy North and Eugenia Walcott. Group members contributed one or two dollars a month each to Jean and he sent money to the Groves, but he was not carrying on any regular programs with the Chicago group.

During this time, would-be Hollywood scriptwriter Diana Huebert, who had had some intense private encounters with Jean before his marriage and again after its end, renewed the hope of a more fulfilling alliance with him. However, by August of 1933 she seemed to have concluded that this was unlikely. In her eyes he had momentarily used her, stirred her to her full feeling with his "terrible genius," but had never really tried to understand her.[2]

The depression, of course, permeated everyone's life. Toomer tried to wring a drop of comfort out of the negative times. A lecture he gave in January, 1933, was titled "How We Can Make Use of the Present Depression," and in it he exhorted his audience to "suffer creatively," gaining energy from depth of feeling, using this opportunity to experience "glow, grandeur, nobility, growth of being." However, even such lectures were not money-makers. In February of 1933 his faithful disciple Carol Bliss was still trying to solicit speaking engagements for him at $100 a lecture. He had been asking $100 to $250 in 1931, but now lecturers were normally receiving $25, and Bliss's efforts were not notably successful.[3]

In mid-1933, everything seemed to have hit bottom. The Chicago group's morale was down, with little input from Toomer; the New York group was asking Toomer for money, and he had none to send. Partly because of the squabble over money, Gurdjieff himself was in conflict with Toomer. He alleged that Jean still had the $2,000 given him in trust some years before as part of a publishing fund, and the master claimed he needed it now in order to survive. Toomer explained that the money was from Mabel Dodge Luhan and was not earmarked for publishing, and he had already sent it, on demand, in small amounts to Gurdjieff.[4] By the end of the year, Gurdjieff, destitute, was selling le Prieuré. In the same year, Boni and Liveright, publishers of *Cane,* went bankrupt and "The Gallonwerps" was rejected by the fourth publisher to whom it had been submitted since it was written in 1927. Meanwhile, Shirley Grove, suffering a miscarriage and feeling too much strain in her per-

2. Diana Huebert to JT, August 18, 1933, in JTP 4:9.

3. JT to Mrs. Lomax, February 19, 1931, in JTP 7:1; MLeS to Caroline Bliss, February 21, 1933, in JTP 1:4.

4. Committee for the New York Group to JT, May 17, 1933, in JTP 7:7; JT to the Committee, May 26, 1933, in JTP 4:3.

sonal life, was tired of being a foster-mother and wanted to relinquish the care of Toomer's year-old child.

In the fall of 1933, hoping to collect some more of Margery Latimer's letters, Jean made a trip to New York, where he stayed through October and November. He was working on other writings also, sending the article "A New Force for Cooperation," rewritten from a 1931 essay, to his agent Max Lieber. During this time, Margaret Naumburg invited him for a friendly lunch "to catch up." They were interested in each other's thinking, but there was no renewal of the old spark. At the end of November, Georgia O'Keeffe came down from Lake George with a packet of Margery's letters for Jean, and he agreed to visit her at the Stieglitz family home, The Hill, at Lake George in December.

O'Keeffe and Stieglitz had been comfortable friends of Jean's for about ten years, and Jean had spent several productive periods at The Hill, which he regarded as a haven, a peaceful place of genuine, honest humanity, where he could write unimpeded and perhaps even inspired by the quality of the company. This time, however, Stieglitz was in New York, and O'Keeffe, staying at the lake with only Margaret Prosser, the longtime family cook, was at a very low point in her life. Tensions had accumulated between her and Stieglitz because of differing personal needs and career ambitions. She had experienced a deep depression about a year earlier and then a seven-week hospitalization for psychoneurosis in February and March of 1933. She was still fighting a slow battle for recovery. Stieglitz, glad to hear Jean was at The Hill, wrote him on December 11, "Georgia has no idea how much she worries me not only now but has worried me all these years. It just cannot be helped."[5] Jean, for his part, was still trying to stabilize his emotional, vocational, and financial situation in the aftermath of Margery's death.

Facing the brittle cold of the Lake George winter, Jean and Georgia found warmth and support in each other. They played with the cats and walked or drove crazily in the snow. She gave him a red scarf for Christmas, and he produced an appreciative essay (later published as "The Hill") on Alfred Stieglitz. After Jean had gone back to Chicago and Portage—Yvonne Dupee had begged him to get back by Christmas—a rush of nine letters to him in January and five in February conveyed the intensity of Georgia's feelings and her appreciation for his help in her recovery. "I miss you. We had duck for

5. Laurie Lisle, *Portrait of an Artist: A Biography of Georgia O'Keeffe* (New York, 1981), 260–65; Alfred Stieglitz to JT, December 11, 1933, in JTP 8:15.

dinner today—even the duck missed you. . . . I wish so hotly to feel you hold me very very tight— . . . All your being here was very perfect for me— I like it that it stands as it is." She showed great tenderness and at the same time an awareness that both needed room to grow. In one letter, she wrote about a dream in which another woman took him away and slept with him "as tho it was her right—I was neither surprised nor hurt." In the same letter, she spoke with awed respect of his center and her own, both of which required total acceptance and careful tending. "We cannot really meet without a real battle with one another and each one within the self"—but at the same time, "I like you much. I like knowing the feel of your maleness and your laugh."

What you give me makes me more able to stand up alone—and I would like to be able to stand up alone before I put out my hand to any one. . . . I want you—sometimes terribly—but I like it that I am quite apart from you like the snow on the mountain— for now I need it that way.

I am tired of cold and wind and snow and being alone—want to lie in hot sun and be loved and laugh—and not think—be just a woman—I rather imagine just a woman doesn't have to think much—it is this dull business of being a person that gets one all out of shape—

My advice to you is to look about for something that is just a woman. The sort of thing I am is no use to you—you need someone near at hand too—judging from your letter—

Jean had seen Georgia's sister Catherine in Portage, and though he noted a family resemblance, felt "Georgia is of another kind, another world."[6] While in Portage he was invited to give a creative writing class in poetry to ten students rounded up, cash in hand, by an enthusiast of his. In April he returned to New York, but he knew he would not see Georgia right away. She was still in Bermuda, where she had gone for sun, color, and escape. A year before, her friend Marjorie Content and Marjorie's teenage daughter picked her up at the hospital and took her to Bermuda for a vacation. This year, while Georgia was away, it happened that Jean for the first time met her friend Marjorie in New York.

This was the same Marjorie Content in whose house Lola Ridge had done the editorial work for *Broom* years before. Although Marjorie never considered herself literary, she had been on the fringes of that world, a partner in The Sunwise Turn bookshop in the early 1920s, during her marriage to Harold Loeb. She and Loeb had now been divorced for several years, and their two children were of college age. Marjorie, separated from her third husband, was living in a comfortable house that her father, a well-to-do New York stockbroker, had

6. Georgia O'Keeffe to JT, January 3, 10, 17, February 14, 1934, all in JTP 8:1; JT to Stieglitz, January 18, 1934, in ASC.

bought her on West Tenth Street. She was graceful, vibrant, the same age as Jean. A professional photographer, she was skilled at woodworking and enjoyed making costumes and props for New York theaters.

Several of Marjorie's friends through the years had recommended Jean Toomer to her. Lola Ridge had said in 1923, "You *must* meet this man!" After Toomer had visited O'Keeffe and Stieglitz at Lake George, Georgia wrote about him in glowing terms ("fascinating—a lot of fun") and urged Marjorie to look him up. Marjorie later spent a summer in Arizona, taking photographs among the Apache tribes for the U.S. Bureau of Indian Affairs, and several summers with the Pueblos near Taos, New Mexico, often with Georgia. For many years she had shared this interest in Indian cultures with Fred Leighton, who also told Marjorie she should meet Jean Toomer. Finally, during Jean's visit to New York in the spring of 1934, Fred called Marjorie and asked if he could bring Jean over. Well prepared, she agreed.

Somehow, from that time on, Jean Toomer and Marjorie Content managed to see each other almost every day. He saw an intense, forthright woman, her dark hair framing her oval face and pulled to a bun at the back of her neck, who had skill in her hands and a great eager warmth for people, an individualist in her choice of flowing skirts and bright colors and American Indian earrings, bracelets, and rings—a person of charm and talent who needed to be reassured of her worth. She saw a tall, urbane, magnetic man giving the impression of wisdom, with horn-rimmed glasses and a trim moustache, his dark brown hair brushed neatly back from his forehead but easily tousled on top. Profound thought had left some furrows on his forehead but an impish smile often lighted his face, and Marjorie thought he "seemed able to see inside me. Seemed to know things about me that I didn't think anybody knew."[7]

By the time Georgia O'Keeffe got back to New York and talked with Jean, early in May, it was clear that things between Marjorie and him were moving fast. Georgia was a bit taken aback but genuinely glad for both of them: "I like it very much that you and Margery [*sic*] have started what I feel you have—I like it for both of you because I feel deeply fond of both of you—and something wonderful should come of it for both of you." Nostalgically, she wished that she and Jean could experience the green of the spring instead of the cold snow at Lake George: "[B]ut it is alright as it is—For both of us it is very right as it is— . . . I seem to be feeling very good in both my body and my mind . . . everything is alright."[8]

7. Information from interview of Marjorie Content Toomer, Doylestown, Pa., June 23, 1978, and photos taken by MCT, May, 1934.

8. O'Keeffe to JT, May 11, 1934, in JTP 8:1.

Gurdjieff, too, was in New York. Toomer was summoned to see him at Child's restaurant, the master's informal headquarters. Further pressure was put on Jean to return any money he had collected and any unsold copies of Gurdjieff's latest work. He was moved to sympathy by Gurdjieff's plight and apparent poor health, and promised to do what he could.

Jean's concentration was in fact elsewhere. He and Marjorie had quickly and thoroughly fallen in love. They found such strength in each other that they planned to be married as soon as Marjorie's divorce was final. When Jean had to go back to Portage at the beginning of June, they arranged to go together. They drove her father's old Packard and kept quiet for the time being about their plans, though they stopped to visit Jean's daughter, who would soon belong to them both. Marjorie had earlier arranged to drive to New Mexico with Georgia O'Keeffe and take a cottage at Alcalde. Now Georgia joined her near Chicago and they drove west. Jean and Marjorie filled the mails and telegraph wires daily until he could finish his business with Margery Latimer's letters and speed to her in New Mexico.

These letters were something of a testing ground for their new and strong but still vulnerable relationship. Both were swept by varying tides of emotion, but Jean clearly kept the upper hand. He discovered that "I have curious deep male feelings about my woman going off out of my immediate world." When two days went by without his hearing from her, he was scared and angry and wrote her a scorching criticism under the salutation "My dear child," which she described as "two pages of such a scolding as I have never had." He accused her of being totally thoughtless and insensitive, enjoying herself while he was suffering: "What in hell was the matter with you? . . . *I can't bear you to disappear.*" At first she was surprised and a little pleased that she was so important, but when the criticism continued for several letters more and she was accused of being fishy and fake, of not paying him enough attention when she was spending most of her time writing to him, sometimes nine, twelve, or eighteen pages, she crumbled: "Here I am—not living—not being—just waiting— . . . please—darling—don't—oh don't do this to me again. Say anything to me when you're there—but let me get thru this time of waiting and separation as best I may." In a different mood he had already answered, "When I thought you might be hurt and I couldn't be there to help you, I felt as if a whole continent were sinking in me, a bright full world sinking into something I could not see."[9]

9. JT to Marjorie Content, June 15, 1934, MC to JT, June 18, 1934, JT to MC, June 13, 1934, MC to JT, June 23, 1934, JT to MC, June 18, 1934, all in JTP 9:3–6.

The letters give evidence of considerable interdependence, beyond the pain of physical separation. She had located a Gregg shorthand book, and during her waiting time she was teaching herself shorthand so she could take dictation to facilitate Jean's writing. In between hurt and angry reactions, she was secure enough to suggest that he should get more of his full feeling-self into his writing, and he agreed. Expressing himself to her had helped free him for writing the introduction he had to produce for the collected Latimer letters: "I *know* that if I hadn't been so free and full in my expressions to you, I'd never have been so free and vital in this. Is it any wonder that I realize how much I need you? How much you are a part of me, the woman-pole of my creation? Together we will do great things, have great living." In turn, she seemed receptive to his psychological diagnosis of her, and it is clear that he had plans to reshape her. He offered the advice that she depended on her body too much, though she used it very effectively, and needed to wake up her mind to function more fully. Finally, after successive explosions of anger, Jean was able to reassure her enough so she could write, "I feel sure—sure—sure of you—of me—of life— and equal to anything. Really intensely happy. . . . You have no idea of the sense of wonder which comes to me—from the conception of being part of you." [10]

By July 1, Jean had finished the essentials of his business with the letters. He stopped for about half an hour to see his daughter at the Groves' place and then was finally on his way to Marjorie. Crossing the Mississippi, he spontaneously began to chant a portion of his poem "Blue Meridian." "I felt," he wrote to Marjorie, "I was engaged in a sacred ritual, in a prayer, in a song of triumph!" [11]

Nourished and encouraged by the warm Southwest and a devoted companion, Jean wrote steadily and was quite hopeful about his prospects at the end of the summer. He sent off "Eight-Day World," a revision of "Transatlantic," the first week of September and promised "The Letters of Margery Latimer" in about two more weeks. "Eight-Day World" was, in his mind, to open the way for a series that would include a rearrangement of his poetry collection "Blue Meridian," two novels then in draft form, and later an autobiography; but Viking Press rejected "Eight-Day World" in November. There were two small successes: Jean's sketch of Alfred Stieglitz written the year before at Lake George was published that fall as part of a collection edited by Waldo Frank. And "A New Force for Cooperation," his long article on personal and social change, was

10. JT to MC, June 21, 1934, MC to JT, June 23, 1934, both in JTP 9:4, 5.
11. JT to MC, July 1, 1934, in JTP 9:6.

published in a London periodical.[12] In addition, Marjorie's divorce was completed at the end of August, and on September 1, Jean and Marjorie were married in Taos by a slightly drunk justice of the peace, with only Marjorie's children and Georgia O'Keeffe in attendance.

Starting back to New York City about a week after the wedding, they picked up baby Margery in Chicago. Shirley Grove resented losing the child, though she had complained about the baby's care earlier, and Max genuinely mourned Margery's absence. In order to ease the transition for the two-year-old who scarcely knew her father and had to take on a new mother, Max and Shirley drove to New York with the Toomers and stayed there for a time. The adjustment was extremely hard for all three family members, just the same. Both parents were about forty; Marjorie was years past her child-raising days, and Jean had never really acted like a father and took little responsibility even now. Little "Argie," as they called her, was used to being the center of attention. She had never been exposed to two adults whose real interests were elsewhere and who in addition believed in more control than her foster-parents had. She made life uncomfortable as only a frightened, unhappy two-year-old can. Nevertheless, Marjorie cared for her with love and tenderness and continued through the years to be a mother to Jean's child. For some months during the next five years, they also took in Edith Taylor's young son Paul, as a kind of companion for Argie and as a help to his mother (Jean's good friend since 1923), who was having a difficult time.

The couple enjoyed for a while a leisure-class life, entertaining artists and dancers in Marjorie's big house, Jean free to write without having to earn a living. Sometimes Marjorie would invite acquaintances from her work in the theater, sometimes Jean would ask his literary friends or people connected to the Gurdjieff work. One night he invited Dorothy Peterson and some other Harlem friends to come to their house. But the melding of their two circles of friends, despite considerable overlap, was surprisingly incomplete. Meridel LeSueur recalls meeting Jean by chance in New York, and he took her to the house to see Argie. Marjorie refused to let Meridel in to see the child, who was sleeping. Meridel left in tears, and that was the last time she saw Jean.[13]

However separate their former friendships remained, Jean and Marjorie settled into a complementary, apparently well matched life together, with

12. JT, "The Hill," in Waldo Frank *et al.* (eds.), *America and Alfred Stieglitz: A Collective Portrait* (Garden City, N.Y., 1934), 295–302; JT, "A New Force for Cooperation," *Adelphi*, IX (October, 1934), 25–31.

13. MLeS to the authors, October, 1982.

deep physical attraction and mutual love and respect, though he was clearly the central figure and she the devoted disciple. She was perfecting her shorthand, taking dictation while he composed, and began typing all his manuscripts. Marjorie's house at 39 West Tenth Street was now Jean's home.

It is interesting that both of Jean's wives had an early exposure to the Gurdjieff teaching and rejected it—Margery Latimer because she feared that it would destroy her writing skill, Marjorie Content because it was too intellectual or esoteric. Yet both later gave their full allegiance to Jean, perforce absorbing his philosophy and becoming clay for his shaping. Marjorie Content had heard Orage lecture in the 1920s and, though rejecting the substance, admired the style, saying, "That man spoke like an angel." She refused to meet Gurdjieff when Jean was in contact with him after their marriage, not wishing to be called an idiot or to be pressed for money, and objecting to the idolatry she perceived around the "master." [14]

During the summer in New Mexico, he spent most of his time writing. He had also tried to lay a foundation for some more Gurdjieff work, though his irritation with the man was growing. His continuing demands, Jean felt, were a case of the strong manipulating the weak and foolish for his own selfish benefit. At the same time he smoothed his passage out of the work by claiming that he wanted to concentrate all his energies on his family. In a letter of August 18 he told this to Gurdjieff and added, "I want to do all I can to help spread the ideas that mean so much to me, that I believe to be the greatest ideas that contemporary man will be privileged to come in contact with." [15] However, he was not actively trying to stir people in Taos. When he talked with Mabel Dodge Luhan, she did not even offer to hold a meeting with Gurdjieff at her house, nor did she think much good could be done in Taos. Worse, in the course of "welcoming" Jean's new wife, Mabel served Marjorie a drink that made her so sick, Marjorie was convinced it was poisoned. In response to Toomer's report on the lack of interest, Gurdjieff canceled his proposed trip to Santa Fe.

In November, there was a new flurry of complaints about Gurdjieff's behavior. Some of the spin-off touched Toomer, blaming him not only for the supposed mismanagement of funds but for the sudden mental breakdown of an erstwhile group member. Jean had already heard that Gurdjieff had made some of Jean's followers who were in New York promise not to have anything to do

14. MCT interview, Doylestown, Pa., August 17, 1982.
15. JT to Gurdjieff, August 18, 1934, in JTP 4:3.

with Toomer—the same kind of vow he had applied against Orage a year before. About the same time, word came of Orage's unexpected death in England. This new series of accusations and events broke Jean's last link to the official Gurdjieff movement. Furious at the criticism, he gathered up documents and canceled checks that proved he had already sent Gurdjieff more than the amount he was supposed to be holding in trust and showed these to Fred Leighton and Gorham Munson, who apparently were satisfied with the proof. He also wrote a detailed letter to Mabel Dodge Luhan, accounting for the $15,000 she had given him nine years earlier for the Gurdjieff work. Finally he wrote to Yvonne Dupee, who was still a good friend of his and still faithful to Gurdjieff, summarizing his position:

G is doing nothing at the present time that I want to participate in or that I want to bring others to participate in. His meetings, for me personally, are lethal. . . . I am saturated, have been saturated for several years—and there is nothing that he is doing that promises to enlarge my capacity. . . . I am not ranting against G, I am giving my opinions and feelings as mine, as coming from me, as having no necessary relation to the reality that is G, to the reality that is the work. . . . I disavow any and all responsibility for those who enter it now, I will bring no new people into it, I will neither persuade nor dissuade old people. I believe that G once had and perhaps still has a very great thing; I am skeptical that he will ever use it. . . . I have only myself, my present best judgements to rely on. Using these, I now withdraw from, or at least will have no active part in the work.

P.S. . . G, for reasons best known to himself, has fallen into the habit of blaming me—or blaming someone—for something that is not that person's fault. Many times in the past he has done it, and I have stood for it—owing to the reasons already given [support of the work and of publishing Gurdjieff's books]. But not this time, in regard to money. Nor this time in regard to insanity either. I am blamed, according to Jerry, for what has happened to E. . . . Well, even Fred puts this . . . breakdown directly at G's door.

But I am tired of being blamed.

I am tired too of the way G swings toward the quarter from which the money comes. . . . I simply withdraw—and hope against doubt for something constructive from the *man* G.

The letter sounds fairly cool-headed, but Yvonne, who knew Jean well, responded as if to an unusual outpouring of emotion: "Of *course* you were furious and you should have been . . . I think you need to be eased a bit and a little reassured about G." [16]

Toomer refused to see Gurdjieff all that autumn, though Gurdjieff was staying in New York with Fred Leighton and, through Fred, had asked to see Jean.

16. JT to Yvonne Dupee, November 25, 1934, Dupee to JT, November 27, 1934, both in JTP 2:16.

Stories were circulating that made Jean think "that G. was like a wheel gone off its axle careening madly down the road . . . smashing into things right and left." In January, however, Fred persuaded Jean to come to a meeting with him, Israel Solon, and Gurdjieff. Toomer was thrown into a crisis of indecision again. "Insane? He was in full possession of every one of his extraordinary faculties. Debauched and slovenly? Nothing of the sort. Afraid of the dark and of being alone? It was ridiculous. Whatever he had gone through, the thing that showed plainly was a decided improvement in every respect." Finding himself again affirming Gurdjieff, Jean arranged that he, Fred, and Israel would give the master a certain sum every week for a month. When the month was up, Jean was courted by Gurdjieff at a lunch, a dinner, and a Turkish bath. Jean gave him more money, believing Gurdjieff was shortly to leave for France. Gurdjieff became confidential, and Jean reminded him that he had once promised to make Toomer the ruler of Africa.

"Something went wrong," he smiled.
"Is my psyche African?" I asked.
"African."
"At different times you have told me it was English and, again, typically American. I don't understand."
"You not as I counted," he said. . . . "You manifest differently at different times, different from what I expected. You not as I counted, and I get angry." . . .
I thought to myself: my psyche African, American, and English, my body with every blood under the sun, my spirit and inner values Oriental, my body and outer aims Occidental, a democratic [sic], an aristocrat, a feudal man, a modern man, my family of the South, I live in the North, what a crock of diverse elements, yet I hang together and am one, I behind the aspects, I through different worlds, I through lives and deaths, I.[17]

Jean was indeed passing through a death from one life into another. In his writing the following summer, he characterized the place of such an event in his life, describing his repeated difficulty in a series of moves from one world to another: "I mean a spiritual and complete severance. . . . When you leave, when all of you goes off into something else, certain deep connections are cut." But he yearned to discover his own integrity amid this "crock of diverse elements" and could not find it in Gurdjieff's shadow. He genuinely enjoyed Gurdjieff, admired and stood in awe of him, later saying he was "on a par" with Buddha and Christ. Now, however, he was disgusted with Gurdjieff's continuing transparent ruses to get more money and dismayed at his own inability to resist. His account of his final break with Gurdjieff was born of this frustration:

17. JT account, written 1935 (JTP 67:2), 24, 46.

"I have reached the limit of my possibilities, for the present. I can do no more for myself in the way of having higher experiences. In the immediate future I, myself personally, do not count." Gurdjieff squeezed passage money out of Jean, claiming he was sailing for France on March 2. In the days following, however, he kept coming back for more money, insisting in this "critical hour" only Toomer could save the work and its leader. Jean decided he had to cut himself free. He acted as if Gurdjieff had in fact left New York on March 2, and made no response to his pleas. He never saw Gurdjieff again, nor did Jean share in his support. But many years later he recognized that he was both "claimed" and "chained" for the rest of his life. [18]

This shift of attention and focus away from Gurdjieff coincided with his shift of location and associations. Even though Jean and Marjorie had tried to provide a bridge for Argie with the Groves, and even though others from the Chicago group (notably Chaunce Dupee and his wife Katharine Green, called "Tockie") came to stay with the Toomers from time to time, there was little real continuation of acquaintances from one segment of Jean Toomer's life to another. It was similar to his leaving the literary world for the Gurdjieff movement, almost stepping into another identity. Indeed, Marjorie had had her own friendships with Sherwood Anderson, Paul Rosenfeld, Stieglitz and O'Keeffe, Lola Ridge, and Margaret Naumburg. (Marjorie had sent her children to Naumburg's school, and she even claimed Naumburg's brother as her first love, at the age of fourteen.) Jean also had his various ties with these people, yet the two never returned to these friendships as a couple. While Jean retained contact with Gorham Munson and Fred Leighton, renewing his friendship with Munson with considerable joy when he returned to New York, the only enduring bridges that were formed across the marriage from one earlier life to another were Mother Latimer (from Jean's) and Lin Davenport (from Marjorie's).

Margery Latimer's mother, who had the largeness of heart to welcome Jean's new wife two years after her daughter's death, began to visit Jean's family every summer. They all called her "Mother Latimer," and after forty years, Marjorie Toomer said of her, "She's just a lovely, lovely woman, . . . a lovely *person. . . .* She never did [resent the remarriage], no, she was very pleased to have Jean marry me. She acquired a new family. We all loved her." [19] In a somewhat psychological balance, though certainly not by design (Jean provided

18. JT, "Book X," 78; JT 1935 account (JTP 67:2, 27:2); JT account, written after Gurdjieff's death (JTP 53:26).
19. Interview of MCT, Doylestown, Pa., November 19, 1974.

Marjorie with a foster-mother, Marjorie provided Jean with a foster-son), Lin Davenport, a young friend of Marjorie's in New York, was invited to come to help work the farm when the couple moved to Doylestown in 1936. There, he became Jean's devoted disciple, both in the physical labor and in the psychological pursuit of Jean's adaptation of Gurdjieff's teachings.

Jean Toomer did indeed continue to pursue Gurdjieff's teachings, after a year or so of moving aimlessly in other directions. The wave of literature friendly to Marxism and the atmosphere in New York stirred his interest in social issues. His response was to reject all class and race struggles, believing that social systems offer incomplete answers. Paul Rosenfeld supported this position: "My objection to communism is just yours . . . that it is an evasion of putting the inner life to rights." Jean's article "A New Force for Cooperation," published in late 1934, developed this idea. In April of 1934, pursuing the same belief, he had called together in New York a group of artists, bankers, and others to suggest the formation of "A Society for the Future," aimed beyond the extreme Right and the extreme Left, which should sponsor lectures, publish a magazine, and have a training school for youth. Unfortunately the proposed content of all this education was vague, and nothing came of his suggestion. A year later, Toomer had come to feel that all one could do, as an individualized person, was to survive, to prepare oneself for functioning in "the coming age, after the deluge, when wisdom has power, . . . when values are moving." [20] That spring of 1935 he had so many discussions with advocates of communism, fascism, monarchy, and Social Credit that he felt bombarded, overwhelmed, and exhausted. It was time to look for a clearer direction.

In the summer of 1935, the Toomers again went to New Mexico and rented a house in Taos, for Marjorie to work on her photography and Jean to write. He was writing, among other things, a play based on the Toomers' experience in Taos and an autobiography explaining how he came to enter the "big blind alley" of the Gurdjieff movement, but these were never finished for submission to publishers. In February, a final rejection of "The Letters of Margery Latimer" laid that project to rest. There were no favorable responses to any of his larger manuscripts. In December, what turned out to be his last published short story, "A Certain November," appeared in the *Dubuque Dial,* whose editor had been a good friend of Margery Latimer's and was eager to have access to her work. Apparently Jean used this to push the publication of his own story, post-

20. Paul Rosenfeld to JT, July 30, 1933, in JTP 8:9; JT, "A Preface to a Place and Function in Society" (JTP 25:17).

poned by the editor for almost a year. (Obscure as the periodical was, the astute editor included pieces in the same issue by William Saroyan and James T. Farrell.) "A Certain November" is a surrealistic combination of non sequiturs and gross scatological images and wordplay. The plot turns on the needs for work, food, love, and particularly warmth. It presents satirically the view of human beings in their usual condition as animallike, of less value than a junked car, and showing no sign of their potential development—"underbaked angeldough."

That same December, on his birthday, Jean made a new resolution:

Suddenly struck by the realization that the mainspring of my life on this earth is wound like the mainspring of a clock to work not endlessly but for a definite brief time and then stop, I have an impulse not new to me but never so strong, to attempt again now what I have made effort to do before, but unsuccessfully, namely, to write *my* book, my one book whose pages will convey the main things I have to contribute to my fellow-men—to begin and finish this writing, whatever else happens, and even though neither the materials nor the form of this book nor my style in language are as ripe and perfected as I would wish them to be.[21]

Although his writing since 1924 conveyed a particular kind of message, Toomer had expected his novels, short stories, and plays to be accepted as literature by the publishing world. He worked very hard for this acceptance, especially after 1929. The year 1936 marks the end of that effort and a redirection toward what might be called pure teaching without fictional or satirical disguise.

That year included, as one such final marker, Jean's last dabbling with drama: a long description of a new kind of theater which would start at ten in the morning and go on until midnight and in which actors and stagehands would participate not for pay but to "contribute to a significant experience." However, no script seems to have been written for this sort of drama. A second milestone was Toomer's last appearance in a mainstream literary publication during his lifetime. Having submitted his long poem "Blue Meridian" (in a collection with other poems) to one publisher after another, Jean had sent it to his friend Paul Rosenfeld, who had published in 1925 an article about Toomer in his book *Men Seen* and who had continued to admire and support him when many former literary admirers dropped away. With Paul's help, "Blue Meridian" was published in 1936 in the last of the *American Caravan* anthologies.[22] Ironically, the poem that marked the end of Toomer's literary career was first

21. JT, "Psychologic Papers," December 26, 1936 (JTP 41:3).
22. JT notes on the drama (JTP 49:14); JT, "Blue Meridian," in Alfred Kreymborg, Lewis Mumford, and Paul Rosenfeld (eds.), *The New Caravan* (New York, 1936), 633–53.

conceived at least fifteen years previously as "The First American." It retraces his steps through Gurdjieff's theory of the universe, which spirals upward in an ever-increasing revelation of spiritual essence, to Waldo Frank's creed of replacing the old gods and myths with new symbols, which in America meant the blending of all peoples into one American race.

This poem was a fitting close to Jean's "literary life," for it encapsulates his movement from Frank to Gurdjieff as his source of inspiration. "Blue Meridian" does not wholly reconcile the new American and the Fourth Way; but in its rambling, Whitmanesque way, it reflects the tension of these influences as well as do any of Toomer's published pieces. Jean perceived this tension in 1924, when the Frank group was breaking up and Toomer, renouncing what he saw as his false role as a New York litterateur, was rejecting Frank also. He wrote to Munson then: "I think that [visiting Fontainebleau] will inevitably subject you to a critical test. It will essentialize and contrast old ways to new. It will pull you between Waldo and Gurdjieff, between literature and a new discipline. But you will not be able to stand these cross-pulls for long. Either you will (inhibit) repress the new, Gurdjieff, etc., and drive again into art, or you will quickly find yourself decided for Fontainebleau." Munson refused the dichotomy, saying that it was characteristic of Jean to build oppositions needlessly and seeing Waldo instead as a step on the way: "Gurdjieff lies beyond Waldo, but the path to Gurdjieff lies through Waldo."[23] But for Jean, the duality continued and was never fully resolved. He struggled with both elements, rejecting along the way both Frank and Gurdjieff but retaining their ideas. Later, though giving his allegiance to another religious system, he spent his years writing tracts that continued to describe a spiritual base he had sought from his two former masters, on whose teaching and message he still relied.

Now, however, another current was moving. Both Jean and Marjorie were restless living in New York and wanted a better environment for their child. Further, Jean's boyhood image of the country estate reemerged, as did his primitivist belief in the mystic quality of the soil, and a lurking dream of establishing a new American Fontainebleau with Jean Toomer as its Gurdjieff. All these forces converged as a practical possibility with Marjorie's father's money. They bought a farm. Toomer in a letter to Chaunce Dupee characteristically described this move as monumentally significant. He was shifting, he said, from a "phase of living without things" to a "phase of living with things": "Long have I lived, first, as unconscious, then as conscious

23. JT to GM, July 14, 1924, GM to JT, July 16, 1924, both in JTP 7:13.

nomad. . . . I have written on the wind, shaped water, planted seeds in space—and the winds will carry, and the water will flow, and the seeds will grow. But now I must concentrate myself and make things manifest in tangible materials. Too few of my fellow men can see and sense and feel and understand what I have done." [24]

On the way to Portage during their whirlwind courtship, Marjorie and Jean had stopped in Paoli, Pennsylvania, at the house of an old friend of Marjorie's, the sculptor Wharton Esherick. Jean had remarked that this part of the country would be a nice place to live. So they returned to the area the following year and found a farm with a good livable house for sale near Doylestown, in Bucks County northwest of Philadelphia. By January, 1936, leaving Argie with their live-in baby-sitter, a young friend from Taos, they were driving down on weekends, stripping off wallpaper and sitting on orange crates until they could sell the New York house and bring their own furniture, much of which was designed by Wharton Esherick. The only "new" piece they bought was an antique cobbler's bench. In April, they hired a local farmer, Ramsey Lewis, to run the farm and began remodeling the dilapidated gristmill. Lin Davenport, fed up with the city and with his job, was asked to come and help. The upstairs was to be living quarters, and there was a large downstairs area. Toomer had in mind, according to Lin, "all sorts of activities, everything from square dancing to philosophical discussion, [but] more on the intellectual than let's say on the manual plane, . . . a place where people could gather for intensive consideration of the problems of man." [25] The main house, where the family lived, was given the name Mill House, and Marjorie designed an emblem for the new project.

Marjorie herself claimed she did not know at the time that Jean hoped to build at Doylestown an institute patterned after Gurdjieff's Fontainebleau. It is true that he thought of many things he did not tell her about. While Lin asserts that Jean worked organically, taking advantage of situations as they developed and letting projects grow naturally rather than forcing them into a mold, Jean did have a plan for his institute at least vaguely in mind. In a talk to a Portage or Chicago group in March of 1933, he had given some examples of trying out desires. For himself, he said, if he got a lot of money, he would probably give it to Gurdjieff. But "I would like to have some kind of Institute, to create books, etc." In December, 1936, as activities were getting started on their Doylestown farm, he wrote to Marjorie's father Harry Content:

24. JT to Charles Dupee, January 19, 1936, in JTP 2:10.
25. Interview of Franklin Davenport, Doylestown, Pa., January 23, 1975.

I have been working as never before in my life. She [Marjorie] has, too. It is not only that my big book is well under way, it is also that the way we live and live together has produced an atmosphere in which more and better work can be done. All who are associated with us seem to feel it, seem to "get going" and really begin doing things. I sometimes feel that what we really have is a sort of school of a new kind, a school in which people learn how to live, not by reading textbooks with a lot of stuff in them which you soon forget, but by seeing living examples, by seeing and learning from real experience and actual life. And when I give rein to my imagination, I sometimes see this place developing through the years into a school or college of a kind never before existing in America. How do you think this sounds? "Content College of the Art of Life". It is of course, only in imagination or when I permit myself to relax from present work and dream of what might happen in the future. If by any chance it ever did happen, I would want the name of Content to figure prominently, because it is owing to you that it is possible.[26]

Partly written as thanks for what her father had already done, this letter could also have been sounding him out for future contributions.

That Jean visualized such a goal is also confirmed by Gorham Munson, a good friend and an astute observer of Jean for many years. Although Jean was happy in New York with Marjorie, "I think he had a dream all this time," Gorham says. "I'm sure— . . . Jean had the idea—that he would eventually establish at Doylestown, on the farm there, an institute for the development of man along the lines of Gurdjieff's estate at Fontainebleau. This was a very ambitious thing to plan, but Jean thought of gathering in people around him, their doing farm work, a lot of outdoor work, and of his being the psychological instructor of young people."[27]

The mill remodeling was finished in the fall of 1936, and Jean swung into a period of intensive action. Part of the recommended program was physical labor, but Lin did most of the farm and garden chores. Jean was photographed working occasionally—shirtless, forking hay onto a wagon; in topcoat and business hat, raking the garden—but Marjorie contended that these were rare examples of manual industry on his part. He did enjoy feeding and admiring his flock of snow-white pigeons brought to them by a Connecticut friend, and he kept the birds until wartime scarcities made supplying feed too difficult. Walking the rural roads nearby, he cut quite a figure, as one of his neighbors recalled: "I thought when I saw him he must have been from either Ethiopia or India. He was narrow, and tall, and black-haired, and walked rather slowly,

26. JT lecture, March, 1933 (JTP 22:7); JT to H. Content, December 22, 1936, in JTP 1:11.
27. Interview of GM by India Watterson, New York, June 27, 1969 (Amistad Research Center, New Orleans).

pondering as he went, meditating, I should say. He always wore a white leather jacket and a black hat, and generally he had on beautiful, what we called Santa Fe trousers that were creamy whipcord trousers—the luxury pants of a cowboy; and he had a black and white coach dog." [28]

But Jean Toomer's forte was within—within the house, and within the mind. He "willed to generate a spiritual form in the midst of the physical," as he states in notes written at the time. Beginning with Lin and Gordon Dupee—Chaunce's son, who was spending the summer there between college terms—Jean wrote several pages a day, then Marjorie would read them each evening and Lin and Gordon would write out their responses. These in turn would be read, discussed, and rewritten. This activity almost magically focused and energized the household, and from it grew, as time went on and with whoever was in residence—Marjorie, Lin and his brother Don, sometimes Marjorie's children Susan and Jim, and Frances, who took care of Argie, as well as other helpers, friends, and guests—instruction and practice sessions in Jean's version of Gurdjieff's theories. Some were modeled after Gurdjieff's and Orage's patterns, some on his own experiments from Portage and Chicago days. He would lecture, with diagrams. Or he would ask a difficult question and elicit alternative suggestions for answers, only to show how foolish each was. Or he would give assignments, some reading a person must do or a paper on a particular topic to write before nightfall, or a deliberate decision that some small action was to be undertaken at a particular time. Or sometimes (but less often than in the hothouse atmosphere of the Portage cottage) he would set up a situation in order to provoke a certain response so the person concerned could observe his or her negative, "disjective" behavior. Even Jean's birthday celebrations were teaching occasions. Jean, sitting in majesty in his white leather chair, gave each guest a book or passage to read and report on (often Jean's own), chosen especially for that individual's good.

This intensive teaching was also being prepared for a larger audience. He turned, as he finally had in Chicago, to private publication. By November of 1936, Toomer had written *Living is Developing* (Psycho-Logic Series 1), the first pamphlet to be published under the Mill House imprint. Its message centers on the potential humanness within each person, which becomes overlaid with false defenses, and on how the individual's condition, whatever it is, can be used in the struggle to overcome the false and regain the true essence: "Crusts and shells and roles and masks, layer upon layer; words and gestures, doctrines and dogmas, layer upon layer . . . Under what debris the human seed." The

28. Interview of Dorothy Paxson, Penns Park, Pa., January 24, 1975.

second in the series, *Work-Ideas I*, was finished in January, 1937. It pinpoints man's difficulty with his two centers, the failure to give sufficient attention to the inner being while the outer (symbolized by materialism, science, and technology) is overdeveloped. Tantalizingly it talks of using tools given by the teacher—but does not give the tools—to get rid of the false layer of discord ("the world of distortion, false egotism, abnormal desires") so that these two centers can develop in harmony. The goal seems to be both individual and social change, the integration of each person and the socialization of all, by which he means coordination with the needs of others and acceptance of mutual responsibility.

Such writing was very satisfying to him. He felt that his great book was developing, his philosophy was being transmitted. His note marking his forty-second birthday on December 26, 1936, concluded: "So, as I swiftly review this year, I can say surely, and with thankfulness to forces both within me and in the great world, that what I have desired all my life is at hand—my being, having moved through the vicissitudes and failures incident to preparation, is at the threshold of its season of full productivity for use."[29]

In March and April, 1937, at the West Tenth Street house in New York, he gave a series of ten lectures which was to sum up his whole philosophy. Lin and Marjorie regularly drove to the city with him, and Marjorie kept notes on his talks as well as on her progress with "the work" that he assigned her on a continuing basis. A talk he gave in May at the Modern School in Stelton, New Jersey, examined the familiar Gurdjieffian theme of the person as a "being inhabiting a body," an egg within a shell. In dealing with children, he said, we normally cultivate the shell, but we should rather consider the body as a mere tool and concentrate our care on developing the inner world.

During this time also, Jean was intensively working with individuals, as was his practice, to lead them to greater self-understanding and shape their characters closer to his ideal. Some of this work was with family members, some with those outside the family. In January of that year, Marjorie's son James Loeb wrote the first of a series of letters to Jean, expressing thanks for the help Jean had given him and asking advice for his problems. He seems to be fully in accord with Jean's philosophy and methods: "I can rightfully feel now that I respect, appreciate, understand, and feel a part of what you are doing in this universe 1937. . . . My trouble lies in trying to find which things in me are false so that I can extract them and then suffer them and weed them out of me. . . . I appreciate the means more every time I think about them."[30] Jean

29. JT, "Psychologic Papers," December 26, 1936.
30. James Loeb to JT, January, 1937, in JTP 6:12.

responded with long and detailed letters (one was twenty-six pages) full of re-assurance, directions, and philosophical discussion.

A second educational effort of Jean's was not equally appreciated, though this did not discourage him. This was his continuing work on Marjorie's character. Orage had long ago told him directly, "We are not entitled to entertain ideas of development or reform for another person. We should not have them. Eliminate them from the man-woman relationship." Clearly Jean had rejected or forgotten this dictum. Once he recorded he was working on a "blind spot" in Marjorie—something she needed to change but did not see the need of changing. Another time he used verbal exaggeration to shock her and "begin the transference and re-location of her center of gravity from outer to inner." At dinner one night in February, with a number of guests present, he told a story about himself, first picturing himself as heartless and cruel to their pet dog, then as acting the good Samaritan to a stranded motorist. Marjorie, shocked at the cruelty, asked him why he had done it, and when he told her he would answer her question in a couple of months, she became angry and accused him of playing a shoddy Gurdjieff trick. In his notes about this incident, he mentions that flare-ups were occurring more frequently between them. He was pleased at the results of this one, deliberately provoked: "This essence-revolt will mark the deep beginning of Marjorie's becoming as fine throughout her entire person as she now is in that real—but usually walled off—part of herself."[31]

It may have been at about this time that notices were sent out to potential participants describing a Care Group of ten or more members that would meet regularly, perhaps weekly, "seeking to find a way . . . of promoting deeper and closer relationships with one another and with all mankind." Perhaps he had this sort of effort in mind when he mentioned the possibility of asking James Loeb and Leila Lane, daughter of Jeremy and Betty, to work with him. The family often invited local people for dinner, and these occasions inevitably became teaching sessions. One who participated recalls: "Margie . . . was a great organizer . . . , she'd get them all storming along, but the people would end up sitting literally at Jean's feet. . . . They'd all cluster around him, and he would talk, or they would talk, and they discussed. . . . The talk that went on was just fascinating. . . . Not one of them seemed to be embarrassed to just open up."[32]

31. JT notes on Orage meetings, April 6, 1926 (JTP 66:5); JT notes, December 26, 1934 (JTP 57:13), October 18, 1936 (JTP 55:14); JT notes for autobiography, February 27, 1937 (JTP 17:2).

32. Invitation to join a Care Group, n.d. [other materials in this file come from late 1930s

But writing was his daily activity, and his efforts to be published were continuous. Haniel Long, editor of the *New Mexico Literary Sentinel* and a friend of Jean's from his visits to Taos, asked for and accepted three pieces, which were printed in July and August. These were brief meditations on evil ("it is simply wrong functioning"), on social activism ("it is like joining the insane activities of inmates of an asylum, when they need rather to be brought to a different reality"), and on other topics such as mislabeling whole organisms by their parts and misunderstanding the person who, seeking higher values, seems not to fit into an ordinary job. Toomer indicated his eagerness for publication when he responded to Long's request. It was a period of extraordinary productivity for him: he had written, he said, "some thousand papers" in that year alone, and though he had arranged these in book form, he would be glad to have parts of the larger works published.[33]

He pointed out to Long an important change by adding, "[F]or writings of this character I am using my full name—Nathan Jean Toomer, or N. J. Toomer—so as to signify the difference between these and some of my earlier work."[34] His sentence here is something of a fiction, because his correct "full name" was Nathan Pinchback Toomer. Although he was christened Nathan, it was not a name he could ever remember being called, since the shift to Eugene was made very early. It is significant that now he chose to make this identification with the name of his father, whom he had never known. This action seems to be an affirmation of his roots, but peculiarly at the same time it was also a move away from the connection to *Cane*.

A mark of this ambiguity is a strange little seven-page pamphlet that is not dated but may have been written near this time in 1937. Called *A Fiction and Some Facts*, it baldly states that Jean's grandfather falsely claimed to be a Negro for political advantage at the time of the Civil War and that whether he, and also Jean, have any Negro blood in their background is questionable. It champions the idea of the new people, the Americans, but the tone becomes querulous when Toomer deals with charges that he is Negro. His wife Marjorie remembered its being printed along with the Mill House press runs, but said she did not like it and tried to quash its distribution.[35]

Toomer's change of pen name was also connected to his image as a writer.

and early 1940s] (JTP 22:28); interview of Georges and Elizabeth Duval, Lumberville, Pa., July 22, 1982.

33. JT to Haniel Long, June 9, 1937, in JTP 7:1.

34. *Ibid.*

35. JT, *A Fiction and Some Facts* (N.p., n.d., [Doylestown, Pa., *ca.* 1937?]) copy in JTP 1:12; MCT interview, Doylestown, Pa., August 26, 1981.

Probably correctly, he surmised that publishers were looking for his old lyrical style of writing, one that he had deliberately abandoned. But publishers, interested in at least breaking even, likely saw little in his current writing that could be perceived as appealing to a large enough audience. Toomer, in his letter to Haniel Long, could have been referring to any one of three psycho-religious collections he had put together that year. One closely related to his lectures and work at Mill House but very difficult to follow was "Psychologic Papers," written as a sort of diary, with each entry dated. It was an experiment in organization, growing out of his belief that something greater was guiding his hand and that therefore the ideas, written down as they came to him, would form an intended—though not readily perceptible—pattern in the reader's mind. Aphorisms ("A man's wife is his most difficult pupil") alternate with anecdotal examples and theoretical explanations. "I do not aim to present a clear mental abstract," he explains in one entry; "I aim to present total man. . . . Thus I have (1) the logic of the mind . . . ; (2) the logic of the emotions; and (3) the logic of the body. Moreover (and this is what will be especially confusing) you will find the psychologic, the form which comes into being, as I pass from one center to the other." In another place he talks about "[a]ssociative, logical, and psychological writing alternating . . . so that the reader cannot 'catalog' but is compelled to . . . form a general impression of the whole."[36]

The whole collection, though it seemed to him to be coming directly by inspiration, in fact reproduces the theory and directions for behavior he was using in Portage in 1931, which were grounded in his work with Orage from 1924 to 1926. Some of Toomer's terms are different, but all the major concepts are there: the world a prison, the human potential caged inside the mechanical person-shell, the false psyche formed within the self, the need to wake from waking sleep, the use of shocks and tensions for growth, the "extraction of psychological substances" from experience, the three-part makeup of the self, and the need for bringing those parts into harmony. In 1930 he had acknowledged, "With certain notable exceptions every one of my main ideas has a G. [Gurdjieff] idea as its parent," but now he seemed to believe he was either original or a direct conduit from a divine source. His figures and images are sometimes vivid and often more acceptable—that is, closer to everyday usage—than the Gurdjieffian terminology, and his exhortations are compelling. However, the instructions are too vague or cryptic for the reader to apply. The problem may have been that he was writing for others, but just as much for

36. JT, "Psychologic Papers," September 9, August 17, 1936 (JTP 41:3, 47:4).

himself: "Being neither scientist, scholar, nor philosopher, but artist, I am not chiefly interested in theoretical structure, . . . but in the function of right thinking as it applies to the creation and the re-creation of man. . . . I do not write so as to make 'systems', nor so as to contribute to psychology or to literature, but so as to contribute to my own development and to the development of those others who find food in my kitchen." Toomer's "diagrammatical writings," in which he "use[s] words, as lines in a drawing, to represent or suggest certain of the essential features of complex realities," may have been valuable tools to his own conscious development, but they remain obscure to the reader. Even Marjorie was not favorable to his scheme for presenting these ideas, and the size of the audience that might be interested in sharing Toomer's self-exploration just did not encourage publication.[37]

That spring, 1937, he sent some of these philosophic or "psycho-logic" papers to William Butler Yeats, noting that the spirit in his writing was the same as that which had moved Thoreau, Emerson, and Whitman.[38] Receiving no reply, he sent them to R. P. Watt and Son, the London firm that published some of Yeats's work. Jean apparently thought his work would be in a comparable category, but the papers were rejected. Some also went to a close associate of Alfred Stieglitz's, Dorothy Norman, who was starting a journal. But Jean indicated that the papers would be published as a book in the late winter or early spring, and on that ground Norman sent them back.

In the same summer, Wharton Esherick's eleven-year-old son Peter came to stay at Mill House rather than going to a summer camp. He helped with the physical work on the farm, and at four o'clock in the afternoon, he shared in the family-community's "deserving time." This was a custom Jean had developed much earlier. He mentions it as part of an early visit to the Stieglitz home at Lake George, when he would pull a bunch of ripe grapes to munch on at about four o'clock. Then, in the winter, when there were no grapes, he would become restless and go get some wine. He could have it if he "deserved to have it, in the sober opinion of O'Keeffe and Margaret [the long-term Stieglitz family servant]." Now almost a sacred ritual in Jean's life, "deserving time" was for everyone a chance to stop work and gather for a drink and a relaxing time. "It needn't be hard liquor but the adults usually would; the children had ginger ale and cookies or something." During these times, Jean began talking to Peter, asking questions that would get him to think and that would develop a particular line of reasoning that Jean had in mind. It was another way of present-

37. JT notes, 1930 (JTP 17:1); JT, "Psychologic Papers," October 28, 1936 (JTP 41:3); MCT notebook, July 8, 1937 (MTC).
38. JT to W. B. Yeats, April 8, 1937, in JTP 10:11.

ing his basic philosophy about man and his place in the world, including such issues as the several functions that make up the self (*Is* Peter his body?); the difference between human beings and animals; the enlargement of one's effectiveness by knowing history, exchanging resources with others, and breaking out of smaller environments into larger; and the necessity of holding all beliefs tentatively until tested by one's experience. Along with the basic Gurdjieffian idea of the three centers of functioning, he introduced that of the various levels of consciousness: "By podding as a pea bursts from its pods for the next stage in its growth from family, community, state, nation, and so on, we are born above the body." [39]

Peter evidently responded alertly and enjoyed his talks; even Argie, only five, asked when her father was going to hold talks with *her*. Marjorie was so impressed that she began taking down the conversations in shorthand. After several had been recorded, she suggested that Jean write them up for publication. He worked on sixteen talks, slightly expanding his own comments but changing nothing of what Peter said. The manuscript was sent to Norton in August of 1937 and was rejected in September. In October, Dutton rejected both "Talks with Peter" and "Psychologic Papers."

"Talks with Peter" was sent off again in November, this time to Macmillan, accompanied by a letter once more raising questions about how to change Toomer's public image:

How to market a book on a basic human theme by a writer who is known to some people as a Negro writer? . . . Whatever I was born and whatever the associations that became linked to my name, I have since developed into a citizen of the world through birth above the body, and all that I write and live is inevitably, from a human being to human beings. This is not simply a "position"; it is a reality. . . .

It might be more simple to discard the name Toomer and take a new name for this new series of writings. A new name, any name, or no name. I am no longer concerned with personal fame; all I want is to put into the world just these very "seeds in a hurricane." [40]

Toomer clearly wanted this to be one of a series of books that combined his crucial experience of transformation and his adaptation of Gurdjieff's ideas. He felt that the public needed these ideas as badly as he wanted to communicate them.

Although the publishers were not convinced, the creative river was still flowing. Chaunce and Tockie Dupee had spent the summer at Mill House, no

---

39. JT, "The Hill" (Typescript in JTP 13:1); MCT interview, November 19, 1974; JT, "Talks with Peter" (JTP 46:1), 96.

40. JT to Mr. Titterton at Macmillan, November 18, 1937, in JTP 7:7.

doubt stimulating Jean to further concentration on Gurdjieffian principles and practices. He worked doggedly through the fall, putting the Gurdjieff material in still another form, a succession of fifty-three segments, each a collection of aphorisms, developing the ideas of detachment from the world, "birth above the body," and use of adversity to attain greater truth. This was designed "for adults . . . who have some realization that man's problems are the consequences of his own psychology, and who therefore desire means more basic than economic and political change." In a note justifying the writing, there is a strange combination of humility and authority. He claims to be of no importance as a person, yet he says he serves as a channel for universal truth. He declares he would not write "were it not for some experiences of a higher order, for the fact that in my soil some sacred grains have been sown, some intuition, and a factor which occasionally operates as if it were the self behind me."[41] Macmillan sent back "Talks with Peter" just in time for Toomer to send them "Remember and Return: Some Means by Which Men Can Mend Themselves, Return to Their Human Natures, and Harmonize Their Worlds." Before Christmas it, too, was rejected.

Some of his enthusiasm by this time had ebbed. He felt that the summer of 1937 at Mill House had not been a true school. Referring to the "present discomforts, bickerings, petty criticisms and irritations among 'adults'" there, he decided that neither he nor other students of Gurdjieff had ever gotten past the kindergarten level.[42] After the publishers' rejections of his Gurdjieffian material, the plan for a Fontainebleau at Doylestown faded as well. Having rejected Gurdjieff the man but still retaining a Gurdjieffian philosophy, Jean found that his big break, either through the publishing world or through his father-in-law's financial assistance, was still eluding him. He was again gathering himself for another flow into the spiritual world, this time in search of a person, or of a group, who might give him the support he needed in the absence of Gurdjieff himself.

Neither as fiction nor as "psycho-logic," disguised or pure, could Jean Toomer seem to get anything through to the audience that he felt was somewhere out there in need of his answers and his methods. Beyond his successes in direct contacts is a looming sense of failure with the larger world. A later diary entry, "Idea of a novel or drama," is perhaps the most telling comment on himself and his publishing efforts: "A man with fine aims and high values works

41. JT to Lois Cole at Macmillan, December 11, 1937, in JTP 7:7; JT, "Remember and Return" (MTC), 34.
42. JT note, July 20, 1937 (JTP 54:5).

and suffers for creative life—events of force. In an age when no one cares, the majority of people simply do not respond to him, while even those who do care (as long as he is present) are not willing to do much, and they soon forget him."[43]

43. JT diary entry (JTP 17:9).

12

Passage to India

The year 1937 was one of intense activity. In terms of contacts with the larger world, 1938 seems almost a blank. But in fact several things were happening in Toomer's closer relationships. Jean was turning back to his most powerful religious experience, the epiphany of 1926. The Toomers were becoming more a part of the community, and Jean spoke out for a local cause; they were also exploring a new religious community, the Quakers. They had to consider the possibility of a new baby. Marjorie was gradually moving away from her devotion to Jean's infallibility, and Jean, lately sounding so sure, was coming to suffer a growing sense of incompleteness, a need for a new infusion or a new system of belief.

Seeking some explanation for the continued rejection of his recent books, Toomer began to believe that these fruits of his seminal experience of "birth above the body" were somehow inaccessible and sterile because he had not written about their source. In one of his letters to Macmillan he said, "Neither in *Talks with Peter* nor in *Remember and Return* have I thrown off all restrictions and allowed the religious base to come through with all possible purity and force. I must develop to this ability." In December of 1937 he outlined what he intended to do. This was preceded by a history of his response to the original powerful experience—the five years of productive work; then a sixth when "my very psyche, all of it, was fatigued" (that was the year of Margery's death, but he does not mention it); then in the ensuing years a renewal, "a flow, indeed a veritable flood of insights, perceptions, and feelings"; then another period of questioning, out of which arose the felt need to record the foundations of his knowledge. When he recorded this experience on paper, he believed, he could go on to write books on spiritual powers, psychology, and society. A fourth, the capstone, would indicate the methods of attaining the goals described in the other three books. In the first few months of 1938 he wrote some seventy-five pages of a book describing his theory of basic spiritual development, and for the next year and a half he worked on recapturing on paper his incredible experience of 1926.[1]

As 1938 began, Marjorie, who had been faithfully taking care of an indefinitely expandable household for Jean's benefit, was several months' pregnant but suffering difficulties with carrying the child. She was forty-three; when they were first married, she had hoped for a child, but by now it seemed too late. Jean, however, felt that the experience, even with its problems, brought some advantages: "Some new and deeper fulfillment has come to her, and she has been more quietly happy than I have known her to be. . . . Now that Marjorie has had the benefit of several months of happiness and fulfillment, it would be a blessing if Nature relieved her, and all of us, of further complications."[2] The pregnancy did in fact end in a miscarriage, putting Marjorie for a time in the hospital. There would be no children from this union.

Soon after they moved to Doylestown, Marjorie was in the market looking for some fish for dinner. There, she met Dorothy Paxson, a woman whom she felt to be a kindred spirit. And Paxson was intrigued with Marjorie's colorful long skirts and distinctive carriage, judging her a gem in a conservative town. Confessing to each other that neither knew much about fish, they continued their acquaintance over a cup of tea. The Paxsons were Quakers, their existence and appearance refuting Marjorie's image of an obsolete sect. On the strength of their new friendship, Marjorie and Jean began visiting the Quaker meeting nearby, the Buckingham Meeting of the Religious Society of Friends. A second attraction was the meeting's small elementary school located next door. Not far removed from its days as a two-room schoolhouse in which an authoritarian teacher dispensed corporal punishment, it had been enlarged and modernized and given a forward-looking principal. The school became the Toomers' choice for their daughter Argie, and it was the focus of much of Marjorie's interest and activity for the next eight years.

For several years of apprenticeship, they went to Buckingham Meeting and sat each Sunday morning in silence. The quiet worship allowed room for an individual's own religious approach, and while neither Jean nor Marjorie had been actively seeking a church home, they found this a satisfying experience. At the same time, with characteristic intensity, Jean was picking up old

1. JT to Mr. Putnam, n.d., in JTP 8:7; JT, "Experience Above Being" notes (JTP 26:7).
2. JT to H. Content, January 24, 1938, in JTP 1:11.

Quaker journals in secondhand bookshops and reading up on Quaker history. The two newcomers took in the full range of larger meetings, the Quarterly Meetings, which included a group of individual meetings like Buckingham located near each other, and the Yearly Meetings in Philadelphia, which gathered together a group of historically and theologically related Quarterly Meetings. When the Toomers were becoming associated with Quakerism, Arch Street and Race Street, the two Yearly Meetings in Philadelphia that together represented the largest concentration of Quakers in the world, were taking steps to come together after a split that had occurred in the nineteenth century. Marjorie and Jean, like many new members, found the differences among the various branches of Friends more tedious than substantive, and the move toward unity could easily be endorsed by such an anti-classificationist as Jean.

Yearly Meeting lasted a whole week each March, and the Toomers took it all in. Marjorie was amazed that even in these big meetings, "anybody could get up and speak. . . . The *democracy* of the whole thing impressed me very much." Occasionally Jean was asked to speak. At Buckingham Friends' School's PTA in January of 1939 he spoke on man's basic struggle—between egotism and "Beinghood" within him rather than between God and Devil outside him. Near that time he also gave a talk to an adult class at Swarthmore Meeting. But they were still not fully aware of the customs of Friends when in February of 1939 he wrote to Howard and Anna Brinton, then directors of Pendle Hill, a Quaker research and study center just outside of Philadelphia, suggesting that he give a lecture there. He included in his credentials some pamphlets of his and a "small book" (probably *Essentials*). But his salutation "Mr. and Mrs. Brinton" showed that he was not familiar with Quaker ways, since Quakers use both first and last names instead of "Mr." or "Mrs." in formal address. Howard Brinton replied that the calendar was full but Jean Toomer was welcome to come to tea any Thursday to hear the scheduled speaker.[3]

Toward the end of 1938, the highway department proposed building a new highway across the land of several farmers, threatening the Toomers' property as well and giving rise to considerable local protest. Toomer wrote an article that was published in the Doylestown *Daily Intelligencer*, January 11, 1939, and reprinted as a pamphlet under the Mill House imprint. In it he suggested that members of the highway department be seen not as enemies but as people, subject like their critics to pervasive cultural pressures. All of us, he said, have

3. MCT interview, November 12, 1974; JT to Howard and Anna Brinton, February 7, 1939, Howard Brinton to JT, February 18, 1939, both in JTP 3:8.

endorsed speed for its own sake, approved of new highways taking others' land if that increased our own convenience, and in general placed mechanical above human values. He pointed out that when machines serve men, this is positive progress; when machines make robots of men, however, this is negative mechanization. He appealed for a joint deliberative process to choose "humanization over mechanization." He sent copies of the pamphlet to highway officials as well as to local citizens and invited both to meetings at which he stressed principles of ecology. His article was well received locally, and some people credit his efforts as having influenced the results. The road was not built according to the projected plan.[4]

As the year turned through the winter, Toomer became increasingly distressed by a mismatch between his image of himself, what he felt he should be doing, and his actual ability to function. In April of 1938 he had written that fourteen years before, he had "received means from an Awake Source," which he had employed ever since, but he was no longer sure that the means were truly effective, since he was not awake yet. "Plainly, unless I do awake within the next year, I should again seek him who is awake." Since then, he had actively pursued prayer and meditation, his prayers directed to "Great Being" or "Indwelling Being." One prayer, written in July, he chose to use as a Christmas greeting in 1938:

> I return to Thee
> By Thy Grace
> Out of the body of this death:
> This is the meaning of the sigh,
> As I breathe again,
> As I lift from labor in oblivion,
>   in a land worse than exile,
>   whose one reality is a nameless dull horror,
> Wherein I have struggled as in a dark river of coils,
>   not knowing those coils from my limbs or my arms from
>   those coils,
> As I lift and sigh, and breathe again,
> And once again glimpse Thy River,
> Thy Meaning and Thy Light,
> And give thanks that I rise—
> One tear in the left eye,
> Falls to the dark river I am leaving,
> As the eye opens to The Life,

4. JT, *Roads, People, and Principles* (Doylestown, Pa., 1939). A copy of this fourteen-page Mill House pamphlet can be found in MTC.

> And I would lift my arms,
>   opened to embrace Thee
> Who have embraced me once again.

But by February of 1939, he was not so sure he was out of the dark river, writing:

> Tired, I have come to the door of the deep rest;
> Exhausted, I have come to the gate of the deep force;
> I have come. I wait.

By March, 1939, he was questioning even his work on describing his mystical experience, wondering if he was using this to strengthen his ego. He began to feel that the Gurdjieff method he had been learning and teaching, which was designed, he believed, for use in active experience, perhaps needed supplanting or supplementing with a method "such as meditation, applicable in quiet moods." He felt that certain changes in his life had brought him to a new state, but he was reluctant to take a different path without the guidance of a wise teacher.[5]

He had also noticed that after each productive, creative period, he was likely to get sick and be unable to work, sometimes for several months. He felt that his work, since it involved the body being passive and the higher self active, lowered his body's resistance. In addition, there seemed to be an oppressive entity just outside him that was keeping him from being effective or even comfortable. He had long thought of his body as a shell or pod out of which one who participated in true Being would be able to emerge at will. This might happen literally, as he felt he had done at the el station in 1926, or it might happen figuratively, as in the Quakers' "centering down." Either way, the body would be clearly ruled by pure Being. But now it somehow seemed that his normal body was too much in the way and that there was a "second body," a kind of envelope surrounding him. Earlier he had thought of this as the "astral body" and believed it was a stage of growth toward larger being, but it seemed now to be against him. At times it became more active, hampering and constricting him. He could not understand this experience, nor could any of his Gurdjieff approaches help him solve the problems it presented. His goal was partly physical relief and partly spiritual enlightenment. He was actively seeking a new way, a new system, a new teacher. In 1937 he had written, "Nor will it help us to go to India. The disruptive vibrations of our civilization have be-

---

5. JT meditation, April 10, 1938 (JTP 56:15); JT poem, July 24, 1938 (JTP 50:37); JT note, February 24, 1939 (JTP 50:63); JT to Mrs. Bailey, December 2, 1938, in JTP 1:3.

come part of our second nature; perforce we would take them with us into the blue silences of paradise."[6] In this he may have been his own best prophet, but now he had gradually become convinced that he had to go to India to find what he was looking for.

Marjorie could not agree. The Mill House experience had grown more and more abrasive for her, though she began it with good will and with faith in Jean's leadership and she had doggedly tried to follow his instructions for her own transformation. Used to spending the day in her darkroom or as she chose, with a maid to manage the kitchen, now she found herself mostly picking, cleaning, and cooking vegetables, washing dishes, shopping, caring for his child and other visiting children, and meeting the many needs of a houseful of assorted guests. To add to her discomfort, she was sometimes rebuffed by Jean when she tried to ask a question during discussion times with guests. She had come to feel that he might be performing more for the satisfaction of the teacher than for the good of the pupil. With his image tarnished, she could no longer believe that everything he did or thought was right and wise. Besides her disillusionment, she knew that Jean had never been good at foreign languages and was worried that they might have severe language problems in the more remote areas of India. He also had real physical ailments and even when well, reacted negatively to situations of physical discomfort such as camping or traveling under less than ideal conditions. Anyone could see how tenuous the world's balance was at the moment. If war broke out, they might not be able to get back—or Jean might decide to spend the rest of his life there in a place fraught with difficulties. She did not want to go; she did not think he could manage alone; there was nothing for seven-year-old Argie to do there but they did not want to leave her behind. Over Marjorie's protest, plans were made for all three to go.

Jean was aware of her feeling. An entry in his journal for August 24, 1939, describes this period: "Marjorie was going to her death. This was her strongest sense of it. I was going to my life. This was my strongest sense of it. I am not overwriting. This is exactly how it was. Our life together at that point was a silent drama of sheer extremes. . . . It was as though doom and salvation were sitting side by side holding hands."[7]

In April, apparently as a kind of rest cure, Jean had gone alone to Bermuda for about three weeks. At that time Marjorie's letters were still tender: "You'll have to conjure up your massage tonight and tomorrow morning I'll have to do

6. JT, "Psychologic Papers," January 22, 1937 (JTP 41:3).
7. JT, India journal (JTP 17:4).

the same sort of trick at 5 AM—turn over, conjure a shoulder and encircling arm—and sink into a second rest." She was still committed to "the work," keeping up discussions and assignments with Lin, and was spending some time typing Jean's manuscript "From Exile into Being." One of her letters to him included a message psychically received by a friend, passed on without comment: "Jean must go to India, because there he will find himself. Marjorie will suffer for awhile—but later she will be happier than ever before." Giving this message little credence, Marjorie was "hoping against good sense—that with a resurgence of vigor—some other event might take place—a major event that would make the Indian search unnecessary right now."[8]

Bermuda proved not enough; Jean insisted on going to India. The money, as usual, had to come from Harry Content, Marjorie's father. He could not really understand the point of the trip, and Marjorie could not wax very enthusiastic, but she did second Jean's request. Although he pleaded financial reverses, Content indicated to Jean, "I can not remember when I ever refused Marjorie, anything that she asked." Jean's effusive letter thanking him for underwriting the trip included the justification:

I have come to a critical pass and am faced with these alternatives; either I go on and up and become virtually a new man fully able to do the work in the world for which I have been preparing all these years, or else I sink back into a condition which I do not want to imagine. . . .

. . . I am deeply convinced that going to India *is* the right thing to do, the only thing to do, and that in a years [*sic*] time other people will be able to realize that it was the right thing, because they will see in me and in her a new vitality, a new energy, a health, a new happiness, an enrichment, and a much greater capacity to be of real service to other human beings.

A letter of further explanation quickly followed, saying Jean was expecting through the India trip to obtain the resources necessary to cope with major world problems. "What I chiefly need is a lot more energy. In other respects I am fairly well equipped. In India, from ancient times, certain men have known how to teach a man to draw on and use the power that is usually locked away under the surface." He suggests that when he has gained this power, "I will be in a position to advance my work in the world so that, among other things, we will derive a living income from it, and I will be able to relieve you of at least a few things that are now bothering you." What was bothering Harry Content was that since Marjorie's marriage to Jean, she had supported the family with the allowance from her father. Almost nothing had come in from

8. MCT to JT, April 24, 25 (quoting letter from Maria), May 4, 1939, all in JTP 9:8.

Toomer's writing—notices report miniscule royalties such as $26.68 in 1936 from *The New Caravan*—and he had not collected money from guests at Mill House as he had from his groups in Chicago. In fact the Toomers were paying Lin Davenport and others for working on the farm and grounds.[9]

On July 19, 1939, the Toomers sailed from New York. In London, Jean was already feeling uncomfortable, and he was having several drinks before he went to bed. The passage by ship was full of annoyances. Late in August, five days after they landed in Ceylon, war broke out. This confirmed Marjorie's fears, but Jean proceeded without much plan, waiting for the meeting with someone as yet unknown who should tell him what he needed to know. Going up the east coast of India, he made arrangements to visit the Theosophical Center at Adyar, Madras, where Laura Chase, an old friend of Margery Latimer's, was living. When these plans were abruptly broken off without explanation, Laura chided, "I am sorry you have gone away so quickly, as I think we have here what you are looking for." But Jean was following another lead. In an ashram in the village of Arunachalla, north of Madras, he sought out a Maharishi Sri Ramanasramam, for whom he had high hopes—not borne out on arrival. After a report of this disappointing encounter was sent to Mill House, Lin reassured him, "So the meeting with the Maharishi was not The Meeting. . . . I do feel that you *will* find it. . . . I truly believe that you will return with all that you have need of." Santiniketan, Rabindranath Tagore's village with the school he had founded, provided a pleasant visit, but that was all. The hope flared again as Jean headed north of Calcutta for Ghoom, a hamlet tucked away in the mountains near Darjeeling. There he spent time with a Buddhist monk, Anagarika Govinda, a former German citizen who had become a British citizen in order to remain in India without harassment during the war. Govinda's life and teaching were attractive to Toomer, but not enough to pass his test of inner, inescapable certainty. Although he considered establishing a study center with Govinda and a Tibetan lama, and although he perceived Buddhism as "by all odds the most genuine, most impressive, the most promising Way that I have encountered" during the trip, he could not commit himself to Buddhism. Such a commitment would require total involvement, including a trip to Tibet and rejecting the Gurdjieff way, which he had followed for fifteen years. Nor was he convinced that Buddhism would provide the immediate help he required.[10]

For a couple of weeks he floated, going to Agra and then Delhi. He asked

9. Content to JT, June 14, 1939, JT to Content, June 13, 18, 1939, all in JTP 1:11.

10. Laura Chase to JT, September 23, 1939, in JTP 1:10; Franklin Davenport to JT, October 18, 1939, JT to Govinda, October 15, 1939, both in MTC.

himself the question others must have asked him: What about Gandhi? He had, he said, met Gandhi all over India, but not in person. In an October letter to Stieglitz, he extolled Gandhi as the one man who was trying to introduce a human element into politics, "*the* man of the India of today, . . . the one world figure that India has produced since Buddha." Then why not try to meet him? He did not know: "All I know is that at the present I am not moved to move any closer to him than I now am." [11]

By early November he had concluded that the kind of man he was looking for could be found only in a large center of population, contrary to his first expectations. The logic seems to be tied closely to Jean Toomer's comfort. Jean had found it impossible to sit cross-legged on the ground or adapt to village facilities. Since, therefore, the only "suitable quarters" for him and his American family existed in large cities, he concluded that a man like him, "a man who had a message to give the world of his time, a man who had a message that could hitch on to me," could be living and working only in a large city. "A life of withdrawal from the world as I have seen it lived in India is not the life for me." [12] This simplified his next moves, as it reduced the number of places he had to visit in search of The Meeting.

By this time, in fact, he was almost convinced that The Meeting would not happen. He had written at the end of October, "If I do not (come) to hate India it will be a miracle of love. (Thus far that miracle has not happened)." Now he was saying that he did not hate India but was taking it as medicine. He was turning back to what he had known before: "My experiences thus far in pursuit of new psychological means have continued to make me realize the excellence of the means I already possess. So much is this so that I have sometimes wondered if, in coming over here, I were in the queer position of seeking to find that which I already have." He implied that the Gurdjieff work had taken him further than any system he had encountered in India, and he overtly endorsed Quakerism: "If Quakerism had the catalytic action that it did in the days of George Fox and Robert Barclay, there would be nothing that we have seen and heard in the East thus far that could be as useful for the right process of American life. Even as Quakerism now is I think it is better for Americans than any religion or way of life that we have seen here thus far." [13]

A week later, from Delhi, he sent a closely typed four-page summary of what he had learned. The nearer he got to exploring other "direct means to

11. JT to Alfred Stieglitz, October 21, 1939, in MTC.
12. JT to "Family in America," November 3, 1939, in MTC.
13. JT, India journal, October 25–27 (JTP 17:4); JT to "Family in America," November 3, 1939, in MTC.

Being," the more repelled he was by the kind of life they required, including withdrawal from the world. As justification, he contended that the world is pressing on us all, and even Easterners cannot keep withdrawing much longer. Before his trip he had been looking for "a means that involves the least possible concern with the body-personality and its world," a means that could be used in silence and meditation. Now he turned again to "psychologic means . . . to be employed in the midst of experience. . . . Instead of asking for Being I am now asking to be made whole. . . . We must be made whole, I think, before we can truly be ready to enter and abide in Being." [14]

Although he left room for the unexpected to happen, he seemed in his November 10 letter to Lin and others at Mill House to be putting the best possible face on a failed mission. A brief stop in Bombay brought no revelation. Nor did repeated visits, back in Colombo, to the ashram of a saintly man called the Venerable Teacher. There were some gains to record by December, however. He felt clear about what he was to do from then on:

The total experiences in India and Ceylon have brought to the fore the excellence for us of America of just the work we have been doing at Mill House these past years. . . . From now on I will be able to accept and fulfill the function allotted to me by great life, without feeling remiss for not seeking a teacher greater than I. I came to this part of the world, as you know, to surrender myself to something greater than I. Such a being, in the flesh, I have not met. The Meeting, as things now seem, was to be a meeting with my own best knowledge, using my own in the non-egotistical sense. [15]

The "outer work" that he saw for himself, in addition to the inner work, may have been indicated by a description in his private notebook. In a November 19 entry, under the heading "Nathan Jean Toomer, Consultant in Human Relationships . . . Racial Relations, Religious Relations, Social Relations," he outlined the kind of reconciling work he would do. He noted that his worldwide experience qualified him for this, and he suggested a fee from those who could pay and free service for those who could not. He imagined his work would be under the umbrella of the American Friends Service Committee, a Quaker organization with which he had become familiar in his growing association with the Friends.

Some personal progress seemed to have been made, too. He believed he was cured of "that curiously distressing physical condition [not further explained] I was in before I left home"—though not with the help of anyone in India whom he had asked about it. In respect to his "second body" problem, "he is as mys-

14. JT to "Our Family in America," November 10, 1939, in MTC.
15. JT to his "family" at home, December 13, 1939, in MTC.

terious and as active as ever, but his activity seems to have become coordinated with the other activities of my totality." And in regard to Marjorie's apprehensions, he was sure that the experience of coping had been good for her. Marjorie, however, could not fully agree. They made their way home, across the Pacific, on erratically available Italian and Japanese ships. When the engines stopped once in mid-Pacific, she thought the end had come. The ship resumed its course, but the sour taste of the trip was still there for her, thirty-five years later.[16]

Despite the determined optimism of his letters to Lin, Jean's private assessment of the venture was bitter. He wrote that he had proved a poor physician in prescribing the trip for himself. In his notebook is this summary:

Nov. 12. In details, so it proved, I had been so wrong as to invite disaster.

Nov. 28. By aim and hope my record was to have been given complete in these simple words—I have entered Being.

Nor was I to have written or even spoken of it. The reality was to have shown in a quiet brightness in my life, as a light that kindled the same light in others, without words. . . .

Instead of saying I have entered Being, I can but say I've been around the world.

It has cost five thousand dollars to complete my disillusionment.[17]

In spite of its apparent failure, the momentum of the India trip carried Jean on for a few months but was brought by midsummer to an abrupt halt which marked for him a new boundary between two successive lives.

Lin Davenport brought their station wagon to the West Coast in January of 1940, and the Toomers then started back across the country. Although Marjorie became seriously ill with a gallbladder attack in Santa Fe, they were all so eager to get home that they went on without waiting for her to recover. In Pennsylvania, however, a heavy snowstorm had blocked a patch of highway, and their car slid into the suddenly stopped car ahead. Limping to the nearest town, Washington, Pennsylvania, they learned that it would take several days to replace their mangled radiator. Jean, undaunted, with his old self-assurance and charm, went to the local college, represented himself as an expert on India, and was immediately scheduled to give some lectures during their forced stay.[18]

Through the early spring, he tackled several new projects with enthusiasm, "re-establishing connections," as he reported in a letter to Gorham Munson, "with the men and movements of my time." By way of implementing his

16. *Ibid.*; interview of MCT, Doylestown, Pa., August 26, 1981.
17. JT, India journal.
18. MCT interview, August 26, 1981.

status as a professional consultant in the art of co-opposition, which he had projected in a statement composed in India the preceding December, he drafted a letter in March establishing or proposing an organization called "The Friends of Being." He conceived this as an association of people who affirmed and pledged themselves to work for "the beinghood of man" and to oppose "anti-being" in themselves and in their friends, who were dedicated to "the creative and balanced development of human beings, as human beings—not as bodies only, not as spirits only, but as beings-with-bodies working out their destinies on this earth, . . . [and] dedicated to the overcoming of separatism of all kinds." Members would use co-opposition and educate others in its practice. At the top of the letter are blanks labeled Director, Associates, Committee, evidently for his name and those of others not yet enlisted. As the business address for this and for his professional consultant operations, he intended to use the house at 39 West Tenth Street, which the family still retained.[19] These proposals are in draft form and were probably never sent out.

At about the same time, he was working on two pieces of writing that came out of the trip to India. The shorter and more finished of these is a drama, called first "The Colombo-Madras Mail," which he started on February 8 while still in Santa Fe. It went through several versions and several titles, including "Tourists in Spite of Themselves" and "Pilgrims, Did You Say?" The characters, completely generic in one version (Mr., Mrs., and Miss European), have names in another (Master, named John; Lady, called Mary; and Missie, called Grettie) but are, of course, Jean, Marjorie, and their seven-year-old daughter Argie. The Sinhalese bearer from Colombo has in all versions his real name, Munasingha. The family suffers a number of minor crises in their compartment on the Indian train—a leaky roof, a siege by coolies, beggars asking for baksheesh, a sweeper coming in to clean the floor, and someone else mistakenly claiming the same compartment—while Munasingha fends off all assaults, and John develops a philosophical discourse about man as the family's dinner is getting cold. Toomer's intention was to bring into sharp relief the greed, rapacity, and oppression among men, which, he felt, existed everywhere but were perhaps more openly manifested in India. He also suggests the physical problems of traveling in India and the difficulty of following any spiritual pursuit in such surroundings.[20]

The second India-based piece was much more ambitious. It was to be a book

19. JT to GM, November 2, 1940, in GMC; JT proposal, March 10, 1940 (JTP 70:1).
20. JT, "The Colombo-Madras Mail" (different versions in JTP 49:2, 49:10); JT's intention indicated in notebook (JTP 17:4).

on India, illustrated by Marjorie's photographs. Far from a travelogue, "The Angel Begori" seems to have been conceived as the complement to the emphasis on despiritualization in "Tourists in Spite of Themselves." It represents the total spiritualization of a trip to India that begins with an angel's invitation to choose a trip to Russia or to India for the purpose of enlightenment. Its form is that of a novel, its characters' names recalling the verbal playfulness of Toomer's Chicago period—the angel Begori, Mr. Philip Gosh, and his friend Bob Gee. The story opens with the words, "'Good Lord!' said Begori; and the Lord, not having been praised for some time, bent down and elevated Begori to the status of an angel." The angel Begori does very little that is miraculous, but from time to time he enables those near him to enter unexpectedly into a sense of temporary participation in a higher state of being. He also provides the funds for the trip, but in an erratic way. Gosh recognizes that this is intended to help him eliminate his unfortunate habit of showing off with money. Philip Gosh, "your aging friend . . . with his stiff legs and medicine bottles" and a somewhat bent body, yearns to enter and leave his body at will. He is surely Jean Toomer. Another character, Lincoln Ahwell, who appears on shipboard with his wife and seven-year-old daughter, is surely Jean Toomer also. And perhaps Bob Gee, enthusiastic and idealistic, is a younger version of Jean. Although there is considerable discussion of philosophy, goals and methods (at one point Ahwell begins, "I have a theory—" and goes on for almost four pages without a paragraph break), the story begins well, with characterization, description, and humor, and arouses some interest in what will develop. However, the 150 pages that Toomer completed take the characters only to the first day on shipboard, and what was to develop once they were on the soil of sacred India remains a matter of speculation.[21]

During these spring months of 1940, while Jean was turning his experiences into writing, presumably cured in India of his immediate ills and ready to begin a new surer concentration on what he already knew, he began instead to have alarming symptoms of physical difficulty. He had several attacks of pain while visiting with Marjorie's father in New York. He had to cancel the talk on India he was scheduled to give for Buckingham Meeting in early May. Referred from one doctor to another, he discovered eventually that one kidney was not functioning. Removal of the kidney was prescribed, and on May 12 he entered Abington Hospital, where he spent six hours on the operating table and five weeks before he could return home.

21. JT, "The Angel Begori," also titled "Exile's Bridge" (JTP 15:1).

This operation seemed to be a watershed of some sort. The kidney had apparently been malfunctioning for some time. Now that the problem had been diagnosed and taken care of, Jean should have been in fine physical shape. Yet he was not; he seemed instead to have been left weaker. His wife felt, on looking back, that this was the beginning of his steady decline in health for the rest of his life, though in some strange way it affected him more mentally than physically: "His *dignity* seemed to have been hurt" was the way she put it. He himself had a sense that he was fulfilling not his own but someone else's fate or karma. He hoped that his undergoing the operation would cleanse the slate, but the following November he noted, "Did not feel purified after operation. Do not yet so feel." [22]

One of his short stories, called "Lump," may illuminate his situation. The main character is "a tall semi-distinguished fellow with a stoop," a serious person in his early forties, who has an irrational fear of hospitals and therefore puts off for a long time the diagnosis of a lump in his mouth. He realizes eventually that he has "a lump in his psyche far larger and more harmful than the lump in his mouth," which is his ego, pride, vanity: "What he did fear, what he did resist with every atom in him was the surrendering of himself to any person in a vital situation. . . . No one should ever dominate him." Curtis, in the story, comes to a happy resolution, able with a nurse's help to submit to being dominated and to laugh at himself. [23] Perhaps what Jean Toomer could do in imagination he could not do in fact. In any case the psychic wound of this operation was so persistently evident to him that ten years later he was seeking relief from it by psychological probing.

On his return from the hospital, phlebitis set in, prolonging his inability to function. He found himself in November in a "curious state," as he wrote to Gorham Munson:

On the surface I feel fairly well . . . ; but the ordeal I underwent was a severe one that seems to have raised hell with my nervous system; my responses are below normal. I *care* as never before; yet, due to some damage to my apparatus that has not yet been repaired, I often act as though I give not one goddam about anything except a book I've begun writing. . . . Damme, Gorham, I even refuse bids to speak—and that is serious!

I was energized, "up and coming" on my return from the East. . . . And then, out of a clear sky, I was knocked down. And now I must again lift up myself before I'll be of any real use to any other. [24]

22. MCT interview, August 26, 1981; JT notebook, May 12, November 22, 1940 (JTP 57:1).

23. JT, "Lump," included in second collection of stories titled "Winter on Earth" (JTP 51:21).

24. JT to GM, November 2, 1940, in GMC.

Toomer's efforts to lift himself up were varied but only partially successful. He shifted the direction of his major writing projects, picking up his autobiography again and a little later developing and expanding that central segment of it which he considered so essential, his experience that began at the el station in 1926. His speaking and teaching grew, taking on a new form and focus. He tried many methods of physical and psychological healing, but ailments began to accumulate faster than they could be cured. He had a number of productive years still to come, but they were wrested out of struggle. From this point on, he husbanded his energy very carefully and could not get away from the image of himself as something of an invalid.

Sometimes it seemed to Jean as if events were pushing him, not necessarily in pleasant ways, in directions about which he had little choice. He described this process in his autobiographies as an illustration of the larger plan for human lives:

Now once again I was being moved by the drive that had never let me come to rest for very long, that had pushed me out of one life and into another, and out of the second into a third, in and out, up and down, through world after world, saying to each in turn—not this, not that. . . .

It makes us enter a world, not because that world in itself is good or bad or indifferent, but because it suits our needs of catharsis-development as of that time. So we enter a world, develop in it, develop through it, and, in time, develop out of it. . . . The essential concern seems to be the unending moving of human beings through life after life, through world after world, towards a long-range objective which remains undefined. [25]

This description referred to events of 1923, but the same sort of thing seemed to be happening to him again. Just as this physical watershed marked his movement from one life to the next, a significant change occurred in the overriding theme of what he was writing and teaching. Primarily psychological up to this period, his work, though retaining much of the same content, now became primarily religious.

25. JT, "The Second River" (JTP 66:8), 29, 31.

V.

THE QUAKER PERIOD

13.

Productive Years

Two of his former lives had roused echoes during this year of 1940, but neither brought much response. In April, Stanley Nott, an editor and an old friend with Gurdjieff connections, came to New York from England and wrote Jean that he would like to see him, but Jean answered that his ill health made it impossible. Again in May, Nott invited him to a benefit performance in New York of music composed by Gurdjieff. At this time Jean was in the hospital, but it is unlikely he would have accepted even if he had been well; he was not interested in Gurdjieff at this period. In the fall, an even earlier life of Toomer's was lifted above the shadows: the New York Public Library invited him as a special guest to a lecture by Langston Hughes about his new book *The Big Sea,* in which Toomer was mentioned. There was little appeal for Jean in this prospect.

However, at midsummer, his shaky physical state and his cutting down on activities and promises notwithstanding, Jean felt clear about one step, and Marjorie united with him. After about five years of attending meeting, they were ready to make a commitment to Quakerism. On August 28 he wrote the note that Buckingham Meeting required for membership: "For some time we have shared the fundamental faith of Friends, and now we are moved to join hands with you as members of the Society. We would also like our young daughter, Margery, to become a member. Please consider this brief note as a request for membership for the three of us." It was promptly acted upon, and the three became official members in October. [1]

In retrospect, Jean Toomer's participation in the Religious Society of Friends

1. Interview of MCT, Doylestown, Pa., August 26, 1981.

could be graphed almost as a bell curve, covering fifteen years. He participated in the activities of the local meeting as soon as he applied for membership, and then achieved prominence in the Quarterly and Yearly Meetings. His major area of work among Friends, as might be expected, had to do with spiritual growth, and during the middle of this period he developed this concern actively among young people as well as adults. The peak concentration of his activities among Friends was about 1947. From then on, he began resigning as chairman of committees and refusing requests to speak, gradually stopping his publication of articles, membership on committees, and finally even his attendance at meetings, including meeting for worship. There were a number of reasons for his withdrawal, both physical and mental. But the contribution Jean Toomer made in the Quaker segment of his life was significant and genuine, and his struggles were heartbreaking.

From a period of listening to and studying the Friends, the Toomers were swept rapidly into a time of active participation. Within little more than a year of their acceptance as members, Jean had been appointed to four committees, one on social service, one to nominate Buckingham Meeting's highest officers, one to compose answers to queries about the state of the Meeting, and one to care for the spiritual life of the Meeting. Indeed he was made chairman of the Social Service Committee almost immediately, and set about planning a series of talks and social gatherings that began in October of 1941. His goal was to use members' expertise and talents (including his own) to deal with topics such as "soil and water conservation, cooperation, nutrition, education, art, religion. . . . I get to do what I can to infuse new life and vitality into the Meeting and to relate the Meeting more fruitfully to the community in general." His own talk, given in November, was on the familiar theme of spiritual development. Asserting "That which truly profits me, truly profits everyone else," he declared that our proper sphere of action is internal rather than external—catharsis-development, integration, unification, working on our own growth to become increasingly able.[2]

The February, 1942, meeting in this series was, at the nudging of the Yearly Meeting Joint Committee on Race Relations, given over to the subject of minorities. Although there was a high concern for race relations in larger bodies of Friends at that period, Toomer's level of racial identification is suggested by his defining minorities as including Negro, German, and Japanese, and by his lukewarm answer in December, 1941, to an inquiry from Philadelphia as to the work his meeting was doing in minority problems and race relations:

2. JT to Betsey Barton, October 11, 1941, in JTP 11:4; JT notes (JTP 28:6).

"Some members of our Meeting, in line with the traditions of their families as well as out of personal concern, maintain friendly and helpful relations with Negroes and members of other minority groups. Our Meeting as a whole has no specific undertaking along these lines, as there seems to be no acute racial problem in our community. However, we are ready to do our best to meet whatever needs may arise."[3]

Jean was given very early a wide range of responsibilities, extending from race relations to concerns about peace and representation of the Meeting at ecumenical gatherings and even to arranging transportation for guests when their Meeting played host to a regional assembly. But the most intense interest for him was signified by his membership on the Committee of Ministry and Counsel. "Unprogrammed" Friends (the pattern of worship adopted at the founding of the Society of Friends and continued by the group to which Jean belonged) do not have any paid or designated minister for a congregation but rely on all members, sensitive to God's guidance, to minister to each other out of a worshipful silence. Among such Friends, this committee is a way of guarding this process. Responsible for the quality of worship of the Meeting and the members' spiritual life, the committee may also offer counseling on individual and group problems. Jean frequently spoke during meeting for worship, and he was soon relied on as a source of wisdom about spiritual matters. He also gave scheduled talks, such as "What Is Religion?" at Buckingham Meeting in January of 1941.

This special skill also received wider recognition. From the middle of 1941, both Jean and Marjorie were regularly appointed by the Monthly Meeting as representatives to Quarterly Meeting, the regional combination of individual congregations that meets every three months to discuss mutual concerns. There at Bucks Quarterly Meeting, Jean's religious messages were notable enough to be mentioned in the minutes of the local Meeting. He was asked, too, to compose answers to the questions about the Meeting's response to the religious needs of its members, answers that had to be turned in at each Quarterly Meeting. Several times his answers were included in full in the Quarterly Meeting minutes. By September, 1943, Jean had been made chairman of the Quarterly Meeting Ministry and Counsel Committee (a position he retained until 1948), and about the same time he and Marjorie were appointed delegates to a special conference on spiritual growth called by the Yearly Meeting. Further opportunities for service in the Yearly Meeting were to develop in 1946.

3. JT to Alberta Morris of Joint Committee on Race Relations of Arch and Race Street Yearly Meetings, in JTP 3:8.

In the meantime, the number of invitations for Toomer to speak was multiplying, and his energy seemed more equal to the task than it had been in that difficult year of 1940. Speaking at local women's clubs and service clubs followed his Monthly Meeting and Quarterly Meeting engagements. A different kind of challenge was presented by the invitation to speak in July, 1942, to the high school section of Friends General Conference at Cape May, New Jersey. This organization, including ten Yearly Meetings spread across North America, then held a national gathering every other summer at Cape May. It represents, as one among several such broad Quaker organizations, a theologically liberal orientation, but holds to the unprogrammed form of worship—the traditional "silent meeting."

For the high school students, Jean drew on the question "Dare we live our Christianity?" as his theme. He chose to focus on the need to face man's double reality—our "sins" (which he did not attempt to define in an orthodox fashion but rather suggested by a list of familiar negatives such as deceit, prejudice, and laziness) and our potential goodness. His charge to the young people was to view man as "an imperfect but perfectible compound," to deal strongly with the negatives but keep their hearts open to love what is lovable in all others.[4]

Toomer's message, the personal quality of its delivery, and his interaction with the young people were so well received that he became a regular part of the summer high school programs through 1948. He and Charles Ingerman, another Friend from the Doylestown area, shared the responsibility for teaching the twelfth-grade class at each biennial summer conference. Jean focused on the spiritual values and Charles concentrated on the pragmatic, privately thinking Jean to be one of the most impractical men he had ever met.[5]

Students who had experienced Jean's leadership in 1942 also asked for him as a keynote speaker for a conference they planned to hold at the Quaker study center, Pendle Hill, in March of 1943. Anna Brinton, who forwarded their request to him, wrote, "I might also add that we are ourselves desirous of making your further acquaintance."[6] This must have been a pleasant contrast to the Brintons' polite rejection four years earlier, when Jean had offered to lecture at Pendle Hill. For at least five successive years, 1943 through 1947, he was also asked to speak to the high school students at George School, a highly regarded Quaker boarding school not far from Doylestown.

His messages to young people through these years clustered around three

4. Talk by JT, "The Unseen Courage" (JTP 27:28).
5. Interview of Charles Ingerman, Doylestown, Pa., January 24, 1975.
6. Anna Brinton to JT, February 19, 1943, in JTP 3:9.

issues, all closely related. The first was growth, and as he pointed out in a talk entitled "Farmers of Men," the goal of Friends, or any religious people, was to lift man above the human condition to a "second birth," to create spiritual man. To achieve this, man has to take responsibility, do the necessary cultivating and planting, make good use of what is given him, but leave the results to God. The second issue was an aspect of the first: the importance of beliefs and choices. Beliefs are to the inner life what bones are to the body; sometimes they are shattered from the outside, but it is both possible and necessary to work at reconstructing them in the best possible form. The decisions arising from beliefs affect not only the self but the whole generation and actually the world. These two issues culminated in the third, prayer and worship as means for establishing a relationship with God, an open channel "to bring the best that is in you into your life, and your life into it."[7]

Another area of service to young people, begun in 1944 and continued through 1949, was Jean's work with the Young Friends of Philadelphia Yearly Meeting. This group included some people of high school age but mainly young adults of college age. Its formation had been partly fueled by the desire to overcome the historic divisions between Arch Street and Race Street Yearly Meetings. The Young Friends hired a college-age person as executive secretary and had an advisory board formed mostly of young people with only two older members. From 1944 through 1949, Jean Toomer was one of these adult advisors. The Young Friends held a number of retreat weekends at a camp or cabin or someone's home, and often Jean and Marjorie would be present, Marjorie quietly in the background—"the one who appeared with nuts and pretzels"— Jean talking, listening, leading inward to the basic resources, the inner light available to each person. He seemed to have a certainty about direction, and a way of getting in touch with divine strength, that the young people were eager for. Contemporary reactions reflect this. One participant wrote him: "[Your words] recalled to me my recent laxness and shortcomings in a very vivid way—and for a moment, at least, filled me with a deep desire to experience the dedication you spoke of. . . . We're very grateful to you." Robert Coe, for some

---

7. JT, "The Silent Meeting," October 11, 1948 (JTP 26:34). Similar thoughts occur in "Contact and Connectedness," Westtown, Pa., May 5, 1948 (JTP 22:36). Other concepts in this paragraph are from notes for the talks "Farmers of Men," George School, April 18, 1943 (JTP 23:27), "Man's Part, and God's," Pendle Hill, March 13, 1943 (JTP 24:42), "What Quakerism Means to Us as Individuals," Young Friends Conference, Moorestown, N.J., April 21, 1945 (JTP 28:14), "Creative Understanding, an Essential of Inward Reconstruction," Cape May, June 25, 1944 (JTP 23:4), and three talks at George School, January 27, 1946, January 14, 1945, and March 12, 1944: "The Importance of Belief" (JTP 24:6), "The Importance of Decisions" (JTP 24:7), and "A Call for Volunteers" (JTP 22:27).

years the executive secretary while Jean was working with the group, wrote to Jean and Marjorie after a weekend seminar: "Besides your intellectual and spiritual leadership, thanks, too, for entering so freely into the informality of the occasion. It was good to have you with us because you were one of us. Probably that type of rapport between leader and group is the essential ingredient to effective ministry."[8]

Others who were young Friends at the time still remember something of Jean's words and style. Sally Fell recalls:

He came across as . . . a very charming, debonair man, . . . [with] a certain . . . charisma. . . . And I think his thinness and his almost ascetic, long beautiful fingers, . . . helped add to the feeling of his being a person of very special spiritual qualities, human qualities, a warmth and openness.

What he was saying was probably in essence not all that different from what we had grown up with in the Society of Friends, but he was saying it in new ways, with a fresh approach and more of an inter-religious, interdenominational approach than anything I was used to. . . . It was more really on openness, and the centering down, and the living close to God. . . . And I remember that Jean used to draw a pie, and divide it into pieces, [to show] how the whole of our life, instead of some little wedge of it, . . . should be God-centered.

Marian Darnell Fuson, executive secretary from 1943 to 1945, speaks of a similar impact: "I think the big thing was his great respect for the resources which come out of silence, or which are tapped in silence. . . . It was great to worship with Jean; he was very strong, he had the feeling of strength; . . . he knew where he was." She credits Jean with support and approval when she was trying to do new and different things, such as speaking out in meetings of austere committees. Besides, "he was fun to be with—had a sort of dry sense of humor, the kind that wasn't exclusive, the kind that wasn't cutting." Ruth Miller remembers Jean from that time as "a very deeply spiritual person," one to whom they could go with any questions, as at one informal session in someone's home when four students were talking about their feelings about religion. In fact Jean had told them that if at any time four or five of them wanted to talk about religion, he would come and be with them, anywhere. At times he talked on a level deeper or higher than the young people could comprehend, but she is convinced that seeing this happen, being aware that there was a more profound level, was important to their growth.[9]

8. Jane Marshall to JT, May 11, 1945, in JTP 7:8; Robert L. Coe to MCT and JT, May 22, 1946, in JTP 1:10.

9. Interviews of Sally Fell, Doylestown, Pa., January 23, 1975; Marian Fuson, Nashville, Tenn., January 7, 1975; and Ruth Miller, New Britain, Pa., January 23, 1975.

The depth of Jean Toomer's ministry and his willingness to take responsibility were quickly appreciated by the adults as well as by the young people. In the summer of 1944, Friends General Conference asked Jean to visit Indiana and Illinois Yearly Meetings. The Conference wanted someone recognized as a solid and communicative Friend to extend the sense of fellowship, to encourage small midwestern Meetings and make them feel less isolated, and to inspire and renew dedication to the religious life. The Toomers made the trip in August, accompanied by Marian Darnell, and replete with extra invitations for Jean to speak at various Meetings. The Toomers' impact was significant: they were invited back by Illinois and Indiana Young Friends for a conference in February, 1948, but had to decline because of Jean's ill health.

Another area of special service in promoting spiritual growth grew out of Jean's leadership in the Quarterly Meeting. On his appointment as chairman (or "clerk," as the Quakers often term this function) of the Bucks Quarter Committee of Ministry and Counsel, he was automatically a member of the Executive Committee of Ministry and Counsel of Philadelphia Yearly Meeting, which met six times a year to guide activities of member Meetings in worship and ministry. Toward the end of 1945 he was invited to take part in a special spiritual life committee. This Yearly Meeting experiment was a response to a challenge by the eminent Quaker leader Rufus Jones, who had asked whether the spiritual condition of members of the Society of Friends was strong enough to meet the current crisis in human experience. Minutes of an early planning session stated, "Twenty spiritual leaders should be drafted right now for visitation to Meetings." As the plan developed, about twenty-five people were chosen who then made themselves available to visit meetings (by invitation) in teams of three to eight. "Our group holds itself ready," a prepared statement said, "to come once or oftener to any Meeting large or small within our limits and to join with them in their search for truth under God's love." [10] They would worship and talk with members, stay in their homes, share problems, and offer counseling. Then between visits the committee would get together to evaluate their experiences and grow closer as a team. Spouses were included in the visiting if they wished to be.

Pastoral care among unprogrammed Friends, like spoken ministry, is the responsibility of all members, but those with a gift for it tend to do more. The work of this Committee on the Religious Life of Our Society, directed largely

10. Minutes of Committee to Further the Concern of Rufus M. Jones, October 10, 1944, Religious Life Committee packet, "The Committee on the Religious Life of Our Society" (both in Friends Historical Library, Swarthmore College, Swarthmore, Pa., hereinafter FHLS).

by Douglas Steere, was a kind of pastoral care for Meetings themselves, provided by a group of gifted Friends drawn from a much larger area. Jean's talent for this service was recognized both at the time and later. Steere gave the Toomers a heavy schedule, writing, "We only work those so hard whom we feel God has a special word to give through them at this time. Please try to swing all you are asked for if you possibly can." After a weekend visit he wrote again, "Your insights so movingly expressed Jean were so invariably sound and deep—yet earthy and plain enough for ordinary people to lay hold of and be helped by." Another participant in a weekend visit wrote Jean, "I am deeply thankful the Divine Source let so beautiful, so simple, so clear an expression on the experience and meaning of worship come through you." Years later, recalling Jean's work with this group, Dorothy Steere felt that Jean was a hidden person in a way. He did not disclose himself very much, but when he did, "he came out of a deep place and as a poet." Douglas Steere then remembered Jean as responding to the slightest touch, "a very highly tuned violin underneath, . . . a very sensitive, beautiful human being." [11]

The Religious Life group, like the Young Friends, had members from both Arch Street and Race Street Yearly Meetings and was part of the movement for eventual unification. This particular group was most active in 1946 and 1947, but Toomer continued his membership on its parent body, the Philadelphia Yearly Meeting section for Ministry and Counsel. Although his physical condition worsened, he served as its assistant clerk from 1947 to 1955, and for several of those years was also chosen chairman of its Executive Committee.

As late as 1951, though Friends were aware that his strength was ebbing, Toomer was asked to deliver a series of lectures as a kind of celebration of the establishment of Doylestown (formerly a subordinate to Buckingham) as a full Monthly Meeting. Each week from May 15 to June 5, he combined his knowledge of religion and psychology to address questions of good and evil in the individual, close relationships between people (particularly parents and children), the uses of suffering, and man's potential for growth. [12]

Although he was not necessarily revered by everyone he worked with through these years, Jean's presence was highly valued in the Religious Society of Friends. He might comfort a Meeting member distraught at the loss of a cherished relative, and in ten minutes she would feel whole again. He might

11. Douglas Steere to JT, February 4, March 26, 1947, Josephine Benton to JT, January 28, 1947, all in JTP 3:10; interview of Douglas and Dorothy Steere, Haverford, Pa., January 24, 1975.

12. Postcard notice (JTP 12:1); JT notes, in possession of Byron Morehouse, Doylestown, Pa.

pick out a word that fascinated him and, in meeting for worship, hold it up and examine it from all sides, lighting up new meanings for those present. "Very slim, very tall, very beautiful, his spirit shone right through his looks." Perceived as somewhat hesitant and shy, not dominating or aggressive, but with a low-key sense of humor, he had a way of making other people feel more capable than they had thought they were. He guided or corrected very gently, with a twinkle in his eye, challenging the hearer inescapably to think about what he said. "He listened," declared one Friend, "faster than you could talk." [13]

He served as a reconciler also. In a meeting for business he might clarify a point to reduce divisive misconceptions, or recall Friends to their shared spiritual base. At least twice this role was officially recognized by Buckingham Monthly Meeting. In November, 1945, the nominating committee found itself unable to bring in names for the Buckingham Friends' School Committee. There was a deep division between those who wanted to keep the same people on the School Committee—it had been the custom to reappoint the members over and over again—and those who wanted some reexamination of policy and personnel. The Meeting named a committee of four people, headed by Jean Toomer, to try to resolve the impasse and to prepare a statement of the Meeting's aims and policies for the school. Jean wrote the final report, incorporating many members' opinions and parts of several drafts. It is a straightforward document about differing views that at the same time praises the strengths and contributions of all parties to the dispute and suggests a process that would combine these strengths, using both experienced and new members. Approved in parts over the next four months, the report was finally given general approval, opening the way for greater participation by members with a variety of views. It served as the basis for the concept of rotating committee membership, which was later taken up by other committees in the Meeting. [14]

On another occasion, Jean, though not appointed to mediate, was recognized as doing just that. In November, 1952, the Buckingham Committee of Ministry and Counsel, meeting under his leadership, felt concerned about the "conflicts of personalities and temperaments" that tended to break out acutely

13. Interviews of Georges and Elizabeth Duval, Lumberville, Pa., July 22, 1982; Douglas and Dorothy Steere; Priscilla Mitchell, Baltimore, Md., May 17, 1983; Edith Passmore, Kennett Square, Pa., June 23, 1978; and Byron and Betty Morehouse, Doylestown, Pa., August 5, 1982.

14. Buckingham Monthly Meeting minutes, November 4, December 2, 1945, March 3, 1946 (FHLS); "Report of the Committee of Four on School Committee" (JTP 70:4); interview of Dorothy Paxson, Penns Park, Pa., January 24, 1975.

in meeting for business and even to have their repercussions on meeting for worship. The Ministry and Counsel Committee, appealing for mutual trust and understanding, offered to meet with any other committee, to "help create an atmosphere favorable for a free and fruitful exchange." The six-page report containing this offer was distributed to all members of the meeting and was appended to the official minutes.[15]

As he was making these contributions through personal contact Toomer was also sending out his ideas in writing to the Quaker community, setting in motion what was to be his last wave of publication. In the fall of 1943, he began to have articles and occasionally poems published in *Friends Intelligencer,* the nationally circulated magazine written for the unprogrammed branch of American Quakers to which he belonged and which was represented by Friends General Conference. By the time his last piece was published, in October, 1950, he had had twelve articles, four poems, and one set of aphorisms in its pages. Giving a message acceptable within the Friends' tradition, they followed a pattern of exhortation that was also peculiarly Jean Toomer: eliminate prejudice and war by awakening individuals to the deeper unity within each of us; let the petty self give way to God. One article, "Keep the Inward Watch" (1945), clearly incorporates the Gurdjieffian techniques of self-observation and of opposing negative practices in oneself: "We must increase our present consciousness and train it to see, to face, to evaluate, to deny or affirm what we find in ourselves." But marvelously enough, its rationale is developed through quotations from William Penn and other early Friends.[16] For purposes such as these, Jean had filled notebooks with quotations organized under various headings, culled from his wide-ranging explorations of early Quaker writings. He was adapting his message skillfully to his audience—he learned by reading and listening to the great Friends past and present. Essentially, though, his basic message was rooted in Gurdjieff's teaching, and he presented this very persuasively in the Quaker community.

In 1947 and 1949, Toomer was invited to write longer statements that were to be published as pamphlets. Friends General Conference requested an introduction especially for young people to the meaning and practice of worship. *An Interpretation of Friends Worship* was completed by October of 1946 and published and distributed in time for a workshop at Pendle Hill in January, 1947, though Jean was not able to serve as a resource leader in person because of his health. In this work, he explains his idea of the "separated self" that stands in the way of the divine spiritual self in us—our body-minds as exiles from God's

15. Buckingham Meeting minutes, December 7, 1952 (FHLS).
16. JT, "Keep the Inward Watch," *Friends Intelligencer,* CII (1945), 411–12.

kingdom. Connecting this view with early Friends' ideas, he describes the purpose of silent waiting: to go through the process of getting the body-mind out
of the way so that the spiritual nature can be awakened. He presents Friends
worship as a way to move from a fragmented existence to the wholeness that is
our proper human state. On the publication committee was one person who
objected to his emphasis on the sinful side of man. Jean defended this by reference to the writings of George Fox, but he also suggested a modification that
proved acceptable. The published pamphlet was called "a significant contribution to the literature on Quaker worship" by the Yearly Meeting.[17]

Toward the end of 1948, Toomer composed his final major message to the
Society of Friends, to be given early in 1949 at the Arch Street Meeting House
to an audience from both Philadelphia Yearly Meetings. According to custom,
the William Penn Lecture, sponsored annually by the Young Friends, who
chose the speaker, was published soon after as a pamphlet. *The Flavor of Man*
spells out Jean's basic understanding of the human situation. In this, as in his
other writings, Jean did not hesitate to use *man* as a generic term. The quality
or "flavor," he says, that makes human beings distinctive is love: "[T]he primary ingredient of man's substance is love, love of God, love of man, and
through love, a sense of unity with all creation." As motivation for seeking this
love, he describes man's discomfort without it as the cause of all contemporary
violence and conflict. He adds to this his conviction that "[t]ime runs out. The
alternatives, I am convinced, are starkly these: Transcendence or extinction."
By references to Brother Lawrence, George Fox, and other towering figures, he
indicates that this essential love is no common everyday love and that attaining
it can be a life's work, or more. Carefully following Fox's description of his experiences, he shows that Fox indicated three levels of existence and the process of
spiritual birth that marks the passage from one level to another. Toomer emphasizes, as did Fox, that attaining even the second level, all that most of us
can aspire to, involves tremendous struggle against the "knot of darkness in
each of us, composed of indifference, inertia, prejudice . . . tied tight by fear,
and by the self-willed, self-sufficient ego," and it also requires God's interven-
tion. His term for this radical transformation, "deep rise," recognizes that one
has to go down through a great deal of negative inner matter before finding the
divine spark, which then carries one up and out—the three stages of "seeking,
ascending, extending. Asking, receiving, giving."[18]

All the fundamental elements of Jean Toomer's teaching are here: the sepa-

17. JT, *An Interpretation of Friends Worship*; Annual Report of the Executive Committee of
Ministry and Counsel, Philadelphia Yearly Meeting, March 26, 1947 (FHLS).
18. JT, *The Flavor of Man* (1949; rpr. Philadelphia, 1974, 1979), 18, 22–23.

rated or exiled self, which needs to discover its larger Being; the struggle required to do so; the world's plight, a result of this separation, which can be remedied only by individuals coming to their shared divine core; the human function of receiving from great teachers and God and then lifting others through the same process.

All these are also elements of Gurdjieff's teaching. Almost everything in Jean's writing and speaking was an echo of something Gurdjieff taught, though details are lost, distorted, or obscured and the terminology is often different. Some parallels are transparent. A statement he wrote for Buckingham Meeting in answer to the Quarterly Meeting queries in 1945 is simply a transcription of Gurdjieff's primary teaching about man's makeup: "Human beings naturally live in three worlds, the physical, emotional and mental. . . . Man's primary need is to find the roots of his life in a fourth world, the spiritual. For us, man's natural habitat is not enough. We are moved towards our divine home." This description was satisfactory to the Monthly Meeting, as shown by the approval recorded in the minutes. The *Friends Intelligencer* article, "Keep the Inward Watch," has been mentioned as prescribing a process similar to Gurdjieffian self-observation. In "The Uncommon Man," Toomer says the human being has three layers: the outer man, who embodies the "common human virtues" (roughly equivalent in Gurdjieff's theory to the personality, which takes its form from social conditioning); the middle man, "full of ill will, hate, greed" (derived from the "instinctive centre"); and the inner man, not usually manifested, which is the "seat of that of God in us"—the "uncommon man" (the faculty of unity and self-consciousness that only a few attain, according to Gurdjieff). Jean's article coincides with the theory in stating that only the inner, uncommon man can overcome the evil of the middle man.[19]

Toomer's position on social action was also similar to one derived from Gurdjieff's teaching: Man has a tremendous responsibility to the universe, but none to social systems. His function is fulfilled in transforming himself. If he achieves this, energies are released that have cosmic consequences. Direct work with politics or economics or social service is of secondary or minimal value.[20] Jean, through his writing and speaking, continued to stress this theme: man's

19. Buckingham Meeting minutes, February 4, 1945 (FHLS, also in JTP 70:6); JT, "The Uncommon Man," *Friends Intelligencer*, CIII (1946), 147–48. For comparison see P. D. Ouspensky, *The Psychology of Man's Possible Evolution* (London, 1951).

20. Interview of Louise and William Welch, New York, June 25, 1982. Also see John G. Bennett, *Gurdjieff: Making a New World* (New York, 1973). It must be noted, however, that both A. R. Orage and Gorham Munson worked hard to change the economic system, so the position described is not universal among Gurdjieff followers.

basic task is to work on himself and renew his right relationship to God. If the world situation is rotten, that is because man is rotten. The first step to peace is to view war as a disease in man. The religious view, in his thinking, requires spiritual actions that are more important than manipulating physical things or societal institutions. "If we are to consider politics [in a Friends Meeting], then surely it should be our aim to come nearer to the Politics of Eternity rather than express views about the politics of time." But in a note in 1947, considering the question of changing man versus changing society, he wrote: "The truth is that *both* approaches are needed. I have stressed the necessity of inward change because it is relatively neglected in our day, because the Friends religion in the beginning gave priority to inner change, and because, incidentally, that is my main way. . . . I think it is only along these lines that our Society can be renewed as an essentially religious body."[21]

It must be said that there are some areas in which Gurdjieff's ideas and Quaker thinking do overlap. For example, Gurdjieff insisted that those he taught should take no one's word but try everything for themselves. From the outset, Quakerism also emphasized direct experience: Friends should not take teachings such as the Scriptures secondhand, on hearsay, but should live in direct contact with the spirit that guided the Scripture writers. In addition, the individual's responsibility for his own development is a tenet of both Quakerism and Gurdjieff's thought. There is no priest or intermediary who can achieve one's improvement, though there is a point, after sufficient effort, when a kind of divine force may intervene.

The concept of reaching for a level of awareness beyond that on which people ordinarily live is also shared by these two systems of thought. It is, in fact, the foundation of all effort in both. Friends express this in the words "centering down" and in the active engagement of unity in worship. It is also a goal, considered by most Friends less attainable, that applies to all of life—in George Fox's words, "I live in that life and power which takes away the occasion for war." Just what is attained at this level of living would be given different definitions by different Friends, but the process involves the self in a larger knowledge of right action, moving the individual will toward being grounded in God's will. Gurdjieff's formulation is much more specific, complex, and staggering in its difficulty. Stages and dangers are identified, and the exercises and activities designed for each stage are, ideally, tailored for the individual by a teacher who has made significant progress on the scale.

21. Buckingham Meeting minutes, February 7, 1943 (FHLS, also in JTP 22:25); JT notes, under title "Convincement" (JTP 70:7).

Many writings by early Friends, as Jean discovered, can be read as describing an actual shift from one kind of consciousness to another, a movement from the scattered, fallible, evil "natural man" into another kind of being that in some way participates in the presence of God. This can be equated to the movement Gurdjieff's followers work for and to the "new birth" Jean himself had experienced. Jean's use of quotations, especially from George Fox, continually underlined this necessary and radical new birth as the forgotten teaching in Quakerism. Other contemporary Friends, too, used imagery implying the need for a different state. Rufus Jones said in one worship session, "We must be shaken awake"; another time, he talked of a ship in a lock being lifted to a totally new level. Douglas Steere compared a salvage ship raising a sunken vessel to the love of God that lifts us up.[22] With these two leading Friends Jean felt in considerable accord.

The segment of the Society of Friends that he had joined in 1940 was a liberal Christian group, with large components of philosophical idealism and social conscience, sympathetic to the movements in physics and psychology that emphasize the nondetermined, nonmaterial aspects of the phenomenal world. Insofar as one could define its theology (a practice discouraged by the Friends' insistence on inner authority and rejection of creeds), its main scriptural basis could be found in the Gospel of John. This gospel's doctrine of the Word, of which Christ is seen as an embodiment but which has a timeless existence, corresponds to the central Quaker belief in the "inward light" as a source of guidance available to all persons of every period. Thus the Quaker, through the discipline of prayer and silent waiting, may come to sense the divine presence, which may include a "leading," a direction for action. Belief in this direct contact between man and God, without intermediary, was surely one of the points that drew Toomer to Quakerism, for it coincided with his sense that he had had a measure of this experience and with his overall conviction that transcendence is man's basic goal. When making notes for a talk in 1945, he listed three major religious aims:

1. Seeking authentic experience of that which is greater than oneself
2. New Birth
3. Being with God and doing his will[23]

The mystical emphasis itself had had a rebirth in eastern American Quakerism in the person of Rufus Jones, its recognized spiritual leader through the

22. Rufus Jones's comments are in two reports on final sessions of Philadelphia Yearly Meeting (JTP 70:6); Douglas Steere quoted in Bucks Quarterly Meeting minutes, November 19, 1946 (FHLS).
23. JT, "Six Aims: What to Stand For" (JTP 26:26).

first half of the twentieth century. With him Jean felt in tune, as they certainly were in their respective efforts to bring others to direct experience of God, though their conceptions of just what this was differed somewhat. Jean believed with Plato, in parallel with Gurdjieff's theory, that the world we know is an exile, a cave, and that our proper domain is beyond it at another level of being. Rufus Jones, in contrast, saw God as part of all His creation and believed that the mystic, after a brief moment in the pure delight of God's presence, was to return to the world to transform it. Jean viewed his fundamental religious experience as a learning episode, in considerable detail: "Through it I learned, by personal experience, whatever I understand about human beings and about our true aims and goals." Insofar as he experienced God, he sensed terror and nothingness rather than love. Rufus Jones, however, had several brief periods of being wrapped in the intense love of God, but there was no unfolding of specific knowledge. He did not believe in the classic "way of negation" in mysticism that views the ultimate as a state of darkness and nothingness. Finally, Jones would have raised questions about the duration of Toomer's experience and the type of process itself. As a teacher of psychology, which was frequently taken up as a secondary discipline by philosophy professors in this period, he was suspicious of visions and trances and would surely have distrusted, had he heard them, some aspects of Jean's account. However, he felt that even the pathological cannot be ruled out of mystical experience if it proves a source of positive, renewing energy for the individual.[24]

There is no evidence that Jean ever explored these nuances of mysticism with Rufus Jones. In addition, he probably did not really recognize some fundamental differences between his philosophy and the prevailing Quaker view. These points of variance are all rooted in his Gurdjieff work, and some people might consider them heretical or dangerous to Quakerism and to Christianity. The first has to do with whether man or God is the primary causal agent. The Quaker process of gaining entry into the spiritual world and the Gurdjieffian exercises toward the same end, aside from the latter's structure and complexity, are different with respect to the role of the divine. In contrast to dependence on human will of a highly developed order, the Quaker believes such movement depends on the divine: God is ready to give insight, help, and direction whenever a person is ready to receive. The human responsibility is to open the door and clean out the room, not to struggle up the ladder. Jean in his Quaker pe-

24. JT to James Loeb, 1941–42, in JTP 6:12. An excellent summary of Jones's mysticism is given in Elizabeth Gray Vining, *Friend of Life: A Biography of Rufus M. Jones* (1958; rpr. Philadelphia, 1981), Chap. 23.

riod, in his personal prayers and public utterances, leaned more than he had in the past toward endorsing the concept of giving way to God's will, but he retained a sense of the need for being in charge, of the person reshaping himself. In a way this may have been a needed stimulus for a somewhat lethargic group of people. Lin Davenport, at least, felt that Jean's major contribution to the Friends was as a "gadfly," offering a "straightforward, hard-nosed approach to life," a nudge to jolt them out of their complacency and get them busy on their essential spiritual development.[25] Yet, when carried too far, this reliance on self could be spiritually dangerous.

The second area in which Toomer followed Gurdjieff and differed from Friends was in his view of a double world, one in which the apparent real was false and the invisible was real. For Jean, this applied on at least three levels. First, a person's inner essence, not only invisible but rarely even operative, is the good; the outer appearance and habits only get in the way. Second, social institutions, external accretions, are distorting, constricting forms. And third, the material world itself, the world of things, is a source of greed and rivalries, an exile rather than a home. He saw the human goal as the ascent to God by detachment from the world: "All of us have in us the potentialities and powers of dying to this little self and being born into a higher consciousness which is, I am convinced, our normal condition."[26] Friends accept the need for another level of experience, but they think the ideal state consists in serving as a channel for divine love and power operating in the world. It is true that Jean found statements about rejecting the world in the writings of early Friends and of classic mystics. These he used as examples. Still, the weight of Friends' history, as Rufus Jones indicated, is on the side of the new man, who with God's help succeeds in driving out the old man and attaining the Kingdom and continues to walk and work with his neighbors, affirming God's presence in the least of them.

The third area in which Toomer's stand reflects Gurdjieff has to do with universality. He did not believe in the doctrine of the Atonement or in Christ as the sole intermediary between humanity and God. In Toomer's view, Christianity was one of many paths to God. He liked to cultivate a reputation as something of an expert in world religions and to speak about what they had in common. In this ecumenism he had a strong ally among Friends in Douglas Steere.[27]

25. Interview of Franklin Davenport, Doylestown, Pa., January 23, 1975.
26. JT to Sheldon Chaney, summer, 1944, in JTP 1:10.
27. Lewis Benson, leader of the New Foundation, one of several Quaker groups which emphasize the centrality of Christ, differs sharply with Toomer on these matters. Benson was a

How did Jean Toomer view Quakerism? Was he using it as a new platform to teach Gurdjieff's theory in a disguised way? It is more accurate to say that he was using Quakerism as a laboratory to test his own ideas, developed from Gurdjieff's teachings, about human needs and potentials. In an essay written in 1948 he summarizes the beliefs he held before he came in contact with Friends: "I had been convinced that God is both immanent and transcendent, and that the purpose of man's life is to grow up to God; that within man there is a wonderful power that can transform him, lift him into new birth; that we have it in us to rise to a life wherein brotherhood is manifest and war impossible." All these beliefs were, he found, supported by Friends. In addition, Friends had developed the meeting for worship and the meeting for business, which gave promise of serving as ways to achieve the goal of "growing up to God." A more informal assessment is given in a letter to old friends from Chicago days: "The Friends of course are a branch of the Christian religion, but there is very little about them to remind me of that 'professional' type of Christianity for which I developed a strong distaste in my earlier years. There is some measure of reality here, a directness, an honesty, a goodness—and, in some cases, a greatness. Here is a way of life, not a preaching, a way of life arising from free association, with a minimum of organization and no priestcraft."[28]

In short, the differences were not obvious, even to Jean, and there seemed to be a good "fit" between what he already believed, what he was comfortable with, and what the Friends stood for. Many of the intricacies of Gurdjieff's system he had already discarded or never fully understood; he had selected, retained, and revised those that seemed valid and useful to him. "It is true," he wrote in 1947, "that in the Gurdjieff work there were methods for breaking and reforming habits and a new coordination. I never knew any too much about them in my mind, though I went through some of them in experience."[29] He had also emphasized the growth of brotherhood when attaining higher consciousness, which causes discriminatory barriers to fall. This re-

Gurdjieff follower in the 1920s, was a member in the 1940s of the Philadelphia Yearly Meeting Committee on the Religious Life, on which Jean served, and in later life was convinced that Gurdjieff's teachings are in fundamental opposition to Quakerism and Christianity, as indicated in conversation and correspondence with the authors, June, 1982–May, 1983. Dr. Gerald G. May, Director for Spiritual and Psychological Guidance at Shalem Institute, Washington, D.C., clarified the opposites mentioned in these paragraphs in an interview, Columbia, Md., June 9, 1983.

28. JT, "Why I Joined the Society of Friends," October, 1948 (JTP 18:19); JT to Eugenia and Russell Walcott, February 25, 1947, in JTP 10:5.

29. JT to Harold Winchester, February 1, 1947, in JTP 3:10.

ceived little notice in the Gurdjieff literature but was a legacy from Waldo Frank. This combination, which he had retained and developed, did not affect the position of Friends. It gave him, rather, a certain authority of knowledge and spice of detail where most Quaker teaching tends to be vague. The result, even with its Gurdjieffian components, must have sounded appropriate and true and given his readers and listeners refreshing hope and guidance. Unspoken, spoken, or written, his message had authenticity. Individuals and groups sought him out and received him and his ideas with gratitude, and the Quaker community, including its spiritual leaders, recognized that and encouraged his participation at high levels. His two pamphlets are held in continuing regard—*The Flavor of Man* has been reprinted twice, in 1974 and 1979, and *An Interpretation of Friends Worship* was reprinted in 1979.

From Toomer's point of view, the Society of Friends had promise, but needed renewal. In his last productive period, it was very much his group. He hoped that all his work on the Friends' behalf would bear spiritual fruit, and, contrary to his experience since 1930, that was what happened. He was publishing; he was invited to speak more often than he had energy to accept; and in his many satisfying individual contacts, he knew he was helping others. Yet the renewal was more important to him than the group identity. "I myself often wonder," he wrote in 1947, "if a new birth of life and power, when and if it comes, will come within any now established religious group. Douglas Steere and Rufus Jones believe that the Friends can be renewed. So do I, so far. Otherwise the heart would go out of my work with Friends."[30]

One of Jean's deepest needs from very early in his life was for the sense of direct experience, being "no man's copy," knowing from the inside. He had tasted this in a small but heady gulp in relation to literature in 1920 and he had sought it ever since in the mystics of all religions. His 1926 experience, growing out of the Gurdjieff exercises, reinforced his years of experimenting with Gurdjieffian methods, but those seemed to lose their efficacy for him by 1939. The dead-end trip to India turned him to an effort more frankly religious than any he had ever made before. It was not just that he used religious terminology to reach his audience; he used it in his thinking and his formulations for himself. His imagery and concepts were much closer now to the biblical "He that loseth his life shall find it" and "The kingdom of Heaven is within you" than to Gurdjieff's non-identification or the development of unity, consciousness, and will. To get inside the religious experience, to be in direct contact with God,

30. *Ibid.*

was his continuing and prayerfully held goal both for himself and for others in the Quaker community.

This intense desire, combined with a deep conviction about human potential and a battery of ideas from both Gurdjieff and Quaker sources, rooted in selected passages from the canon of Quaker prophets and communicated with Jean's continuing skill for imagery and words, made Jean Toomer a loved and respected spiritual leader in the Society of Friends. In some ways his most fulfilling time, it became also, in the conflicts and strains it concealed, his most tragic.

Mill House, early 1970s
Photo by Cynthia Kerman

Jean Toomer and Lin Davenport pitching hay, 1936
Photo by Marjorie Content Toomer, from Marjorie Toomer Collection

Jean, Marjorie, and young Margery Toomer with bearer Munasingha, Ghoom, India,
1939
From Marjorie Toomer Collection

Toomer with his pigeons, 1936
Photo by Marjorie Content Toomer, from Marjorie Toomer Collection

Jean Toomer, 1947
Photo by Marjorie Content Toomer, from Marjorie Toomer Collection

At Mill House, 1940s
Photo by Marjorie Content Toomer, from Marjorie Toomer Collection

Marjorie and Jean Toomer (*right*) at Doylestown Meeting, August, 1950
Courtesy of the Spruance Library of the Bucks County Historical Society

The barn remodeled into the Toomer house
Photo by Cynthia Kerman

Jean Toomer, about 1955
Photo by Marjorie Content Toomer, from Marjorie Toomer Collection

14.

The Unreceived Message

It is rather curious to trace the second life coexisting for all these years with the public Quaker figure of Jean Toomer. This shadow life was the private self of body and mind, of which few people were aware.

Through the fall of 1940 and the winter following, Jean struggled to pull himself out of a state of depression. Although his malaise seemed somehow connected with his kidney operation, he was seeking a psychological or a spiritual solution. In November he noted his physical symptoms: a flare-up of the eye inflammation that had long plagued him and an intestinal congestion on the right side. This was a localized strain and tightness, a kind of knotting up, accompanied by a contraction of the abdominal muscles, which would relax only at his conscious command. It was a variable condition, better on some days and worse on others. He also observed a lack of responsiveness: compared to the way he had been ten or fifteen years earlier, he saw himself as "emotionally dead."[1]

As time went on, his sense of being paralyzed or imprisoned grew more extreme. He felt he had spent all his energies against unfair odds: "I gave lavishly to hold myself up for eight years when I was being bent down by a burden [the unrecognized kidney problem]. I used the remainder to sustain the operation that removed the burden." In January, 1941, he referred to his psychological death. In February he wrote, "I have attempted the almost impossible. I have been bombed by the world and torpedoed by my own sins. . . . I am a sinking ship." In March he said, "This is no pit, no prison; this, I think, is my grave. . . . I am kept afloat by mind and will only. If these give out I will

1. JT notes, November 22, December 30, 1940 (JTP 57:1).

sink—or be taken over by a higher power." [2] In a three-pronged attempt to cure himself, he took up the practice of self-observation he had learned from Orage and Gurdjieff, which he had dropped in 1929 or 1930; he explored his shortcomings critically; and he began working on a book.

His first speculation on the cause of his problems was rooted in Gurdjieff's theory, according to which there are several bodies that may be developed besides the physical. The proper development of the emotional self contributes to the formation of the "astral body." Toomer wondered if the astral body could undergo a period of sudden growth when—as with the physical body at puberty—its normal functions were suspended or awkwardly performed. If so, he might not be ready for stronger feelings because his astral body was still unfinished. [3]

His second insight on his failures was psychological, dealing with the disjunction between what he wanted to say and what people wanted to hear. What was there to keep him writing, if no one felt a need for it? Also he seemed to lack an ability "to create *forms* for my overwhelming wealth of material." Soon after, his self-analysis cut even deeper. He believed he had acted out of a compulsion to appear commendable in other people's eyes and, by this, had "bankrupted my soul." Now, confident he had discarded this compulsion, he would begin to accumulate inner wealth. Five months later he reminded himself, "I am in dis-grace [out of grace] because I have resisted God's power, set myself up as an authority and would call attention to and win praise for *my* power and exploits." [4]

The book into which he poured his energy and hope for himself was another attempt at his autobiography, his perennial production. Now, however, he called it a "dangerous experiment." The early pages of this version contain the words, "I who write this am dead. . . . There is a stone in the doorway of my tomb which I must remove before I can resurrect. This book is my hand taking hold of the stone, rolling it away." [5]

Why should this, his sixth major attempt at writing his life story, carry so much peril and promise? Toomer, after struggling against the difficulty of the task but becoming convinced of its necessity, had started his first version of his autobiography in 1929. "Earth-Being" was a fairly straightforward account of events and his feelings about them. It was approximately 250 pages long and

2. JT notes, December 30, 1940 (JTP 57:1), January 24, 1941 (JTP 57:2), February 20, March 1, 1941 (JTP 57:3).
3. JT notes, December 30, 1940 (JTP 57:1).
4. JT notes, January 7, 9, 1941 (JTP 57:1), June 2, 1941 (JTP 57:4).
5. JT, "Incredible Journey" notes February 12, May 15, 1941 (JTP 14:3).

dealt with the time from his grandparents' days through his childhood in Washington. He sent it, hopefully but fruitlessly, to a publisher in September, 1930. During the next two years he developed what he called "Outline of an Autobiography," rewriting some of the early parts but expanding on his adolescence and his search for meaning in literature. His next effort, about the time of his marriage to Marjorie Content in 1934, was directed to the issue of rooting in his life story the explanation of his attitude toward race and class differences. "On Being an American" described individuals and cultural surroundings more fully than did any of the other versions. In November, 1934, he gave up this writing project because he was afraid its format subordinated the greater elements (his spiritual development, for instance) to the lesser (his racial conditioning and the events bearing on that). Besides, the whole web was so complex, he could hardly isolate a single segment. The next year, however, he tried again. "Book X" was another rendering of his high school and college years, and he intended to bring it up to the present time, showing how a self could swing away from the cultural norm and, becoming individualized, contribute to the creation of a new order.

Involved in preparations for a new phase of work at Mill House, and perhaps dissatisfied with his efforts so far, Toomer then dropped work on autobiography until the end of 1937. At that point he decided to write the section around which everything else turned, his experience of "birth above the body" in 1926. He worked on this tremendously difficult description for over a year, producing a rough draft by March of 1939, then laying it aside to get ready for the trip to India.

What was different now—even if we take into account Jean's penchant for exaggeration—that made his new venture into autobiography so fraught with danger? His notes, and the direction his narrative took, suggest several possibilities.[6]

First is the effort to bring his characters to life. In earlier versions, he had written about his family and friends mostly in terms of their effect on him, as conditioning agents of various sorts. This way of using people had, he felt, been destructive: "I have buried them, and so I have died. I, thinking to save myself, have sunk with them." Now he was trying to see their inner motivations. In some instances, he used a second-person narrator and spoke directly to a character, for example, his father. In concentrating on his own psychosocial development, he was also examining that of the other major characters in

6. This analysis depends, of course, on accurate identification of which notes were written at this time. See Appendix for a discussion of this problem and for the dates and location of the various autobiographies.

his tale. His re-creations of their personalities could be right or wrong, and if indeed he was to live or die by this, it was a risky effort. Besides, in looking at these significant people more intensely, he might discover flaws and tensions in himself that he had not been aware of. He thought he had never hated anyone; but in the writing, such a feeling might be uncovered. This must then be disclosed: "So help me God, these are to be honest pages."[7]

Honesty would also force him to tramp again through tender territory—how should he state his racial background? This was not an outward problem in his life and could largely be ignored; yet raising the issue again could make it one. That its place in his life was not fully clear even to him is suggested by the fact that he wrote and rewrote the section on ancestry. In one version he quickly takes the reader to the divine ancestry of all human beings. In another he emphasizes the common life-force in people and their responsibility to all mankind. In a third he examines realistically the difficult choices, in American culture, for people with Caucasian features who have some connection with the Negro world. In a fourth he uses anthropological references to point out the staggering number of ancestors we all have and the certainty that we are all of mixed blood.[8]

Perhaps the greatest risk was that he would fail, that he would not find a way out. He saw his life up to that time as having been partly directed, partly accidental, partly chosen consciously, a process of finding himself and losing himself over and over again. Now he was up against a blank wall and realized he was trapped, in prison. By transforming this experience into the universal, demonstrating that all men are "bound and shackled, cramped and well nigh strangulated by the terrible thing that has happened to human life and is, I do believe, largely of our own making," he hoped to get out. He saw the book as a devotional act for freedom and deliverance. Showing others how, from time to time, "I transcended the limitations of this ordinary waking-state and experienced a life more real, a being more true, a world more free," he might himself find a way of following that road again.[9] But if not—what then?

The overall title was "Incredible Journey: The Life and Death of Jean Toomer; an Autobiography." Quotations Toomer noted for possible epigraphs are "Know thyself," "Know the truth, and the truth shall make you free," and "'The world is a bridge; pass over it, but build no house thereon'—Jesus." In his section and chapter titles, death and resurrection are the controlling images. Although he

7. JT notes, March 15, 1941 (JTP 57:3); JT, "Incredible Journey" notes (JTP 14:3).
8. JT, "A Leaf Thinks of the Tree," "Family Tree," and other notes (JTP 14:3).
9. JT notes (JTP 15:2); JT notes, February 19, 1941 (JTP 14:3).

had taken the name Nathan when submitting manuscripts to a publisher in 1937, it was only now that he thought of the name change as a mark of a hoped-for new birth, and he expected that it would be his name until death. "I am tired of minor changes of all kinds, but with my whole heart would welcome a major transformation, a radical sharp rise upwards into a new being, a new consciousness, a new birth, a spiritual birth effected by the love and light of Christ and God's transforming power. . . . (I trust that (Nathan) Jean Toomer will be my final name until I recover my being-name, or until long hence I receive my heavenly name.)"[10] To friends he remained always just Jean Toomer, but the official name he used in all his contacts with Quaker organizations was N. Jean Toomer. It was a kind of sign of his new identity.

So he began. In the interest of factual accuracy as well as personal honesty, he looked up background information for the first time. He sent an inquiry to the directors of the cemetery in New Orleans where his mother and grandparents were buried; he wrote the Health Department in Washington for the information on his parents' marriage license; he burrowed in archives in Philadelphia for records of manumissions; he gathered together the old letters and other papers he had saved from being burned when his grandmother's things were sorted out after her death; he read reference and history books on his grandfather's period; and he noted recent addresses of relatives and childhood friends for possible further information.

During the next several years, the writing was fitted around other activities. He was still working on this autobiography as late as 1948, but never brought it to as full a form as some of the other versions. Pieces were written and rewritten many times, but rather soon he turned his attention to the independent development of the 1926 segment. Only eighty-three pages of finished manuscript of "Incredible Journey" seem to exist, and they are a bare beginning on an extensive plan covering his life through 1924—all of this was to be only the first "book" (called "Earth-being") of five, according to the outline made in February, 1941. It is evident from his section titles that this book was to show his exile from his family, then his exile from the path of other young people his age and his frantic search for what he should be. It was to paint him as a lover and as a religious man rather than as a thinker or creator of literature. "Book of Searching and Finding," the last section of this first part, was to cover his "discovery of Gurdjieff and learning the method," with its final chapter called "Ramp of the Bridge." This evidently was to lead into his projected second

10. JT notes, February 17, 1941 (JTP 14:3); JT, "Incredible Journey" (JTP 14:3), 34–35.

book, "The Bridge of Exiles," in which he is lifted from Hell to Purgatory and then has his first taste of "the Universe," only to lose it again in the third book, "Death and Imprisonment." Although it is guesswork to connect these titles with specific years of his life, one can assume that "The Bridge of Exiles" would cover the high point in 1926 and take him perhaps through some successful early teaching experiences. The final three books, "Death and Imprisonment," "Revolt of the Soul," and "Re-Birth," cannot be exactly placed in his personal history. Perhaps the last was to describe a period still in the future as he started writing.[11]

And the results? Not publication. Some piece of autobiography was rejected by Harper in December, 1941; there is no record of his submitting any part later. Probably, however, publication was not his primary goal. He may have come to some new appreciation of his family, and he was certainly made more acutely aware of all the strains in his racial and cultural background than those who saw him simply as a spiritual Quaker leader would have guessed. He made again at least one contact with his relatives. He wrote in 1944 to Aunt Nettie, Bis's wife, saying he expected to come to Washington in a year or so and would see her then, but he never did go back. As for the fulfillment of his greater goal, the new birth, one could not say that was really achieved through his work either, though in the letter to Nettie, Jean makes a grandiose statement about his progress:

I've been on an inward search, on an adventure into the deeper realms of living, in search of the meaning of this life, trying to find the basic causes and some of the basic cures of the ills and problems from which the entire human world is suffering. . . . I've been very active; but the action has not been of the kind that immediately shows on the stage of life. Little by little, however, I've been "coming back," as they say. Several months ago I finished a book, and when that book is published I expect to enter upon a new phase of life.

His notes to himself, however, did not reflect arrival at this stage. In August, 1941, he had written, "This is not my life; this is my atonement." At the same time he held a continuing conviction that his life was "preparing for an un-named performance" and so must be protected.[12] The autobiography, however, was never brought to its final chapter, and throughout the time he was writing it, Jean's notes expressed the continued longing for a replacement of self by a new man, one flooded with the life and power of God. The death image less-ened in intensity and the search shifted in method, but the desire for transcen-

11. JT, tables of contents (JTP 14:3, 19:5).
12. JT to Nettie Pinchback, October 12, 1944, in JTP 11:4; JT notes, August 25, 1941 (JTP 57:4).

dence never ceased. Neither death nor rebirth but something more like purgatory seemed to be his lot during these years of the 1940s.

There were mundane issues occupying him at the same time, related to financial limitations. Early in March of 1941, he reluctantly told Ramsey Lewis, the farmer they had hired when they bought the property, that Lewis would have to leave. Lin Davenport had married, and he and his wife wanted a place of their own and felt they could manage the farm. They moved across the road from Mill House and took over Lewis' job. In August, Jean and Marjorie were driving out to the West Coast, when they got word in Salt Lake City that Marjorie's father was dying. They flew back to New York, but did not arrive in time to see him before he died on August 14. Harry Content's finances and family relations were such that Marjorie's inheritance was fairly limited in comparison to the allowances she had formerly received, and Jean from then on felt the pressure of what he called "reduced circumstances." There was no longer a girl to help regularly with Argie—by now called "Arge"—or with the housework; only the three of them now were occupying the big house in Doylestown. The New York house had been maintained for their occasional visits to the city. Lin Davenport's mother, who had originally been the housekeeper, lived there, and sometimes James Loeb and other friends or relatives stayed for short periods of time. Now the house had to pay its way or be put up for sale. The farm at Mill House, too, had never broken even, but Lin was working hard to make it less of a financial drain. And Jean was seriously trying to gather materials that could be published and bring in some money. Beyond this, he still cherished the dream of "some kind of a center, a 'cell of awareness,' here at Mill House,"[13] which would somehow not only make spiritual use of the space there but produce enough income to carry the property and the family.

It was probably this sense of financial need that stimulated him to send the autobiography, still unfinished, to a publisher. He also put together a new arrangement of some of his poems, under the title "Blue Meridian and Other Poems." Harper rejected this too in December, noting that the quality was good but it would be risky in terms of sales. But besides his autobiography, he was concentrating on "From Exile into Being," the account he had begun in 1937.

Toomer had become increasingly convinced that the central mystical event of his life in 1926 had to be told so that readers would see the basis for the rest of his teaching. The actual experience of his birth into a higher consciousness

13. JT to Betsey Barton, October 11, 1941, in JTP 11:4.

and his oneness with all mankind and its larger source, accompanied by the awareness that the divisions between people were idiotic and that most of their daily interactions were petty, was proof for him that these conclusions were grounded in the universe itself. Once accepted, these ideas could be the foundation of much more positive human behavior, eliminating war, racial discrimination, economic exploitation, and all the major ills of society. And if people could be convinced of what had happened to him, he thought, they could be convinced of the truth of the principles inherent in his "birth above the body." So, parallel with his spiritual teaching and ministry among Friends, despite his growing physical weakness, he tried his best to communicate this experience, crystallizing his intentions from his trip to India.

Into early 1944 he worked on shaping this account. For the next four years he was to suffer the hopes and pangs of encouragement, revision, and rejection of his manuscript, which he called at first "The Second River" and later "From Exile into Being." The collection of aphorisms written in 1937, "Remember and Return," had been the philosophical outline of his conclusions about his 1926 experience. But during the 1940s, his main effort was toward getting his basic account of that seminal event published.

At the same time he moved to activate the "cell of awareness" he hoped to establish at Mill House. In October, 1942, he began a series of meetings with the six residents there (counting Lin and his wife Ellen, though they lived across the road, and Lin's brother Don and his wife Polly). He called it a study of "the Work," the term used to refer to the Gurdjieff method, and began with the standard outline of man's three centers, each divided into three subcenters. As homework, he asked participants to try to describe themselves in terms of which centers were strongest in them and give evidence for their conclusions. Also they were to try to visualize themselves from the outside (*e.g.*, "There goes Marjorie"), a basic exercise in non-identification. Marjorie kept notes on these meetings, and after the first one she recorded, "For some reason he got 'power' over most of us and I fell asleep—also Don and Polly." But she tried her best to remember the main points and did better that time than most of the others in doing the homework. During the next several months Jean continued to develop his theory and some elementary exercises. Each person needed a fundamental "I" to control the petty desires of the three centers and should recognize this development as the most important duty of this life.[14] The ideas he concentrated on had been included in his more complex lectures of 1937, a

14. MCT notebook, 1942–43 (MTC).

time when Mill House was most active and flourishing. Jean was also repeating the concepts and practices he had stressed in his early teaching in Chicago.

The "cell of awareness," however, apparently did not grow and divide, as Jean must have hoped it would. Nor could it be a source of income while the participants were family members and those who worked the farm for them. Some people may have experienced growth, but Marjorie, at least, was discouraged about her general state by the following April. "The work" was neither interesting nor enjoyable enough to draw her into it, and nothing she did through it lent warmth to anything else.[15] In the spring of 1944, Lin Davenport, who had been Jean's strongest supporter in the work, moved away after unsuccessfully trying to make the farm pay. Without him, there was no nucleus around which to build.

Jean, meanwhile, was giving more talks to groups of Friends and to wider audiences. But he was still troubled by some aspects of his physical state. He ordered Thomas Sugrue's life of Edgar Cayce soon after it was published in December of 1942. Cayce, a psychic, had been widely recognized for his diagnoses and prescriptions for the alleviation of physical problems. When in a simply induced trance, he needed only a person's name and location to be able to describe that person's condition and what should be done to correct any problems. Sugrue's book, which tells how Cayce discovered his ability and gives a number of case histories, impressed Toomer. Further, Jean was drawn to Cayce's religious and service-directed orientation. Jean wrote Cayce in March, asking for a "physical reading," and a day in June was set for it. In a letter of April 19, Toomer summarized his difficulty:

At present . . . and indeed for some time, my life and work have been hampered by some physical irregularity that seems obscure. . . . [First,] I cannot even do such a simple thing as mow the grass of the lawn without getting tired and having to stop and rest. . . . This lack of physical energy and endurance is a quite evident feature of the condition.

A second evident feature is that I have considerable difficulty getting to sleep of nights. That had been so for some years prior to the [kidney] operation, and has been more so since.

Now for the obscure feature. I feel that there is some kind of irregularity in the condition or the functioning of the vital organs in or around the small intestines. There is a tension there, a sort of contraction. Often I have the thought that this contraction, or whatever it is, is the seat of all the other difficulties, and that if I could straighten this out, the rest would follow.[16]

15. *Ibid.*
16. Thomas Sugrue, *There Is a River: The Story of Edgar Cayce* (New York, 1942); JT to Association for Research and Enlightenment, Virginia Beach, Va., April 19, 1943, in JTP 1:2.

Jean's "reading" occurred on June 22, 1943, at 10:30 A.M.—Cayce in his headquarters in Virginia Beach, Virginia, and Toomer at home in Mill House. After receiving it and following the directions, he reported the results to Cayce in September. Toomer had been surprised by two parts of the diagnosis: "that toxic forces through the system and poisons pressing on my nerve centers were chief among the causes of my trouble" and that his body lacked, in Cayce's words, "the vital energies to renew the activity of the glands in the organs themselves." He was also surprised at Cayce's "unusal [*sic*] knowledge of my body to know, as the reading did, that vitamins, taken in in this manner could disturb the equilibrium. I had experienced this sort of thing before. Whereas, most of the people I know can take vitamins in large quantities without feeling the slightest disturbance." Cayce had prescribed purifying the alimentary canal and treatment with ultraviolet rays. This produced some changes for the better, reducing the intestinal tension. Jean thought if he could follow the prescription more faithfully, even greater improvement would result.[17]

He wanted to continue his relationship with Edgar Cayce, and he asked for a check reading and for a life reading. The check reading would have been a second evaluation of his physical condition after a period of treatment. Cayce's life readings, however, though still centered on the individual who applied, purported to give information derived from a person's past lives on earth. These readings were meant to draw together and describe the elements that were actively influencing one's present life or that should be utilized for the soul's growth. But the biography that caught Jean's attention had also attracted many other people to Cayce's work, and he was inundated with requests for readings of all kinds. Cayce began to schedule more and more hours a day for readings, and became exhausted. In September of 1944, a year after Jean Toomer had sent his first report after Cayce's prescription, he wrote Cayce again specifically requesting a check reading. But Edgar Cayce had a stroke that same month. He gave no more readings, and died on January 3, 1945.

Jean did not have an excessive interest in psychic phenomena, but he did believe that they could give evidence of potentialities beyond those normally exercised and that such phenomena could be related to religious experiences. He had written a warm and encouraging letter to Dr. J. B. Rhine, head of the investigations into parapsychology at Duke University, in 1939. As he said in his April, 1943, letter to Cayce's organization, "I have long been sure that man has powers above those ordinarily exercised and have been on the lookout for records of human contact with 'that of God.'" Without rejecting the usual

17. JT to Edgar Cayce, September 4, 1943, in JTP 1:8.

channels for learning and curing, he was open also to the unusual. He may have thought he needed to try all kinds—his illnesses were not easily cured.

One further observation he made in his September, 1943, letter to Cayce suggests a continuing problem, reflecting his complaint in 1940, that could be physical or psychological: "I am particularly eager to know how to help bring the sympathetic and cerebrospinal systems, the liver and the kidney circulations, into harmony. For some time I have been aware that, in my terms, my mental and emotional systems were by no means as coordinated as they ought to be." Although he seemed to have moderate success with the Cayce treatment, his ability to follow instructions was, from his own viewpoint, limited, and Cayce himself could give no further guidance. The problems Jean identified at this time were not fully solved, and the road ahead was to be marked by many other treatments for the same and additional difficulties. In the meantime, Marjorie faithfully gave him his "treatment" each night at bedtime—a kind of body-rub, though not a real massage, which she continued for years.

Through this period, there were many light moments, too. There was much day-to-day living to be done; grandchildren began to arrive on the scene; and Jean had not lost his penchant for clowning. A few vignettes will give some of the flavor. Although not given much to exercise, Jean took some walks on the beach during brief family vacations at the shore in the fall of 1945 and 1946. In January, 1946, he was persuaded to go sledding with Marjorie and Arge on the occasion of a new snow. Early one January morning, when Marjorie noticed a small intruder in their bed, Jean got up, armed himself with gloves and a pillowcase, then cornered the mouse and dumped it out the window.

Marjorie's son James Loeb, after he got out of the navy and became a civilian pilot, lived at Mill House for a time with his wife and small son. In 1946 they found a house nearby but remained in close contact with the family. Jean maintained a playful correspondence with Jim, including two absurd "invoices" to acknowledge gifts or hospitality, one of which is partially quoted here:

To James J. Loebuck, Vice Pres. (retired)
The Slinky Swamp Aviation Bog,
Mosquito Meadow, New Jersey . . .

I Slinky Chicken (skin and meat useful in the construction of plywood airplanes) . . .
Several dozen Boggy Eggs . . .
2 shipments of bomb-shell Beer (good for war against mosquitoes, indigestion,
    bogs, swamps, and depressions) . . .
I have the honor, sir, wherewith to submit my check . . .
                    J. Jean Roomer

For a time, there were two families with toddlers in the Toomer establishment. Marjorie's daughter Susan also moved into Mill House in 1946 with her little daughter, and soon after had another baby. The grandchildren called Jean "Goppy." He teased them and played with them, but insisted that they be fed and put to bed before it was time for his dinner.[18]

Other children joined the party now and again. Paul Taylor, who was called "Polo," the son of Jean's long-term Gurdjieff friend Edith Taylor, had stayed at Mill House sometimes as a child. He was just a little older than Arge, and when he came back in 1947 he was much impressed with Jean's wisdom and with Arge's beauty. Jean wrote him with sage advice about both—Polo should wait awhile to judge how that wisdom, or that beauty, might fit into his life.[19]

When Mother Latimer died in 1947, Jean had to deal with the matter of Arge's inheritance from her. A few stocks and the family home were left to Arge and Margery Latimer's sister Rachel. Jean tried to be generous to Rachel and considerate of his own family's limited resources (they were already dipping into capital for living expenses). But he apparently felt free to make all the decisions without consulting Arge, though she was now almost fifteen. At one point he wrote to the lawyer, "I know that young Margery would share my desire [for Rachel to keep the house] could she understand things. As it is, she will take my word for it."[20]

Young Margery was now ready for secondary school. She had attended Buckingham Friends' School from the beginning of her schooling. Natural progression led her to the nearby Friends boarding school when it came time for high school: this was George School, where the Toomers knew many of the faculty and Jean had frequently given talks. She applied in the spring of 1947 for admission in the fall, and in connection with this, two troubling incidents occurred.

The Quaker community at this time was in a situation many considered hypocritical. By basic principle and long heritage, Friends bore continuing witness to the full equality of all persons and had worked publicly for the rights of blacks. But they also had acquired a backlog of cultural sludge, and in many of their institutions, particularly their schools, no blacks were admitted. In many cases, despite agitation by concerned Friends, Quaker schools lagged

18. JT to James Loeb, December 30, 1946, in JTP 6:13; MCT to her daughter Susan, September 6, 1945, February 1, 1946, both in possession of Susan Sandberg; interview of Susan Sandberg, Doylestown, Pa., March 20, 1983.

19. Paul Taylor to JT, September 6, 1947, in JTP 11:4; JT to Taylor, September 13, 1947, in JTP 10:11.

20. JT to Dorothy Walker, May 23, 1947, in JTP 10:6.

until after public schools were forced to integrate by the Supreme Court decision of 1954.

How Jean Toomer was classified racially by his friends and acquaintances during his Quaker period is an interesting question. Most did not realize until they had known him several years that he had any black forebears. They could not remember later how they had learned or deduced this, and when they found out, it made no difference to them. Many were quite open to racial diversity. They may have thought he was of East Indian extraction, or perhaps they thought nothing of his race at all. Marjorie's custom of wearing American Indian jewelry suggested connections with exotic cultures other than the black. Some did not want to bring the realization into full consciousness, thinking either that he wanted to "pass" or that if his black heritage was recognized, other people would react negatively. Still, to other good friends, he spoke openly of his family and childhood. But while Margery was growing up and while Jean was himself delving into his own mixed background, he had not spoken to his daughter about that background or even, through her early years, let her know who her real mother was.

When, in this rather curious situation, George School received Margery's application, the School Committee asked one of its members, Will Eves, to go to Jean and ask directly if he was Negro. Eves did so, and the answer he received satisfied him that Jean was not. When he reported this to the committee, they admitted Margery.[21] Whatever Jean's actual words and however clear the incentive for a negative answer, his motivation was probably much more complex. The question would have called forth his lifelong effort to transcend the racial labels he considered artificial and false, and no doubt some disgust at the school's policy, as well as his genuine sense of the irrelevance to his concerns of the minimal part of his makeup that derived from his black heritage.

No further problem or question was raised about Margery's attendance by George School, where she was a student from 1947 until her graduation in 1951, though the school did not openly admit any black American students until Julian Bond enrolled in 1952. The racial issue was brought up again, however, out of concern for Margery herself. The school librarian, who knew the family, realized that there was a collection of Negro poetry in the school library which contained some of Jean Toomer's poems from *Cane*. She surmised that it might be a shock for young Margery to come on this volume unawares and find her father represented as a Negro; so she went to the Toomers to communicate her concern. At some point Margery had to know, but up to then, as

21. Interview of Marian Fuson, Wallingford, Pa., March 13, 1983.

the librarian correctly guessed, she did not. Perhaps Jean had felt that his background was part of a past incarnation, of no concern to her. Perhaps he was unthinkingly repeating his grandfather's silence about personal history as he himself was growing up, which had forced him finally, at the end of his high school years, to ask the vital questions about his heredity.

It is symptomatic of the strange cultural and moral dilemma about race of which Jean was sometimes the unwilling center that the librarian's knowledge about the book made no difference to Margery's status at the school. When questioned about this many years later, the librarian said, "She wasn't a Negro. . . . I mean this—*Cane* really wasn't written by the person we knew, you see? I mean it's as if there were two Jean Toomers. . . . He was a *most* interesting and complicated person." [22]

The Jean Toomer operating through the mid-1940s was most interested, not in his racial configuration, but in making his extraordinary experience of 1926 a source of enlightenment to a large audience. By October of 1943 he had finished the draft of "From Exile into Being" and was revising and editing it with Marjorie's help. In May of 1944, after what he considered two years' constant work on it, he sent the manuscript to Harper. With their response in August came some reports from readers. One was quite favorable, calling the account fresh and authentic, though the reader did not regard Toomer's experience as startling. A second was mixed, noting that Toomer "writes well, simply, persuasively, charmingly . . . [but] repeats and repeats to the point of tedium" and suggesting more stress on elements that would make the book more "familiar and acceptable to the Christian reader." A third was totally negative, calling the book dangerous and insisting that what was needed were, instead, "First Principles, Right Morals, and valid methods in that one thing necessary—prayer." [23] In any case, Harper's decision was negative, and Toomer next sent the manuscript to Dutton.

In the following month he also let his friend Denver Lindley read it. Lindley was a member of the Wider Quaker Fellowship, a group loosely associated with the Society of Friends. He had been at the retreat center of the well-known mystic Gerald Heard and was just publishing an article on devotion in the *Friends Intelligencer*. He was also an editor at Appleton-Century. The dilemma Jean felt when Lindley liked the manuscript, which was still in the hands of a rival publisher, was soon resolved. Dutton returned it with a rejection in October. Jean had already asked Lindley to send it to Gerald Heard to see if he

22. Interview of Edith Passmore, Kennett Square, Pa., June 23, 1978.
23. Readers' reports, June 10, 1944 (JTP 65:22).

would write an introduction, and this was done, Lindley now gladly assuming the role of sympathetic editor. Jean, having discovered Heard in 1938 through Georgia O'Keeffe, admired him and had corresponded with him but had never met him. He and Marjorie had hoped to visit Trabuco, Heard's retreat center, in the spring or summer of 1944, but did not get there.

Unfortunately, Heard's reaction, which included the impressions of four or five other people with whom he had shared the manuscript, was severely critical. There was no question of his writing an introduction. "As it stands it won't do"; the book was lacking "in style, in vividness, in power to give conviction." Yet there were, he felt, "fine, true, and deep things in it." He suggested that it be cut 50 percent and put in a biographical framework—in other words, rather than the experience being its own proof of validity, the life must prove the experience valid. Felix Greene, a friend of Heard's and Toomer's, also read it. He thought that the reader would need additional material to fit what happened to Jean into other mystics' experiences and also to relate the event to the ordinary person's life.[24]

Jean, though somewhat taken aback, took the criticism in good grace and began with some enthusiasm to rework the material into a three-part book— the second would be a simple account of the experience, and the first and last would be expanded along the lines Greene suggested. At a dinner with Stieglitz and O'Keeffe in New York at the end of January, Jean explored further the direction his book should take and the implications of Gerald Heard's response. Jean, though he thought Heard had been unduly stiff and cold, continued to look up to him as an "extra-individual." As for Georgia, the old warmth remained: she, as he said to Lindley, "has been one of the few people on the inside of my life and work, and this for many a year. She is 'family.'"[25]

Through correspondence and conferences during the winter and into the spring of 1945, Lindley encouraged Jean to expect publication by Appleton-Century when he had completed the manuscript according to his new outline. In the midst of a flurry of Friends activities in the summer of 1945, Jean's creative writing energy seemed to be overflowing, and for more than a month he worked steadily and satisfyingly on this project. Toomer's method of writing was not what could be called disciplined—he did not set aside certain times for writing, but proceeded on impulse or inspiration. As he reported to Lindley in August: "This is how I seem to work. Three or four months, not much

24. Gerald Heard to Denver Lindley, November 15, 1944, enclosed in Lindley to JT, November 22, 1944, in JTP 1:2; JT to Lindley, January 2, 1945, in JTP 6:11.
25. JT to Lindley, January 30, 1945, in JTP 6:11.

doing—except interior work, and sometimes not that. Then along comes a phase in which I do all and more than I could have accomplished by working at a steady but comparatively pedestrian pace for several months. Given one more period like the present one, and the book should be finished. But how long will this last? When will the next come?" In March, 1946, Lindley asked Toomer about his progress on the manuscript, indicating that the deadline for the fall books was approaching. At this point Jean had to confess that the Muse had not been kind. He had not had a creative spurt since summer and still had twelve chapters to rewrite—which would take him to the middle of May unless creativity sprang to life and brought results sooner.[26]

But on April 5, Lindley sent Jean the bad news that he was leaving Appleton-Century for Henry Holt. He offered to give Toomer's material to his successor at Appleton or to take it with him to Holt. Unfortunately Jean had as yet no signed contract with Appleton. Although the new editor there wrote (addressing his letter "Miss Jean Toomer") offering a contract when the manuscript was ready, Toomer felt he would have a better chance with Lindley, who had nurtured and encouraged the book all through its development. Gorham Munson, who had also read and commented favorably on the manuscript, recommended his keeping it with Denver Lindley. Jean therefore withdrew it from Appleton and had his revised version hand-delivered to Lindley at Holt on May 26.

By July, having had no word except the acknowledgment that the manuscript had been received, Toomer was uneasy and wrote a letter of inquiry but decided not to mail it. On August 6, he sent a brief note to Lindley, asking if the book was in difficulties and proposing to call him shortly. On the same day, Allen Tate, instead of Denver Lindley, wrote Toomer from Holt to inform him that the manuscript was rejected. There was a certain irony here: Tate, who had actively and unsuccessfully sought to meet and encourage Jean in 1923 and 1924, was the one in 1946 to deny his long-held hope of publication. Jean immediately sent the manuscript to Harper for a second consideration in its revised form. But he could not escape a crushing sense of betrayal—his good friend Lindley not only deserted his cause but suddenly dropped out of the picture with no explanation. Not until the following February, after mediation by Betsey Barton, a mutual friend, but apparently still without a word from Lindley, did Jean tender a renewal of contact with Lindley on a friendly basis.

By that time, Harper had reviewed and rejected the manuscript, but with long and constructive comments to which Toomer responded with thanks. He

26. JT to Lindley, August 7, 1945, March 26, 1946, both in JTP 6:11.

said he was convinced then that the account of his experience should be put aside for a time:

I regarded that book as my seed-book. And I felt that certain sections of it, those dealing with my personal validation of the possibility of a new birth, freedom, kinship, brotherhood, being-continuity, the real existence of love and God, etc., to have some real meaning for others, in their own right. But . . . if the record was not understood, no good would be served. . . . When I read the reports of the readers . . . I saw at once that the publication of the book, in its present form, might throw any number of readers off, and impede far more than aid my service to others.[27]

He also said that he would send it back to Harper when he had reworked it to his satisfaction. He had sent along with it a collection of poems that he called "The Wayward and the Seeking." Some of these were newly written, some were from the 1930s, and some went back to his days in Chicago. Harper rejected this at the same time. Three months later, by May, 1947, he sent both manuscripts to Longmans, Green. In July, both came back again with rejections.

In his correspondence with publishers, he seemed to understand what he needed to do to communicate to his readers this intense message he had long had within him. But even given the help of editors genuinely interested in what he was saying, this clarity melted away under his peculiar inability to evaluate his own writing. Somehow he could not see the presentation from the reader's angle. Marjorie, when she first typed it, had suggested—in vain— that he separate the narrative from the insights gained. His imagery could still be compelling, but tone and point of view are inconsistent. Vivid description gives way to a didactic lesson or a line suddenly addressed to the Deity:

So was I visited by Grace. For the Power is Grace when it manifests to us. (To be in the Power is to be Grace. To be out of the Power is to be in dis-grace. Dis-grace and exile are one and the same condition.)

So Grace, as a bright hand with prescient fingers, worked in my total human being.

So the Power touched this life, touched it perfectly, radically changed it without halt or flaw, effortlessly wrought an intricate and sweeping revolution, ordered everything, opened the creature to the creator within and brought me, together with that manifesting being, through the initial stages of the unimaginable.

O wonderful that Power![28]

The general account, with its exquisite detail, has the ring of utter veracity and depicts a person uplifted in awe and humility. But the interlarded comments and the set of short essays at the end present ideas in such authoritative and

27. JT to John Chambers at Harper, January 31, 1947, in JTP 1:9.
28. MCT to JT, May 5, 1939, in JTP 9:8; JT, "From Exile" (MCT), 8.

sometimes pompous ways, they seem to come from a different person altogether, and their connections with the experience are not always clearly made.
Given Toomer's shifting rhetorical sands and a subject matter outside general
experience, it is difficult for a reader to feel anything solid underfoot.

Many disappointments had come to Jean Toomer in letters from publishers.
The final rejection for this, his "seed-book," was perhaps the most crushing.
He put the manuscript away in July of 1947, and this was the last time he sent
a major work to any publisher.

Much later Lin Davenport made an observation about Toomer, as he was
reflecting on this period. Lin, after being as close to Jean for eight years as
anyone except Marjorie, had moved away from the area in 1944 and then returned in 1952. When he came back he noticed a major change—something
more than natural aging. "In his later years, every time I saw him, I had that
really very strong sense, something has gone that was there before. . . . The
doctors never knew what the hell was wrong with Jean. . . . The medical ailments or problems . . . could never satisfactorily account for what was happening in, let alone the total man, but just the physical body." Without ever
pinning it down, Lin had a hunch that "at some point in Jean's life something
really disastrous took place in his inner life. . . . I feel something happened
inside which . . . resulted in this decline of the whole man, the physical, the
mental, the— . . . The thing which was the most sad was the going out of the
fire. . . . If I'm right, and it's only a guess, . . . whatever it was that began to
quench the fire, well, then, everything went with the fire, you see, including
the body and everything else. So who knows?" [29]

This progressive series of rejections—the raised hopes, the reworking, the
apparent betrayal by a friend, the further reworking and final rebuffs for this
manuscript that carried the very heart of Toomer's life experience—may or may
not have been what began to quench the fire. But it was very close to this time
that a clear downturn can be observed in three areas, his activities, his perception of his spiritual state, and his health.

In connection with writing or speaking, he characterized himself in the fall
of 1947 and in the spring of 1948 as being in a "period of low-ebb of energy, a
stubborn state that so far has defied my efforts to work out of it." In June of
1948 he wrote, "There's something new, some new means, some new direction, some new form of life that I must have, lest I find myself over long in the
desert and myself become in time among the living dead. . . . I am waiting for

29. Interview of Franklin Davenport, Doylestown, Pa., January 23, 1975.

something to click in me. Then I'll move." [30] He had been responsive to other requests as well as to those of the Friends, and within the last twelve months he had written an appreciative piece on Alfred Stieglitz just after his death, which was accepted by the magazine *Twice a Year*; spoken at a community worship service sponsored by the Council of Churches in Woodstown, New Jersey; given the sermon at a Vassar College Sunday service; reviewed a new translation of Jakob Boehme for Harper; and given a talk entitled "Poetry and Spiritual Rebirth" for the Catholic Poetry Society in New York. But from this time on, he accepted fewer of these outside invitations, and in addition he began to resign from long-standing commitments for the Friends and refuse short-term ones.

His inner life and his view of himself had undergone some searching and change, too. He had early seen his need to overcome his inflated egoism, but he was sure this could be done, as indicated in "The Days Ripen," a poem published in the *Friends Intelligencer* in January, 1944:

> I am thy man, be thou my God.
> Had I learned to say this years ago,
> Already it might have come to pass;
> But in those green days of my life
> The little will was rife
> To think and dream and work so hard
> Myself to be a god to men,
> Myself to do without Him.
> Not that, not that, little self.
> This is it: I am thy man, be thou my God.

A note in 1945 underlined this position. He recognized that he could not say what he had really meant to those he tried to help. "What pretension, then, to say or feel that I helped them. This conceit, this illusion, but keeps one from realizing the need of and desiring to yield to God's power." A short note in 1946 again warned of his tendency toward the false face: "I do not want to build up a dignified front, a noble exterior. That I can do, but it is an unrewarding strain. I want to be held up by the living substance of my depths." [31]

As 1946 went on, a time he described to Douglas Steere as "curiously broken," when "deep plowing" was occurring in him, Jean showed a growing uncertainty about the outcome of this struggle. He wrote a number of poems

---

30. JT to Katherine Karsner, May 27, 1948, in JTP 3:11; JT to Chambers, June 13, 1948, in JTP 1:9.

31. *Friends Intelligencer*, CI (1944), 39; JT, "This Is Thy World" notes (JTP 27:6); JT, meditation, March 4, 1946 (JTP 25:13).

at this time, mostly religious; selections from three will illustrate his state
of mind.

> My life is not clear:
> I have used soap and water,
> Chemicals and fire
> Generated by friction,
> Mind upon mind,
> Heart upon heart,
> Will upon problems.
> Still my life is unclear.
>
> God make me clear.

A second poem, reworked in three versions, develops the thesis: "It is not guaranteed that God will break our crust,/And free the spirit prisoned in our cells."
And among the poems gathered for "The Wayward and the Seeking," most of
them more notable for their autobiographical than for their literary value, is
"Witness," a summary of his condition, in which he is almost fiercely clinging
to the hope for renewal:

> It is by death of self that man ascends,
> And man himself must snuff the self;
> It is by rise of man that God descends
> And makes new members of the kingdom.
> My friends have seen the stiffening
> Of joints, the gathering deficiency,
> The death mask settle on my face,
> And may have known it was my inward work;
> Have seen me struggling through my night,
> The day delayed, and I in death
> An uninviting witness of the way;
> More than dying I cannot do,
> I cannot will myself into new life.
> Unshakable my faith that the miracle
> My powers cannot make will be wrought
> By laws of being and God's grace—
> Another being will come to life in light,.
> The spirit sing, love rejoice in God and men,
> And I in life a glowing witness of His way. [32]

By 1947, his hope and faith subdued, he felt a strong need to get away for the
summer, "lest the coming winter really get me down." He and Marjorie went
out to New Mexico, their first time there since 1940 and Jean's last trip west. It

32. JT, poem fragments (JTP 50:43); JT, "Witness" (JTP 50:64).

failed to fulfill: "I came to the big land and vast places to find God, or to be found by Him; I found, instead, a thief." Through these years when he was working hard to perfect his account of his central experience, he was clearly making a conscious effort to submit his self-will and self-importance to a larger power he thought of as God. Still he had cherished the thought that he had some special way to serve, one that would be recognized when his spiritual growth was sufficient. This conviction grew increasingly difficult to maintain in the face of multiple rejections and lessening energy. In the fall of 1947, after a moving Religious Life group retreat weekend, he wrote: "I have tried to live self-sufficiently for myself. Now when I realize I cannot do so, I offer myself to God. I have tried to live for myself, and in doing so have injured my body. Now I offer my broken body to God. I did not offer it in my youth. I did not offer it in the vigor of manhood. Now I offer it in this battered and weakened life. If he accepts it, then will I know that He is merciful, and that His grace is for all." [33]

His words "broken body" and "battered and weakened life" indicate the third major aspect of Jean Toomer's life that seemed to shift at this time. His health, which had occupied him intermittently in the past few years, from now on became almost a full-time concern. Sometime after the partial respite he experienced with the Cayce treatment, through the winter of 1944–1945, he noticed immense fatigue after each period he spent responding to a request to write or speak, and he was having more trouble getting to sleep. Martin Vorhaus, a close friend in Buckingham Meeting who was a doctor, diagnosed the problem as gallbladder dysfunction. Jean was again confident that at last his underlying illness had been identified, but the pills prescribed did not bring a quick cure. A little intestinal flu at Christmas of 1945 and general malaise in February, 1946, were additional discomforts. Toward the end of 1946, dietary restrictions, part of the continuing treatment of the gallbladder, made it difficult for him to stay away from home for more than a day at a time. In early 1947 he began mentioning his "uncertain" physical condition as a reason for not accepting future commitments. He realized now that his body—or his attitude toward it—could be a prison. After talking about the "wear and tear" on his body in a letter to the Walcotts, describing a deficiency of hydrochloric acid and anemia as well as the sluggish gallbladder, he wrote:

That doggoned business sometimes stops my mental functioning in any creative way, and constantly gives me the sense that there is something in my own innards that I must overcome if I am really to do anything. . . . I can't tell from one day to the next whether I'm going to be up or down. . . .

33. JT to Herbert Seligmann, December 13, 1947, in JTP 8:12; JT, New Mexico notebook, 1945 (JTP 13:11); JT, "I Come to God," October 7, 1947 (JTP 24:1).

Faith is needed, and prayer too, and the quiet constant effort to keep oneself open to the renewing powers, not to close oneself against them, not to let our illness seal us within it.[34]

Sometime in 1947, Toomer was diagnosed as having arthritis also. For years he had had a slightly stooped posture. He was a tall man, six feet one, and he wrote standing up at a desk in the dining room. This may have intensified his tendency to lean his head and shoulders forward, as would his habit of looking over the tops of his glasses when in conversation. Now a stiffening of the back and shoulders seemed to be accentuating the stoop. In the fall of 1947, after his return from New Mexico, he tried two treatments at once, one for the gall-bladder and the other for arthritis. His analysis of the results sounds like a disaster report: "Back toward the end of September, I began to be tied in knots. I tried two treatments, which I thought would complement each other. Instead, they conflicted. . . . For a while I was going around like an old man, 90 at least." In addition, the fall had brought a major renovation of the house, including the modification of a small outbuilding into a workshop and retreat for Marjorie. This increased Jean's torture: "Just at the time when the house was most broken up, my body felt most broken up. As the house looked, that was just how I felt."[35] He had lost weight, having little enough to lose, and the doctor ordered him to rest and eat and turn down all engagements.

Thin, long-legged, almost birdlike as he stood on the beach in the summertime, he had always had a somewhat frail appearance. In winter he went to meetings with a scarf around his neck, wrapped up against the chilly buildings. Even in his active period his energy was limited. A friend observed, "He had to garner his strength; he lived sort of on the very edge of what he had, all the time."[36] Now he had to really take time off to recover. In the course of 1948 he became convinced that he had to spend full time working on his body, in order to be able later to work with his mind and spirit. He was launching himself, as it later appeared, on a final frantic race between development and extinction.

34. JT to Russell and Eugenia Walcott, February 25, 1947, in JTP 10:5.
35. JT to Seligmann, December 13, 1947, in JTP 8:12.
36. Interview of Dorothy Steere, Haverford, Pa., January 24, 1975.

VI.

EFFORTS TO ESCAPE

15.

Body-Bound

In June of 1948, Jean Toomer was like a ship becalmed, in dead, unmoving waters, waiting for the wind to blow from any direction. He saw a curious parallel between this time and his state in 1924, just before he committed himself to the Gurdjieff movement, "the conscious evolution of consciousness."[1] In both these periods, the need to attach himself to something had at least two sources, the desire for growth and the desire to be healed, but their relative weight had changed. In 1924, though he could see splits in his personality that needed mending, his overwhelming drive was toward growth and transcendence. In 1948, however, the need for wholeness was so desperate, he felt that his growth—or even his use of his talents to benefit others—could not proceed without it.

From his childhood he had had the trait of giving himself totally to one enthusiasm after another. Now in his last years a parade of enthusiasms again began, each taken up with great expectation that it was the answer, each involving almost full-time concentration while it lasted, and each fading away after a season of excitement.

The first of these, in the summer of 1948, was a specific repetition of 1924, for he again tried the Alexander method, which he had sampled briefly before his first plunge into the Gurdjieff stream. This was a system of retraining the body for better coordination of bones and muscles, partly by letting go of unhealthy positions and mechanical reactions. Developed by Frederick M. Alexander in the early years of the twentieth century, it had proved useful in teaching schoolchildren, actors, and dancers, as well as patients with several

1. JT to John Chambers, June 13, 1948, in JTP 1:9.

kinds of bodily dysfunctions. It emphasized optimum posture, natural motion, balanced distribution of energy between physical, intellectual, and emotional functions, and conscious control of mind and body. It is easy to see why it sounded to Jean like a hopeful procedure for working on his arthritis and inner imbalances.[2] He found a teacher in New York—his old friend Alma Frank, Waldo's second wife—took a room at the Beekman Hotel, and consecrated his summer to learning the new coordinations.

Getting the rigid, mechanical self out of the way and allowing a deeper self to operate the body must have seemed familiar to Toomer, and he found the process interesting. Although the teacher produces changes immediately with the method, they do not become permanent until much practice has eliminated the old habits. There was no startling difference, inward or outward, when he came back home, but he kept doing the exercises (which were more sedentary than strenuous) for a year or more and felt some improvement. The stoop, the stiffness, and the inner congestion, however, remained to plague him.

His eye inflammation also flared up again in December, robbing him of almost a month's work on the William Penn Lecture, which was to be ready for the printer in early February. When the lecture was given at the end of March, 1949, Toomer displayed some loss of his faculty for judging an audience. Speaking in a meetinghouse that echoed with the rattling of streetcars outside, on a night that proved to be extremely hot, he went on for more than two solid hours. Marjorie, sitting in the front row, could do nothing to signal him to stop; he was completely carried away by a sense of inspiration, a feeling that something greater was speaking through him. One or two members of the audience were similarly impressed, but some, though they agreed the material was worthwhile, thought Jean went well beyond the bounds of consideration for those listening to him. It was a pattern he was beginning to show also during informal evenings at home, talking on and on about his own interests. Some of his friends asked themselves, "Why bother to go over, just to listen to Jean talk all evening?" He showed this tendency also in his notes to himself and sometimes in telephone calls, running on with what seemed a compulsive verbosity. A handwritten, undated note he tucked away in his private tin box could well describe this time:

Furiously running from boredom.
A feverish activity which springs not from his source, but from a continual energy . . .

2. See Michael Gelb, *Body Learning: An Introduction to the Alexander Technique* (New York, 1981).

Talks to forget himself. Frantically desires to. Argues where his intelligence must tell him argument is futile.

Tremendous need for contact with people. Something needed which life as yet has not given. Mal-adaptation. Mind in conflict with soul.[3]

Jean by now was on the track of another method of healing and growth, which he saw as combining the psychological and the religious, a frank attempt to get at his physical problems by psychological means. He had been studying the work of Carl Jung for two or three years, and in the spring of 1949 he sought out a Jungian analyst. He believed that what Jungians called the "unconscious" was, in his own terms, "the dark aspect of the Within"—that is, a facet of the latent divine power but one that religion largely ignores. On June 10 he began his analysis in nearby Germantown, working steadily through the summer, though Marjorie had wanted to go to New Mexico. In late August he vacationed briefly at a beach in New Jersey while she went to the Poconos. Then he returned to the full-time occupation of keeping a journal, recording his dreams, and going to sessions with his analyst two or three times a week. Even such formerly central activities as the Religious Life Committee retreat were excised from his schedule. By fall he was fully involved and convinced that this new method was working. Already an easing of some tightness had brought greater openness between him and Marjorie. "It is a deep sea diving that I am doing, a going down into my own knot of darkness as never before. . . . This would seem to be my religious crisis. . . . I have no doubt that it is caused by the rather acute emergence of some unresolved matters in the unconscious that have been there since my early boyhood and which have not been touched by such inward practices as I know and could engage in."[4]

In the course of the analysis, based largely on Jean's dreams, several themes became prominent, somewhat to his surprise. One was his emotional involvement with Gurdjieff; another was his confused racial identification, which proved a much livelier issue than he had thought; and a third was the "king-priest" image. There was also his absorption with the question of fighting or submitting. With this focus on aggression, predictable in psychoanalysis, appeared an equally predictable concentration on sex, but of course each of these had the Jean Toomer stamp.

The eruption of Gurdjieff into Jean's dreams was not unrelated to outside events. Although he had sought no contact with Gurdjieff for years, others had

---

3. JT to Russell and Eugenia Walcott, February 15, 1949, in JTP 10:5; interviews of MCT, Doylestown, Pa., March 10, 1983; Douglas Steere, Haverford, Pa., January 24, 1975; and Lawrence and Ruth Miller, New Britain, Pa., January 23, 1975; JT notes (JT tin box [MTC]).
4. JT to Douglas Steere, October 15, 1949, in JTP 3:11.

tried to keep him in touch. He was aware that Gurdjieff had been in New York in the winter of 1948–1949, returning to France in January, and that there was an effort to raise money for the publication of *Beelzebub's Tales*; by the end of September, Toomer had not responded to two appeals to subscribe. With these reminders, his first recorded dream about Gurdjieff occurred in July. In it, Jean, held down on a bed, is powerless against Gurdjieff's attack. About two weeks later in another dream, Gurdjieff is putting something big and round, edible and very desirable, into Jean's mouth, requiring him to swallow it whole. Jean somehow believes he can do this, "even though it be belief in the seemingly impossible." In a third dream a month later, Jean wants to be helpful to Gurdjieff and Gurdjieff kisses him.[5]

Just past the middle of October, in response to further pressure in the non-dream world, Jean wrote Paul Rosenfeld to make it completely clear that he was not going to help with any Gurdjieff projects: "When I was an active agent I liked it too. It was my meat and bread and life. [But now] I just don't want to get involved in any way, either financially or as an agent helping to circulate that sufficiently potent material." Ten days later, he had a phone call from Dorothy Wolfe, who as Dorothy Hunt had first encountered the Gurdjieff teaching through Jean's group in Harlem, to let him know Gurdjieff had died. Two weeks after this he had another dream. Many of Gurdjieff's followers are looking with awe at some wonderful items he has left that give great power or understanding. One is a kind of folder, and each page presents a small part of a picture of a beautiful place of worship (temple, church, or mosque). The viewer has to put all the segments together in his mind; the folder carries the saying, "You have not seen the whole until you have seen all the aspects." Shortly after this, in another dream Jean does not obey an order Gurdjieff gives him. Gurdjieff grabs Jean and they tussle. "Suddenly I feel a burst of angry power and try to get G. into a position so that I can give him a decisive sock on the jaw."[6]

As he talked this series over with his analyst, she pointed out the contrast between the first one, with Gurdjieff on top, and the last, when Jean is putting up a fight. Jean saw many reasons for his being angry at Gurdjieff: "No adequate individual teaching. No career. I [was] left with nothing I can carry on by myself, and function with in relation to others." She agreed that his resentment had some foundation: the same time and devotion spent in becoming an

5. JT to Paul Rosenfeld, October 19, 1949, in JTP 8:9; Lord Pentland to JT, September 28, 1949, in JTP 4:3; dreams of July 8, 21, August 28, 1949 (JTP 33:1).

6. JT to Rosenfeld, October 19, 1949, in JTP 8:9; note of phone call, October 30, [1949], N of E (JTP 54:8); dreams of November 4, 17, 1949 (JTP 33:2).

analyst would have made Toomer a fine one. She paid little attention, however, to the dreams showing awe and respect and appreciation for the marvelous gifts Gurdjieff brought. In February, though Jean persistently refused to subscribe, Dorothy Wolfe sent him a copy of *Beelzebub's Tales*. In May, Jean reported a final dream, of Gurdjieff on his deathbed. He was not sure whether this meant the end of Gurdjieff's unwanted power over him, or the end of his hope in the Gurdjieff work and what it could do, but the dream brought deep sorrow at the death of his "great hope in the twenties, for all mankind." After this one, Jean resolved to bring no more dreams about Gurdjieff for discussion, since the analyst "can't begin to understand" what the whole experience had meant to him.[7] The ambivalent reluctance that he felt in his first contact with Gurdjieff, about submission to "the most powerful man I have ever known," the fear of being hurt or violated, was clearly still with him. But the dreams also give a strong impression of his attraction to Gurdjieff's elusive but mysteriously fulfilling offerings.

Dreams about race, a second prominent theme, spanned the whole period of the analysis. In several of them, he sees one or more black people in some public place and wonders whether he should speak to them; in each case, he does. One dream takes him back to a friendly gathering of white and black friends at his grandparents' old apartment in Washington. But the most intriguing are those in which Toomer's own identification is called into question. In one such dream, Jean is on a segregated train in the South. He intends to travel as black, but the sight of a "common type of Negro" slouched in that section makes him feel he does not belong there. When the conductor greets him as a white person, he feels committed to traveling as white. He then goes to a white restaurant, but feels uneasy until a dog and the dog's owner both accept him as white. Again, he is pushed into joining the white group. Finally, considering himself white, he sees several rough-looking white sailors on a bench in front of him. He has a feeling that "I have gotten myself into the company of . . . a bunch of pretty crude fellows." A similar dream, about two months later, contained even more tension. He is traveling on foot through the South, again accepted as a white but holding back from proffered friendships because he knows what these friends would feel if they knew "there is some Negro in me." His old friend Ken (Kennedy from high school days in Washington) joins him. The real Ken had insisted, when Jean tried to persuade him to think of himself not as black or white but as American, that such a position was all right for Jean "because I was white. It was . . . not possible for him. He was a Negro." The

7. N of E, December 9 [1949], May 12 [1950] (JTP 54:8).

dream Ken goes around willingly with Jean, but when a group of white men enter a room where the two are, Ken jumps up to be respectful. Jean is disgusted by his playing the role of "Negro puppet to white masters." Later Jean approaches a street corner where Ken and a white friend of Jean's are standing; he waves to Ken and the white man waves back. He cannot talk to either of them without "getting into complications over Negro and white" so he goes on and speaks to neither. The dream proceeds to two dead ends: a passageway that leads inside a prison, and a tenacious white girl with whom he is dancing, who only hangs on tighter when he tries to get away to avoid the impending sexual consummation with its racial complications.[8]

His analyst felt that in racial matters he had made his peace with the outer world but not with the inner. In one of his dreams the analyst herself appears, showing him two luminous circles moving toward each other, which represent the white and Negro worlds, and telling him they have never before come together inside him. In the dream, "I do not see the unification actually accomplished, but have a sense that this simple yet profound, this obvious yet mysterious, occurrence is in progress." He wanted, and tried, to bring these parts together. He began to see a "weakly inferior colored boy" inside him, who had hidden away and never grown up, and he now promised himself to grant this boy "full membership in the psyche of the present individual," for the sake of himself, the blacks, and the whites who had created this mutilated boy. He agreed he must have deliberately kept whites he knew from mingling with blacks he knew in order not to stir up this conflict in himself between the capable adult and the inferior-feeling colored boy. By March, his analyst thought that though the problem was not solved, Toomer was showing some progress.[9]

A third theme that received much attention in the analysis was Toomer's image of himself as a priest or king, in some sort of elevated, ruling position, with skills superior to those of the people about him. This image was no stranger to Jean Toomer's perception of himself since the days of the Black Prince in Chicago, but it had been latent in more recent times, the Quaker minister predominating, in a humble search for God. Now it came again to conscious recognition in full force. Only a few dreams about this experience are recorded, but it became an almost obsessive refrain in his notes in the spring, when he was losing interest in recording dreams but was writing voluminously in his journal. Several dreams in the summer and fall obliquely refer to this

8. Dreams about race, June 16, 29, July 23, October 13, 17, September 4, 11, 1949 (JTP 33:1), and November 30, 1949 (JTP 33:2).

9. Dream of October 11, 1949 (JTP 33:1); JT notes, September 11, 1949 (JTP 33:1), March 16, 1950 (JTP 54:8).

image. One, for instance, describes his wearing a black scarf or cloak: "Dressed according to what I am. Proper. Sober dignity and vitality." In a powerful dream in November, Jean is high on the outside of an ancient stone church or cathedral and knows that as priest he is required to come down almost magically. He starts down the wall with flying leaps, balancing miraculously on each place his feet must land. When he reaches the bottom, there is a great musical chord, which he sings at the same time, then a happy commotion of friends in the courtyard. Part of his success lies in his skill, and part in the "unseen forces, guides, supports" to which he as priest has access. In an initiation dream about a month later he is led through passageways and concealed doors, then carefully examined by a black man to make sure he has no "colored blood," and finally admitted into the inner life of the place, which is doing some special, secret work. [10]

The last-mentioned dream suggests a connection that Toomer's later notes make more explicit: that he had to move into the white world to claim his "proper" status. According to his perception, he could not see anywhere in the black group "my kind of life, the life I was seeking": "To hell with whites as such, but I appreciate and respond to the *kind* of life that was being lived, for example, in the Conference on Religion and Psychology. . . . I'm believed by some to belong to what I don't belong to. . . . [On the contrary] I belong *only* to the kind of life I'm now speaking about . . .—but I'm not quite in it, not accredited as is my due." Somewhat ironically, it was his affirmation of the black aspects of himself, when he wrote *Cane,* that led through the white literati to his acceptance into the inner circle of those who were seriously seeking the meaning of life. Almost immediately, he recalls on thinking of that time, his intense union with Margaret Naumburg took him beyond that affirmation. "[B]y the transforming experience through love, the opening, the rise," he was accepted into the elite world, and then he was completely alienated from his recent black identification by the "stupidity" of those who made much of it after the publication of *Cane.* [11]

The validity of this memory of his motivation is underscored by two dreams he recorded in March of 1924, six months after the publication of *Cane,* when he was living with Margaret Naumburg in Reno. In both, blacks figure prominently but Jean is not one of them. In the first, he persuades a real Negro to do away with two false ones, who have painted their faces black. In the second, Jean is master of a large castle and, with great dignity and power, ejects a

10. Dreams of August 27, 1949 (JTP 33:1), November 8, December 19, 1949 (JTP 33:2).

11. N of E, May 6, February 1, [1950] (JTP 54:6).

crowd of blacks from his cellar. He torments one of them with some kind of magic, then flies into the sky while a black gargoyle face grins at him from a totem pole. The persistence of his black identification and his rejection of it are evident in these dreams, and the process by which the king-priest establishes himself, getting rid of the black elements, is clearly displayed in the second.[12]

Since that early day, however, though he had moved in the circles he had chosen, he was dissatisfied with his reception. Now he felt he was "discounted" by Gurdjieffians, by Friends, by others, even Gorham Munson. He resented the fact that Gerald Heard and Paul Tillich, instead of Jean Toomer, had been asked to speak to the upcoming Conference on Religion and Psychology. This conference was an annual gathering, begun about ten years earlier by a group of Friends interested in Jungian psychology, held on the Haverford College campus. They invited speakers or leaders who were experts in the interplay of psychology and religion. Jean, of course, felt that this was just his area. His first reaction to this imagined snub was an aggressive "I'll show them all!" Next he questioned why: had he not yet grown enough to be an "insider," or had he fallen from what he was in a former life? Then a more logical analysis led him back to the inner blockage where his search had begun: "I cannot get what I want to have (what *belongs* to me) because I cannot give (fully) what I have to give."[13] He did not seem, as he wrote, to see his illness as an excuse for his lack of achievement, yet from time to time he had caught an awareness that something in him did not *want* him to be well.

The two high points in his analysis occurred, strangely enough, at opposite poles of this struggle about being given due recognition. He classed them together in his mind as emotional experiences, but he apparently did not compare them. In October he noted that, because of the analysis and the Alexander exercises but not as a direct result of his will, his body suddenly was able to stretch up and out, a glorious sample of what he was hoping for. At the time, he considered the old stooped posture a "setup built to compensate for lack of basic power." The new man that had arisen had "no need for teaching or being looked up to, . . . no offense that I am not star-rated." Instead, he had an "[a]ppreciation of actual sufficiently high regard and desire for my presence and services." By spring, however, this lack of star rating was again uppermost, and a similar sense of his body straightening out and feeling power was read as a confirmation of his regalness. A dream of himself as a king fed an

12. JT notebook, 1924 (JTP 57:8).
13. N of E, April 21, [1950] (JTP 54:8), May 5, 12, [1950] (JTP 54:6).

outpouring of emotion. He recalled that Mother Latimer had said he came "from a line of princes": "If I *were* as much of a king in the world as I am in myself, how wonderfully I would function. . . . If I, being what I am, having my understanding, impulses, aims, were to have a king's power—position—means, I *would* serve my people to promote in them the purpose and meaning and . . . fulfillment of human life. Non-egotistically, I could be a deeply wonderful king-priest-medicine man, *if* I had means proportionate to my being. . . . It is when this recognition is . . . *denied,* that I buck." [14] This concept seemed to be very close to the core of his identity: he could not let it go.

Two other areas of concentration were represented quantitatively by the largest number of dreams—sex and aggression. Many of the recorded dreams centered on sex. Few represented participatory situations, and most of those were with a person he did not feel fully attracted to; in more, he was an observer. Some were symbolic and some involved former friends or members of his family. Sex was a continuing problem and joy for Jean Toomer and those close to him. Many women found him overwhelmingly charming; some sought him out; but sometimes his attentions were distinctly unwelcome. Now as this life history came into view through his dreams, the analyst offered two insights. One, a slight leaning toward homosexuality, was a surprise to Jean, but he recognized it as a true part of his personality. The other, which surfaced in dream images of his wife and two daughters in the household, was an unresolved Oedipal conflict. He accepted this, too. A clue was his jealousy of Marjorie's daughter Susan while she was being courted by the man who became her second husband. Jean noted then how he had felt when his mother was being courted before she remarried—he was afraid some man might take her away.

Two of his early loves appeared in his dreams also. Phyllis Terrell, the girl for whom he claimed to have quit the University of Wisconsin, was twice visible but unattainable; and Emily Otis, his golden girl of 1930, became the embodiment of his anima, his ideal, his soul. The anima in Jung's theory is the feminine principle, usually hidden in a man, the unconscious reflection or obverse of the conscious, revealed side of the personality. Jean could think of nothing more likely to heal all his ills than an evening with his anima, someone like Emily. After dinner, dancing, and lovemaking, he would get a good full sleep and all would be well. In the real world, however, the analyst assured him that he could not play out these fantasies. He noted angrily: "[She] 'goes

14. N of E, October 1, [1949] (JTP 54:8), May 6, 5 [1950] (JTP 54:6).

into', again, what I know from my own experience better than she can tell me, men at my age [are] attracted to young girls. Repetitious drivel."[15]

It seems, both from the number of dreams concerned with the final problem and from the many notes related to their analysis, that the question of fighting or fleeing, aggression or submission, was another issue of continuing importance to Toomer. Early in his discussions with the analyst, he fitted to his memories the concept of a castration complex, which for him explained in part his feelings about race, women, and his health. He believed its origin was in his mother's seduction of him (these are his words, but the sense in which he means them is not clear) and her later rejection of him, leaving him with a continuing fear of being rejected, especially acute because of his color. The racial issue, with its combination of servility and aggression, could be a projection in his case (as the analyst suggested) of the conflict between him and his mother.[16]

Toward women this sensitivity was apparent also in his cutting himself off, often by teasing, when he felt hurt or vulnerable—something he realized he did not do with men. A general fear of being knocked down made him frequently adopt a pose of resignation or submission, as he had at the time of the kidney operation, which caused him to feel helpless or caught. During that hospital stay, he recalled, the head nurse told him he was one of the best patients they had ever had, but the price he paid for repressing his feelings was a continued "lump in the unconscious."[17]

The body, too, was involved in this castration complex. According to his analyst, everyone has a dichotomy between body and spirit, but Jean had more than the usual opposition between the two, and a dramatization of the relation with his mother as well. His neurosis impeded the body, and Jean was therefore overdrawn toward his body. As Jean considered this he connected his forward-bent head with an attitude of resignation, with "a notion I've bent over to duck my head to escape blows from the world." In his childhood, his body had become helpless in order to win his mother back, and he now realized that this kind of hazard was still with him. Each of the two times, in October and in May, that he had felt most healthy, straightened up, and invigorated with a rush of energy and insight, his gallbladder within a few days had given him

15. N of E, May 20, [1950] (JTP 54:7), May 10, 12, [1950] (JTP 54:6), June 21, [1949] (JTP 33:1), November 13, [1949] (JTP 33:2), February 15, [1950] (JTP 54:8), July 25, [1950] (JTP 54:7).

16. N of E, September 19, [1949] (JTP 54:8).

17. N of E, February 21, [1950], September 27, [1949] (JTP 54:8).

enough trouble to end the good period. Perhaps, he thought, it was his neu-rosis in a last-ditch fight against the constructive forces working in him.[18]

Although a few of the dreams contained the kind of monsters and lurking shadows that used to fill his recurrent nightmares in childhood, many more seem to indicate his resistance to the state of submission. In these, he is fight-ing, either with fists or guns, sometimes in league with other men, sometimes alone. In life, too, as his analysis progressed, this resistance seemed to in-crease. In March of 1950 he made a note, "Tired of writing and speaking for no monetary return. . . . Tired of not hurting other people but hurting myself by repression." In less than a month, when Marjorie responded to his negative comments about a cause dear to her heart by accusing him of being a fake and calling his spirituality a sham, he reacted with a physical blow. About three months after that, his resistance to his analyst, waxing and waning through the spring, grew so strong—particularly when she began advising him about his writing—that he broke off all connection with her and ended his venture into analysis.[19]

One more major feature of this period needs to be mentioned: his struggle to conquer his bodily symptoms, which came to be centered in the monumental effort to get a full night's sleep. In brief, everything that he had complained of in the past decade (except the eye trouble, which came and went erratically) continued to be wrong with him. He had the congestion in the lower ab-domen, which now he connected with the gallbladder; he had the stiffness in his shoulders and back, and occasionally in one leg, with the increasingly bent-over posture; and he had the persistent problem with what he called his "sec-ond body."

In the matter of the second body, it was hard for him to get understanding or sympathy. Doctors could not be helpful; his analyst would not consider the subject; Marjorie did listen and try to understand, but she could not really imagine how it felt. She suggested that he simply lie quietly in bed when he could not sleep, but for him this did not feel possible. When he went to bed, the second body seemed to tighten about him and grip him so, there was no hope of sleep until he deadened it with whiskey and sleeping pills. Sometimes when he had had a good, releasing day, he thought it would let him alone, but that almost never happened. Only once, at the time of his king-priest experi-

18. N of E, May 10, [1950] (JTP 54:6), October 7, November 9, December 3, [1949] (JTP 54:8).

19. JT's childhood nightmares are described in "Earth-Being" (MTC), 111–14. Other notes are from N of E, March 7, 30, [1950] (JTP 54:8), July 25, [1950] (JTP 54:7).

ence in May of 1950, did he note major relief of this kind, that the second body was actually moving freely. Ordinarily what he did in the day seemed to have little effect on his nights—on the contrary, the nights were controlling the days. Unlike most people, who rest at night to get through the day, he tried to gather energy during the day to get through the night.[20]

What he took to deaden the second body at night also kept him knocked out in the morning and often impaired his functioning over long periods. He was well aware of this and was actively working to reduce his intake of whiskey and Seconal. Several times he put off taking the sleeping pills until he could stand the pressure no longer. One night in early May, though he had noted a few days before that the second body was "now larger, with increased activity and increased tightness at night," he decided to try going to bed without either whiskey or Seconal; he had never dared before. He recorded that his second body tightened "but not unbearably so," and for two hours he lay there before taking any whiskey. Thereafter he drank a little at two-hour intervals and used some Ketochol but no Seconal. Both he and Marjorie were pleased with his fortitude, and each night for the next several weeks, he tried to do the same thing. But though he was determined and desperate, the rally was brief. He continued the battle for years, measuring his progress against his consumption of these damaging drugs, but the pills and potions, in a strange alliance with his second body, proved tougher than his resolution and became more and more destructive of his life.[21]

Clearly the year of analysis had shaken his foundations, making him question the sincerity of his calling to minister to others, the reality or fiction of his king-priest image, and even his basic ability to do the things he thought he could do best. At one point he pictured himself as a priest-martyr, always an alien, and concluded, "I had a destiny—and I've missed it." At the end of the sessions, however, though he knew he still needed more therapy, he was asserting again his hope for himself as a counselor—if possible, one who was paid. He had toyed with the idea of how good he would have been as a psychoanalyst, but he realized that he was too old to start the years of training required. Still, he knew that his counseling had helped people in the past. In addition, Jean was increasingly troubled that the family was living beyond its income, that he was the most expensive family member, and that over the years he had made little or no financial contribution.[22] Now, in the late spring of 1950, a technique appeared that gave promise of meeting these several needs.

20. N of E, May 6, 7, [1950] (JTP 54:6).

21. N of E, May 3, [1950] (JTP 54:6).

22. N of E, April 19, [1950] (JTP 54:8); JT to Howard Schubart, December 14, 1949, in JTP 8:11.

At the end of May a friend of Jean's, Bill Cleveland, had showed him a new book, *Dianetics* by L. Ron Hubbard. Bill and his wife were already excited about the pseudopsychological technique it described for uncovering the hidden wounds in a person's past that control present actions and emotions. (At first said to be a scientific system, but not endorsed by psychologists or psychiatrists, dianetics has since gone through several metamorphoses to become the Church of Scientology.) Toomer, studying the book, was immediately interested and, disillusioned by now with the analysis, arranged for a trial session, together with Bill, on the third of July. Subsequently he went back to Elizabeth, New Jersey, for further sessions about three times a week through the fall, and from January to March he took a six-week training course to prepare himself to be an "auditor," able to give the "runs" that he had found so helpful. He also hoped that his cash outgo would become an inflow.[23]

From the time he entered this new experiment, Jean expected to be shot straight back to the beginning of his life: "I may contact the painful root of my racial conflict." He also expected the trouble to be connected with his mother, perhaps even prenatal. Later, in the course of his "runs," many of these deductions were in fact made from the fragments of phrases that brought surges of emotion as the sessions touched different levels of memory. In his first session, it was suggested that his mother's dying of peritonitis after acute appendicitis was related to Jean's gallbladder congestion in the same area of the body. Several later sessions brought sensations of an injury to his right side, with the recurrent indication that this had happened before he was born. From the phrases expressed in connection with this sensation, Toomer came to believe that his mother had arranged, and then halted, an abortion: "No, no—don't stick him . . Take it out of me. God forgive me . . . I must have been out of my mind." Other phrases that seemed to relate to the same period he connected with his racial pain—for example, his mother saying, "Get out of here, you black bastard," presumably to his father. Various other sessions recalled injuries to his right side: the time he fell out of the tulip tree, the time he was pushed down by a bully after his illness. He also saw an analogy between vomiting, his body's route to illness and attention as a child, and his mother's sick headaches, her way of retreating from her father's high-handed orders. Jean got a tremendous release and outpouring of energy from the first few sessions, and was convinced that he had found the "chief source of psychosomatic trouble: congestion, abdominal spastic, impeded breathing, difficulty functioning by day and sleeping by night, hitherto inexplicable reduction of aware-

23. N of E, May 26, [1950] (JTP 54:6), July 1, [1950] (JTP 54:7); JT notebooks (JTP 69:1, 69:5, 69:7, 69:6, 69:9).

ness, alertness, ability, functioning, even possibly the damage to the tube outlet of the right kidney, solar plexus damage, lack of 'guts,'—all due to that
original damage to no. 1 area . . . me bent over—after strain in meeting for
worship—arthritis, etc."[24]

After the first flush of success with this new treatment, however, as had happened with other curative experiments, his physical difficulties overtook him
again. His gallbladder was first to act up, then the second body, then his right
hip joint went "out of whack." Doubts about the system immediately arose in
him, and he slowed his participation but persisted. He soon discovered that he
could both provide and receive immense satisfaction in serving informally as
an auditor for someone else. Great stores of energy seemed to be available for
this, even when a friend called on him to do it late at night. His life through
the fall of 1950 was a pendulum from functioning to nonfunctioning: brief
contributions to Friends circles, sometimes painfully given, sometimes easily;
backing out of family, religious, and social commitments and even appoint-
ments for sessions in dianetics; and then for a time, full energetic participation
in the almost daily round of auditing and being audited. He offered "runs" to
family members, and had one two-hour session with his daughter Arge, in
which she "said more as to what she felt than she's said to me, or in my presence, during her entire life!" It was certainly communication on a different
level from his frequent greeting to her, "Well, are you Passion, Romance, or
Glamour today?"[25]

During his good period in the spring he had made a speech on psychology to
a community group and had written three or four articles. September of 1950
saw his last published article, in which he seems to be struggling to justify and
accept the problems in his life. Now he was doing little public speaking
and less writing. In the late spring of 1950 he had gone back to his friend
Dr. Vorhaus with a request for something to help him sleep. He was now
taking, at various times of the day, hormones, vitamins, folic acid, and anti-
spastic medicine as well as the whiskey and Seconal, and periodically in-
dulging in varieties of food, such as bluepoint oysters and shrimp creole,
which he later regretted having eaten. In January of 1951 he had one in-
conclusive session in New York with a doctor who had ties to the Dianetics
Foundation. He listed himself as practicing "Psychosomatic Medicine" and

24. N of E, July 2, [1950] (JTP 54:7); JT notebook, February 18, 10 (ellipses in original),
1951 (JTP 69:9), November 2, 1950 (JTP 69:5), October 9, 1950 (JTP 69:1).

25. JT notebook, October 14, 1950 (JTP 69:1), October 16, 1950 (JTP 69:5), January 2,
1951 (JTP 69:6); interview of Margery Toomer Latimer, Doylestown, Pa., June 23, 1978.

explored some implications of Jean's second body and his sleeplessness. Then, having decided to become a professional in dianetics, Jean began the training course at the foundation school in New York.[26]

Within ten days after Toomer finished his course, the Dianetics Foundation schools in New York and New Jersey closed down, broke, and Ron Hubbard, amid mutual recriminations, opened a new Dianetics Foundation in Wichita, Kansas. Although Jean thought his training was adequate and he had already gotten good results as an auditor, there was no longer a support system to help him get started with clients. Most auditors who had been paid had worked through the foundation. Moreover, the rumors and confusion surrounding the breakup did not enhance the already low esteem in which the organization was held—Jean was no longer mentioning dianetics among Bucks County friends and neighbors. For these reasons, though he worked a little with individuals in an informal way, the training was a failure in terms of providing him a way to make a living. Neither did it prove a means of curing him. The insights he had gained, though they may have helped his understanding, did not translate into permanent bodily improvement. In fact his image of himself as an auditor, at the completion of his training, was that he was working not "on difficulties that traditionally are in the fields of medicine and psychiatry, but with those in the fields of creative experience and the religious life."[27] There was little clear demand for such a service.

Many times in the past Jean had experimented with nutrition. He had, for example, concentrated on athletics and diet in both high school and college, and had cured himself in Ellenville after his too-frantic schedule led to a break-down in 1918. Now, through the following winter and into the spring of 1952, he turned his self-curative efforts to the field of nutrition. He read, experimented, and kept records on the effects of various nutrition supplements and vitamins, along with the battery of medicines and the liquor that were his constant companions. He continued trying to cut down on the whiskey he drank at night. In April he noted some success with this and some relaxing of the abdominal contraction—temporarily believing that he had found the answer to a long-standing problem.[28]

26. JT notebook, October 9, 12, 14, 1950 (JTP 69:1), October 25, 1950 (JTP 69:5), January 2, 1951 (JTP 69:6), December 9, 1950 (JTP 69:7). The article is JT, "Blessing and Curse," *Friends Intelligencer*, CVII (1950), 576–77.

27. JT to Stan Waldrop, March 26, 1951, in JTP 10:6; JT to Douglas Steere, July 16, 1951, in JTP 3:11; JT to W. N. Scott, July 9, 1951, in JTP 8:11.

28. JT notes, January–April, 1952 (JTP 17:10).

No solution, however, lasted for long, and December of 1952 saw him swept unexpectedly into his final series of attempts to restore body and soul—back, indeed, almost to where he had started. The curious cyclical sense he had had of a repetition of 1924, which began his recent round of desperate experiments, now brought him again to its identical 1924 conclusion—Gurdjieff.

16.

Return to Gurdjieff

As it was the impact of a man—its powerful leader—that first drew Jean Toomer into the Gurdjieff movement, it was again a man and not a book that brought him back. In November, Marjorie and Jean made casual plans to go to New York for several days, visit friends and see a show. Fred Leighton had in the meantime sent Jean a copy of a recent book on Gurdjieff's teachings, written by John G. Bennett, an Englishman who had worked closely with Gurdjieff toward the end of the master's life.[1] Jean had glanced at it and set it aside without much interest. But when Fred wrote him that Bennett was to give a series of lectures in New York, one scheduled for the evening of the very day the Toomers planned to arrive, Jean decided to attend. At that lecture his impression of Bennett's "inner freedom" and "quietly sustained feeling of joy" was overwhelming. Toomer was suddenly certain that Bennett had received some teachings denied to Toomer himself. He was filled with longing to reach such a state, "a level sensibly higher and much more stable than my own." Next day, when Toomer, Fred Leighton, and Gorham Munson met for lunch with John Bennett, Jean learned that Gurdjieff had in fact begun in about 1942 to develop some rather specific teachings in Paris and had trained several people to transmit them. Jean was irresistibly drawn. He now had no questions about returning to the fold: he wanted only to catch up with what he had missed, to "be given another chance *to be*. To evolve. To become of use to myself and others."[2] Now, after Gurdjieff's death, Jean was

1. Probably John Bennett, *What Are We Living For?* (London, 1949).
2. JT to Eugenia and Russell Walcott, March 24, 1953, JT to Mme. de Salzmann, March 24, 1953, both in JTP 11:7.

coming back. Ironically, if he had turned in this direction when in 1948 he began casting about for a new means of salvation, he could presumably have worked with Gurdjieff himself in New York. But his feelings and motivations had to go through other stages before he could return.

He began immediately, learning voraciously from Bennett for the two weeks before the latter returned to London, then becoming a member of one of the groups set up as an outgrowth of Bennett's lectures. Under the leadership of Mme. Jeanne de Salzmann, to whom Gurdjieff had given the care of the work, some sixty people of the hundred or so who applied were selected to meet regularly and learn more about the system. Toomer was in a group led by Mme. de Salzmann and another Paris-trained leader. In the summer, when both had gone back to Europe, the leadership of his group passed to Louise Welch, who had worked with Orage and Gurdjieff and also with Ouspensky and Mme. Ouspensky after 1941, when they came to the United States and set up a center at Mendham, New Jersey. In spite of his shaky health, which had often interfered with his getting to Quaker gatherings in Philadelphia or dianetics sessions in New Jersey, Jean managed to go to New York every week for these meetings, usually staying in Fred Leighton's apartment overnight, missing only one Wednesday evening in his first six months.

A primary factor in his urgency was certainly his need for help in his struggle for a sound body and mind. Despite his forays during the past four years, riding off in all directions in search of a solution, he seemed no better off than before. Louise Welch sensed that Jean had "a kind of depressed feeling that he would never again find the right search for the truth." Later he described his 1952 state: "I had come to the end of my rope" and "I had come to the point where I could not go on without [the work], could hardly even barely live." In addition to his group participation, he had individual interviews with Mme. de Salzmann and wrote long, detailed letters to John Bennett. With both of them he explored his "second body" problem and for the first time got an answer that promised hope: a way to practice "deep relaxation" of the autonomic nervous system. Since Dr. Vorhaus had moved away, Jean began seeing Dr. William Welch, Louise's husband, who was also in the Gurdjieff work, for medical advice. In July both he and Dr. Welch were pleased to note that his nighttime whiskey consumption had been reduced by half. When after the initial burst of energy his physical problems began again to overcome him in the summer and fall of 1953 and brought him to a low point around Christmas, it was Dr. Welch who diagnosed the difficulty—Jean's stomach had dropped below its normal position—and prescribed an abdominal support and some exercises. For a time, Jean rejoiced that the "real" source of all the trouble had at last been discovered.[3]

Of course physical relief was not Toomer's direct goal in returning to the Gurdjieff work. His primary concentration was, in Gurdjieff's phrase, on "the hope of consciousness," which, as Louise Welch later described it, had suddenly dawned for him again: "I had a feeling that this [hope] was what Jean was experiencing but with more depth because he had already gone through his doubts and disillusionments and all that. He was no longer a naive young man in search of spiritual truth; he was a disillusioned man looking for objective truth." Jean wrote to John Bennett, "During these past three and a half months more 'newness' has come into my life than during the past fifteen years." His work on combating the mechanicalness in himself brought him by midsummer to some real insights: that in his earlier teaching he had lacked inner strength, unity, dependability and that he lacked genuine understanding, though sometimes real teaching happened through him. "There was the real thing—and, there was the mere role. And back and forth I'd pass, from the sincere ability into the pretense. . . . Back and forth, with my awareness too sluggish to detect the change from the one to the other, most often." More than ever before, he committed himself to attaining a real and permanent "I" above and beyond his many inconsistent, partial selves, though he recognized that he would not achieve it: "It is probable that in this life I shall never be able to attain more than a closer approach to a real 'I.'"[4]

Such an image of cool steady wisdom, not tangled with emotions or reacting mechanically to events, must have been quite attractive as he struggled through the summer and autumn to inch away from his old patterns. From the end of June to the end of August, Marjorie was in New Mexico, helping care for their friend Maria, who had been injured in a fall, and seeing Georgia O'Keeffe and other old friends. Jean had to cope with a mixed household of Arge (convalescing from a chipped ankle bone and suffering at least two other crises during the summer), a young woman helper-boarder with her small undisciplined daughter, assorted dogs and cats, and, in the mill nearby, Susan and her husband Sandy and their brood, now four children.

A faint track of *Cane* arose from that summer and spread, like a comet's tail,

3. Welch interview; JT to Mme. Ouspensky, January 18, 1953 (first draft), JT to John Bennett, February 20, March 20, 1953, all in JTP 11:7; JT to MCT, July 26, 1953, in JTP 11:8; JT to Mme. Ouspensky, February 1, 1954, in JTP 11:10.

4. Welch interview; JT to Bennett, March 20, 1953, in JTP 11:7; JT to Mme. de Salzmann, June 1, 1953, in JTP 11:8.

over these years. In Abiquiu, Marjorie saw two copies on Georgia's bookshelf. She seized one and showed it to Maria, who was excited on reading it. Maria and another of their old friends in Santa Fe, Joe Foster, who had been Jean's roommate in his earlier life at the University of Wisconsin, suggested that it should be put out in paperback. Joe was prepared to get in touch with some publishers and try to make arrangements, but Marjorie asked him to wait for Jean's permission. This was probably one of the heavy burdens she laid on him that fall, the push to make decisions he was not ready to make. This one apparently never was made while he lived, as the first paperback edition of *Cane* came out two years after his death. Yet the copyright had been renewed in 1951, and Jean, putting together promotional material for the workshop he was to give in the spring of 1954, listed his authorship of *Cane* ("a collection of poems and sketches") along with *Essentials* and *The Flavor of Man*, thereby publicly linking three of his various lives.

When Marjorie came back she too was trying to change old patterns in the hope of increasing communication and real companionship with Jean. But he felt that he was under attack, as a series of his notes reveals:

Sept. 29 '53 Sequence of events: contending with myself, very difficult contending, during those difficult sessions with M; contending with myself to move my body into taking a daily walk, however it feels, . . . moving myself to write papers necessary for my course . . . ; moving myself to go places, out at night, etc., when everything in me pulls against it, almost cries against it. And some results, to date . . . : a slight gain in inner strength, a definitely better bodily tone. . . . The desired prospect—my being able to get a restful sleep of nights (without poisons), get up relatively early, walk, work, eat well, get a more balanced functioning inwardly and outwardly.

Nov. 28 '53 Energy at *low* ebb. So little. Rotten physical states. Rough emotional times. M ramping (let up now) ever since returning from southwest. Nothing is right. Money. Finding a new place to live.[5]

In December and January he suffered through company, his abdomen often so contracted that he did not feel like sitting up or talking. Persistent work in his groups through the ensuing year brought small advances and records of unexplained downswings and upswings. A wisdom-tooth extraction left him in pain for more than a week. In May he felt a new awareness that even when his physical state was not good, his psyche could still be active and present and did not have to be the body's slave. In August, he spent a few whirlwind days writ-

---

5. Correspondence between JT and MCT, June-August, 1953, in JTP 9:7, 11:8, 11:9; JT notes, "Experiments, 1953–54" (JTP 17:7).

ing four long-postponed letters, culling and disposing of "useless manuscripts," and persuading Marjorie, Arge, and other residents outside for a game of softball.

Then in the fall, after a difficult trip to New York with Marjorie and Arge, a lingering cold turned into such discomfort that Jean called a local doctor and, feeling too shaky to drive, asked Marjorie to take him for his evening appointment. She sat in as he listed for the doctor all the poisons he was taking. There seemed nothing earth-shaking about the doctor's diagnosis of an intestinal virus or his directions to come back in a few days for a barium enema. But there was something about that evening visit that caused a psychological upheaval. After he got home he felt a fluttering and heaving in his solar plexus, turned face down on his bed, and gave way to repeated yawns and tears.

What was happening may have been what he had sought in the great campaign to free his emotions thirteen years before. Perhaps it arose from Marjorie's concern for his health, expressed in her driving him over and sharing the consultation, which forced him to be fully open with her as well as with the doctor. Perhaps his efforts to become more aware had led him to see her more clearly— he had already begun tentatively to express some of his appreciation of her difficult situation in the household, and she to respond. Then a few days later, talking to someone else, he suddenly had an image of himself blaming his body, his wife, everything but himself for his troubles. This was the complete opposite of what he had believed about himself. He saw now that his usual practice was escaping rather than contending: "I am nothing but a shell of a man. I am hollow. A pose. A false front." He had an almost physical sense of this shell cracking to expose the horrifying truth of weaknesses and fears that had armored themselves with self-complacency and thus shut him off from real emotion and honest relationships.

With his usual dramatization, he pictured the battle begun by this new awareness as a hand-to-hand combat between the positive forces struggling for life and "those weaknesses, those sometimes almost overpowering emotions, that strong pull downwards towards extinction." And finally he felt success: "My horse has come out of the stable," he wrote to Mme. de Salzmann,

only it was much worse than a stable, it was a prison. It was locked in there. . . . Now it lives, and so I live, for that is where I am alive. . . .

I had known for years that, except for brief occasions, my emotions and feelings, especially my better quality feelings, had been in retreat from my wife. . . . Now I also recognized how much they had also withdrawn from some other people and situations. It was an awful dead condition, and I could do about it nothing whatsoever. . . .

Now that my feelings are somewhat free and alive again, I wish and hope and pray that never again will they go into retirement.[6]

What resulted from this remarkable opening was, as Louise Welch remembered much later, a time when there was a real change in both Jean and Marjorie: "Marjorie looked like a young girl," and both seemed young and happy after having regularly looked exhausted. It happened about this time that Louise had invited Marjorie over for tea and then to take part in her group meetings. Marjorie for the first time was willing to be in a Gurdjieff group, becoming one of a small number meeting with Louise on weekdays in Princeton, and even feeling that "a miracle had happened to me." Jean realized that he himself had been the block to her earlier participation, and he felt humbly grateful for the brokenness in him that could open the way for her. The two found a warmth and closeness they had not shared for some time. They had come to an agreement about the problem of living space. Susan's family, crowded in the mill, had found a house about seven miles away. Mill House and the mill, now too complicated for Jean and Marjorie to take care of, would be sold and the old barn on their property would be remodeled into a smaller place for them. Jean found that his "second body" problem abated when his emotions were set free. He also was able to reach out again in small ways to the Meeting and the community. In March of 1955 he composed a letter of invitation, on behalf of Buckingham Meeting, to encourage friends and neighbors to attend their meetings for worship, and he was one of a "selected list" of local notables interviewed by the Doylestown paper about his views on the best way to bring peace.[7] In the picture published with this interview, he was the image of a good gray Quaker, with his rimless bifocals, his neatly clipped small moustache, his slightly gray hair conservatively cut, and his sober expression. He had, however, essentially left the fold. His lively interest and his waning energies had for several years been focused elsewhere.

In the meantime, as always with him, hand in hand with Jean's concern for his inner transformation had walked his concern for his outer role. He was troubled, in his first few months back in the Gurdjieff work, by resentment at being "outside," a beginner, behind others—yet he had for years chosen to separate himself from that community. His position in the hierarchy was somewhat anomalous. He was put in an elementary study group, but in some ways

6. JT notes, August 26, 1954 (JTP 17:8); JT journal notes, February 7, 1955 (MTC); JT to Mme. de Salzmann, November 8, 1954, in JTP 11:10.

7. Welch interview; JT to Mme. de Salzmann, November 8, 1954, in JTP 11:10; JT journal notes, March 3, 1955 (MTC); Buckingham Monthly Meeting minutes, March 6, 1955 (FHLS); "'Voices for Peace VI': N. J. Toomer," Doylestown *Daily Intelligencer,* May 26, 1955, p. 11.

his former status was acknowledged. The private luncheon with Bennett the day after the lecture was one such indication, as was Mme. Ouspensky's invitation the following January to come to Mendham for the celebration of Gurdjieff's birthday. John Bennett kept up a detailed advisory correspondence with him and, by May of 1953, was asking when Toomer would again be ready to begin teaching. Jean was eager to do so, but felt he should keep "low" for a time, as he felt too much fluctuation in his physical condition and mental state to be dependable just yet.[8] By that fall, however, he was experimenting with leadership, giving directions (without official permission) for a subgroup led by a friend of Fred's in New York and starting a course that he hoped would gather some possible Gurdjieff adherents near Doylestown.

Some poets, artists, and intellectuals living in the area had started a reading group the year before, to explore various aspects of art and thought, and in the fall of 1953 they set up a series of seminars and workshops. Toomer was asked to give an eight-lecture course on the spiritual development of man. His course, as he summed it up, "fell in between a G. group and a series of lectures. Not so good. But, some few really touched, and these may come to form the nucleus of a G. Group. This too foreseen." Although he had mentioned George Fox, the Bhagavad-gita, and Jean Toomer's life story in his lectures, most of the time was spent on awareness exercises and the theory of four states of consciousness.[9]

He followed this with a second course in the spring of 1954, this too under the aegis of the Bucks County Workshops, with paid enrollment but offered at Mill House. Called "The Reintegration of Ourselves," it was even more frankly than the first workshop based on explaining the Gurdjieff theory of man. By this time Jean's group leader in New York was "warm and pleased that I, to whom so much was given, am again in the current in the work. . . . I too am glad." In the midst of this eight-week period, Toomer asked Mme. de Salzmann "if I may have my own gathering in the country" for reading Gurdjieff's books. She agreed, provided he only *read*: if anything more was to be done, he was to ask someone else to help. From this seed a group began, continuing to meet in the Toomer home, which lasted about two years and represented Jean's final effort at teaching. Louise and William Welch soon joined the group and helped with the leadership. Jean continued to study the writings of Ouspensky and Bennett, and in the summer of 1954, Fred Leighton showed him a transcription of Gurdjieff teaching the French group in 1943–1944. This fascinated him and almost seemed to transmit a certain new

8. JT to Bennett, May 26, 1953, in JTP 11:7.
9. JT notes (JTP 28:8, 54:2).

energy. Toomer was still "a man of enormous magnetic excitement" when it was awakened, "great charm, great capacity to affect people, to make them think and feel," and some in that small band still resounded to his impact many years later.[10]

Jean assigned readings to the group—Gurdjieff's writings, Quaker material, Thomas Sugrue's life of Edgar Cayce, John Bennett's books, Gerald Heard's works, accounts by the classic mystics, depending on what he felt they needed. He repeatedly went over Ouspensky's second lecture in *The Psychology of Man's Possible Evolution,* which dealt with the four states of consciousness and the need to balance the physical, mental, and emotional centers before even the second of these states could be attained. At first, Marjorie read these books aloud, until members had time to secure their own copies. Other group members suggested related philosophical works to read, and they would discuss the readings with one another between meetings. The exercises, however, were private and were given individually. "Jean knew each one's weaknesses," reported one member, Miryam Ralph, "and what had to be sharpened and developed." She added, "It was the greatest thing that ever happened to me in my life, was to become a member of this."[11]

At the same time, Toomer's physical state was interfering more and more with his effective functioning. His hard-won emotional freedom was a variable quantity, often replaced with the old tensions. Louise Welch would regularly call to ask how Jean was before she came for a group meeting, because sometimes he did not feel well enough to handle the questions and then it would be her task to do so, "although we always preferred he do it because he always brought a great vitality to it." After the period of renewal marked by the "release of his horse," from late 1954 on into 1955, his good times grew less and less frequent. When the Toomers moved to the renovated barn in August of 1955, he was still functioning fairly well, but after that his downswings seemed to be deeper. Some days he would feel good enough to go to New York, some days he would feel so bad that he could do nothing but rest all day. He gradually found it almost impossible to sit up; he could only stand up or lie down. He could no longer go to Friends meetings or participate in outside activities. When he received company or led his group, his usual position was lying on a wooden-backed couch perpendicular to the fireplace in the living room. A few years earlier he had had a time of excessive verbosity, but he now

10. Ruth Ikeler to JT, March 18, 1954, in JTP 1:7; JT notes (JTP 26:9); JT notes, March 18, April 21, 1954 (JTP 17:8); JT notes, August 16, 1954 (JTP 67:1); Welch interview.
11. Interview of Miryam Ralph, Pipersville, Pa., March 21, 1983.

spoke less and less until he came to be almost completely silent. To some of the members, he was just as inspiring without speaking: he "could lie there and look very fragile, like Gandhi; . . . he would sparkle even though he couldn't move . . . and could make a point to each of us with a single word that would be important the rest of our lives." [12]

What finally ended the group was fragility, both Jean's and the group's. One couple, Tom and Jeanne McCormack, left town with a change of jobs; two other couples separated; there was no energy to recruit replacements. And Jean found that the groups took so much out of him that he felt he could not go on. He sent the members to another leader sometimes, then gave instructions to one of the members to continue with the group. In 1957 the Welches moved from Princeton to New York. It was then too difficult for Marjorie to continue her group meetings with Louise, and impossible for Jean to stir so far from his couch. But as late as 1958, Louise wrote and asked him to try to give an exercise to the group, as she felt that he would do it more effectively than the member who was acting as leader. Jeanne McCormack, too, still depended on him for instruction. She wrote him from Indiana of her concern for his health and her ongoing efforts to practice what he had taught her. After she came back to visit him in September of 1957, a visit "that meant and means so very much, a transfusion in effect," she tried to start a Gurdjieff group with a nucleus from the Quaker Meeting in Lafayette, Indiana. Her group met for about six months before it faded away. [13]

The small remnant that was left in Doylestown drew around Jean to support him. They would bring vitamins, afraid he was not eating enough, and would try to help Marjorie with various tasks, to relieve some of her burden of caring for him. They began to see Jean sometimes in much less flattering situations, and two of them at least felt called to send him loving but sorrowing advice. One shared with him her experience of dealing with anguish by silent surrender or one-word prayers.

But alcohol, barbiturates, calmers, tranquilizers, I have come to see, for me, are a small suicide; the desire to escape pain and tension. Pain and tension are part of growing when used with understanding.

You have a gift, perhaps what Christians call grace, and certainly it is painful, and sometimes one expects madness, but it seems to me a small price to pay for being open, receptive, and prayer does help.

12. Welch interview; Ralph interview.
13. Ralph interview; Louise Welch to JT, June 14, 1958, in JTP 10:8; Jeanne McCormack to Ikeler, September 22, [1957], in JTP 11:4; McCormack to JT, May, 1957–March, 1958, in JTP 7:6.

The other regretted having had no transportation when he needed her to "pull you from a depressed or lonely state":

Much to my chagrin it has come out how far you journeyed into the night. Whatever forces pulling you or gravitating you to destruction counter balances for equal construction. . . . Do you get into these states purposively and then they get out of control—You recognize your limited physical reserve? . . .

Alcohol is a false stimulant and depressant—also cause of impotency and repressed sexual drives expressed thru violent aggression is thrusted against the very ones who care the most . . .

There has been nothing written which you have not hitherto been informed.—But when a teacher—a man—performs commonly as an adolescent boy he needs an emotional spanking.

Jean—please ask and answer this question—When a better quality of your good self is in the state for it—"Jean—now—when your other depressed side gets the upper hand—what do you really expect of your friends?" When you know the answer let us know—we can carry out orders better than floundering around.[14]

This recognition of Jean's two separated selves seems to be the key to understanding, if it is possible to understand, his last years. On one hand were the destructive times referred to; on the other was a great quietude that had come over him, a withdrawal that some thought had a spiritual quality. Friends who came to visit would see him lying fully dressed on the couch, sometimes speaking a few words, sometimes getting up without explanation and going to his room. Or Marjorie might wave a good friend on to his bedroom, white and spare as a monastic cell, where he would be lying with his hands folded, looking up at the ceiling. The guest's presence might be acknowledged by a brief warm sentence or a pat on the hand. Jean's eating became likewise ascetic, a meal reduced to one grape and a square of cheese.

What was going on inside this inscrutable exterior? Jean's flow of correspondence and personal notes dried up after the last great surge of energy in 1955, so further interpretation must depend on outside observers. It is reasonable to expect that his struggle toward understanding, control, and self-development continued as long as he was able—as did also his love for adulation and the bodily addictions against which his struggle had been directed. All these tendencies were indeed inferred or read directly by various people who saw him. One friend, Miryam Ralph, believed that his eating habits were his training for the life of the spirit, a development for rebirth, preparing his physical body so there would be very little left of it. But she also recognized that he became

14. Ikeler to JT, n.d. [ca. 1957] in JTP 11:4; Rene [later Miryam] Ralph to JT, July 30, 1958, in JTP 8:8.

very irritating in his fussiness about food, and that alcohol was his undoing. Louise Welch, too, saw his quietness as a preparation for another stage of being, that he was becoming less active and more contemplative: "He was understanding directly many things that had once been subjects for wordmaking, but no more—for that, perhaps they were even too profound." In 1937, Jean had written a description of such an activity, the "apex-function of the human mind":

I love inner-action more passionately than I used to love love. It is this that I want for myself and hope for everyone. . . .

Never am I in such *real* contact with surrounding people and the outer world in general as when I ponder. . . . It will seem paradoxical to many, I know. . . . They picture the in-man as closed off, walled in. . . . Yes, the inner-active man does shut out the *nonessentials* of the world—and for the very reason that he is prepared to contact what is essential. . . . [By pondering] the essence of the inner man—his best fruits— are rendered available and ripe to give to the world. Through it, moreover, we can contact still higher powers.[15]

It may be that this kind of activity was sometimes going on. Marian Fuson reported a visit during this period, when Jean did not eat with the guests but came in after lunch and then as suddenly left to go back to his room: "It was a strange thing to me, because there was a currentness for someone who was rejecting the current world—that is, the answering of letters, the keeping up with things: he was quite current on people we had known together, in the Young Friends movement, for instance. . . . He was quite *there*, while we were together; and my feeling was that this was a *choice* on Jean's part—that what he was *current* on was his choice." Still, Louise and others, while suggesting that something deeper was occurring, recognized that there were times when Jean was simply fatigued, depressed, and hemmed in by his "irascible body," as Dr. Welch called it. Some friends, however, felt that his behavior had nothing to do with a religious search and simply signaled a "denial of life, an abdication from the human race," a giving up, a "copping out." Many were critical of his refusal to try to exercise, and some heard him admit that he was his own worst enemy. And some suspected it was simply Jean's old game of playing a role, now the mysterious guru who had found he could be the center of attention just by lying there and doing nothing.[16]

15. Ralph interview; Welch interview; JT, "Psychologic Papers," March 21, 1937 (JTP 41:3).

16. Interviews of Marian Fuson, Nashville, Tenn., January 7, 1975; Sally Fell, Doylestown, Pa., January 23, 1975; Georges and Elizabeth Duval, Lumberville, Pa., July 22, 1982; Susan Sandberg, Doylestown, Pa., March 20, 1983; Nancy Geiger, New Hope, Pa., March 24, 1983.

He did not keep himself totally without communication; the decrease was gradual. Around 1956, Dr. Welch persuaded him to write an account of his first summer at Fontainebleau. This was assigned primarily as therapy, since Dr. Welch saw that recalling these memories and producing a written manuscript brought Jean temporarily back to life. He had worked sporadically on an account of his experience with the Gurdjieff movement ever since 1950, shortly after Gurdjieff's death, and he started in 1953 the account of that first summer at the institute. Polishing this piece for Dr. Welch was his last literary effort. Jean wrote only a few letters in 1957 and 1958. To a letter from Buckingham Meeting in January of 1957 regretting his illness (on the occasion of a short hospital stay), he composed a very fitting answer. He wrote a few notes, both serious and light, to old friends and to Arge when she was away, who as she grew up decided she wanted to be called Margot (perhaps emulating her father's name changes). He enjoyed watching the ball games and keeping track of the statistics. But he was more and more confined to his house and shut off from people he had known. John Bennett came again to New York from England about 1958, but Toomer did not see him then, though Fred Leighton was in contact with Bennett. Bennett was introducing Gurdjieff followers to a method of spiritual training called "Subud" that promised direct contact with a "Supreme Power that works for good . . . [a] spontaneous working of the Holy Spirit in the soul of man." It seems that Toomer at an earlier stage would have been eager to explore this potential route to his lifelong goal; but he made no such move in 1958, and when in 1960 or 1961 the opportunity was offered him directly, he declined.[17]

His withdrawal from life included a withdrawal from connection with Friends. From about 1955 on, he had scarcely been seen in Meeting, and at some point (certainly by the time he was not answering letters at all), he stopped paying his quarterly assessments. Probably for these reasons, though no one can remember his actually leaving the Society of Friends, the Yearly Meeting records show that in 1961 "he resigned or was released" from membership in Buckingham Meeting. But on this point the Monthly Meeting minutes for November 11, 1962, have a contradictory note. The Committee of Overseers had been considering lifting the assessment requirement for aged members and in this connection gave special attention to Jean Toomer: "They recommended that Jean Toomer be considered a full member of Buckingham

17. Welch interview; Ralph interview; John G. Bennett, *What is Subud?* (New York, 1959), 2, 3.

Monthly Meeting until his death and not be requested to contribute financially. Meeting approved the recommendation." Thus, though he had clearly
committed himself to the Gurdjieff work, he was less clear about leaving the
Society of Friends. In the face of his de facto withdrawal, his Meeting chose to
retain his membership.[18]

A final effort by the outside world to reach him was made in the years shortly
before 1964. Most of his literary acquaintances of the 1920s, particularly those
involved in the Harlem Renaissance, had lost track of him long since, in his
successive transformations through several lives. Some thought it better not to
know, presuming he had "passed" into the white world. But among those in
this group who still felt awe at the contribution Jean had made in *Cane* was
Arna Bontemps, compiler of many anthologies of black literature, author
in his own right, and at the time a librarian at Fisk University. The wife of a
physics professor at Fisk was Marian Darnell Fuson, who had earlier been
Young Friends executive secretary, closely associated with Jean and Marjorie
Toomer in the Philadelphia area. When a faculty member saw one of Jean
Toomer's Quaker pamphlets lying on the Fusons' coffee table he said, "Good
heavens! Jean Toomer! Why, he's disappeared!" Marian, however, said he was
very much alive and hardly in hiding. Word got to Arna Bontemps, and eventually he got Jean's address from Marian and wrote to him. When he got no
answer for some time, Marian suggested that he write to Marjorie, as Jean was
not answering letters. The contact was thus made around 1960.[19]

Bontemps was most interested in getting Toomer's papers for the Fisk University library. Jean, though barely communicating at this time with Marjorie
or anyone else, was not averse to having his papers go there, but he stipulated
that he would not sort or prepare anything. Fifteen cartons were shipped to
Fisk in December, 1962, and some more about a year later. These contained
practically everything that he had written or collected up through 1963,
though a friend who sometimes stayed with Jean was hired to do some sorting
and packing. Jean, usually lying inert on his bed, was pacing the floor as the
two women went through his private records of his life, disposed of a few clip-
pings or multiple copies, and packed the materials for shipment.[20] Marjorie
retained duplicates of a number of Jean's manuscripts, and the rest of the papers

18. Helen Brink (Philadelphia Yearly Meeting Membership Records) to Lewis Benson,
May 10, 1983, in Benson's possession, Moorestown, N.J.; Buckingham Monthly Meeting
minutes, November 11, 1962 (FHLS).
19. Fuson interview.
20. Geiger interview; MCT to the authors, August 4, 1983.

went to the Fisk collection, where there were already echoes of the charmed circle of the 1920s in the many Stieglitz photographs that Carl Van Vechten had persuaded Georgia O'Keeffe to give to Fisk after Stieglitz's death.

Before the papers were sent, William Hubben, who had edited the *Friends Intelligencer* and published many of Jean's articles, looked over Toomer's writings to see if he could put together some cogent collection, presumably on a spiritual or religious theme. He concluded that he could not. There is a secondhand report that when Jean was told this, he grunted, "Couldn't find anything—must not be very much there."[21]

Most observers were reluctant to try to distinguish the physical from the mental in Jean's progressive deterioration during his last eight to nine years when very little of his former self was available to the world. But his physical problems could not be denied, and Dr. Welch thought they were sufficient explanation of his condition. Jean had a long-drawn-out destructive kidney disease; after one was removed, the other was not functioning properly. His capacity for alcohol decreased as the kidney function worsened. And he had difficulties with his gallbladder and stomach, and of course other infirmities and frustrations of old age crept up on him as they do on everyone. In addition, the arthritis compressed his vertebrae and crippled him.[22]

Perhaps because Jean Toomer had wanted so much, had expected so much of himself, negative behavior became very strong as these positive possibilities began irrevocably to slip away. It was in a measure what he had foreseen when he had turned inward in the desperate effort to work on himself with every tool at his disposal, aware of his addictions and failings but still hoping for growth, still hoping to fulfill a destiny of outstanding service to mankind. Not only was he withdrawn, an uglier side appeared. Retreating and attacking became alternate, separate ways of acting, and an obsession with sex was often evident. All three issues, prominent in his self-exploration at the time of his psychoanalysis, now were turned to the outside, displayed in crude, raw form. In the battle between body and mind, which his analyst had recognized as acute in him, the body appeared to have conquered. In Gurdjieffian terms, the moving center, emotional center, and sex center had taken over anarchic, uncoordinated control in his personality, displacing the intellectual center or any higher organization. It was often alcohol that roused him from his regular supine state to activity, sometimes in profanity or scatological speech, sometimes in attempted sexual pursuit of the person who was taking care of him. Sometimes

21. Geiger interview; Ralph interview.
22. Welch interview.

he was playful, but at other times he was threatening. He would contrive ways to get more prescriptions and more liquor than Marjorie allowed him, even though she kept these things locked up and he could not stir out of the house. He would call a taxi driver to bring him some or persuade the kindhearted occupant of the downstairs apartment to do so. Marjorie, finding that she could not leave him alone, hired someone to stay with him when she had to be away. Sometimes the situation was out of control by the time she returned. The combination of whiskey and barbiturates knocked him out so completely that at times he would fall and not be able to get up again. At night, without her hearing aid, Marjorie could not hear him fall, and she could not lift him without help. Finally she was unable to cope with these problems, and about 1962 she and Susan found a nursing home for him. Because he was unhappy there and begged to come home, and had shown considerable improvement through forced detoxification, she took him back; but after a time a similar round began again. After another stay and return home, he was placed again in a nursing home about 1965, and he began to enjoy himself, joking with the nurses and calling up local stores to order expensive delicacies to be charged to Marjorie and delivered to him. But even then, he impressed one nurse as one of the kindest, nicest patients they had in the home.[23]

There, Jean Toomer died, complex and contradictory to the last, on March 30, 1967, at the age of seventy-two, of congestive heart failure, arteriosclerosis, pneumonia, and uremia.

23. Sandberg interview; Geiger interviews, March 21, 24, 1983.

VII.

SUMMING UP

17.

Issues and Institutions

Some lives are best measured not by accomplishments but by failed attempts, not by trends they set but by issues they helped to define. Jean Toomer's life touched so many central issues and so many personages in American culture that it is difficult to assess his importance other than by commenting on his role as an uncomfortable inhabitant of our times. His life helps to illuminate the lives of those whose existence is more muted, who ask questions but do not commit their lives to the answers. He lived in extremes and combined the seemingly contradictory: arrogance and self-doubt; absolute confidence in leading others to self-knowledge and a perpetual uncertainty of his own identity; desire for leadership and reliance on the largesse of others to keep him housed and fed and ascendant; a vision of himself as the paradigm of the universal man and a lifelong struggle to synthesize the fragmented parts of his unfulfilled self.

Jean Toomer is best known as a writer, though when one contrasts the amount of writing published to the amount unpublished, he could be judged as a comet that had one burst of glory before burning up. He is recognized, and criticized by many, as a person who tried to detach himself from racial labels. He is increasingly becoming known as a pioneer Gurdjieff teacher, though the Gurdjieff method still stands on the fringes of acceptability and the quality of his leadership has been questioned. Finally, he is remembered as a leader in the Society of Friends, though he became a Quaker rather late in his life and withdrew from participation a decade before he died. How, then, does one finally measure a man whose potential seemed to have little fulfillment other than searching for it? We must, to finish the story, compare his intentions with his achievements. And for those who believe that the quest itself is its own reward, or that the mark of the saint is in the struggle toward perfection, there may even be in Jean Toomer a model for success—particularly when the goal is a kind of Grail.

In this case, the quest had a literally superhuman goal: to transcend the human and enter another realm of being. In some form or fashion, this was what he sought all his life from adolescence onward, whether he measured it in self-awareness, a new level of consciousness, a feeling of being "inside" a creative process—or called it a new birth of participation in God's presence. Midway in his life he summed up his major efforts: "the vital issues of art, literature, psychology, cultural criticism, personal relations, religion, and consciousness," like a quiver of arrows, all pointed one way, the "straight and main direction of my life," the goal of which was transport beyond himself into something larger, more ideal, more unified, more directly connected with the heart of the universe.[1] Related to his need for integration of his conflicting selves, this goal in his successive incarnations forced him to confront a number of issues and institutions.

The question of race, though a reverberating issue for Toomer, was a detour from his point of view. He spent a lot of time expounding his theory of racial irrelevance in order to get on with more important things. At one point he said, "It is clear that the world is not going to let me whole-heartedly pursue other interests until I have given it some new facts and creative attitudes towards race." At another time he referred to race as "one of the hurdles I must jump. . . . I had need to clear up and cut away, among other constrictions, the, for me, false factors of Race." His intention here, in terms of institutional impact, was simply to expunge society's image of race as an important factor in classifying people. Classification, for Toomer, seemed to be the nemesis of mankind, a reflection of intellectual empty-headedness. In a statement written soon after the publication of *Cane,* Toomer satirized man's false need to classify things. In "The Fable of the Creature," some high-minded individuals with magnifying glasses and a dictionary are examining an insect:

> Suddenly one of us declares authoritatively: "I have it! It is a cockroach!"
> "So it is!" we all exclaim. "It is a cockroach!"
> At last we understand.
> We shake hands and look knowingly at the thing we understand.
> The tiny moving creature goes about its business, being what it is.[2]

1. JT notes (JTP 26:2).
2. JT notes, August-September, 1930 (JTP 17:1); JT, "Notes on Race" (JTP 26:2); JT, "The Fable of the Creature," July 11, 1930 (James Weldon Johnson Collection, The Beinecke Rare Book and Manuscript Library, Yale University, New Haven).

This campaign against classification certainly had a personal basis. Toomer felt a conflict between his image of himself and what he perceived as society's image of him. In 1930 he wrote, "My desire to be dominant . . . will not allow of my being colored." He saw the racial label as a smaller constricting box within the constrictions all humanity suffers in its earthly form. There were also psychological factors, which will be discussed more fully later. But his position had a larger frame of reference. He believed that everyone's physical, emotional, and mental development was narrowed by society's labeling: "I would liberate myself and ourselves from the entire machinery of verbal hypnotism. . . . I am simply of the human race. . . . I am of the human nation. . . . I am of Earth. . . . I am of sex, with male differentiations. . . . I eliminate the religions. I am religious." [3]

He was not seeking a shift in a category attached to his own name, such as from black to white; he wished to be neither white nor black. The vision of the universal man was the benchmark of his identity, and perhaps he accurately perceived himself as the embodiment of the greater American soul, a concept that Waldo Frank and others continued to encourage. Toomer's appearance, he noted, caused various people on separate occasions to think that he was of eleven different nationalities. As for biological forebears, he could not be sure but was probably somewhere between one-eighth and one-sixteenth black. And he had lived among blacks, among whites, among Jews, and in groups organized without racial labels around a shared interest such as literature or psychology, moving freely from any one of these groups to any other. One mark of membership in the "colored" group, he said, was acceptance of the "color line" with its attendant expectations; neither his family nor he had ever been so bound. To be in the white group would also imply the exclusion of the other.

> What then am I?
> I am at once no one of the races and I am all of them.
> I belong to no one of them and I belong to all.
> I am, in a strict racial sense, a member of a new race.

This new race of mixed people, now forming all over the world but especially in America, "may be the turning point for the return of mankind, now divided into hostile races, to one unified race, namely, to the human race." It was a new race, but also the oldest. The different racial and national groups could still contribute their distinctive richness: "I say to the colored group that, as a human being, I am one of them. . . . I say to the white group that, as a human

3. JT notebooks, 1929–30 (JTP 17:1); JT lecture, "What I Believe," *ca.* 1929 (JTP 28:7).

being, I am one of them. As a white man, I am not one of them. . . . I am an American. As such, I invite them [both], not as [colored or] white people, but *as Americans,* to participate in whatever creative work I may be able to do."[4]

Thus Toomer propounded the rather unpopular view that the racial issue in America would be resolved only when white America could accept the fact that its racial "purity" was a myth, that indeed its racial isolation produced blandness and lack of character. On the other hand, racial purity among blacks was just as much a myth and only encouraged defensiveness and unconscious imitation, like that of an adolescent who defines his revolt against his parents by the very values he is trying to renounce. Race, he said, was a fictional construct, of no use for understanding people: "Human blood is human blood. Human beings are human beings. . . . No racial or social factors can adequately account for the uniqueness of each—or for the individual differences which people display concurrently with basic commonality."[5]

The search for identity, for a unifying principle in himself, had led him past the partial identification of race, an external aspect, to an inward core that we all share. In *Cane* and particularly in the character Kabnis, identity was regional, connected with the earth by roots going into the soil; ten years later, Toomer had a new vision of attachment, not to the soil but to the air. No longer struggling to touch the earth or find his cultural forebears, he rejected tangible, physical identities in favor of the universal spirit. He made a similar observation about Alfred Stieglitz, describing him favorably as "rooted *in himself* and to the *spirit* of the place. . . . Not rooted to earth; rooted to air." Toomer aspired toward what he felt Stieglitz had already attained, "a never broken relatedness to a universal life."[6] This kind of attachment, of course, was congenial with the Gurdjieffian view of finding the way through self to the universal, which is greater than self.

The religious basis for this position became stronger after Toomer's 1926 experience, in which he had a vivid image of his life blending with the lives of all people of every kind and condition. This vision demonstrated that humanity was united through its connection with divinity, a principle that all the major world religions espouse but few in practice embody. It was therefore not just race but also nation and class as artificial barriers between people that Toomer was trying to cast down. He gave this antibarrier idea specific form in an article published in 1934, proposing a new religion. Noting that humans have

4. JT, "The Crock of Problems" (JTP 32:7), sec. 10, pp. 15, 16, 26, 17.
5. JT, "Incredible Journey" (JTP 15:3).
6. JT, "The Hill," in Frank *et al.* (eds.), *America and Alfred Stieglitz,* 297; JT to John Chambers, August 11, 1946, in JTP 1:9.

trouble getting along because they are focused outward and are competing for physical resources, he suggested focusing inward as the solution. In this new religion, man would be rooted to his own energy, the source of which is his shared humanity, rather than to an energy derived from a specific locale or people. In this "super-conscience that lives in essence" would be found "a world-religion, complete enough to include all people, true enough to strike deep root-energies, sufficiently empowered to unify each individual in himself."[7]

In the context of a religion in which the way to the divine is through the individual, it is not irrationally arrogant of Toomer to see himself as the embodiment of the universal man physically as well as mentally and spiritually. It is also not surprising that Toomer resorted to the aphoristic statement as encompassing truths about himself and the universe around him, or that he should name his book *Essentials*. Thus his "I" becomes Everyman: "I am of no special field. I am of the field of being."[8] His belief that he could not be located within traditional definitions and classifications was one to which he remained true for his entire life.

How are we to evaluate this position? Did it have an impact on the culture? Toomer did not expect his self-definition to be accepted easily. In his early life as a writer he had shown the difficulty of blending racial diversity into a positive self—indeed, his characters in *Cane* reinforce the archetype of the "tragic mulatto." In his writing in the late 1920s he recognized the pervasiveness of racial antagonism and aggression. In a long, well-reasoned article written in 1928 he describes the varieties of race problems and their becoming culturally set and calls for applying behavioral conditioning and "selective fusion on the basis of biological fitness" to achieve their solution. Cynically he recognizes that "liberal opinion and intelligent humanism affect the race question just about as much as they affect the practice of business and the politics of the Republican and Democratic parties."[9] Yet he envisions an increase in fluidity, a greater spiritualization of the culture, which, combined with natural mixing, will bring about the result he desires.

No one can say that this has happened. The progress in race relations has come largely through the passionate self-affirmation of blacks as a positive group—certainly a powerful, needed, and constructive step. In such a climate it is not surprising that Toomer's position against separateness and racial defini-

---

7. JT, "A New Force for Cooperation," 31.
8. JT, *Essentials*, 24.
9. JT, "Race Problems and Modern Society" (Typescript in MTC), 33, 29, also in Baker Brownell (ed.), *Problems of Civilization* (New York, 1929), 67–111.

tion was maligned both during his lifetime and later. One of the kindest things said about his racial stance by a black critic is Alice Walker's comment in her review of *The Wayward and the Seeking*: "'Cane' was for Toomer a double 'swan song.' He meant it to memorialize a culture he thought was dying, whose folk spirit he considered beautiful, but he was also saying goodbye to the 'Negro' he felt dying in himself. 'Cane' then is a parting gift, and no less precious because of that. I think Jean Toomer would want us to keep its beauty, but let him go." [10] The implication is that an individual has to be on one side of the line or the other. The prevailing American attitude still is that the line between black and white is inexorable and that if one is a little bit black, one is all black.

Yet Jean Toomer's perspective is so logical, as well as so congruent with teachings of all great religions, that it cannot be ignored. Indeed, there are others who have taken a similar position, in varying ways. Poet Robert Hayden was distressed that Arna Bontemps, a colleague of his at Fisk University, was putting together anthologies of "black poetry." Of mixed blood himself, Hayden did not want to be pushed to claim one part of his heritage and disclaim another. At the cost of forgoing recognition until he was past fifty, he refused to be classified as a *black* poet and insisted, if identification was necessary, on being called a *poet* whose cultural roots were partly in the black community. Ralph Ellison, affirming the southern black elements in his heritage, at the same time affirms his roots in Emerson and in all the history of the English-speaking world. James Baldwin calls on American whites to recognize that they are slaves to the image of blackness in themselves. James Alan McPherson, a winner of the Pulitzer Prize in fiction, has written, "In the gradual elaboration of basic rights, an outline of something much more complex than 'black' and 'white' had begun. . . . [In the new citizenship arising] each United States citizen [could] attempt to approximate the ideals of the nation, be on at least conversant terms with all its diversity, and carry the mainstream of the culture inside himself." [11] All support the concept of mixture, the fundamental quality of all Americans' participation in each other.

The failure is not in the concept, but just where Toomer placed it, in the bounded attitudes of individuals and the difficulty of overcoming cultural conditioning. As long as society does attach such value judgments to skin color, it is almost impossible for a lone individual to effect the obliteration of those

10. Alice Walker, "The Divided Life of Jean Toomer," *New York Times Book Review*, July 13, 1980, pp. 11, 16, also in her *In Search of Our Mothers' Gardens* (San Diego, 1983), 60–65.

11. Interview of Marian Fuson (a friend of Robert Hayden's), Nashville, Tenn., January 7, 1975; McPherson quoted in Marilyn Ferguson, *The Aquarian Conspiracy* (Los Angeles, 1980), 142.

judgments. The growing assumption that being black has a positive rather than a negative value rating is an important step, but should this be society's final position? Interviews of Toomer's friends often brought out the statement "And I didn't know he was black until several years later, but of course that didn't make any difference to me." Jean Toomer would have thought that this view, prevalent in the milieu in which he lived in Bucks County, simply continued the mistaken notions he had tried to correct. His failure to change these individuals only reflects America's failure to change its own attitude toward race. Toomer thus represents a touchstone in American culture. His was a valiant and sustained effort toward a sane position, which may find a sounder emotional basis when the race word *black* has positive associations for all of American society.

Along the route to his goal, this detour aside, Jean Toomer took on three institutions: the literary world, the Gurdjieff system, and the Society of Friends. How did each of these fit into his search, and what impact did he have on them?

Transcendence, involving as it does transition between modes of being, entails changing the ideal into the real and the real into the ideal. To understand literature from the inside is to participate in another level of consciousness; to bring this level back to earth is the writer's exacting, impossible task. Toomer endorsed this view of art as a religious experience and the writer as a prophet, whose words are God-given and therefore belong to a special order of things. He wrote to Sherwood Anderson that art "in our day, other than its purely aesthetic phase, has a sort of religious function. It is a religion, a spiritualization of the immediate." [12] Much of his correspondence with his literary friends contained discussions of the function of literature and art, which helped to shape the prevailing radical literary view that Waldo Frank, in particular, represented.

Toomer was also working out, in his early writings that eventually became *Cane,* the problem of self-identity. He was trying to meld the fragments of his heritage into an emblem of the universal man. Much of the greatness in *Cane* stems from this impassioned effort. If Toomer spent a lifetime searching for identity beyond the limits of a divided self, his book reflects that fragmentation and the attempt to bond the pieces into a meaningful whole. Many tensions—between blacks and whites, rural and urban people, blue blood and peasant, the idealized and the cynical—were as much a part of the fabric of Jean Toomer as they were of *Cane.* And, as in the book, the attempt to blend

12. JT to Sherwood Anderson, December 18, 1922, in JTP 1:1.

the opposites was never fully realized. Yet the measure of success—the ideal shining in startling flashes through ordinary words in extraordinary juxtaposition—was a harbinger of the book's impact, for *Cane* anticipated what would appear a generation or two later in the literary world.

Three kinds of influence can be observed from Toomer's published writings. One is his personal interchange with writers in his own circle. Second, still direct though unchosen, is the fanning out of his reputation and style in the Harlem Renaissance and its recent revival. Third, somewhat more amorphous, is a sort of echo in the more distant reaches of the American literary scene.

First, as part of the literary milieu of New York for a brief, spectacular time, Jean was not only a taker but a giver of the messianic fervor that Waldo Frank's circle of friends helped induce. Going back to one's "primitive" sources to find new value in art and culture was not unique to Frank, Munson, Crane, and Toomer, but their cross-fertilization kept the impetus alive. It is impossible to read Frank's *Holiday* without thinking of Toomer, or to read "Kabnis" without referring to Crane's poem "Black Tambourine." Even after Jean moved on to the Gurdjieff work, he did not renounce his literary friends, nor did he stop engaging others in discourses on culture, literature, religion, and art.

Second, and ironically, since Toomer himself discounted the Negro movement during the Harlem Renaissance, it was this movement that most clearly showed his literary influence. *Cane*'s exaltation of the "primitive," its lyrical penetration into the juice of the "dark purple ripened plums," the souls of the slaves and descendants of slaves; its sordidness and cruelty in human relationships; its yearning for something like love but more than love—all these are reflected in other writers of the renaissance period. Toomer's work itself was kept visible by those promoting the Harlem Renaissance or influenced by it. Although Toomer became indignant at the process, Alain Locke, both in his writings and in his discussions and lectures, helped remind the public of *Cane* throughout the late 1920s and 1930s. Younger writers such as Langston Hughes and Wallace Thurman maintained Toomer's visibility by their references, even when Hughes chided Toomer for abandoning Harlem for greener pastures and Thurman despaired at the general descent of the Harlem Renaissance into mediocrity. Thurman's book *Infants of the Spring* was based on his observation of writers and artists in a loosely knit bohemian group that had perhaps started when Toomer first attempted to establish a Gurdjieff group in Harlem. The protagonist states, "I don't expect to be a great writer. I don't think the Negro race can produce one now, any more than can America. I know of only one Negro who has the elements of greatness, and that's Jean Toomer." Others who came to New York to seek inspiration from black writers—Ann

Petry, for example, first arrived in New York in the mid-1930s and began her writing career there—fed on their admiration of Jean Toomer's works.[13]

As part of the larger group of writers, such as McKay and Hughes, who turned to more "primitive" sources for inspiration, Toomer also has had international recognition. Through the salons held by the Nardal sisters, René Maran, and others, artists from Africa and the West Indies had access to Americans such as Alain Locke, who continued to be among the foremost proponents of Afro-American culture. Léopold Senghor, Aimé Césaire, and Léon Damas, recognized as the founders of the Negritude movement, used Toomer and other writers as touchstones in their own efforts to elevate black national culture and art in their developing nations. Senghor, long a fighter for black nationalism and pan-Africanism and the president of Senegal for many years, recalls what it was in the poems of *Cane* that inspired him to translate many of them into French: "What are the characteristics of this poetry? It is essentially non-sophisticated like its African sister. It remains close to song. It is made to be sung or recited and not to be read—thus the importance of the rhythm—Negro rhythm, so tyrannical under its aspect of freedom—thus the importance of its music, so difficult to retain in translating Toomer." If one translates Senghor's poems into English, there are echoes of rhythm, image, and tone that recall Toomer:

> Ah! perhaps tomorrow the purple tune of your flute
>   will still forever.
> That is why my rhythm becomes so pressing and my
>   fingers bleed on the khalam.
>
> Perhaps tomorrow my friend I will fall—oh!—
>   on the unappeased earth
> Regretting your dropping eyes and the misty tomtom
>   the surrounding rounds of mortar.
> And you will regret in the half-light the
>   burning voice that sang of your black beauty.[14]

Jean Toomer as an important figure in American letters had a resurgence in the 1960s when the awareness of black history and culture intensified and his works were made available at Fisk University. Critics such as Robert Bone and Darwin Turner presented a measured and carefully researched view of Toomer and his literary influence that extended beyond the New Negro movement.

13. Wallace Thurman, *Infants of the Spring* (New York, 1932), 221; interview of Ann Petry, Old Saybrook, Conn., June, 1981.

14. Léopold Senghor, "Trois poètes nègro-américains," in *Poésie 45* (Paris, 1945), quoted in Lilyan Kesteloot, *Black Writers in French*, trans. Ellen Conroy Kennedy (Philadelphia, 1974), 73; Senghor's poem, from *Chants pour Naëtt* (Paris, 1949), translated by Richard Eldridge.

Thus the third element to be noted about Toomer's writings of the *Cane* period is a matter not necessarily of influence but of resemblances and echoes. He totally shifted the forms of southern regional writing. For all their insight into culture and character, writers such as Kate Chopin and Charles Chesnutt never captured the complexity and fluid interplay of soul and soil that exist in Toomer's pages. He was one of the first to bring to fruition in his creation the tangled contradictions of the southern heritage. Jean Toomer was of a southern aristocracy, from a proud and famous family, with manners and wealth and servants. He had his myth and his downfall in his grandfather's lost position, his mother's two disastrous marriages, and the poverty and deterioration that marked his grandparents' later years. And he bore the brand of the interracial love-hate that is the South's special tragedy. He anticipated Faulkner, Carson McCullers, and Flannery O'Connor in the intricacy of his characters' confused desires, the symbolic warping of the body in a situation that warps the soul, the clarity of vision that refuses to take sides, that pities and penetrates and illuminates.

In terms of vehicle and style, Toomer was far ahead of his contemporaries. The subtle movement of *Cane,* from realism to surrealism, from country to city to the city man in the country, from character to caricature, serves at its best to make "things unseen to men . . . tangibly immediate," as his ancestors' soil does for the poet-observer in "Fern." Toomer was building a new form, as Robert Bone has suggested, with Stein's wordplay, Pound's images, and Eliot's mythic reverberations—translating the personal, racial, and human experience into symbolic event or encounter. Followed later by Ralph Ellison and John Cheever, Toomer made events melt into a surrealistic dream with symbolic significance. Like Donald Barthelme and Richard Brautigan, he placed non sequiturs in matter-of-fact prose, gave to logical impossibilities a colorful life. In all these ways he stood alone in his time, and he was a beacon to the future. He wrote of himself in 1930, and could have written in 1923, "I am not a romanticist, I am not a realist—in the ordinary sense: I am an essentialist, a spiritualizer. . . . I am a poetic realist. This means two things. I lift facts, things, happenings to the planes of rhythm, feeling, and significance. I clothe and give body to potentialities." [15]

Toomer's art was not always controlled, particularly as he later came to let the symbolic outweigh its embodiment. Even his efforts during the period of his total immersion in literature were not fully satisfying, but they were powerful.

15. JT, "Earth-Being" (MTC), 18. Some of the description of *Cane* in the preceding paragraphs is adapted from Cynthia E. Kerman, "Jean Toomer?—Enigma," *Indian Journal of American Studies,* VII (1977), 67–78.

At the end of his initial writing stage, Toomer's vision, like Kabnis', remained unfulfilled—his search was incomplete but his journey was over. Art for Toomer was an attempt at absolution, transcendence, salvation, whereby he could solve the problem of his identity through words, working out a verbal equation. Writing was therefore for him a torturous creation; when words could not fill the void, they riddled him with feelings of inadequacy.

At a time in 1929–1930 when he was reflecting on his past and present, Toomer stated that he was primarily a lover, second an understander, and third "a person concerned with incorporating my ideas and ideals in living." With his characteristic intensity, the understander and translator of life into words, dissatisfied with his art, turned to the translation of psychological potentialities into life. It was the second main stage of his journey. His move from the New York literary life to the international Gurdjieff life was a change only in method, not in goal. Literature for Toomer was a way to organize one's ego to keep it from the brink of chaos, and to create a form that would convey to the reader this experience of chaos trembling into order. It would then lift him to an elevated state by its aesthetic perfection. The Gurdjieff system, in turn, appeared to be a supreme method of organizing the self. One works with what is there, gets rid of disabling habits, balances and blends the parts, then moves to a new level of consciousness that should take over harmonious direction of the organism and may gradually come into communication with a higher level of being. Each step upward in a vast unending interconnected cosmos provides more potential for effective functioning, knowledge, and power. To understand and teach such a system, to practice and help others practice it, seemed to offer the chance to create new potentialities in the shape of human beings. The goal of merging the real and the ideal was thus also incorporated in the Gurdjieff work. Toomer did not give up the process of creativity, but he changed its object. "Once a man has tasted creative action," he writes, "then thereafter, no matter how safely he schools himself in patience, he is restive, acutely dissatisfied with anything else. He becomes as a lover to whom abstinence is intolerable." Jean continued to participate in the creative process by making himself and the selves of others the art form. In this way, he could bear directly on those who came in contact with him and could create a dialogue that no literature once written can effect, or so he felt.[16]

Toomer wanted to be in the inner circle of Gurdjieff's coterie, privy to secrets and capable of passing them on to disciples in the lower echelons. How did he in fact stand in relation to such a complex system? He was not a remark-

16. Quotations from JT, "Earth-Being," 15–16; JT, "From Exile into Being, or The Second River" (JTP 37:8).

able intellectual, though he studied deeply whatever interested him. He was intense and concentrated, as Gorham Munson has noted, but he lacked a broad background that could have given him a sophisticated basis for comparison and judgment. He had no systematic knowledge of philosophy, psychology, literary criticism, art, or music, but he was thoughtful and often asked deep questions. He was not afraid of any subject, but he was often unwilling to pursue it systematically. "Jean had a good mind," reports Munson. "Perhaps it was a little slow, . . . but he had a good mind; he used it hard. . . . He was a very interesting talker on intellectual topics, but [at] the same time, . . . he wasn't particularly incisive or penetrating, not at all brilliant." [17]

Toomer himself noted late in his life that he used to think that learning a method or theory was pointless; he wanted to move immediately to results. Therefore he never really learned to play the piano or knew what was happening in the physics and chemistry lab; he never became a musician or a scientist because he skipped the fundamentals. Even in writing itself, he misused several verbs and pronouns through the years, produced many inept fragments, and frequently misspelled random words. An insight during his analysis in 1949 focuses an emotional spotlight on this question. It is an abbreviated note relating to his "hatred of the cold white mind, efficient, arrogant . . . calculating in its manipulations." This mind could occur in either whites or blacks, he notes. "I [am] not able to compete with that mind. My qualities [are] superior to it in a human sense, but it is dominant in the world. . . . It has hurt me. I hate it." [18]

Jean therefore had no pretensions to intellectual interpretation or abstract analysis of the Gurdjieffian or any other philosophical system. He painstakingly made notes when he was with Orage, and followed these closely when he began leading groups himself. Later, when he tried to write out his own adaptation of the system, much of the material on the process was the same, but theoretical refinements and abstruse details, such as the theory of the octave and the meaning of the enneagram, were eliminated. Toomer was never successful at transmitting much in writing in the way of psychological theory. Although Gurdjieff and Orage insisted that pupils should not believe any statement until they tested it for themselves, phrases passed down from these leaders tended to become laws. By the time segments of Gurdjieff's system, whether or not identified with the master's name, were described in Toomer's

17. Interview of GM by India Watterson, New York, June 28, 1969 (Amistad Research Center, New Orleans), 6–7.
18. JT notes for article in 1940s (JTP 53:22); JT note, December 6, 1949 (JTP 54:8).

words, they included little to compel belief except the confident authority with which they were stated.

The evaluation of Jean Toomer as a Gurdjieff leader is somewhat equivocal. James Webb, in his monumental but in no sense official book on Gurdjieff's work, has called him "the most senior 'pupil-teacher' of Gurdjieff's ideas in the United States" after Orage's departure. However, Gurdjieff followers agree that Orage was so outstanding, no one can really be compared with him, and, in any case, Toomer was doing no organized teaching after Orage left in the fall of 1931. Michel de Salzmann, son of the woman who headed the work after Gurdjieff's death, later became one of the directors of the world network. He lists Toomer among a very few writers in whose work "today the tree [of Gurdjieff's teaching] has borne fruit": "For us, the only true creativity is influential and gives testimony to the life of a teaching. We find much more alive [than anecdotal or historical accounts of Gurdjieff] . . . the works of those who, because they were especially linked to writing, tried to pass on what they understood in a form that was original and appropriate to them. Let us name here A. R. Orage, Jean Toomer, P. L. Travers, and René Daumal, among others [including] Maurice Nicoll." It is true that Toomer's book *Essentials* was highly valued by many people, most of whom already knew Jean personally. Louise Welch remarks that in it, "I thought he touched something both genuine, and genuine to the Work." His Mill House pamphlets, Gurdjieffian in inspiration though not in name, were launched with considerable hope, but their trajectory was very short. Little else he wrote that was derived from Gurdjieff's ideas was considered worthwhile even by Gurdjieff followers.[19]

Toomer's main contribution to the Gurdjieff movement was not made through his writing. His strength was rather in the application, in the individual approach within the group, and in the designing of experiences that put people in new situations and made them test new behaviors. It was also in his personal charisma. "He was beautifully at ease as he spoke," Arna Bontemps wrote after his brief experience of Jean's Gurdjieff leadership, "calmly fluent, uncommonly serious for one who seemed to have so much going for him, and soon he had all of us eating out of his hand, as the expression used to be." Another observer, after a first session with Toomer, wrote of his awe and bewilderment: "Bewildered is an ungracious term but the prophets who heard

19. James Webb, *The Harmonious Circle: The Lives and Works of G. I. Gurdjieff, P. D. Ouspensky and Their Followers* (New York, 1980), 413; Michel de Salzmann, "Footnote to the Gurdjieff Literature," *Parabola*, V (August, 1980), 98; interview of Louise Welch, New York, June 25, 1982.

the voice of Jehovah (or whatever the Psychiatrist would say they did hear) were also so. I am not suggesting that you are J. . . . But I have never found so much illumination—or even been allowed to come so close to the light and even warm my hands at the flame—in so swift a space before." His followers were totally dedicated to his leadership, and Jean had here an immediate and lasting personal influence. For all his self-doubts, he did project himself as one who knew the inner world with an absolute certainty: "He saw the connection, he put it all together. More than anyone I have ever known Jean knew what and where Man was, what he could become. As Jean moved we were ready to move. He opened doors we were ready to walk through, he rang bells we were ready to harmonize with." [20] The impression of having knowledge beyond the normal level was no doubt reinforced by his mystical experience in 1926. Although he did not directly use this in his teaching prior to the late 1930s, for him it formed an incontrovertible fact that would have been fundamental in any consideration of the potentialities of human consciousness.

Jean Toomer's impact on the Gurdjieff movement, therefore, was real. It was not as inflated as he had fantasized on the train to Chicago in 1926—"Toomer the Chicagoan" did not take his place in history. But he extended the movement geographically beyond the New York intelligentsia and incorporated a group of people who would not otherwise have been involved, some of whom were changed, they believed for the better, for the rest of their lives. His energy, attractiveness, inventiveness, and authority could gather up scattered people looking for self-improvement or more meaning in their lives and sweep them into a group that promised—and sometimes delivered—just that result. Toomer was not a primary or a fully submissive channel, he never belonged to the innermost circle, and his personal quality did not approach Orage's. But in the exploratory years, when the form of the teaching was being worked out on both sides of the Atlantic, he was chosen, and served well, as an expander and transmitter of the work. Although he was cut off from developments and quite outside the movement from 1934 to 1952, he was welcomed back when he was ready to return.

As the Gurdjieff practices seemed to lose their energy for him at the end of the 1930s and he swung from a psychological to a religious emphasis, he again combined an approach through writing with a personal ministry, and he allied himself with another institution—one that had a clearer form and more accessible history than the Gurdjieff movement did. In terms of his progression

20. Arna Bontemps, "Remembering *Cane*," *Banc!*, II (May, 1972), 10; Stephen [?] to JT, October 30, 1932, in JTP 8:15; Franklin Davenport, "Mill House," *Banc!*, II (May, 1972), 6.

toward his goal, Quakerism was another method for finding wholeness, now identified even more with the concept of transcendence. Again, too, there were two sides to his goal: spiritual growth for himself and a hope of transforming others. He wanted to renew and energize the Quakers, to call them back to what he felt was the early Quaker experience of the divine presence. So he took as a method and tried to learn in practice, refine, and communicate to others the process of the meeting for worship, which he recognized as the heart of what Friends were about, and he had considerable success. He cared little for exploring theological niceties, but he was most interested in how people used their opportunities to learn and grow. In turn, Friends regard Toomer not primarily as one who expounded new doctrine but as one who stimulated spiritual experience.

His approach and theory differed in some ways from those of most Friends, but the differences were largely invisible in Toomer's work as a Quaker leader. They did not serve to shift the preponderance of opinion in his direction; perhaps instead they lent a certain energy to his formulations, a novelty and force. He was a well-accepted minister, in the Quaker sense of one who seems to be in touch with heights and depths of wisdom. He spoke often by invitation and could usually be expected to have something to say in almost any gathering. He added to the useful body of Quaker writing, showing good judgment in what he sent out for publication. These writings were not aimed at developing a theology but pointed rather toward changing people's behavior. They display his gift for the startling or memorable image, often grounded in his own mystical experience. Both here and in his speaking, this experience, though not described in detail, was always there to indicate the possibility, the reality, the taste of the new birth to which he was calling his audience. He is remembered for making vivid the potential levels of being, showing how to draw on the "springs of wisdom whose sources lie beyond the restrictions of this three dimensional world." In his own words, he was "pointing to the next higher terrace of our ascent to God," explaining the need for "re-connecting the outer man with the inner man who *now is* connected with the divine principle and in whom *now* resides functions such as universal love and universal conscience."[21] In addition to his words, the power of his personal magnetism, his "spiritual, fey quality," suggested an otherworldliness that intrigued his hearers and drew them often to their own search.

21. George E. Otto, "Religious Society of Friends," *Banc!*, II (May, 1972), 8; interview of Ruth Miller, New Britain, Pa., January 23, 1975; JT to John Chambers, January 31, 1947, in JTP 1:9; JT to Howard and Anna Brinton, February 7, 1939, in JTP 3:8.

This quality had a genuine basis in his own constant effort to touch the life of God. Toomer must have been one of those whom Douglas Steere had in mind when he wrote, "Many among us have heard the 'words that are not heard with ears,' and others have known inwardly the transforming power of the ever renewing revelation of God, and have been drawn by it to recast their lives." Jean recognized, and taught, that there is a more frequently accessible kind of "liberation from the prison of our ordinary selves" than the sudden illumination.

Sometimes I have a sense of a sacred current, an undercurrent perhaps, a love and beauty that break in upon us unexpectedly, rising to the surface and then all too swiftly disappearing into the mysterious depths. Sometimes I am dimly aware of a pulsing Life that presses in upon our lives and tugs at us as if to draw us out of our small selves into its vast reaches. And sometimes I have the recognition that my creativity (creative force) is but a tiny expression of the unimaginable creativity that sweeps through the whole world. At those times my life and its purpose seem part of a mighty life and purpose.

If I try to put my meaning of God in intellectual terms, I might express it this way. God is the vast living Reality of which we, in our real natures, are parts. The fact that we are tiny parts, mere pin-point particles, is less important than the fact that we are parts. Religion and art are to me the ways and means by which we grow and awaken to a realization of what we are essentially, and our inherent relation to all the rest of the creative order.[22]

Jean's participation in this current, when it occurred, made those about him aware of their potential for an everyday kind of mysticism—if not a greater one.

Impact he certainly had on the Society of Friends, but not enough to suit his yearning. He had failed to transform and renew their spiritual life, and on a personal level he had neither transformed nor renewed his own. He sensed no large acceptance of the mysticism he felt was an inherent part of Quakerism. Eventually, whether by enforced inactivity or choice, he was thought to have withdrawn from membership by 1961, but he had ceased to be a participating member years before that. One former Young Friend, looking back, wondered if Toomer became discouraged because he saw so little real change in people after working with them for years. Another acquaintance felt that he withdrew because some people put his race above his contributions in evaluating him. In 1946 Jean wrote, "I know how it feels to have a message and to find that one's own religious group is, by and large, indifferent." Later he made a note to himself: "Did I expect too much of Gurdjieff and the G. work, the Society of

22. Report of the Religious Life Committee to Philadelphia Yearly Meeting, quoted in *Friends Intelligencer,* CVI (1949), 681–82; JT, untitled notes (MTC); JT "The Way Out," in possession of Margery Toomer Latimer, Pineville, Pa.

Friends, psychoanalysis, and, still earlier, writing and the literary world? Perhaps. Certain it is that I was disappointed in all of them, to some extent." [23]

What was, in the end, the broader influence of Toomer's transforming experience in 1926? He saw it as an innately valid religious experience, proving truths that fitted both with the Gurdjieff system and with Quaker beliefs. To outsiders this was not so clear, and close friends of his among Gurdjieff followers differ in its assessment. One saw Jean's experience as "a moment of what Gurdjieff means by self-remembering"; another was embarrassed that someone so knowledgeable in the work would take the event so seriously and so without humility, believing he had really attained being-consciousness. Orage and Ouspensky both indicated that being-consciousness could be achieved only for brief moments until one had reached a high level of control through long practice. Among Quakers, Jean expected interest in the detailed account but perhaps opposition: "The central attitude of my book is so contrary to the prevailing ones that I am sure it will not be readily appreciated by very many. . . . Since it is out of the familiar frames, I do not expect it ever to be generally accepted." [24] The manner of his observing and sensing, as well as his assumption of the foreignness of the everyday world, did not fit the expectations of Friends. Although they speak of "centering down" or a "covered Meeting"—meaning a direct contact with God—they do not picture when they "wait on the Lord" anything so specific, intense, and lasting as Jean's experience.

Can such an experience carry credence for anyone beyond the person to whom it directly comes? William James asked this question in 1902, and it is likely that no better answer has been given since. He said that a mystical state may well be absolutely authoritative for the person who experiences it, but it carries and need carry no automatic authority for anyone else. However, the many testimonies to such states require the untouched to concede the possibility of "other orders of truth" beyond the rationalistic consciousness. In addition, the repetition of certain patterns across many experiences suggests a pantheistic and optimistic universe where power resides in something other than the naturalistic, material realm. [25]

Perhaps for the reason James mentions, as well as the elements of "misfit" that Toomer himself recognized, Jean was unable to get his account published and it was never known in detail among Quakers. The power of his own experi-

---

23. JT to Rowland Morgan, March 13, 1946, in JTP 7:11; N of E, July 19, [1950] (JTP 54:7).

24. JT to Chambers, October 7, 1946, January 31, 1947, both in JTP 1:9.

25. James, *Varieties of Religious Experience,* 405–20.

ence could not convince other people of the ethical theories and moral behavior he believed it indicated. His "conversion experience" could not be transferred to others through the medium of the printed word.

Jean Toomer's effects on various American institutions appear, in sum, to be noticeable, but all fall short of what he hoped. His impact on individuals—much more important to him than institutions—and his primary effort to build himself have yet to be examined. Yet besides his very real legacy to the literary world, the Gurdjieff movement, and the Society of Friends, and despite divided opinions about his stand on race, he performed a service in bringing society up short against some major questions. How can the human community retain the strength of ethnic contributions without being destructively separated by the differences? Which is more important, aesthetic beauty or the human experience it conveys? How can new forms be found to contain and communicate chaotic emotions and social forces—in words? in changing people? in changing social systems? What are viable logical and emotional sources of moral actions? What is the greatest possible goal for humankind?

The questions will endure longer than any one individual's answers. But Jean Toomer's answers, in some strange ways, seem to have anticipated developments in each of his fields by a generation or more. In his writing in the early 1920s he foreshadowed the mythic reverberations and the casting aside of traditional realistic constraints and language taboos that became more generally evident in the literature of the 1950s and 1960s. In his groups in the late 1920s and early 1930s he anticipated the work of experimenters in group dynamics and of many humanistic psychologists of the 1960s and 1970s. In his fumbling but persistent efforts to reach different levels of consciousness, potential capacities, to connect mind and brain, the personal and the cosmic, to match the inner development of the human spirit to the outer in a struggle to save the world, he anticipated a movement of the 1980s. This movement draws together basic research in the mind-brain relationship, right and left hemispheres, biofeedback, the new physics of consciousness, the holographic model of reality, and the many new techniques for personal transformation that combine physical, mental, and spiritual components.[26] The role of the artist-prophet, who sees through and beyond society, may have been better filled by Jean Toomer than he could have guessed.

26. A description of this movement is given in Ferguson, *The Aquarian Conspiracy*.

18.

Person to Person

At some point in his life Jean Toomer set down two columns entitled "Women I Have Known" and "Men I Have Known." He listed, beginning with his grandmother and grandfather, ten women and fourteen men: Nina Emily Pinchback, Phyllis Terrell, Margaret Naumburg, Edith Taylor, Mabel Luhan, Yvonne Dupee, Bertha Ochsner (who became the wife of Douglas Campbell), Eugenia Walcott, Alma Wertheim, and Clare McLure; P. B. S. Pinchback, Henry S. Kennedy, M. L. Ehrlich, Waldo Frank, Gorham B. Munson, A. R. Orage, G. I. Gurdjieff, Hart Crane, Melville Cane, Paul Rosenfeld, Alfred Stieglitz, Fred Leighton, Douglas Campbell, and Charles Dupee. The list is undated, but the omission of certain significant names, such as the two women he married, suggests that it may have been made in 1928 or 1929. His highlighting these individuals and the range of relationships represented by this list illustrate both the importance of people to him and the different ways in which he related to them. In an undated note he once declared that people had always been the center of his life—"not God, not art, not literature, not money."[1] These people influenced and shaped him, and he in turn had a memorable impact on the lives he touched. As he was many selves in succession, he impressed others in many different ways: artistically, philosophically, sexually, psychologically, religiously. In all his self-described functions, as a lover, an understander, and a translator of potentiality into actuality, he was dealing with people. In those dealings, there was power.

Being a lover was a very congenial role for Jean. At least four of the women on his list, and others not on it, spent a season or more as his sexual partner.

---

1. JT notes (JTP 13:2, 15:13).

Because of his "exaggerated sense of privacy" he deliberately excluded "love stories," except for oblique references, from his autobiographies. Letters in his files and reports from interviews, however, fill in some details of these experiences. In general he was not shy about endorsing love's power and attraction for him: He called himself a lover primarily, and only secondarily listed his other qualities, saying, "In so far as I have been moved by inner impulse, my turns, returns, leaps and crossings have followed love. And as with them, so my sufferings and joys have sprung from love's defeats and fulfillments." Loving, too, was a way of transcending, thus fitting into his overall search. He was carried away by love before he got caught up in literature; love helped break up his first college year; and it gave him his greatest sense of experiencing another world prior to the mystical event in 1926. Speaking of this love, he wrote, "There was transport, there was rapture, once or twice there was revelation . . . But it came to an end. I want it to last, never ending. I want to rise there and remain there. I have no taste for anything else. I want to *be* there."[2]

He was what any age would call a good lover. He knew how to use his natural charm and sustain his attraction with both the obscure and the famous. This is not to say that he was an indiscriminate womanizer. He mostly kept to a sequential monogamy based on sincere regard, and when he strayed from this, he took himself to task. "It has always been with me," he wrote, "that the love of one person tends automatically and organically to exclude love for others. In fine, though I may love many, one after another, I am usually faithful to the one at the time."[3] Toomer had a way of looking and reacting, often described in letters to him, that showed exceptional empathy and understanding. Gorham Munson commented that any woman Jean loved was a fortunate woman. Jean encouraged intimacy and strong feeling, which quite naturally overflowed into uninhibited actions that combined physical, intellectual, and emotional trust.

Some who responded with this kind of love mentioned it when they wrote him. One said in the spring of 1928: "Oh Jean, Jean how I love this earth—the mountains, the sky, the sea. I wish I could love man the same way but I can't—only you. Sometimes it is enough to know you as I have. When I think of you everything is so beautiful, so simple, so right." The first time Margery Latimer was close to him, she felt melted down and turned into a young shoot of corn warmed by Jean's sun. Another admirer who renewed an intimacy with Jean after Margery's death wrote him with regret after it ended: "Even that nite last winter when I went with you to your room—I felt any woman would have

2. JT, "Book X"; JT, "Earth-Being" (MTC), 15; JT, "Incredible Journey" (JTP 15 : 1).
3. JT, "Outline of an Autobiography" (JTP 14 : 1).

done. There was one moment of understanding. God, Jean, what a pity! Only one man knows the feeling capacity which is mine because he had the terrible genius of bringing it forth in me."[4] Margaret Naumburg, Mabel Luhan, Georgia O'Keeffe, and Marjorie Content all, in turn, wrote to him how they were captured, held, and fulfilled in this closest of relationships with him.

Toomer's attraction, however, was strong even without direct sexual engagement. People depended on him for consultation, intimate advice, affection, and understanding. In his early days as a Gurdjieff leader he was adored, for instance, by Elise Bunnell, a young widow who became a participant in the Portage experiment. Cabling money to Jean at Fontainebleau in 1929, she added, "But there you are so wise and kind and all seeing—You always do make everything seem right—which is one reason why I miss you." Three years later, during Margery Latimer's pregnancy, Elise Bunnell could write, "You still seem my best friend and the only sane person in a world of rather mad people." Eugenia Walcott commented, "There's so many unexpected facets to you, Jean, which I suppose are a part of what makes you irresistibly charming." Yvonne Dupee enjoyed his company, meeting him regularly for lunch or dinner several times a week until Margery Latimer's sudden prominence in Jean's life in 1931. Much later in his life, too, Toomer was sought out for warmth and comfort. A member of Buckingham Meeting, in her thirties at the time and needing emotional support her family could not give, went to him at his house after her favorite aunt died. "And he . . . was tall and absolutely loomed in the doorway, to me, and I was down on the bottom step, and I can still see him. . . . He didn't say anything. He just stood there. He could see I was distressed, I was in tears, and he just held on to me like this and . . . kept hugging me and patting me on the shoulders, until I could eventually get out what the problem was." She concludes, "It was the only place I really wanted to turn, at a time like that."[5]

Yet implicit in Jean's way of loving women was his philosophy of the ideal man-woman relationship. He rejected the notion that intelligence or superiority is concentrated in either sex, but he retained far more of a "type" image about gender than was consistent with his abandoning all arbitrary categories in his affirmation of the universal man. A most thrilling element for him in the first Gurdjieff demonstration he saw was the dance called "The Initiation of

4. [?] to JT, March 14, 1928, in JTP 7:3; [?] to JT, August 18, 1933, in JTP 4:9.
5. Elise Bunnell to JT, August 20, 1929, summer, 1932, both in JTP 1:7; Eugenia Walcott to JT, summer, 1929, in JTP 10:1; interview of Elizabeth Duval, Lumberville, Pa., July 22, 1982.

a Priestess," which clearly enunciated the male and female roles, the men dynamic and thrusting, the women lyric, "purified by devotion and aspiring," according to his description. He continued to claim that men and women each have a "basic nature" appropriate to their sex, and he blamed "mal-conditioning" for the kind of protest he saw arising in feminist women—including Margery Latimer, before he took her in hand. "Instead of being a hunter of women," he wrote, "the married man should be a hunter of understanding. No woman should be a huntress at any time of her life." Woman must clearly be feminine and subordinate, man actually the "lord and master," as he stated in a letter to Marjorie Content a few weeks before their marriage: "Above all, you must keep your womanness. . . . Woman must give herself to man—if he can take her. Then she may give herself to the world all she can. . . . Only by man's functioning in relation to her can she function." Earlier he had written, "From a woman I demand rightness of response, meaning, that I look to see if her responses to things, people, events, buildings, books, correspond to mine."[6] He took this line strongly when he advised male friends who were having trouble in affairs of the heart: all would be lost if they were not completely firm about who was in charge. Yet he was never a rough "macho" type—Lin Davenport described him as a "gentle man with force." And in some situations, when faced with illness or emergency, for instance, he was quite at a loss and Marjorie much the more competent. His attitude toward the sexes may have grown partly from his interpretation of Gurdjieff's teaching, partly from the patriarchal conditioning in his grandfather's house, and partly in compensation for some of his own tendencies to withdraw from potential conflict or rejection and his resulting fear of being submerged and subordinated.

These attitudes naturally had their effects on his marriages. For the brief span of the first one, it seems that Margery Latimer acceded fully to Jean's being Pygmalion. She was willing to have him shape her attitudes toward her body and her being, and even allowed him to direct her in the area where she probably had better judgment than he—her writing. She looked on him as somebody who "straightens everything out for people" and who could do "miraculous things." She accepted his requirement that she write about positive rather than negative experiences. When he promised to provide the conditions she needed to finish her book before her baby was born, she believed he would.[7]

6. JT Autobiography (JTP 16:9); JT, "Portage Potential" (MTC); JT, "Functions of Man to Woman" (JTP 23:38); JT to MC, June 20, 1934, in JTP 9:4; JT notes, 1930 (JTP 17:1).

7. MLT to Laurie B. Latimer, January 13, 1932, MLT to Jessie Overholt, January, 1932, MLT to Ruth Ware, January 8, 1932, all in JTP 6:1.

Marjorie Content also slipped into a fully subordinate role, captured by Jean's magic and believing implicitly in his power and wisdom. However, when cracks appeared in this magic image, her strong individuality began to assert itself and there came to be areas of competition and strain. It is interesting, for instance, that observers who were primarily Jean's friends have remarked that his teaching in the Doylestown period was inhibited by the presence of so many of Marjorie's old friends, while from her perspective the overwhelming crowds she had to care for were *his* friends and disciples. Although the two were congenial and enjoyed each other, their temperaments were very different. Marjorie was more outgoing, outspoken, and social-action oriented, and Jean more inward-turning, philosophical, and in need of periods of aloneness. This made them complementary but also caused friction in their life together, particularly as she became less certain that Jean had the key to the One Right Way. The most difficult question she had to deal with as time went on was whether she was valued for herself or was being used.

This question persisted in its crudest form because of their somewhat unusual arrangement that the wife provided all the income throughout the marriage. In this case, it did not seem to be a problem in the early years. Marjorie, fully dedicating herself and all she had, made Jean a partner in financial decision-making and in every way head of the household. In later years, however, as other irritations grew, this one loomed larger until it weighed on him fairly heavily—toward the end of his productive years, he had to admit that nothing he produced had brought in any money. She certainly was glad to be able to free him to write; but as years went on without confirmation of his work from major publishers, she may have felt at some level that he was taking advantage of her. And he must have felt a dependence unwelcome to one who believed in the man's strong leading role.

Important as women were in Toomer's life, his list has more men on it than women. The list of men also contains more people he clearly regarded as models—Pinchback, Frank, Orage, Gurdjieff, and Stieglitz. Some of these, too, provided the warm, strong, male friendship that seems to have been a vital ingredient in all of Jean Toomer's lives. From his childhood and youth he had valued male friends, including Dutch and Kennedy. Out of his literary period grew the involvement that bordered on spiritual brotherhood with artists such as Waldo Frank, Hart Crane, and Gorham Munson. From his Gurdjieff work came the attachment to Douglas Campbell and his lifelong friendship with Fred Leighton, with whom he shared roars of laughter over matters only they could understand, whenever they got together. In his Quaker period arose a warm fondness between him and Douglas Steere. There were others, such as

Jeremy Lane and Lin Davenport, who were younger and stood to him somewhat in the relationship of disciples.

Friendship sometimes took the form of mutual financial aid, apart from the support given Toomer because of his teaching. In Jean's youth, he and his friend Kennedy had an informal understanding that each could call on the other for money almost as needed, and Kennedy reminded him of this even after Jean had moved on to his next life: "Jean, old cockroach— . . . Say bo! You know it is no use of you needing anything and going without, when your old pal is in funds. . . . You know old pal that what's mine is yours, so don't hesitate."[8] Jean felt free, too, in the later 1920s to ask Paul Rosenfeld for money.

Toomer continued to lean on others in this way, particularly in the years from 1931 to 1934 after he stopped teaching in Chicago, during his first marriage and shortly after. Margery Latimer had only modest resources, and publishers were not taking the writing by which Jean hoped to earn a living. So, though he was no longer making a direct contribution to their lives, he was dependent on gifts and loans from acquaintances and followers from his days as a Gurdjieff teacher. At about the same time, however, he was coldly unhelpful to his last surviving family. Uncle Walter, administering Jean's grandmother's small estate, found that he could not keep up the mortgage and tax payments on the house she had owned, which was now partly Jean's. First he asked Jean for help with these payments and got the reply that Jean had no money. Meanwhile, Walter had lost his job and borrowed all he could, but he wrote Jean in January, 1931, that his own home "is your permanent home as long as I live. . . . Now don't stand on any ceremonies—come home if things are tough for you or if you want to rest." Jean failed to answer a series of increasingly desperate letters, until Walter decided to sell the grandmother's house and could not even locate Jean to secure his approval. Walter was still out of work when the house was finally sold and the proceeds calculated. On getting this news in February, 1932, Jean telegraphed immediately, asking Walter to send him the check for his share.[9]

When Marjorie Content married Jean, she discovered that because of his extensive one-way exchanges, he owed a great deal of money to a great many people, which she paid. After this time he was generous to his good friends, though he did not respond to every appeal, turning down in particular those coming from or on behalf of Gurdjieff. But he loaned some money to the Mun-

8. Henry Kennedy to JT, July 20, 1923, in JTP 11:2.
9. Walter Pinchback to JT, April 20, 1929–February 14, 1932, in JTP 8:6.

sons at a time of need; when Fritz Peters, whom Jean had known at le Prieuré and in Chicago, called on Toomer in an emergency, he wired some money immediately. And when the son of one of his closest friends from Chicago days asked for help with financial and career problems in his college years, Jean was generous with both time and money. Of course, both were in more plentiful supply at this stage of life, thanks to Marjorie.

Throughout his lifetime with both male and female friends, Jean frequently was a loving, understanding counselor. He often did not do this well within his own family and sometimes his advice was given unasked, yet this ability was exceptional, one for which he was most valued by his friends. Beginning with his long talks with his friend Ken when they were in high school, he came to believe that he had a gift for helping people. The early stages of most of his love affairs included thoughtful prescriptions for the growth of the beloved's mind or the better harmonizing of her organism. (This continued despite Orage's specific advice to Jean that instruction in "the Work" and personal love life should be kept strictly separate.) People in the Chicago groups relied on Toomer for advice about their careers and guidance when their marriages were in difficulty. Jean described in a 1934 letter how he had spent a long time with a couple in his group, talking over their problems. Next day "they told me how differently they felt, how everything was really all right now—thanks to me, their friend, their brother, their father. And I, looking at them, hearing their thanks, felt very still and humble." At another time, when one of Fred Leighton's marriages was breaking up, both Fred and his wife Lucy turned separately to Jean. Fred wrote, "You are the only person I know who could (if anyone can) . . . contrive some shock or condition" to enable his wife to reorganize her emotional state. Lucy had earlier written him: "You are the only person I know that I can come to with a problem and receive real help—not mere advice, mere consolation." [10]

Not everyone received Toomer's counseling and teaching with equal eagerness. The warmth that some felt in him was balanced by the coolness and detachment sensed by others. Some listeners resisted him as he had resisted Gurdjieff, and some questioned whether his work with people bordered on manipulation. Personal qualities in Jean and ideological derivations from the Gurdjieff work combined to make this a real issue, and his wife Marjorie served only as the prime example of a general phenomenon.

10. JT to MC, June 17, 1934, in JTP 9:4; Fred Leighton to JT, February 9, 1932, Lucy Ann Leighton to JT, January 6, 1931, both in JTP 6:6.

In a sense, Jean Toomer used everyone he knew. His purpose and destiny were so overriding that everything else was secondary, and part of his destiny was to change other people's lives. Some Gurdjieff methods for doing this lent themselves to a kind of distortion, and on occasion Toomer thus defended petty behavior with lofty excuses. One such method was to administer "shocks" to certain individuals so a person might move from a plateau to the next stage of growth. Toomer sometimes used social occasions for this kind of lesson. He once chided a friend for charging him with unkindness when he had become angry at her. No matter how he behaved, she was to keep faith that his intention was to help, "however much you understood that intention, whatever my means of attaining it." [11] Clearly an uncontrolled outburst of temper could be covered, after the fact, with this explanation. His wife and her daughter were particularly vulnerable to this, and they came eventually to mistrust his intentions and his judgment.

Another Gurdjieff method involved the effort to live at a different level of consciousness and to work actively on oneself, which necessarily draws attention away from the intimate involvement with another. A letter to Jean from John Bennett in 1953 offers an illustration:

There is a very important task for you to accomplish in getting the right relations between your wife and your work. It is another example of G's favorite conundrum of getting a sheep and a wolf and a cabbage across a river. . . .

To succeed in the task you have to convince *all three parts* of your wife that the work will not come between you. She must think and feel and sense that she receives more and not less from you.

Now you cannot accomplish this by *quantity.* . . . Only *quality* will help. Quality means attention. It means self remembering. It means a far greater effort to enter into *her* emotional situation.

. . . Such a task . . . belongs to what G.I. used to call: "Externally play role, inwardly not identify." But the role must be so perfectly played that no one can possibly see the conscious work. This means that you must *at all times,* genuinely *feel* what you are doing.

That is the extraordinary part of such a task—that if you forget and are careless for one minute, you undo the result of many days or even weeks of work. [12]

It is easy to interpret this crudely as advocating deception, but there was something more subtle meant, which perhaps only an initiate could fully explain. One loves but does not love at the same time, because one is removed from the loving and exists in a sphere of larger intention. One must be detached from

---

11. JT to Dorothy [?], January 16, 1936, in JTP 8:11.
12. John Bennett to JT, February 12, 1953, in JTP 1:3.

any emotion, yet move in the human world where emotions are the springs of action and the bonds of community. Jean could no doubt understand the paradoxical nature of this instruction from his mentor, but in practice the lines separating genuine fully felt caring, caring and being detached at the same time, and playing the role for its effect may have been dim.

In one other area, his loving effectiveness may be questioned—his role as a father. It seems clear that the love was there but did not quite know how to show itself in this relationship. Jean acted toward his daughter more as a teacher than as a father, speaking to her in abstractions before she was ready for them and leaving the responsibility for everyday discipline and nurturance to Marjorie. Between this high-level esotericism and a low-level teasing and fun-making, Jean seemed to have difficulty in entering constructively into his daughter's life. However, he proved to be a foster-father much appreciated by Paul Taylor, who lived with the Toomers for several years in New York and Doylestown, attended Buckingham Friends School, and returned for visits in his adolescence and adulthood. He later remembered with gratitude and some wonder Jean's association with him.

In sum, many people looked to him as one who could diagnose and treat psychological ills: "In dragging this defective machine into the Universal Workshop I not only want to have it put in running order. I want to know what is the matter with it. . . . Can you, sometime when it is opportune, give me your expert opinion." Later in his life he was called on for more spiritual than psychological counsel, but he continued to communicate a sense of deep understanding, even in a brief contact: "You would certainly have the feeling that he was very much in tune with you"; he was "a mountain of strength to all who knew him." One friend of his later years concluded, "I think he loved everybody, and . . . he didn't love them for any particular reason, he loved them for their diversity." [13]

The lover, the understander, the translator of ideals into visible form— Toomer in all these ways aimed at translating behavior into the ideal. As a teacher, he was accomplishing this translation. His teaching, after he left the path of literature, was his way of following out his aim to "build a world"—to actualize the ideal. He did not, however, see himself directly as a world-saver: "Civilization still needs to be 'saved,' though I do not now and never have seen myself as a 'savior' of such a mad elephant. One has to be an elephant to mea-

---

13. Lea [?] to JT, June 16, 1930, in JTP 6:5; interview of Byron and Betty Morehouse, Doylestown, Pa., August 5, 1982; Harold Perry to MCT, April 7, 1967, in MTC.

sure up to an elephant, and I am but a lamb—with a dash of goat." [14] He intended rather to build a world of those people directly related to him and transformed by his teaching. They ideally would help others to be transformed. Although his aim was more grandiose than the visible results, he made a difference. In spite of all his excesses and failings, those he touched were changed because of him. In fact, he was sometimes able to inspire in others what he failed to achieve in himself.

It is intriguing that when Jean was drawing away from writing as a career in favor of shaping people's psyches, many of those he shaped turned to writing, through some had never tried it before. Dorothy Peterson, who had started in Jean's Harlem group and maintained a correspondence with him after he left New York, was one of these people. Afraid to show her writing to anyone else, she had sent him one piece, and confided in 1928, "I don't think anybody has ever done for me in my whole life anything that I value as much as I do your last letter. . . . I don't even know how I came to show you what I had written, except that you must have gradually been building up in me a confidence in your ability to tell me the truth without hurting me. That seems to me very wonderful." Again in 1931 she exhibited her reliance on his insights, sending him the draft of a book "because you will know what it was I wanted to do, and you can tell whether I have, in any degree, succeeded." [15] Something about Toomer seemed to lead his followers to the craft of words. Self-exploration, reporting, fiction, criticism, and poetry flowed from various members of his Chicago groups, too, as a response to their work with him.

Many people declared their indebtedness to Jean for insights that changed their lives. One friend in 1927, at the beginning of a seven-year correspondence, wrote, "For the first time in my life I begin to love God, through you. It seems that only since I have begun to realize you and love you as a higher being has the idea of God begun to hold emotional meaning." Katharine Green believed that the Gurdjieff experience through Jean Toomer was "the most important thing that had ever happened" to her, and that without it her life would have remained hopelessly snarled. Yvonne Dupee wrote that her surviving the Portage experiment made her feel free and able: "I have gained a new sense of power . . . a sense of iron and steel. . . . I have an added self-respect, a feeling of a new kind of dignity and some right to it." Margery Latimer had a new orientation to the community she lived in: "Jean did this beautiful thing to me—I had always been set off from the people, never really with them—

14. JT to Betsey Barton, January 31, 1945, in JTP 11:4.
15. Dorothy Peterson to JT, November 10, 1928, December 22, 1931, both in JTP 8:4.

and then when I formed the group for him in Portage for the Gurdjieff lectures and got in touch with people that way—O when I turned and saw them all at the wedding I felt in a way I had never felt, as if I were some part of them venturing out into the universe and as if they were giving me away to him and to the world." Others in the Portage experiment also expressed gratitude for their new insights and growth, both then and later. Elise Bunnell wrote in 1967, "Although it has been many years since any of us has seen him he at one time influenced us all for a better life. He will not be forgotten." [16]

Jean's later experiment with the "cell of awareness" at Mill House was summarized by a reporter writing a feature article forty years after the fact: "The point is not that these groups failed to become permanent institutions. What is remarkable is that they existed at all. During their short hours upon the stage they seemed to capture something fragile but profound in our society—a sense of self-sufficiency, fellowship and harmony." Lin Davenport, who worked with Jean in this group and is perhaps the sole thoroughgoing disciple of his Gurdjieff-based psychological teaching, has thoughtfully assessed its results in his life:

Jean's ideas and Jean's attitude, his philosophy, for me at least, clarified and articulated what I almost at once affirmed as, this is the way it is. And I would say that the importance to me of this association with Jean was that because of this clarification and because of this complex and very broad spectrum, basketful of understandings and attitudes, that it left me with an awfully solid sense of what I was, where I wanted to try and go, and a security which I say with all humility, a security which is very very rare, a security based on a set of values which don't change, at least they don't change for me.

So that this security, perhaps it's a kind of self-confidence, it's enabled me to be an extremely low-profile, quiet nonconformist, when measured by what the world considers the conventional yardsticks. But it's enabled me to live what has been to me a very satisfying life, with no feeling that I . . . had to persuade other people to live my way. . . . I think the best short way of stating what I'm trying to get at now is that I think because of my relationship with Jean, it sure stabilized and secured me as an individual.

Paul Taylor, also shaped by Jean in this period, wrote after Jean's death, "I mourn Jean as I would a father. . . . I later learned to respect, though I never could emulate, the strength of his moral and intellectual convictions. I would have wanted to please him somehow by being a better son for him—to reward

16. Harriet [?] to JT, June 27, 1927, in JTP 8:9; taped interview of Katharine Green by Robert Twombly, Briggsville, Wis., March 21, 1975 (State Historical Society of Wisconsin, Madison); JT, "Portage Potential," 317; MLT to Jessie Overholt, January, 1932, in JTP 6:1; Elise Bunnell to MCT, April 4, 1967, in MTC.

the faith he always seemed to have in me." Even Susan Sandberg, who took Jean on in adolescence as a stepfather and was never bowled over with his charm and power as her mother was, recalls the wisdom and enduring usefulness of Jean's teaching that one should use every experience, whether bad or good, for learning and growth.[17]

Beyond the period of Jean's active psychological teaching, a number of people have also testified to the power he had in making them aware of the spiritual potential that lay within them. Perhaps the most vivid description is by someone who was a young member of Buckingham Meeting late in Jean's period of work there. She felt that Toomer was the source of her first "real insight into a sort of light from within. This sort of thing [was] a spiritualness that came from inside the body, which each person had sought for. . . . And I used to feel a lot more that way when I was close to him and talking with him than anybody I can think of." She believed that through Jean's help she achieved a connection "not so much to any man-made religion, . . . but an individual sky-hook. . . . And he had it; everybody could have it. . . . And it didn't depend on anything else except what you set up between yourself and whatever it was you wanted to hang on," whether that was outside you, above you, or within you. But this was not everyone's reaction. At least one Quaker couple spent an evening at Jean's fireside, watched him holding sway over an "admiring bog," and never went back. But at his death, one friend wrote of having long missed "the Jean, whose mind and spirit we all loved and admired so much." Another called him "a great man, almost in spite of himself. . . . I do not lose sight of the angel-devil—still this must be said." Even his wife Marjorie, with all her knowledge of his many sides, could still say of her earlier years with him, "For many years I thought Jean was practically a god." And in her later years, she had "seen and felt the life and power" in him, declaring that he and Douglas Steere "are the only two in the Society of Friends who speak with the life and power."[18]

Jean Toomer had more awareness of his faults, even of his falseness, than most people around him knew. The many selves warring within him, the boundless ego that he tried to supersede by a new birth above the body, continued to fragment him to the end. But he was a sensitive instrument for love

17. Fred Fiske, "Toomer Started Bucks Refuge for Human Development in '30s," Doylestown *Daily Intelligencer*, July 19, 1975, p. 3; interview of Franklin Davenport, Doylestown, Pa., January 23, 1975; Paul Taylor to MCT, April 10, 1967, in MTC; interview of Susan Sandberg, Doylestown, Pa., March 20, 1983.

18. Duval interview; Amelia Swayne to MCT, [1967], Ruth Ikeler to MCT, [1967], both in MTC; interview of MCT, Doylestown, Pa., March 20, 1983; JT notes, May 3, 1950 (JTP 54:6).

on many levels. His special sensitivity and intensity were shared with people near him, so they could participate in his vital life. In 1934 he wrote,

We never know we are beings till we love.

And then it is we know the powers and the potentialities of human existence, the powers and the potentialities of organic, conscious, solar, cosmic matter and force.

We, together, vibrate as one in harmony with man and with the cosmos.[19]

When he was able to let love flow through him, others too were lifted up to places they could not have gone without him.

19. "Sing Yes!" from the 1934 unpublished collection "Blue Meridian and Other Poems" (JTP 50:5), also in a different version in *W&S*, 205–207.

19.

Struggle Toward Sainthood

Many questions about Jean Toomer's life remain. In examining his public accomplishments and his private friendships, we have looked at only the external side of his lifetime search. The core, the essential element around which everything else revolved, was his effort to transform himself. We can grant his outward efforts a moderate success, but when we look at the whole curve of his life, including its dismal end, we have to ask if any word but *failure* can be applied. He wanted to be "one of the world's greatest writers and greatest men." He wanted to be one who had the answers to all the problems of existence. He wanted to be a spiritual giant, in constant intimate contact with God. He was none of these. Yet his whole life was a struggle toward these ends. Why, with such promise, such devotion, such proven abilities, was there so great a gulf between what he believed was possible in self-development and what he seemed able to achieve?

Although no human personality, much less one as complex as his, can ever be laid open to full understanding, a critical look at the psychological, physical, and spiritual aspects of his struggle may help us to see Jean Toomer more clearly and to begin on an answer to this question.

Basic to his life enterprise was the search for identity. He defined it in these words: "I assume that identity is the predetermined and highest goal of the human unit (not the I and I's that I am now aware of, but the highest potential-I). . . . I assume that the godhead is the end, I assume it is the beginning, hence I hold that beginning and end are one."[1] As the goal of transcendence was the positive incentive that drew him through the different segments of his

1. JT, "Beliefs and Assumptions," n.d. (JTP 22:21).

life, the negative incentive was the necessity that pushed him toward this same goal. He needed transcendence because he needed wholeness. He had to transcend, first, the warring of his many contradictory selves.

Everyone shares the condition of having personality elements at odds with one another. In fact this is so universal an experience that in their teaching, Orage and Ouspensky often began by describing this conflict to show everyone's need for attaining a unified "I" that would rule these many selves. But the degree of contradiction in Jean Toomer's case is so extreme as to be unique. He pointed this out many times, with perhaps a wry pride. One of his most complete summations occurs in his introduction to "Earth-Being":

Towards life in general I have three pairs of main attitudes. I see it as comic and tragic, as chemical and sacred, as natural and divine. . . .

I am both pessimistic and optimistic, a realist and an idealist. I am an egotist; I can be genuinely humble. I am promiscuous; I am single. I have regard for nothing; I am devoted and sincerely deeply care. To care for—this is one of my main feelings. I am crude and cultured, weak and strong, slow and quick, without morality but with conscience—and all of these in extreme degrees.

I am complex and involved; I am quite simple. I am secretive and revealing, round about and direct. I am concentrated, diffused; formed and unformed. I have essential organization. I am chaotic. I can work intensely. I am lazy and heavy with inertia. I can rise from the depths of inertia to the height of force. When idle I too am sex and a stomach. I am younger than a child and a thousand years old.

I am a chicken; I am a hawk. A sheep, a wolf. A reliable person and a pirate.

I am a home-man and a wanderer, a patriarch and a lone nomad.

A devil and a saint.[2]

The devil-saint image was depicted symbolically in one of his early notebooks, "Characters," as two triangles superimposed to form a six-pointed star. The one pointing up is labeled "The Black Saint"; the one pointing down, "The Black Devil." The middle section, of course, is shared territory.

Together with this cauldron of impulses and behaviors Toomer's personality contained a tendency to tip dangerously in one direction or another. This was illustrated in his tremendous successive enthusiasms—for body building; for girls and women, one after another; for socialism; for music; for his major areas of concentration, writing, the Gurdjieff method, the Society of Friends; and then for the various cures he attempted for his ills. It was also illustrated in his sudden rejections, of a sequence of colleges and of most of these "bumps" of excitement, one by one. Indeed, the strangely segmented nature of his life is a product of this pattern of one enthusiasm displacing another.

2. JT, "Earth-Being" (MTC), 18–19, most of this also in *W&S*, 20–21.

While his 1930 self-description seems to show a tolerant amusement for the warring doubleness in himself, his actions belie such complacency. The best of his literary efforts embody the search for completion, for integration. His repeated reaching out to one system or another shows a clear need for placing his concepts in an organized framework. His yearning to transcend the fragmented human presence by entering another, nonmaterial world is a way of stepping from multiplicity into unity. In fact, early in his second marriage he outlined this problem in the hope his wife might help him get out of his depressions: "By type I am by turn creative and fallow, intense and relaxed, high up and let down, functioning and strained. My fire burns and then it must be quenched lest I burn up. My best work is done in what might be called intensive spurts." In tennis or schoolwork it was the same: he was "in form" one day and out the next, active and then inert. He could not learn by steady application but only suddenly, in a swift flash. Emotionally, difficult periods would unexpectedly be supplanted by comic moods. "My own life has been so varied and disconnected that it sometimes seems to me that I have used most of my energies in welding myself together. . . . These efforts have deposited in me a deep area of fatigue. . . . When I drop I not only drop into the tiredness of the moment, but into the fatigue of my entire life-struggles."[3]

A few examples, supplementing incidents reported throughout this account of Toomer's life, will illustrate his unease with fluidity and instability. Robert Bone has suggested, with considerable insight, that it was Jean's experience of being carried away by emotion in his encounter with Margaret Naumburg that led him immediately to seek an anchor such as he perceived in the Gurdjieff method—a controlled way of evaluating and changing behavior. Jean's ecstatic description of this experience lends much credence to this possibility: he was indeed, he says, carried to a level where he had never been before, and his fall from that height forced on him a total reorganization. Again, at several periods of his life he regretted his lack of control over the writing process that was so essential to his being. One instance occurred when he was trying to finish editing the Margery Latimer letters and join Marjorie Content in Taos: "[The editing] simply required the sustained application of my ordinary, that is, usual mind—and this mind, pretty well trained, is more or less entirely at my service. . . . But to write the introduction required creation, the functioning of my unusual mind, my essential brain—and I do not and as yet cannot control this Mr. Brain."[4]

3. JT notes, 1934 (JTP 27:35); JT notes, 1929 (JTP 15:13).
4. Robert Bone, *Down Home: Negro Short Fiction, from the Beginning Through the Harlem Renaissance* (New York, 1975), 229; JT to MC, June 21, 1934, in JTP 9:4.

Sometimes he assumed a philosophical detachment from the strain of this conflict between freedom and control: "It is a universal issue, not peculiar to the artist only, for all men are subject to the contest between chaos and cosmos, between destructive and constructive tendencies. . . . Productivity versus licence, productivity and licence—it is certainly a big and vital theme, one which interests me tremendously, and one of these days I hope to do a work that will go to the roots of the matter in a complete way. There's no end to the drama of it." At other times he put it in more personal, frightening terms: "A new man is born when one realizes his ability to reconcile. This marks the end of the fear of being torn apart, which fear, along with the fear of losing one's head, operates to paralyze man."[5]

In the latter part of his life, the extremes were still there to haunt him. Sometimes when he spoke in meeting for worship, his message was an effort to work out this problem. One listener reported, "One day he was saying that he couldn't understand, himself, why he could feel such empathy for the underprivileged and the people caught up in wars, . . . and at the same time . . . even harbor the thought to poison the water supply of Doylestown. And you can see that was a shocker. . . . But the point was, he was struggling with the extremes of his nature, in trying to understand it." Later he continued to be troubled by uncontrollable ups and downs, his functioning and nonfunctioning, and planned to talk to his Gurdjieff group leader about "my too great an instability." But the devil and the saint continued their uneasy association in Toomer until the end.[6]

From a psychological viewpoint such a record, clearly showing wide mood shifts that are not solely the result of outward situations, indicates some kind of affective imbalance. Dr. Gerald G. May, a psychiatrist who has reviewed the elements of Toomer's life, suggests a likely possibility. What Jean Toomer manifested may have been something of the type of condition that used to be labeled "manic-depressive" and is now called "bipolar affective disorder," or it may have been the milder version called "cyclothymic disorder." If the family history were to reveal a similar pattern, the diagnosis would be strengthened, since there is often a genetic component in these disorders. There is nothing in the record to indicate that Jean's mother or maternal grandparents experienced these extremes of behavior. However, the way Jean's father swept into Washington in a whirlwind of spending, energetically courted and married Nina, and then as suddenly swept out again, certainly suggests a periodicity of intense

5. JT to Harrison Smith, July 29, 1933, in JTP 8:14; JT, "Psychologic Papers," July 31, 1936 (MTC).

6. Interview of Byron and Betty Morehouse, Doylestown, Pa., August 5, 1982.

advance and withdrawal. What we know of him is not enough to validate a hypothesis, but it does provide some support. And Jean, in one respect, equated himself with his father: "Both mother and father were heart people. I mean that emotions, feelings, were the ruling forces of their lives. . . . So with me."[7]

It is not necessary or reasonable, even if we accept such a label as a working hypothesis, to brand Jean Toomer as mentally ill. All such disorders exist on a continuum among people, in some cases making a person completely nonfunctional in the everyday world, in others making one only slightly deviant. It is clear that Jean functioned well in many ways; that he was somewhat deviant— otherwise he would not have been so interesting; and also that in certain areas, something in him did interfere with the abilities he wanted so much. What such a hypothesis can do is to identify a possible source for those elements of his personality that seemed intractably to stand in the way of what his best self tried to achieve. It can also provide a framework in which some of the contradictions and mysteries fall into a logical pattern.

The key to this pattern is the connection between excesses and curbing them. The perception of excess or abandon in oneself is frightening and leads to the need for control. In addition, the psychodynamics of Jean's childhood would have strengthened this need in him. From his birth he had no secure placement, as his mother was cast loose; he had no real position in the family, no clear racial identification, no geographical anchor, no father. In a sense, he had no mother—she was treated as a teenager, took little responsibility for him, and was in danger of slipping away at any moment, as she did in marriage and eventually in death. In such a fluid world he had to find something firm. He was left very much alone and had to make his own forms and rules. At the same time, not feeling that he was loved without question, he was convinced that only by being different or special could he be loved. The lack of secure attachment to anyone else would also give him the kind of dependence on and love of self that could predispose him toward some traits of the narcissistic personality.[8]

In his autobiography, Toomer takes pains to list the ways he was left unusually alone as a child and the ways he had always felt unique, "isolate," "out-

7. Interview of Gerald G. May, M.D. (Director for Spiritual and Psychological Guidance, Shalem Institute, Washington, D.C.), Columbia, Md., June 9, 1983; JT autobiography, 1929 (JTP 17:1).

8. The psychodynamic analysis was outlined by Dr. May. In addition, many parallels between Toomer's traits and those associated with the narcissistic personality disorder, and their possible connection with his childhood pattern, have been pointed out by clinical psychologist Kathleen Peoples, a mental health counselor at the University of Pittsburgh.

side the run of common affairs." A series of other memories suddenly fit into this pattern of discomfort with emptiness and his need to be in control. A 1929 notebook entry mentions his irritation in Paris because he has a hard time keeping track of the points of the compass there. He couples this observation with a description of his general uneasiness if, in a room anywhere, he does not know whether his chair faces north or south and what the geographical layout of the city and the surrounding area is. In his recollections of childhood, certain types of commands—those suggesting that he was incapable of doing a task or needed policing—provoked rage and a refusal to obey. Clearly, those orders which questioned his own ability to control what he was doing were isolated in his mind by means of a defensive overreaction. He felt his place in his child-community had to be as a leader, wholly withdrawing when that place was no longer available to him, and seeing himself then as "the deposed solitary keeper of a kingdom that had broken and gone forever." Even in infancy he remembers requiring adults to "display a subjects-to-king attitude"— he speaks of becoming able to "rule" his nurse, mother, and grandmother at a tender age. A little later, he concocted complicated schemes to induce guilt in his elders while maintaining his own innocence—a manipulative control. In contrasting his formal (useless) learning with the self-guided, informal, useful kind, he again shows his preference for being in control. He talks of the delight of breaking rules: "It is the *thrill of independent power* exercised by a man of the human aristocracy who knows that the taboos were made by his ancestors, men of his psychological class, not for him but for the herd." In explaining the appeal of military drills or gymnastic exercises or hierarchical government, he says, "I hate institutions but I love structures."[9] The emotional basis of his lifelong search for structure and order and also of a contradictory value, the delight in breaking rules, is now discovered in his need for control, which arose from his own unstable temperament and was compounded by his free-form childhood.

Even Toomer's penchant for giving names to everybody is a way of conquering. From the time of Adam, the naming of creatures has been a sign of sovereignty over them. Ralph Ellison in *Shadow and Act* explores "the suggestive power of names and the magic involved in naming," speaking particularly of blacks' need to reclaim their own names because names shape reality. Jean himself wrote, "The giving of good names is one of the happy ways men have of appropriating things, of humanizing them. . . . Indeed if the name is fine

9. JT, "Earth-Being" (MTC), 168–69, 171–72, 203, 43, 145, 165–66, much of this also in *W&S*, 62–64, 40, 46–48; JT Paris notebook, October 20–23, 1929 (JTP 69:13) (emphasis added); JT, "Book X."

enough the giving of it and use of it seems almost to make the thing a part of us." Thus, in yet another manner, he managed those around him. Another dimension of the same process was Jean's own sense of being nameless: "I responded equally well to all my names but probably, in my deeper moments, regarded myself as the nameless." [10] This suggests a feeling of being lost, disconnected. More profoundly, however, he eluded others' naming and devised schemes so he could not be controlled but instead took on the aura of the mysterious power that is in control of all. Later he used this power to name himself.

The need for control, of course, had its inner effects too. He could not let excess emotion carry him away. He speaks of putting up barriers to his feelings in anticipation of his mother's marriage, so that he was almost callous when she died. In his time at the College of Physical Training in Chicago, "to protect my deeply impressionable nature from receiving too strong and too many shocks, . . . I deliberately set about the forming of a buffer, of a protective mechanism, resolving to meet the world with, and to let it touch me only through, my mind." [11] This protective mechanism had become so strong that in 1953 he felt that his only hope of salvation was to break it down.

In other areas, this emotional regulation probably affected his view of reality. For instance, he did not recognize until very late in life the painful residue of racial conflict that was still within him and was connected with a sense he had that his mother had rejected him. It may have been the suppression of this pain that kept him less than open with his daughter about her background, and perhaps less than aware of the societal racism around him. This is evident in his depiction of the "gay, bright, sweet life" of the upper-class blacks in Washington during his teenage years—a time when Mary Church Terrell, a good friend of the Pinchbacks', took her two daughters (Jean's friends and early loves) out of that very society to Oberlin for a year so they could experience what it was like to live away from the daily burden of discrimination. Alice Walker has noted other such blindnesses in Jean's account of his life, such as his not recognizing why he was brutalized on the playing field at Wisconsin, where he was perceived as an Indian. [12]

Jean's contradictory needs to be in control and to be loved were further confused by racial factors. He wanted to be submissive and please others, but this posture carried the stigma of a slave stereotype. He also wanted to dominate and lead, using what he considered male strength as well as the power of an

10. Ralph Ellison, *Shadow and Act* (New York, 1964), 151; JT, "Portage Potential" (MTC), 15; JT, "Incredible Journey" (JTP 15:4).

11. JT, "Outline of an Autobiography" (JTP 14:1), back of 26.

12. Terrell, *Colored Woman,* 244; Walker, "The Divided Life of Jean Toomer," 11.

exceptional person. Society seemed to reserve both these roles for whites. His way of getting past these dichotomies was to rise above the racial barriers—to unite the warring parts of himself by negating the cultural expectations that supported them.

The pendulum swings of Jean's temperament were surely a factor in his problems with his writing—as well as in his successes. He recognized their part in his spurts of inspiration, but not in his lack of control over the product. The genius he displayed at his best came largely from his unusual intensity of feeling and experience, which took him beyond the normal boundaries between material and nonmaterial, between animate and inanimate, between possible and impossible. But this free-flowing imagery, in his best writing, was contained in a subtly formed pattern, which in *Cane* was a circle of journey and return. He had at the time been extensively studying literary masters and was working closely with other writers who were shaping their materials with equal care. He applied these models to his own writing, and he also sent his work to Waldo Frank for critical review. Later he cast his models aside. He never really adopted Ouspensky's elusive but highly demanding requirements for producing objective art. Rather, he set out on his own track, which meant that his writing was either too loose or too controlled. Several of his friends noted these qualities at different times, particularly the overcontrol as his intent to instruct overrode the free-flowing imagery that had been his strength. Gorham Munson called his later writing "wooden." In 1928, Margaret Naumburg, who had resumed a friendly correspondence with Jean about writing and publishing, wrote her frank response to a manuscript of his: "Maybe what you have written down is the skeletal material for you to build your book on. I feel as though a good deal of what you've done is Jean thinking aloud, but not yet ready for publication, for an audience. . . . It is not fleshed out as it should eventually be." She admonished him to make it not sociological but personal. A similar comment came from Marjorie Content in the summer before they were married: "It occurs to me that you have been writing too much from your head—not that I am all for emotional writing . . . but I don't think you need worry about the head part being left behind—The teacher or rather the educator will never be lost in your work—but the way for that same educator to reach people is by uncontrol and spontaneity of expression—Give the artist in you freer rein." The opposite swing of the pendulum is illustrated in Toomer's correspondence with Harrison Smith, a publisher's representative, about his novel "Eight-Day World," which he had at one time called "Transatlantic." In a letter of seven single-spaced typewritten pages (itself a symptom of excessive enthusiasm), Jean writes,

You ask, "haven't you dashed at it too wildly, with a flaming imagination that opens the throttle wide and forgets to put on the brakes around the corners?" And I meet this by saying, firstly, . . . I'll be glad to tone down and haul in wherever I can; and, secondly, . . . owing to my personal psychological necessity, I *simply had* to open up and let fly. The trouble with the books of mine you've seen prior to Eight Day World was precisely that . . . I held in too much. . . .

Eight Day World is my book of license. Let me have it! Let me have my fling! I promise that my next book will be a book of discipline!

He says in the same letter that he had tried for two months to rewrite the book "in a straightforward realistic manner," but as it lost its faults it lost all its glories.[13] Pushed by these psychological imbalances, Jean clearly was not able to make the delicate reconciliation between freedom and form that is the essence of the work of the artist.

Toomer's intentions for his writing changed after 1923, but was his ability to structure his work affected also? It is difficult to gauge the effect his involvement in the Gurdjieff movement had on his writing. The process of self-development envisioned in the system appears to involve a high measure of control, though ideally this control is given over to the evolved essence, what we might call the best self of the person. One can, similarly, call Toomer's writing during his Gurdjieff period overcontrolled and empty of life. But his summary of the effect the Gurdjieff work had on him, written when he thought he had left it behind, indicates not increased control but rather a new man full of new material to express "because he *has to.*" "Between 1924 and 1932 I went on a far journey into strange lands of experience (so much so that all or most of my internal parts were dissassociated and recombined into new formations)— and only this year have I come back, so to speak, to the world of usual earth-life—and I've come back a very different person from the man of 1923—and this relatively new person is just beginning to write. And this *is not* fantasy or symbolism; *it is actual, real.*"[14]

There is probably no simple correlation and may be no causal connection, but Toomer's writings that were clearly derived from his Gurdjieffian world view seem most to display undigested combinations of elements—fantasy, humor, satire, didacticism, perhaps some tender imagery—each cut short before it could be developed in a satisfying way or logically related to the whole. There seems to be a curious lack of judgment about the works, or little understanding of how the reader would perceive them. The success of his earlier

13. Margaret Naumburg to JT, June 6, 1928, in JTP 7:19; MC to JT, June 19, 1934, in JTP 9:4; JT to Harrison Smith, September 9, 1933, in JTP 8:14.

14. JT to Smith, September 9, 1933, in JTP 8:14.

writings and of his later pieces on Quaker themes, when he was least actively pursuing the Gurdjieff teaching, lies both in their intensity and in their whole-ness—the development of an image or an idea until it is complete. To achieve this kind of balance over the churning chaos—to let it go, then wrap it up—required a supernormal effort on Jean's part. Perhaps also it needed dedication to an ideal of beauty or divinity beyond the goal of self-improvement. Or per-haps a trusted, sure-eyed critic: a Waldo Frank or a William Hubben.

The second major factor in Jean Toomer's personality was his drive toward leadership. This was an aspect of his need for control that blossomed with a grandiosity of its own and, like his mood swings, was both a blessing and a curse. His extreme dependence on his self-image—and on others' acceptance of that image—for his sense of self-worth reveals traits of what may have been Toomer's secondary impairment, narcissism. But again and again, Jean recog-nized this drive, and the ego inflation that came with it, and he tried to tran-scend them. "I was not selfless then, nor have I since so become—and this despite the fact that in time I came to see clearly that it was up to me, not to express, not to repress, but to overcome my own ego," he wrote of his early childhood. He even recognized its basis, as is shown in an undated note:

> Without pride, he is inert, timid, and inconsistent.
> With pride active, he is active.
> He wants protection. [15]

Yet much of the time he was in the grip of the image of himself as a leader, a prophet, one given a high destiny by fate—and one who thus had authority and controlled his environment. In various ways he was acting out this role in all his incarnations. When he gave himself the name Jean, he was playing at being a poet. As soon as he encountered the Gurdjieff work, he nibbled at leadership, becoming a teacher before he was ready. Its capstone for him, the experiment in Portage, made him unabashedly not only the unquestioned cap-tain of the ship but the creator of the new world its passengers had chosen to enter. When he joined the Quakers, he was an immediate expert.

His self-advertising was sometimes unrestrained. Introducing himself to the sponsor of a talk he was to give in Chicago in 1930, he called himself a psychologist, creator, and aesthetic critic, and he added, "Since 1923 I have been, to use the words of others, 'one of the most creative and critical of the younger men in American letters and art.'" To a publisher's representative in 1933 he wrote: "The big writers of this age and their books *do go over* with the

---

15. JT, "Incredible Journey" (JTP 14:3); JT notes (JTP 13:6).

reading public and they do make money for themselves and for their publishers, as well as become important factors in the cultural world. I am of that clan. I state it nonegotistically. I know the force that is in me. . . . I am going somewhere—and I'm going to take a fair portion of the world with me." A little earlier, he put these thoughts in a private notebook:

Never in my life have I experienced utter despair. . . . Something in me has always been convinced that I am a child of great destiny, that I have a star, that I am led on by it towards a great fulfillment.

Nature in America experimented for three hundred years and with millions of blood-crossings to produce one man.[16]

Some disciples, such as Jeremy Lane, helped feed this "messiah complex" in probably unwholesome ways. Soon after Margery Latimer's death, Lane showed his dependence on Toomer: "More and more I feel you a man of destiny. . . . And I will be preparing myself as well as can be, for a readiness to your command." He saw in Jean the possibility of a savior, "a man of world power. My constant wish is to be really alive then, alert, and able to function with you. . . . I am thankful that you are in the world." Sally Fell, who was a Young Friend in the 1940s, also reported, "At the time, I thought he was the Messiah—we all felt the same way." Even psychic messages may have intensified the image. A medium in Fort Atkinson, Wisconsin, transmitted two such laudatory messages:

[1931] Toomer is great channel because physical make up is peculiar and sensitive to great degree. This sensitiveness has been well tempered, and thru hard discipline is now asset. Body has become fine instrument. Force is increasing. Very great change is for him.

[1933] Have full trust in Toomer. He is going up to strong position.[17]

Jean Toomer's need to be seen as an authority or high priest both augmented and undermined his teaching. Part of his problem was that this image was not all false. He was too good too soon. He put real magic in his writing; he had a gift for reading people; and his charm was powerful, compelling. He learned how to use these in stimulating ways. But because much came easily, as F. Scott Fitzgerald points out in his essay "Early Success," he was led to depend on what seemed his destiny, to rely on inspiration rather than discipline, to feel that the

16. JT to Josephine Beardsley, November 1, 1930, in JTP 1:3; JT to Smith, September 9, 1933, in JTP 8:14; JT notebook, 1930 (JTP 17:1).
17. Jeremy Lane to JT, September 17, 1932, in JTP 5:2; interview of Sally Fell, Doylestown, Pa., December, 1985; Libby Damuth to JT, September 30, 1931, July 29, 1933, both in JTP 2:1.

river would carry him on to its grand predetermined ends. And also, the weakness underneath—the personal chaos that he felt would follow if he were not in complete charge—made him vulnerable.

The shy, frightened boy inside him therefore bristled at any allegation that Jean Toomer was not as good as the image or was not sincere in the role. Both his own and observers' reports are remarkably pointed in attesting to his emotional eruption whenever a question was raised about his honesty or sincerity. Gorham Munson reports that Jean took criticism very well in general, but "he did get angry and suppressed anger in the Gurdjieff work when people criticized . . . his pretentions, let us say, of leadership." In an early notebook, Toomer records "the confession of my last spiritual weakness: I still retain shreds of desires to hurt people . . . when they doubt my complete frankness, my overwhelming honesty." The greatest upheaval recorded in the course of his marriage came as a result of Marjorie's calling him a spiritual and religious fake, not living what he professed. Thirteen years earlier he had written "Idea for a Drama," in which the main character is a man whose life and strength are based on utter candor. His wife's best self recognizes and values this, but when she wants to cripple him she makes it seem that he claims omniscience, ignoring his careful statements that he does not know; she insists on accuracy of fine detail when he does state a fact; and she reminds him that he is biased. How his drama ends is a question: he may regenerate her, she may defeat him, both may be defeated.[18]

Such reactions, of course, were not what he intended. As late as 1955–1956, when he was writing the account of his first trip to Fontainebleau, he reminded himself of the proper, creative reaction to criticism or difficulty. It was a saying of Gurdjieff's which was displayed in the Study House and which he had repeated many times since in his own notes:

"You are here having realized that you have only yourself chiefly to contend with. Therefore thank those who give you the opportunity."

As time passed, and changes occurred in me, this saying came to mean more and more. . . . What a remarkable attitude. And how difficult to apply.

In some cases he seemed able to make good use of this technique. But in the long haul—"how difficult to apply."[19]

The strength of his defenses would suggest that the same motivations that gave Toomer the desire kept him from the achievement. Tragically, again and

18. Interview of GM by India Watterson, New York, June 28, 1969 (Amistad Research Center, New Orleans), 13; JT notebook (JTP 55:6); N of E, May 6, [1950] (JTP 54:6); JT "Idea for a Drama," March 15, 1937 (JTP 55:14).
19. JT, First Trip, 14–15.

again, he recognized that this overriding need for the appearance of greatness superseded performance itself, but he could not overcome it. A scarcely disguised description of himself in the would-be novel "Portage Potential" gives a fairly clear view of this recognition:

The man was a writer. He could use words rather well. . . . [His books] contained vivid perceptions and sensings, sincere feelings, clear understandings, and, though there was a bit of posturing in them they sprang . . . from a sincere desire to communicate what he believed to be important. . . . But this writer had in him a number of properties—among others, a large dose of egotism which made him wish to appear as one of the world's greatest writers and greatest men. Related to this wish was the fear that he did not look the part, and that if anyone should meet him without "knowing who he was" he would make a poor impression.

In sad hindsight after Jean's death, Gorham Munson offered this conclusion:

Jean pretended to be more than he was. He assumed the development and psychology beyond the point that he had ever reached; he ascribed to himself powers and knowledge which he had not really attained. Some would say he had a fantasy which he truly believed in, a fantasy about himself as a master of psychological knowledge. It doesn't seem to me that he could have deceived himself to that extent. He play acts as a spiritual leader. I don't want this to sound . . . hostile or too critical. . . . In the Gurdjieff work we were told you can't be too skeptical. Jean was not skeptical enough about himself. The Gurdjieff work tends in your study of yourself to show up that you are a nonentity, that you cannot do anything, that you are determined, that you are automatic, that you are a mechanical being. Jean knew a good deal about that, but Jean would somehow not accept his being a nonentity. Instead of that, he stepped across to being somebody, to accepting the claim to himself, "Well, I have developed. I am a being in a higher state of consciousness," and that was a lie, you see, and it distorted Jean's relationship with his old friends, perhaps his relationship with Marjorie Content. In the end, Marjorie Content rebelled against this, and Jean told me himself, . . . "I have put on too much of an act."

Louise Welch, his fellow learner in the 1920s and his teacher in the 1950s, put it a little more kindly:

It's an interesting thing that some people are either born, or however it comes about, magnetic; and they have an influence over other people, sometimes long before they're wise enough to make the right use of that influence. Also having that quality makes one wish to be worthy of the admiration and so on that one gets from others.

I think in Jean's case it began with a magnetic quality and it continued with his really wishing to find his way to being as wise as those people thought he was. . . . I think he realized at a certain point, . . . he needed to understand more himself. [20]

20. JT, "Portage Potential," written 1931–32 (MTC), 64–65; GM interview, June 27, 1969, p. 19; interview of Louise Welch, New York, June 25, 1982.

This was certainly part of the story. In his Quaker years he was searching with a much greater humility than before, but somehow he still clung to the vision of his greatness. When it failed, he tended to retreat into a martyr's position as the misunderstood prophet. There is a kind of irony or self-fulfilling prophecy in the school theme he wrote in the fifth grade, about the time he turned twelve. "The Venetian Etchings of Whistler" contained the sentences: "What true innovator has stood forth unchallenged by contemporaries? What man of genius has not been hounded and persecuted by his own age? It is a truth and a deplorable one, that the message of a great man will, as a rule, find a receptive ear only in some later generation."[21] With such a view he could always salve his bruised ego.

His unremitting need for control had its impact, too, on Jean's relationship with his body. Perhaps the earliest example is his childhood illness, deliberately brought on to keep his mother close when he feared losing her. When he was in high school, he battled against what he perceived as sexual excesses by taking up rigorous body-building exercises. The need for order and discipline was probably a large, and unrecognized, factor in his choosing to attend the American College of Physical Training in Chicago, which proved to be his longest-lived college experience. The same desire is also reflected in his continuing experiments with nutrition. Several times he chose to cure himself by devising certain diets, contrary to the advice of doctors. He had a theory that if appetites were left alone, they would correctly tell people what, and how much, to eat. He applied this theory to the selection of food for the community in the Portage experiment (using his own appetite, by definition the purest, as the guide), and sometimes applied it negatively to veto what Marjorie had carefully prepared for his dinner. And in the early 1950s he tried a number of vitamin and nutrition supplements, keeping careful records of amounts and results. The Alexander technique, with which he worked in 1922 and again in 1948, was another kind of body control. And the Gurdjieff method involved dances and physical labor and constant efforts to balance the physical in a harmonious and precise way with the mental and emotional functions.

Further, Jean showed an intense sensitivity to pain and other physical symptoms, a quality that was part of his pattern of extremes and also represented his tendency toward narcissism. At one point he made a note of the dark imaginings that arose when he had to have routine blood and urine tests. Even after the blood was taken and he knew there was "practically nothing to it," he kept

21. JT school notes (JTP 13:6).

imagining: "Maybe the puncture in the vein isn't healing properly. Maybe it will have to be done over again. Unholy cow!"[22] His hypochondria was no doubt one of the factors that drove him continually to concentrate on his body, pyramiding into psychosomatic ailments that combined with those of purely physical genesis to cripple him, even though he noted early that focusing on the body was a false use of energy.

One of these crippling ailments was the phenomenon he called his "second body." While it is hard to construct an image of what Gurdjieff may have meant by "astral body," what Jean experienced in no way resembles what the term means in psychical literature. It is rather more likely, according to Dr. May, that Toomer's second body was a "psychologically determined symbol of his own inhibition of himself," that is, a projection or externalization of his need for control. Its source was "the very thing in him that never lets him just be who he is and relax." Dr. May bases this theory on the fact that the second body seemed to Jean to become most active when he was trying to go to sleep. At this "Freudian time," when the conscious mind lets go and gives way to dreams, the controlling ego is most threatened. If, therefore, it can contrive a mechanism to keep the body awake, it wins—and what more appropriate form than an outer constricting shell?[23] Another clue supporting this idea is Toomer's own observation that when his emotions were released, his second body gave him no difficulty. Jean was truly caught, though he never saw quite how, in his own net.

In contrast to his effort to control his body, it was often the body that signaled the need of more control. Besides the periods of inaction that regularly followed the periods of high functioning, there were at least five times in Toomer's life when he suffered a fairly serious physical collapse after a time of frenetic activity. Two of these, the bout with atheism in 1916 and the time in New York in 1919 when he was holding two jobs, taking music lessons, playing tennis, and going to lectures all at the same time, also involved an experience of mind-body dissociation. The others occurred in 1921 when he was writing madly in Washington, in 1923 after his emotional roller-coaster meeting with Margaret Naumburg, and in 1940 after the exhausting and unsatisfying trip to India.

A final consideration in the interplay of body and mind in Jean Toomer is the role of alcohol. For most of his life, Jean was a jolly social drinker. Prohibition created only slight difficulties in his getting beer or liquor and made him more

22. JT notes, February 20, 1955 (MTC).
23. Dr. May interview.

exuberant over the possibilities when he got outside its bounds, as in Canada, for example, or on board ship. He often mentions drinking as a pleasurable activity in his letters, and it is so portrayed in the shipboard novel "Transatlantic." It became the main feature of his afternoon "deserving time" and functioned as a reward, at other times, for hard work or for enduring difficulty or nameless vicissitudes of existence. None of this in itself is particularly excessive. There are no reports before the last decade of his life that he was out of commission because of drinking too much. Some are reluctant to identify him, even at that period, as an alcoholic. A family history supporting alcoholism would make this likelihood stronger, but the available records contain no such indication. However, his friends knew his proclivities. Eugenia Walcott wrote him after he had driven off to Toronto in 1929 with Douglas Campbell, "I don't see why you didn't leave a stench of alcohol instead of gas behind you—I wouldn't put it past you running on beer the last two hundred miles." His preoccupation with drinking and using it as a reward are attitudes that are part of the pattern of an alcoholic. A playful paragraph from a letter to Marjorie Content in 1934 is an example:

When I take this to the station, shall I stop in a tavern and get still another glass of cold beer? It's very hot and sultry and close here tonight. . . . I've been working hard. Don't you think I'm deserving? Don't you think I *might* stop at that tavern and put my head in just to see *if* they have any beer? It is right on the way to the station. When I come back, I *have* to pass right by that beer place. Don't you think I might? Just to see if they have any? Just to taste it to see if it is the kind I like? Just to drink a glass to see if in truth I am deserving? Don't you think? [24]

Whether or not Toomer had a genetic predisposition to react excessively to alcohol, it seems clear that as time went by, alcohol had an increasing effect on him. Even by 1929 he noted, "Alcohol producing a condition in which my techniques of control no longer work." Dr. May believes that Jean's liver and gallbladder problems could well have been brought on by years of drinking. Ironically, alcohol can also cause sleeping problems. In using whiskey to get to sleep, he may have chosen as a cure the very agent causing the difficulty. Sustained use of alcohol causes cumulative damage, robbing the brain of its capacity for judgment and organization. The sad pattern of his last years, when a friend said that "he seemed to have lost all his self-respect," represents just this damaged state. [25]

24. Eugenia Walcott to JT, summer, 1929, in JTP 10:1; JT to MC, June 27, 1934, in JTP 9:6.
25. JT note (JTP 69:13). Dr. May outlined the psychological connections and medical analysis of likely effects of alcohol at Toomer's level of consumption.

From the perspective of his last years, Toomer's attention to his body seems to have been a failure, resulting in an ever-worsening condition; but no one can know what his state would have been without it. The effort to control the body by the mind and will, perhaps misdirected and eventually lost, was a hard-fought battle. He asserted the unity of mind and body, perhaps because his mind and body were at war.

Jean Toomer's spiritual journey remains to be examined. He wanted to be a whole person psychologically and physically; but fundamentally, his goal was higher than either of these. His conception of harmonious development had to include, and give highest rank to, the spirit. In "Beliefs and Assumptions," he wrote that spirit is the "highest factor in the human unit, for it and the god-head are indeed identical, the body being the lowest factor in the human unit, for it and the godhead are most separated. The body then should be strictly subjected to the needs of those factors that are higher than it." A friend who worked with him teaching Quaker young people, when asked what Jean's main goal was, replied, "Maybe—maybe Jean was trying to save his soul. It sounds hoary, but that old salvation thing I think was always there." Did he succeed? The same friend thoughtfully answered, "Religiously he always reminded me somewhat of a ship that likes to go to sea but doesn't like to anchor—you know, restless at anchor; some ships are. And he was always reaching out; he was very deep into Quakerism, he was very deep into the Gurdjieff movement; he was experimenting religiously. I don't think he ever actually found himself." In Jean's own view, he came to see himself not as God-taught or God-filled but "pointed towards God, at best." And by 1951 he was resignedly writing, "Perhaps . . . our lot on this earth is to seek and to search. Now and again we find just enough to enable us to carry on. I now doubt that any of us will completely find and be found in this life." In an ironic way, "Myself," a verse Jean wrote in an early notebook, prefigures this life quest:

> When in quest of vain endeavor,
> Seldom finds, but tires never.
> Thus into grey mists I fly,
> Nothing gained but always try.
> Each hour to live as life ordained,
> Myself to be, or die to gain.[26]

It was not that he believed in instant conversion; he understood it would be a long, hard journey: "The old person has a terrific hold on us. He or she does not

26. JT, "Beliefs and Assumptions" (JTP 22:21); interview of Charles Ingerman, Doyles-town, Pa., January 24, 1975; JT to Floyd Sandberg, January 28, 1951, in JTP 11:4; JT, "Adolescent Notes" (JTP 13:6).

give up easily. Having lived and been with us for twenty, thirty, forty years, he will not die in a night. Even if we die daily he will not die until the days have become years. Nor is the new person made in a day or a night. This making of oneself is a life-time occupation. It is a life-time devotion." [27] But when he came to the end, he did not seem to have arrived. Hard as he tried all his life for personal growth, dedicated as he was to God's work, and inspiring as he was to many people, no one has seriously nominated him for sainthood. The skeptical characterize him as a fake saint; the more charitable call him a failed one. Anyone aware of his persistent devotion must ask why.

The clue may be found even in some of the preceding passages. "To save his soul," finding *himself,* "Myself to be," "This making of oneself"—all contain the concept of the spiritual journey as a *means* to self-expression or personal advantage. If one believes that the essence of self and the godhead are identical, or even that the route to God is through the self, this image of the spiritual search is natural. But to carry it too far, to substitute the self for God as the goal, may be to abort the search. Dr. May identified the characteristic he called "willfulness" as distinguishing Jean from classic mystics. In spite of Toomer's lifelong yearning to be drawn into God's presence and used by God's will, he was blocked by the need to remain in control. For him, spiritual insights became not ends but means for self-expression. "His own need to be the special one, the one in charge, was so strong that it spiritually remained the obstacle all his life. He had all the accoutrements of the spiritual life without the real surrender." Even during the experience that Jean felt was the high point and proved the possibility of transcendence, he was very aware of self—albeit a transformed self—from beginning to end. This self was still in full control, moving his body from a distance. The basic mystical experience, in contrast, is unitive, giving a sense of oneness with God: "In real unitive experience the sense of one's self stops. The mind pauses in all of its activities that define *you*." [28]

Jean's own description of his personal search underlines this analysis: "I can almost say that in every respect I have *made* myself." He had formed his body-mind "after having come to feel that I had no mind at all. I have made my feelings out of emotional chaos. This making has resulted in a strength which is priceless, but it has also resulted in fatigue." All his life he had been "panting to catch up with myself." When his body expanded, his spirit "has taken sudden leaps, . . . consciousness has expanded and all of me has had to run and

---

27. JT, "Portage Potential" (MTC), 243.
28. Dr. May interview.

race. . . . My life has been a series of revolutions." Such a sense of personal power surely leaves no room for God, and Jean recognized this at one point, when he was writing of having helped people: "What pretension, then, to say or feel that I helped them. This conceit, this illusion, but . . . keeps one from realizing the need of and desiring to yield to God's power." Rather than yielding to God's power, for most of his life he saw God as leaning only on him. He had brought this concept into full conscious acceptance just before his peak experience in 1926. Instead of depending on others for help, he told himself, he must "die to all happy accidents, identify with no one, . . . allow no 'reaching out.' . . . Allow no expectancy of aid or help." He had thought that "life would help the organism," but now he knew that "I must help it, and must prepare myself in order to be able to help God. The prospect is at once terrifying and liberating. I, single and alone in this vast universe—all points of which are equally 'remote.'" [29]

The same failure to yield himself was evident in the human leadership to which Toomer gave allegiance. Although he looked up to and learned from Waldo Frank, Frank was really a way station, in Toomer's mind, to greater things. "I . . . had to pass through Waldo," he wrote. Even Gurdjieff, of whose undeniable power Jean stood in awe, was a method for attaining his own ends. And each of the women Jean loved, though he loved them sincerely, also represented the meeting of a need at a certain stage of his life, was used for this purpose, and then (excepting his wives) put aside. He disclosed this attitude in a 1930 note describing the phases of his development-search. The first phase was what he called searching in experience: "Seek and find and search with a woman who can energize him. . . . Books, art, study—these will be subordinate, if not completely laid aside for the time. Margy." The second was "the phase of purest zeal," searching "in a special set of conditions with a special method. A woman is not necessary for this, and, unless she can take a subordinate position, she will be a hindrance. Gurdjieff." In the third phase, searching "in speaking and writing," a woman is necessary only as the "companion of other hours, the soft gay atmosphere of his body and feelings. He will not wish to probe life very deeply and continuously with her. . . . It is not a question of more or less love. It is a matter of loving in another way. Emily." [30]

Toomer's inability to surrender to God was related to his inability to love people fully and unconditionally. To do this requires having received that kind of love in early childhood. If we think of the situation in Jean's infancy, we can

29. JT notes, 1934 (JTP 27:35); JT, "This Is Thy World," 1945 (JTP 27:6); "Tennants Harbor" notebook, April 10–11, 1926 (Typed copy in JTP 66:2).

30. JT notes, "New York Aug-Sept 1930" (JTP 17:1).

see that a mother so harried as his could not have tenderly and single-mindedly cared for her child. He believed that the failure of her breast milk warped him, but this was only a symptom of her general anxiety about her marriage, her financial security, her father's anger, and her whole future without the support of the loving husband she had counted on. When, in turn, Jean was taken back to his grandparents' house, his acceptance was patently conditional: all evidence of his father had to be removed, and he should become as exactly like his grandfather as possible. It is no wonder that such a child could never relax in the secure knowledge of being loved for himself, but had to struggle all his life to be something better. If this was combined with a bipolar disorder, which required him in controlling himself to control those about him, it is clear why both real intimacy and his lifelong goal of transcendence remained beyond his reach.

It may be that unconditional love was the gift Margaret Naumburg gave him. We can only speculate, but if so, given his history, this would explain the fireworks she set off in him and his ecstatic sense of being lifted into another realm.

How much did Jean Toomer understand of all these constrictions and contradictions? It is, in the end, impossible to know. He was both enhanced and impaired by his psychological makeup. The bonds were his daily companions, but how they were fastened or unfastened continued to be an unsolved problem. He flavored the search, however, with humor. "I can never forget," remarks a long-term associate of his, "the recurrent twinkle in his eyes as he quizzically remarked the all too frequent follies of human frailty. At times he just seemed to be smiling at his own part in these shortcomings while he continually essayed their elimination!" At least twice he seemed almost able to take the last necessary step. During his analysis, for a moment he could relax and just *be,* no longer needing to be star-rated. And again, there was the glorious period during his return to the Gurdjieff work when his "horse was out of the stable"—his emotions released—and he found that love could flow to and from him. But the old patterns closed in again. He knew his lower nature well, and his higher nature less frequently, but "at least he was acquainted with his higher nature," as Louise Welch puts it. "I feel towards the end of his life he was moving much more into his comprehension of himself, . . . trying to move towards true integrity." Having "suffered to the core for salvation," she added, "Jean was an old soul."[31]

31. George E. Otto, "Religious Society of Friends," *Banc!,* II (May, 1972), 8; N of E, October 1, [1949] (JTP 54:8); Welch interview.

It seems as if, in the final irony, the *determination to be* robbed him of the *ability* to be. The discovery and nurture of his inner essence and its best functioning in a larger spiritual world were his goals from beginning to end, but his need to be in charge was so strong that submitting to that larger spirit did not come until his body forced it on him. By that time, his capability for higher functioning had been eroded along with his will. But the lifetime effort was magnificent and unceasing.

At the conclusion of Jean Toomer's life, his friend of forty-five years, Gorham Munson, was preparing a manuscript about the 1920s entitled "The Bridge of Estador" (the title was taken from one of Hart Crane's poems describing human achievement). Toomer's death evoked from Munson a thoughtful review of Jean's life. Later he made it a postscript to his early essay "The Significance of Jean Toomer," which had been published in 1925 and again in his book *Destinations* in 1928.

The Postscript, which follows, was written in 1969:

After many years of invalidism, Jean Toomer died in obscurity on March 30, 1967, in a Pennsylvania nursing home. The following year a leading publisher discovered *Cane* and reissued it in a library of perennial books by such authors as Mark Twain and Booth Tarkington. This was a singular sign of faith in the permanence of *Cane* inasmuch as the book had sold only a few hundred copies on its first appearance forty-five years earlier.

The reissuance of *Cane* was at once highly acclaimed. The book was ranked with Richard Wright's *Native Son* and Ralph Ellison's *The Invisible Man,* and Toomer was included among the leading figures—Langston Hughes, Countee Cullen and others—of the "Negro Renaissance" of the 1920's.

Toomer was at last granted importance for his literary accomplishment. But my 1928 essay was not so much concerned with the significance of Toomer's literary achievement as it was with the significance of his symbolic promise. The reader may ask if Toomer lived up to the significant promise which I asserted for him in 1928. At the time I was thinking of the example of Katherine Mansfield who had achieved a new vision of art during her stay at the Gurdjieff Institute in Fontainebleau-Avon. I thought that Toomer would be a parallel example of an artist reaching a profounder apprehension of Beauty which Plato called the Splendor of Truth.

Toomer filled a filing cabinet with manuscripts but most of them failed to reach publication. In 1931 he was the author of *Essentials,* a privately printed book of aphorisms and definitions he jotted down during his years as a leader of groups who were studying the ideas of Gurdjieff. But *Essentials* and the few stories he did publish and the unpublished plays and autobiographical pieces were none of them impressive. They were quite different from *Cane.* In fact, Toomer was no longer drawing on the strength of his roots in Negro life and had abandoned his lyrical vein. He was attempting many times to write beyond his power. His attempts at allegorical writing were often wooden and even embarrassing.

During these years Toomer had become a professional seeker of self-knowledge and a professional striver for self-development. In 1925 he had formed a Gurdjieff group of Harlem writers and intellectuals. In 1926 he had moved to Chicago and there conducted Gurdjieff groups until 1931. Shortly after, he married the novelist Margery Latimer, and set up a small "institute" at Portage, Wisconsin. This "institute" ended with the death of Margery Latimer. Toomer moved to New York and then to Doylestown, Pennsylvania, and continued his study and practice of the Gurdjieff system. For several years he dreamed of establishing a sort of "institute" at Doylestown, but it was never to be. Instead there came the breakdown in health, the long bedridden years, and the visits to nursing homes.

Thus Toomer's career after the brilliant beginning was one of comparative literary failure, and it will be only natural that some will say that his comparative failure as a writer and his decline in health deprive him of the sort of significance I have claimed for him. They will even say that his quest for the miraculous was his ruin as an artist. I do not think so. I have been frank about Toomer's later years precisely because his significance of endeavor and promise remains despite one's disappointment in his actual achievement. We must realize that there are many casualties on the road to self-development. Almost all the aspirants to becoming new men fail to cross the bridge. Very few indeed reach the Promised Land.

Jean Toomer was a casualty on the Bridge of Estador. His significance abides in his valiant attempt to "Walk high on the bridge of Estador, / No one has ever walked there before." [32]

The tremendous difficulty of this search was always present to Jean, and never more so than in his last years. He never found out how to escape, but he learned a great deal about endurance. All the contradictory pieces of self ached and strained to be one whole, and to stop struggling. Yet he knew that suffering was essential, both in Gurdjieff's philosophy and in his own. He remembered Gurdjieff's saying, "We can have no bread without baking: knowledge is the water, emotions the flour, and suffering the fire." He himself had written in 1931 that "the one fundamental rebellion, the one conscious tragedy, on earth" was to rebel against suffering the necessary purification that would bring us back to ourselves. One of his last writings deals with this question, and it could well stand as his final testimony. It is the letter he wrote to Buckingham Meeting on January 22, 1957, in answer to their note of sympathy about his illness:

A friend once said to me—I do not know which of our afflictions God intends that we overcome and which He means for us to bear. Neither do I know. But this is certain: Some I have overcome, some I continue to bear.

32. GM, Postscript, printed for the first time here by the kind permission of Elizabeth Delza Munson, from whose collection of Munson papers it was taken. In the interest of accuracy, the error in sequence of events in Munson's fifth paragraph should be noted: the Portage experiment, intended for the summer only, ended *before* Jean's marriage to Margery Latimer. This was a period when Munson did not see much of Toomer.

This too I know: there is that in us, call it the spirit, which is not now and never has been all caught up in the earthy troubles of our bodies, emotions, and minds. And so it is free to undertake God's business for men on this earth.

Whoever has this career has everything that he can have. Whoever lacks this career lacks everything, no matter what else he may apparently possess.

in fellowship—

Jean[33]

Jean Toomer had a glimpse of God. A saint in his yearning for perfection, he was blocked by factors that came into his life so early and so strongly that he could not get past them. He had an expanded set of human failings; he had an inordinate ambition. He took these factors and made the most of them, using them grandly while he foundered against them. His successes, though only partial in the world's eyes, were thus a triumph of the human spirit. Declaring that "[t]he process of life is accidental *and* automatic *and* conscious—all three obtaining in the complex nature of reality,"[34] he maintained a strange combination of convictions about man's place in the universe. He believed in the prison of social conditioning; in a broad scheme of predetermination that included glory as well as doom; and, paradoxically, in human beings' fundamental responsibility for their own development. But somehow in his life he proved the validity of all these contradictory concepts. Blessed with powerful gifts and bound with a special set of physical, psychological, and cultural chains, Jean Toomer freely took on himself the task of breaking those chains and broke himself in the striving, leaving all about him luminous fragments of life.

33. Gurdjieff's aphorism is in a note Toomer made, probably in 1954, headed by the words "G—received by me 1929–30" (JTP 17:8); JT quotation from "Portage Potential" (MTC), 152–53; JT to Hilah [?], January 22, 1957, in Buckingham Monthly Meeting minutes, FHLS.

34. JT, "Book X."

APPENDIX

A Note on Toomer's Autobiographies

To determine which of Jean Toomer's many notes belong in which version of his autobiography is not an easy matter. In the files of the Jean Toomer papers, a manuscript may be complete in one folder, extend over many folders, or appear in two or more widely separated boxes. Some are titled, some are not; some are dated, some are not; some can be internally dated; some were written over a period of several years. Often the same title is applied to different segments written at different times. For instance, "The Second River" is a revision of "From Exile into Being" and a first title for "Why I Entered the Gurdjieff Work"—the two manuscripts covering totally different experiences. "Earth-Being" was a title given to the autobiography written in 1930, but it was also given to a section of "Incredible Journey," written from 1941 to 1948. In our best judgment, from internal and external clues, the major autobiographies and their relationship to the materials in the Jean Toomer Papers are as follows:

"Earth Being"	1929–30	JTP	15:1, 5–9
Also in MTC			17:1
			19:2–4
"Outline of an Autobiography"	1931–32	JTP	14:1
"On Being an American"	1934	JTP	15:2, 10, 11
"Book X"	1935	JTP	16:1
"From Exile into Being" (with revisions as	1937–46	JTP	20:1–4
"The Second River")			21:1–9
Also in MTC			37:1–4, 8
			38:1–7

Bibliography

WORKS BY JEAN TOOMER

Books and Pamphlets

Cane. Foreword by Waldo Frank. 1923; rpr. New York, 1967. Introduction by Arna
    Bontemps. New York, 1969. Introduction by Darwin Turner. New York, 1975.
Essentials: Definitions and Aphorisms. Chicago, 1931.
A Fiction and Some Facts. N.p., n.d. [Doylestown, Pa., *ca.* 1937?].
The Flavor of Man. William Penn Lecture. 1949; rpr. Philadelphia, 1974, 1979.
An Interpretation of Friends Worship. 1947; rpr. Philadelphia, 1979.
Living is Developing. Doylestown, Pa., 1937.
Roads, People, and Principles. Doylestown, Pa., 1939. Also in Doylestown *Daily Intelli-*
    gencer, January 11, 1939, p. 1.
Turner, Darwin, ed. *The Wayward and the Seeking: A Collection of Writings by Jean Toomer.*
    Washington, D.C., 1980.
Work-Ideas I. Doylestown, Pa., 1937.

Poetry, Fiction, Drama, and Essays

"American Letter." Published as "Lettre D'Amerique," translated by Victor Llona, in
    Bifur, I (May, 1929), 105−14. Essay.
"As the Eagle Soars." *Crisis,* XXXIX (April, 1932), 116. Poem.
"Authority, Inner and Outer." *Friends Intelligencer,* CIV (1947), 352−53. Essay.
Balo. In *Plays of Negro Life,* edited by Alain Locke and Montgomery Gregory. New
    York, 1927. Play.
"Banking Coal." *Crisis,* XXIV (June, 1922), 65. Poem.
"Blessing and Curse." *Friends Intelligencer,* CVII (1950), 576−77. Essay.
"Blue Meridian." In *The New Caravan,* edited by Alfred Kreymborg, Lewis Mumford,
    and Paul Rosenfeld. New York, 1936. Poem.
"Brown River Smile." *Pagany,* III (Winter, 1932), 29−33. Poem.
"A Certain November." *Dubuque Dial,* IV (December, 1935), 107−12. Short story.

"Chips." *Friends Intelligencer*, CIV (1947), 705. Aphorisms.

"The Critic of Waldo Frank: Criticism, An Art Form." *S4N*, No. 30 (January, 1924). Essay.

"The Days Ripen." *Friends Intelligencer*, CI (1944), 39. Poem.

"Easter." *Little Review*, XI (Spring, 1925), 3–7. Short story.

"Gum." *Chapbook*, No. 36 (April, 1923). Poem.

"Here." *Friends Intelligencer*, CV (1948), 280. Poem.

"The Hill." In *America and Alfred Stieglitz: A Collective Portrait*, edited by Waldo Frank et al. Garden City, N.Y., 1934. Essay.

"Istil." *See* "York Beach."

"Keep the Inward Watch." *Friends Intelligencer*, CII (1945), 411–12. Essay.

"Meditations: Evil." *New Mexico Literary Sentinel*, September 7, 1937, p. 8. Essay.

"Meditations: From a Farm." *New Mexico Literary Sentinel*, August 31, 1937, p. 8. Essay.

"Meditations: JT and PB; Make Good." *New Mexico Literary Sentinel*, July 20, 1937, pp. 6, 7. Essays.

"Mr. Costyve Duditch." *Dial*, LXXXV (1928), 460–76. Rpr. in *The Wayward and the Seeking*, edited by Darwin Turner. Short story.

Natalie Mann. In *The Wayward and the Seeking*, edited by Darwin Turner. Play.

"A New Force for Cooperation." *Adelphi*, IX (October, 1934), 25–31. Essay.

"Open Letter to Gorham Munson." *S4N*, No. 25 (March, 1923). Essay.

"The Other Invasion." *Friends Intelligencer*, CI (1944), 423–24. Essay.

"Oxen Cart and Warfare." *Little Review*, X (Autumn-Winter, 1924–25), 44–48. Essay.

"Prayer." *Friends Intelligencer*, CV (1948), 121. Poem. Not the same as "Prayer" published in 1923 in *Cane*.

"The Presence of Love." *Friends Intelligencer*, CI (1944), 771–72. Essay.

"Race Problems and Modern Society." In *Problems of Civilization*, edited by Baker Brownell. New York, 1929.

"Reflections." *Dial*, LXXXVI (1929), 314. Aphorisms.

The Sacred Factory. In *The Wayward and the Seeking*, edited by Darwin Turner. Play.

"Santa Claus Will Not Bring Peace." *Friends Intelligencer*, C (1943), 851–52. Essay.

"See the Heart." *Friends Intelligencer*, CIV (1947), 423. Poem.

"Something More." *Friends Intelligencer*, CVII (1950), 164–65. Essay.

"Spiritual Scarcity." *Philadelphia Inquirer*, March 28, 1949. Essay.

"These Three." *Friends Intelligencer*, C (1943), 647–48. Essay.

"Today May We Do It." *Friends Intelligencer*, CII (1945), 19–20. Essay.

"The Uncommon Man." *Friends Intelligencer*, CIII (1946), 147–48. Essay.

"White Arrow." *Dial*, LXXXVI (1929), 596. Poem.

"Winter on Earth." In *The Second American Caravan: A Yearbook of American Literature*, edited by Alfred Kreymborg, Lewis Mumford, and Paul Rosenfeld. New York, 1928. Rpr. in *The Wayward and the Seeking*, edited by Darwin Turner. Short story.

"Withered Skin of Berries." In *The Wayward and the Seeking*, edited by Darwin Turner. Short story.

"Worship and Love." *Friends Intelligencer*, CIII (1946), 695–96. Essay (forms section of *An Interpretation of Friends Worship*).

"York Beach." In *The New American Caravan,* edited by Alfred Kreymborg, Lewis Mumford, and Paul Rosenfeld. New York, 1929. Novella, originally entitled "Istil."

Major Unpublished Works

"The Angel Begori." Unfinished novel, 1940. Jean Toomer Papers, Collection of American Literature, The Beinecke Rare Book and Manuscript Library, Yale University, New Haven (hereinafter cited as JTP).

"Blue Meridian and Other Poems." Poetry collection gathered in different versions in 1931, 1934, 1941. JTP.

"Book of Aims." Essays, 1938. JTP.

"Book X." Segment of autobiography, 1935. JTP.

"Caromb." Novel, 1932. JTP.

"The Colombo-Madras Mail" or "Tourists in Spite of Themselves." Play, 1940. JTP.

"The Crock of Problems." Extended essay, 1928. JTP.

"A Drama of the Southwest" or "The Elliotts." Play, 1935. JTP.

"Earth-Being." Autobiography, 1930. JTP and Marjorie Toomer Collection, in possession of Margery Toomer Latimer (hereinafter cited as MTC). Full version unpublished, though large excerpts have been printed in *The Wayward and the Seeking,* edited by Darwin Turner.

"Eight-Day World." Revision of novel "Transatlantic," *ca.* 1934. JTP.

"The Elliotts." *See* "A Drama of the Southwest."

First Trip to Fontainebleau. Autobiographical account, 1955–56. Copy given to authors by Dr. William Welch.

"From Exile into Being," also called "The Second River." Segment of autobiography, relating mystical experience, 1937–46. JTP and MTC.

"The Gallonwerps." Play (1927) converted to novel, 1928. JTP and MTC.

"Incredible Journey." Autobiography, 1941–48. JTP. Excerpts in *The Wayward and the Seeking,* edited by Darwin Turner.

"The Letters of Margery Latimer." Edited and with introduction by Jean Toomer, 1934. JTP.

"Lost and Dominant," also called "Winter on Earth." Short-story collection, 1929. JTP. Includes three stories previously published and the following unpublished stories: "Break," "Drackman," "Fronts," "Love on a Train" (also called "Skilful Dr. Coville"), "Mr. Limph Krok's Famous 'L' Ride," "Pure Pleasure," and "Two Professors."

"Lump." Short story, *ca.* 1936. JTP.

"Man's Home Companion." Short story, 1933. JTP.

"Meridian Hill." Autobiographical short story, *ca.* 1921. MTC.

"Navarin." Collection of poems and prose, 1930. JTP.

"The Negro Emergent." Essay, *ca.* 1924. MTC.

"On Being an American." Segment of autobiography, 1934. JTP. Excerpts in *The Wayward and the Seeking,* edited by Darwin Turner.

"Outline of an Autobiography." Autobiography, 1931–32. JTP and MTC. Excerpts in *The Wayward and the Seeking,* edited by Darwin Turner.

"Over the Shining Waters." First version of novel "Transatlantic," 1929. JTP.

"Paul Rosenfeld in Port." Review of Rosenfeld, *Port of New York,* 1924. Alfred Stieglitz Collection, The Beinecke Rare Book and Manuscript Library, Yale University, New Haven (hereinafter cited as ASC).

"Portage Potential: An Adventure in Human Development." Account of Portage experiment, 1932. JTP and MTC.

"Psychologic Papers." Essays, 1937. JTP.

"Remember and Return." Aphorisms, 1937. JTP and MTC.

"The Second River." Autobiography, 1952–54, covering period 1914–26. Also called "Why I Entered the Gurdjieff Work." JTP.

"The Second River" (1937–46). *See* "From Exile into Being."

"The South in Literature." Essay, 1923. JTP.

"Talks with Peter." Essays, 1937. JTP.

"Tourists in Spite of Themselves." *See* "The Colombo-Madras Mail."

"Transatlantic." Second version of novel "Over the Shining Waters" (1929), later revised as "Eight-Day World." JTP and MTC.

"Values and Fictions: A Psychological Record." Essay, 1925. JTP and MTC.

"The Wayward and the Seeking." Collection of poetry, 1947. JTP.

"Why I Entered the Gurdjieff Work." *See* "The Second River."

"Winter on Earth." Collection of short stories, 1936. Title also used as alternate for "Lost and Dominant" collection, 1929. JTP.

WORKS BY OTHERS

Selected Criticism and Biographical Sketches of Jean Toomer

Banc!, II (May, 1972). Fisk University Library; Special Collections issue on Jean Toomer.

Bell, Bernard. "Portrait of the Artist as High Priest of Soul: Jean Toomer's *Cane.*" *Black World,* XXIII (September, 1974), 4–19, 92–97.

Benson, Brian, and Mabel Dillard. *Jean Toomer.* Boston, 1980.

Bone, Robert. *Down Home: Negro Short Fiction, from the Beginning Through the Harlem Renaissance.* New York, 1975.

Bontemps, Arna. Introduction to *Cane,* by Jean Toomer. New York, 1969.

———. "The Negro Renaissance: Jean Toomer and the Harlem Writers of the 1920s." In *Anger and Beyond: The Negro Writer in the United States,* edited by Herbert Hill. New York, 1966.

———, ed. *The Harlem Renaissance Remembered.* New York, 1972.

Boyd, Ernest. "Aesthete: Model 1924," *American Mercury,* January, 1924. Also in *The American Twenties,* edited by John K. Hutchens. New York, 1952.

Braithwaite, William Stanley. "The Negro in Literature." *Crisis,* XXVIII (September, 1924), 204–10.

Bush, A. M., and L. D. Mitchell. "Jean Toomer: A Cubist Poet." *Black American Literature Forum,* XVII (Fall, 1983), 106–108.

Candela, Gregory. "Melodramatic Form and Vision in Chesnutt's *The House Behind the Cedars,* Dunbar's *The Sport of the Gods,* and Toomer's *Cane.*" Ph.D. dissertation, University of New Mexico, 1981.

Christian, Barbara. "Spirit Bloom in Harlem. The Search for a Black Aesthetic During the Harlem Renaissance: The Poetry of Claude McKay, Countee Cullen, and Jean Toomer." Ph.D. dissertation, Columbia University, 1970.

Clark, J. Michael. "Frustrated Redemption: Jean Toomer's Women in *Cane*, Part One." *CLA Journal*, XXII (1979), 319–34.

College Language Association Journal, XVII (1974). Special June number on Jean Toomer.

Collins, Paschal. "Jean Toomer's *Cane*: A Symbolistic Study." Ph.D. dissertation, University of Florida, 1978.

Dillard, Mabel. "Jean Toomer: Herald of the Negro Renaissance." Ph.D. dissertation, Ohio University, 1967.

Dorris, Ronald. "The Bacchae of Jean Toomer." Ph.D. dissertation, Emory University, 1979.

Durham, Frank, ed. *The Merrill Studies in "Cane."* Columbus, Ohio, 1971.

Eldridge, Richard. "Jean Toomer's *Cane*: The Search for American Roots." Ph.D. dissertation, University of Maryland, 1977.

———. "Unifying Images in Part One of Jean Toomer's *Cane*." *CLA Journal*, XXII (1979), 187–214.

Frank, Waldo. Foreword to *Cane*, by Jean Toomer. New York, 1923.

Goede, William. "Jean Toomer's Ralph Kabnis: Portrait of the Negro Artist as a Young Man." *Phylon*, XXX (Spring, 1969), 73–85.

Griffin, John C., Jr. "Jean Toomer: American Writer (a Biography)." Ph.D. dissertation, University of South Carolina, 1976.

Gysin, Fritz. "Jean Toomer." In his *The Grotesque in American Negro Literature: Jean Toomer, Richard Wright, and Ralph Ellison*. Bern, 1975.

Harris, Trudier. "The Tie That Binds: The Function of Folklore in the Fiction of Charles Waddell Chesnutt, Jean Toomer and Ralph Ellison." Ph.D. dissertation, Ohio State University, 1973.

Johnson, Isaac J., III. "The Autobiography of Jean Toomer: An Edition." Ph.D. dissertation, Purdue University, 1982.

Kerman, Cynthia E. "Jean Toomer?—Enigma." *Indian Journal of American Studies*, VII (1977), 67–68.

Krasny, Michael J. "Jean Toomer and the Quest for Consciousness." Ph.D. dissertation, University of Wisconsin, 1971.

McKay, Nellie. "Forerunners in the Tradition of Black Letters." *Harvard Educational Review*, LI (1981), 158–62.

———. *Jean Toomer, Artist: A Study of His Literary Life and Work, 1894–1936*. Chapel Hill, 1984.

McNeely, Darrell. "Jean Toomer's *Cane* and Sherwood Anderson's *Winesburg, Ohio*: A Black Reaction to the Literary Conventions of the Twenties." Ph.D. dissertation, University of Nebraska (Lincoln), 1974.

Munson, Gorham. "The Significance of Jean Toomer." In his *Destinations: A Canvass of American Literature Since 1900*. 1928; rpr. New York, 1970.

Nwankwo, Nkem. "Cultural Primitivism and Related Ideas in Jean Toomer's *Cane*." Ph.D. dissertation, Indiana University, 1982.

Pinckney, Darryl. "Phantom." *New York Review of Books*, March 5, 1981, pp. 34–36.

Quirk, T., and R. E. Fleming. "Jean Toomer's Contributions to the *New Mexico Sentinel*." *CLA Journal*, XIX (1976), 524–32.

Rosenfeld, Paul. "Jean Toomer." In his *Men Seen*. New York, 1925.

Rusch, Frederik. "Every Atom Belonging to Me As Good Belongs to You: Jean Toomer and His Bringing Together of the Scattered Parts." Ph.D. dissertation, State University of New York at Albany, 1976.

Scruggs, Charles. "Jean Toomer: Fugitive." *American Literature*, XLVII (1975), 84–96.

————. "The Mark of Cain and the Redemption of Art: A Study of Theme and Structure of Jean Toomer's *Cane*." *American Literature*, XLIV (1972), 276–91.

Singh, Amritjit. *The Novels of the Harlem Renaissance: Twelve Black Writers, 1923–1933*. University Park, Pa., 1976.

Story, Ralph. "Master Players in a Fixed Game: An Extraliterary History of Twentieth Century Afro-American Authors, 1896–1981." A.D. dissertation, University of Michigan, 1984.

Taylor, Carolyn. "Blend Us with Thy Being: Jean Toomer's Mill House Poems." Ph.D. dissertation, Boston College, 1977.

Turner, Darwin. Introduction to *Cane*, by Jean Toomer. New York, 1975.

————. "Jean Toomer: Exile." In his *In a Minor Chord: Three Afro-American Writers and Their Search for Identity*. Carbondale, Ill., 1971.

Twombly, Robert C. "A Disciple's Odyssey: Jean Toomer's Gurdjieff Career." In *Prospects: An Annual of American Cultural Studies*, edited by Jack Salzman, II (1976), 437–62.

Wagner, Jean. "Jean Toomer." In his *Black Poets of the United States: From Paul Laurence Dunbar to Langston Hughes*. Translated by Kenneth Douglas. Urbana, Ill., 1973.

Walker, Alice. "The Divided Life of Jean Toomer." In her *In Search of Our Mothers' Gardens*. San Diego, 1983.

Wallace, Carolynn. "Jean Toomer: Death on the Modern Desert." Ph.D. dissertation, George Washington University, 1981.

Sources Consulted on Gurdjieff

Anderson, Margaret. *The Unknowable Gurdjieff*. London, 1962.

Bennett, John G. *Gurdjieff: Making a New World*. New York, 1973.

————. *Is There "Life" on Earth? An Introduction to Gurdjieff*. New York, 1973.

Gurdjieff, George I. *Beelzebub's Tales to His Grandson* (*All and Everything*, First Series). New York, 1950.

————. *Meetings with Remarkable Men* (*All and Everything*, Second Series). 1969; rpr. New York, 1974.

McIntosh, Mavis. Interview, Sag Harbor, N.Y., August 1, 1982.

Munson, Elizabeth Delza. Interviews, New York, July 7, 1978, June 25, 1982.

Nott, C. S. *Teachings of Gurdjieff: A Pupil's Journal*. London, 1961.

Orage, A. R. *Selected Essays and Critical Writings*. London, 1935.

Ouspensky, P. D. *In Search of the Miraculous: Fragments of an Unknown Teaching*. New York, 1949.

————. *The Psychology of Man's Possible Evolution*. London, 1951.

————. *Tertium Organum*. Translated by Ouspensky and E. Kadloubovsky. Rev. ed. New York, 1981.

Peters, Arthur [Fritz]. *Boyhood with Gurdjieff*. New York, 1964.
————. *Gurdjieff Remembered*. New York, 1971.
Views from the Real World: Early Talks of Gurdjieff. New York, 1975.
Webb, James. *The Harmonious Circle: The Lives and Works of G. I. Gurdjieff, P. D. Ouspensky and Their Followers*. New York, 1980.
Welch, Louise. *Orage with Gurdjieff in America*. Boston, 1982.
Welch, Louise, and William Welch. Interview, New York, June 25, 1982.
Welch, William J. *What Happened in Between: A Doctor's Story*. New York, 1972.
Zuber, René. *Who Are You Monsieur Gurdjieff?* Translated by Jenny Koralek. Boston, 1980.

General Related Studies

Bontemps, Arna. *One Hundred Years of Negro Freedom*. New York, 1961.
Boyle, Kay, and Robert McAlmon. *Being Geniuses Together*. 1938; rpr. Garden City, N.Y., 1968.
Carter, Paul J. *Waldo Frank*. New York, 1967.
Cowley, Malcolm. *Exile's Return*. New York, 1934.
Du Bois, W. E. B., and Alain Locke. "The Younger Literary Movement." *Crisis*, XXVII (February, 1924), 161–63.
Ferguson, Marilyn. *The Aquarian Conspiracy*. Los Angeles, 1980.
Frank, Waldo. *Holiday*. New York, 1923.
————. *Our America*. New York, 1919.
Giles, James R. *Claude McKay*. Boston, 1976.
Haskins, James. *Pinckney Benton Stewart Pinchback*. New York, 1973.
Hughes, Langston. *The Big Sea*. New York, 1940.
James, William. *The Varieties of Religious Experience*. 1902; rpr. New York, 1936.
Johnson, James Weldon. *Along This Way*. New York, 1933.
Kesteloot, Lilyan. *Black Writers in French*. Translated by Ellen Conroy Kennedy. Philadelphia, 1974.
Latimer, Margery. *Guardian Angel and Other Stories*. 1932; rpr. Freeport, N.Y., 1971. Rev. ed., Old Westbury, N.Y., 1984.
Lewis, David. *When Harlem Was in Vogue*. New York, 1981.
Lisle, Laurie. *Portrait of an Artist: A Biography of Georgia O'Keeffe*. New York, 1981.
Locke, Alain. *The New Negro: An Interpretation*. New York, 1925.
Loeb, Harold. *The Way It Was*. New York, 1959.
Luhan, Mabel Dodge. *Lorenzo in Taos*. New York, 1932.
May, Gerald G., M.D. *Will and Spirit: A Contemplative Psychology*. San Francisco, 1982.
Munson, Gorham. *The Awakening Twenties: A Memoir-History of a Literary Period*. Baton Rouge, 1985.
Perry, Robert L. *The Shared Vision of Waldo Frank and Hart Crane*. Lincoln, Neb., 1966.
Rosenfeld, Paul. *Men Seen*. New York, 1925.
————. *Port of New York: Essays on Fourteen American Moderns*. New York, 1924.
Simmons, Reverend William J. *Men of Mark*. 1887; rpr. Chicago, 1970.
Sugrue, Thomas. *There Is a River: The Story of Edgar Cayce*. New York, 1942; 2nd ed., 1945.
Terrell, Mary Church. *A Colored Woman in a White World*. 1940; rpr. New York, 1980.

Trachtenberg, Alan, ed. *The Memoirs of Waldo Frank*. Amherst, Mass., 1973.

Vining, Elizabeth Gray. *Friend of Life: A Biography of Rufus M. Jones*. 1958; rpr. Philadelphia, 1981.

Weber, Brom. *Hart Crane: A Biographical and Critical Study*. New York, 1948.

————, ed. *The Complete Poems and Selected Letters and Prose of Hart Crane*. New York, 1966.

————, ed. *The Letters of Hart Crane, 1916–1932*. New York, 1952.

Index